The Joan Palevsky Imprint in Classical Literature

In honor of beloved Virgil—

"O degli altri poeti onore e lume . . ."

—Dante, *Inferno*

The publisher gratefully acknowledges the generous support of the Classical Literature Endowment Fund of the University of California Press Foundation, which was established by a major gift from Joan Palevsky.

This book has been published with the financial support of the Dipartimento di Ateneo per la Didattica e la Ricerca of the Università per Stranieri di Siena and the Research Projects of National Interest Program (PRIN 2010–2011).

Shameless

Shameless

The Canine and the Feminine
in Ancient Greece

With a New Preface and Appendix

Cristiana Franco

Translated by Matthew Fox

UNIVERSITY OF CALIFORNIA PRESS

University of California Press, one of the most distinguished university presses in the United States, enriches lives around the world by advancing scholarship in the humanities, social sciences, and natural sciences. Its activities are supported by the UC Press Foundation and by philanthropic contributions from individuals and institutions. For more information, visit www.ucpress.edu.

University of California Press
Oakland, California

Library of Congress Cataloging-in-Publication Data

Franco, Cristiana.

   [Senza ritegno. English]
   Shameless : the canine and the feminine in the ancient Greece : with a new preface and appendix / Cristiana Franco ; translated by Matthew Fox
      p. cm.
   Based on the author's thesis (doctoral)—Università di Siena.
   Includes bibliographical references and index.
   ISBN 978-0-520-27340-5 (cloth, alk. paper) — ISBN 978-0-520-95742-8 (pbk., alk. paper)
   1. Dogs—Mythology—Greece. 2. Dogs in literature. 3. Women—History—To 500. 4. Women (Greek law). 5. Greece—Social conditions—To 146 B.C. 6. Dogs in art. I. Fox, Matthew (Matthew Aaron), translator. II. Title.
PA3015.D64F7313   2014
880.9 3522—dc23   2014000727

Manufactured in the United States of America

21 20 19 18 17 16 15 14 13 14
10 9 8 7 6 5 4 3 2 1

In keeping with its commitment to support environmentally responsible and sustainable printing practices, UC Press has printed this book on Natures Book, which contains 30% post-consumer waste and meets the minimum requirements of ANSI/NISO Z 39.48-1992 (R 1997) (*Permanence of Paper*).

CONTENTS

Shameless is a study of representations of the dog in ancient Greek texts under-taken from an anthropological perspective: that is, it not only attends to explicit authorial statements (the judgments and conscious views that writers and thinkers expressed about dogs) but also aims no less at recovering implicit knowledge, that body of presuppositions, beliefs, and prejudices relating to dogs that lay behind most of the assertions and images that the ancients made and that were rooted in specific modes of everyday relations with the animal. In short, the work tries to identify and illustrate with available sources—literary texts, myths, proverbs, anecdotes, fables, spontaneous metaphors, and comic jokes current in the repertoire of popular culture—the forms of knowledge and ideological projects at play within discursive practices where the dog figures in some relevant position.

The questions I posed for myself were the following: Why do Greek sources offer such divergent representations of dogs, as in, for instance, the conspicuous contrast between Argus—one of the few creatures Odysseus sheds a tear for in the *Odyssey*—and the dogs of Actaeon? Why was *dog* an insult, despite the regular presence of dogs in Greek life? Why was the first woman, Pandora, equipped with, among her other perilous resources, a "doggish mind [*kyneos noos*]"? And why are so many negative female figures portrayed with canine traits?

In the British and American tradition of expository writing, it is normal to set out one's thesis statements at the head of the work, anticipating the conclusions toward which the subsequent pages will then progress. Holding the reading in suspense of a resolution, as in fiction, is not considered good scholarly practice. The present work instead follows a writing tradition more typical in Continental scholarship, one conceived as more of an investigative work, in which the hypothesis—the idea that gave rise to the research—is presented as a riddle to be solved, and the argumentation then guides the reader along the pathway that led the researcher-detective toward the solution of the case.[1]

The idea of presenting the results of my study in a form that in some fashion retraced the course of my research—begun in 1998–99 in the doctoral program at the Center for Anthropology and the Ancient World at the University of Siena—seemed to me both more enjoyable and more informative, since it also described the labyrinth through which I had to wander and made apparent that degree of serendipity common in any exploration of the mysterious workings of a distant and foreign culture. Besides, in Italian editorial practice, the form of a study—even scholarly ones—is not necessarily divorced from concerns with stylistic pleasure or the reader's entertainment.[2]

The interdisciplinary nature of the work, combining classical studies with perspectives and concepts derived from anthropology, interpretive semiotics, human-animal studies, and gender studies, made it seem best in the end to present the results in terms accessible to nonclassicist readers, so all the more technical questions have been removed from the main text, and discussion of specific problems of interest only to specialists has been placed in the notes.

Impatient or disoriented readers, preferring to get an overall picture of the work's structure and a statement of its results, may want to begin with the last section, "Conclusion," which briefly sketches the themes and arguments that the work traces out. Classicists interested in delving into the ancient sources and philological literature on which I have relied for my interpretations will find this information detailed in the notes.

Although it maintains the overall structure of the original, the English translation of the text is nevertheless different from the original Italian edition in several respects. Above all, in the years since the book's first release, I've run across several ancient sources that had escaped my notice or that I had not thought of using but which now appear significant. These have been taken into account and are discussed in the present edition. The text has also been revised and updated as far as possible in light of articles and studies that either appeared after the Italian edition was published or did not receive the attention they deserved when I drafted the original book. In particular, the bibliography relating to the dog in Greece has been much expanded.

Finally, I have supplemented the present edition with an appendix that aims to illuminate the theoretical and methodological coordinates by which I conducted my research, the conceptual tools I turned to as I worked on the text, and the intellectual traditions with which my research wishes to engage in dialogue. In particular, it outlines a framework of results and possibilities that a transdisciplinary perspective inspired by anthrozoology and human-animal studies seems to offer for the development of new ways to study animals in the ancient world.

This volume thus represents a significant expansion and updating of the Italian original.

Habeat sua fata libellus.

Siena
August 12, 2013

PANDORA AND THE FIRST MISADVENTURES
OF THE HUMAN RACE

There was a time, says Hesiod, when human beings lived happily, in complete harmony with nature and the gods. Human life was without sadness or toil, food came spontaneously from the untilled earth, and neither sickness nor old age existed. Everything was so perfect that even the more pleasant disturbances, such as desire and hope, were unknown to those blessed ancestors. But one day this happiness, complete and without blemish, suddenly fell to pieces: through a mistake of Prometheus, humans and gods came into conflict, and the human condition was condemned to the discomfort of uncertainty, to that ambiguous mixture of good and bad, of joy and suffering, that characterizes to this day the imperfect and ephemeral existence of mortal creatures.[1]

Let us look at exactly how this came about. Gods and men—at this point humans were only male—were preparing to dine together one day near Mecone. Prometheus, the Titan who harbored a strong fondness for mortals, had the unfortunate idea of favoring them to the gods' detriment. He slew an ox for the feast, then divided out two portions, one for the gods and another for men. In one he grouped all the best parts, muscle and fat, which he wrapped in hide and covered with the animal's stomach to make them appear less appetizing. In the other portion he placed just the bones, but covered with white fat so as to seem more desirable. The Titan then turned to Zeus and invited him to choose which portion he preferred, certain that the king of gods would fall into his trap and select the pile of fat-covered bones.

But this undertaking had a most unfortunate outcome. Sensing the trick, Zeus accepted the challenge. He chose the worse portion anyway but removed the layer of fat from the pile of bones, and, with the swindle unmasked, he decreed an ingenious punishment, one destined to lay humanity low for good. The lord of Olympus decided that from then on, at every sacrifice the gods would take the bones of the slaughtered beast burned on the altars, while to men would go the meat.[2] But in exchange he would hide forever the grain and the fruits of the earth. Men would no longer be able to gather these without effort, but only through toil and suffering, with hard labor in the fields. A punishment fitting the crime: for the meat hidden by Prometheus, Zeus hid fruits and crops from men.

Nevertheless, the wretched toil of agricultural labor seemed to Zeus a penalty still too lenient for the protégés of Prometheus. The father of all the gods decided to double it by inflicting a further and fatal concealment: he made fire vanish from the earth as well. This time the philanthropic Titan did not passively accept this state of affairs. Taking a hollow reed, he managed to capture a glimmer of flame and brought the precious spark back to mortals. Men thus owe to him at least their abilities to cook their food, forge metals, and fire clay.

But for this second of Prometheus's clever tricks the human race received another and still more frightful malady. Angered by the theft of fire, Zeus decided to counterattack with a third move, this time decisive, that put an end to the struggle forever and relegated men far from divine happiness. To this end he conceived a marvelous invention, a "dizzying, invincible deception"[3]: he created Pandora, the first woman, progenitor of all the women to come. Woman, an insidious creature destined to enter the houses of men, turned out to be so clever that no man has ever been able to escape her, because she is so irresistibly attractive that all who see her "feel great joy," because, even if she is ruinous, they love her, "embracing in love their own evil,"[4] and because men must reproduce through her, who gives birth to children and grandchildren, in order to escape eternal death and the extinction of the species.

What punishment could be harsher? With Pandora—calamity made woman, a living disaster who, by opening the jar in which they were held, scattered every sad misfortune into the world—Evil makes its entrance among men, clothed in divine beauty, with the seductive appearance of a desirable good: they will crave to have it near, dote over it, and bring it into their homes. From that moment they will be no longer, as at the beginning, human beings (*anthrōpoi*) pure and simple, but instead men (*andres*), for the "race of women" will barge in and install itself within the human race, splitting it into the two complementary halves of men and women.[5]

THE "BITCHINESS" OF WOMEN

To fabricate the first woman, Zeus assigns each god a task—hence the new creature's name is Pandora, "she who was a gift of all [the gods]," or perhaps "she who received from all [the gods] a gift."⁶ The job of shaping the first material goes to the divine artisan Hephaestus, who must mix earth with water and give the clay the seductive appearance of a young woman ready for marriage—and his models are the immortal goddesses. At this point his job is done, and around this marvelous automaton the other gods begin to busy themselves, each one ready to contribute with their own specific skill. Athena attends to the woman's education, which in the ancient world essentially consisted in teaching her to work the loom.⁷ Aphrodite busies herself in giving Pandora an irresistible charm, pouring over her head that delicate grace (*charis*), a seductive submissiveness, that provokes torments of desire.⁸ But the ambiguous power of eroticism is not the only evil component in this first bride's trousseau. To finish off the wicked work of Zeus, in steps Hermes, whose job is to give Pandora "a bitchy mind [*kyneon noon*] and a thievish nature."⁹ And so Zeus's instructions come to an end.

Of what exactly does this contribution requested of Hermes toward the making of woman consist? What does Hesiod mean when he attributes to Pandora the temperament of a dog and a strong propensity to steal? Concerning the deceitful and thievish (*epiklopos*) nature of women, we don't need to look far for explanations, since other passages in Hesiod's poems clearly illuminate his opinion on the matter: for a husband, a woman means another mouth to feed. In a rural economy based on male labor, woman is the parasitic element that uses up the supplies stored away with so much toil by the men.¹⁰ In Hesiodic morality, founded wholly on the necessity of agricultural labor, woman constitutes an unproductive element. To cultivate the fields means to earn a living through honesty and justice, and so, those who, like a wife, eat bread without having plowed, reaped, or gathered, live by robbery. It is in this sense, then, that Pandora has the soul of a thief. And naturally, Hermes is the one who gives it to her, since he is the thief of Olympus, the patron god of thieves and the protector of scoundrels.¹¹

As for the adjective *kyneos*, "of or like a dog," which Hesiod used to describe the mental disposition characteristic of woman and which I have chosen to translate— here at least—with the colloquial word *bitchy* for reasons that will become clear, it is certainly used as a term of disparagement. But perhaps it is less generic and banal than a modern reader may be inclined to think. The Greek word for dog (*kyōn*), as well as a number of others derived from and formed with the same root, *kyn-*, was frequently used as a term of abuse and disparagement: when one wanted to offend someone, one would address them with words such as *dog, dog face* (*kynōpēs* and, in the feminine, *kynōpis*), or *dog fly* (*kynamyia*); one might use the not very flattering phrase "nothing is more dog [*kynteron*] than you"; or again, an ugly and grievous situation was "most doggish [*kyntaton*]." So, no doubt, when Hesiod calls the nature that Hermes gave to Pandora *kyneos*, he does not mean it as a compliment to feminine nature. But still, there are reasons to believe that with this choice of term the poet is engaging with a larger cultural tradition that connected women and dogs in a subtle and subterranean relationship.

In the ancient Greek imagination the figure of the dog seems, in fact, to be interwoven with the disparaging discourse on the nature of woman in a far from casual manner. While it is true that the insult *Dog!* and its derivatives are used to address a wide variety of things—humans but also actions and sensations—in many situations, it is also true that in the Homeric poems more than half of their occurrences are directed at women or, in quarrels on Olympus, goddesses, such that the suspicion arises that this kind of verbal aggression was heard as particularly suited for censuring the behavior and attitudes of women. Moreover, the dog appears as a paradigm for the base nature of women in two cornerstone texts of Greek misogyny. Besides the Hesiodic account of the creation of Pandora, the theme recurs in the Homeric episode dedicated to Clytemnestra's crime: a murder so heinous that it turns the queen of Argos into the source of the bad reputation of the entire female race.[12] In this well-known passage of the *Odyssey,* Clytemnestra, the treacherous wife and assassin of her husband, is defined by the shade of her dead spouse as "dog-faced," since one can imagine nothing "more terrible and more doggish," Agamemnon adds, than a woman who kills her own man.[13]

In short, the Greek tradition attributed some sort of canine nature to both women, whom it remembered as prototypes of feminine unreliability. And then there is Helen, another mythic figure of feminine betrayal and inconstancy, who is called *bitch* and *dog face*—she is, in fact, the one designated *kyōn* and *kynōpis* most often in the Homeric poems.[14] If we add to this the fact that the only mythical figures with definite canine attributes in Greek culture are female, and all of them by nature disturbing—the Erinyes, goddesses of vengeance; Hecate, goddess of the crossroads, who wanders through graveyards by night; destructive monsters such as Scylla and the Sphinx; the raving bacchantes possessed by Dionysus—we get a clear enough picture of how in Greece the negative side of the representation of dogs maintained a special relationship with the darker aspects of the image of woman.

My aim is to substantiate this claim and to trace the possible reasons for such a persistent symbolic connection. But to reach that point will require a long circuit to reconstruct the cultural imagination of the dog, which was founded on the unique types of relationship that the Greeks had with the animal. Only after the terms of this relationship are understood will it become possible to propose an explanation of how and why dogs came to have a special association with a certain image of the feminine. Before dealing with this issue, then, the investigation will wind through a path traced out by ancient sources relating to dogs: from Homeric epic to jokes of the comic poets, from proverbs transmitted by poets and paroemiographers to metaphors of the tragedians, from Aristotelian treatises to fables in the Aesopic tradition. Through the full range of available texts and evidence, I will try to reconstruct the vast set of opinions, notions, and beliefs that characterized dog-human relationships and thus constituted the entry *kyōn* in the ancient cultural encyclopedia.[15] This will afford an understanding, first of all, of precisely how the dog was suited to provide material for so many elaborations of a negative character, which will then permit us to determine the thematic and semantic spheres in which the image of the dog appears in the symbolic language of poetry, fable, and myth. Only then will we have the necessary context for identifying the workings of, and the reasons for, the peculiar connection between the representation of dogs and the image of women. After this, in the last chapter, we'll meet up again with Pandora and her "bitchy" nature.

A few preliminary notes before getting to the heart of the problem. First, the owner of the dog will be referred to as *master,* despite my personal preference, to reflect the Greek usage (*anax, despotes*). Second, the human element in the interspecies relationship will be designated as *man,* quite intentionally. Certainly ancient Greek women had relationships with dogs, but there is no evidence for this in literary sources, based on which this investigation has been made. It is the male gaze that constructed the cultural representations we will be dealing with, and it is the male view on dogs (and women) that we will be discussing throughout this book.

Moreover, Nicole Loraux has aptly noted that "for the Greeks *chiennerie* speaks to the feminine,"[16] and in the course of examining the ancient sources we will have the opportunity to appreciate the senses in which this statement is true. The disparaging French term *chiennerie,* unfortunately, does not have an equivalent in English (or Italian), and our lexicon does not even have a neutral term to designate "canineness," the set of traits that characterize the cultural concept of the dog. Thus, for convenience, these characteristics, with their negative connotations, will at times be designated by the term *bitchiness* (*cagneria* in Italian), a coinage that, while perhaps sounding a harsh note, nevertheless compensates with the double advantage of both conveying a strongly disparaging meaning and carrying a feminine connotation. (Later on in the study, however, *cagneria* will be rendered as *doggishness,* for reasons that will become clear.)

One cannot forget, after all, that the combination of negative connotation and femininity is not a phenomenon that relates only to ancient Greek "bitchiness." The Italian *cagna,* for example, like the English *bitch,* is both much stronger and a more effective insult than its masculine counterpart, *cane* ("dog"). For this reason, I suspect that this investigation into the dog-feminine pairing in ancient Greece will also offer some valuable starting points for reflection on the prevalent phenomena of symbolic intersection between animal, insult, and femininity, widespread as these are in other and more recent cultures.

1

Offensive Epithets

A DESPISED ANIMAL?

The Greeks' habit of speaking ill of women is notorious. Perhaps less notorious is that they were also strangely accustomed to speaking ill of dogs. As the prologue notes, *kyon* (the vocative form of *kyōn*)[1] was an insult, one that could apply to a person who was greedy, cowardly, treacherous, irritating, or vulgar. In ancient comedy, many sarcastic remarks leveled at impudent women and greedy demagogues play on the figure of the dog. In Aesop's fables, the dog strikes no better figure, being implicated in stories about unworthy behavior and symbolizing opportunism, greed, or cowardice. Does this mean the dog was a despised animal? Did the Greeks perhaps—like the ancient Hebrews and some peoples in Islamic traditions today—feel disgust for dogs?

This is in fact the prevailing view. Despite slightly varying conclusions, scholars have so far assumed that if *kyon* is an insult, this means that in Greece the dog was despised, or at least found particularly repugnant in some aspect.[2] But this apparently straightforward thesis does not stand up to a simple objection: ancient sources do not confirm this alleged contempt for the dog. Indeed, one finds no traces of it in the Homeric poems, where *kyon* is an uncommonly frequent insult. So how can this riddle be solved?

One proposed solution notes the frequency with which the epic poems evoke dogs in threats of outrageous treatment of corpses. When a Homeric hero wants to terrorize an enemy, he threatens to cut him down and leave his corpse to the beasts, and in most cases the beasts assigned to the horrible dismemberment of the dead are dogs. Thus, it is argued, the dog in Homer is clearly the necrophagic, corpse-eating animal par excellence, and from this repugnant aspect arose the insulting use of *kyōn*.[3] This is possible. But why then did terms such as "vulture [*gyps*]" or "raven [*korax*]" not figure among insulting expressions as well? This explanation only restates the problem without resolving the contradiction: why among necrophagic animals was it just the dog—the one closest to and a co-worker of humans—who earned the unenviable role as a term of insult?

Moreover, the sources do not confirm even the presumed discredit that necrophagy cast on the whole canine species. True, in some cases dogs were excluded from sacred spaces for reasons of ritual purity: for example, we know they were not allowed to enter the Acropolis of Athens or to touch ground on the island of Delos.[4] But certainly it cannot be said that dogs were impure animals *tout court,* excluded from all sacred spaces. In some sanctuaries, for example those of Asclepius, they were not only tolerated but even venerated as belonging to the god and as a source of healing.[5] Again, if dogs were considered impure per se, the Greeks, so preoccupied with risks of contamination, surely would not have kept them indoors, as was indeed frequently the case. In fact, it seems that in Greece the category of impure did not apply to any animal species.[6]

To get around this problem, some scholars propose a second theory, which nevertheless only shifts explanation to a chronological axis: the dog, they say, was not well favored in the epoch prior to which our first sources date. The Homeric use of *kyon* as an insult would thus be a linguistic relic of the Mycenaean period, a holdover from a time when the dog was not yet completely domesticated and was therefore perceived as an unreliable companion.[7] The expression, then, would have persisted as a fixed formula after the animal's change in status. According to others, the origin of the insult *kyon* might be located still further back, within the formative period of Indo-European languages, or else looked for in neighboring cultures, such as those of the Near East. In the first case, the Greeks would have inherited it from their Indo-European ancestors; in the second, they would have imported it from the Near East during the epic's protohistory. In either situation, the insult would have entered Greek usage purely as a desemanticized expression,[8] and this would explain why, in the formative period of the Homeric poems, the denigrating use of *kyon* no longer corresponded to an active attitude of contempt for the dog.

It seems quite clear from this brief survey that in the absence of concrete proof, the idea that using *kyon* as an insult must necessarily correspond to a general repugnance for the dog is untenable, and indeed contrary to the evidence of ancient sources, or can be accepted only at the price of unprovable hypotheses: references to prehistoric origins lost in the mists of time or appeals to distant cultural influences from the East. But if commentators have not doubted the correctness of this assumption—the necessity of a link between the use of the animal term as an insult and some disrespect for the animal in question—it is because of its apparent self-evidence. For example, the fact that one is not being complimentary when one calls someone "a worm" is most obviously explained by an intention to compare one's interlocutor with an animal traditionally conceived as slimy, slow, and primitive, helpless but infesting, and associated with foul-smelling putrefaction. But on closer inspection, not all cases of insult using animal categories can be so easily explained.

The assumption that an offensive use of an animal name implies bad repute for that animal within the human community arises from a specific way of analyzing and classifying the mechanism of insult. The offense of an animal category arises from a metaphor of the antonomastic variety: that is, the reason an animal name functions as an insult is that it is traditionally associated with at least some element of a negative character, which becomes the key to the offensive metaphor. For example, with the insults *ass* and *pig* (in Italian as in English), the operative traits are, respectively, stupidity or stubbornness and filthiness or gluttony.[9] Thus to tell someone, "You're a pig!," amounts to saying "You're filthy" or "You're a glutton," like the filthy and gluttonous animal, through antonomasia.

This way of analyzing the offensive figure, while correct, has its limits. First, it tends to resolve the metaphor into equivalence without explaining what communicative advantage the figurative expression may have over the literal.[10] Second, it poses serious problems to someone who wants to identify a term of equivalence for the metaphor *dog*. Even in many languages that use this term of abuse—Italian, German, English, and Russian, besides ancient Greek and Latin—if one tries to specify in each case what exact negative property or properties hold the key to the outrageous metaphor, one is faced with quite a quandary.[11] In Italian, for instance, the insult *Dog!* does not seem to yield to any easy analysis. One can use it for quite disparate reasons of hostility and resentment, from an unjustified racism that figures the unwanted foreigner as a "bastard dog" to the pain of a betrayal suffered by a traitor who is a "damn dog," not to mention that the insult *dog* appears in one of the most common blasphemous expressions in the Italian language. In all these cases, what is the negative cultural trait traditionally associated with the dog that might constitute the metaphor's key element? To what specific negative feature or features of the animal are we alluding when we call someone a dog?

The situation is no different with the Greek insult *kyon*, for which it is very difficult to identify a precise literal equivalent. When ancient commentators were faced with annotating a passage containing this insult or one of its derivatives, they explained that to call someone a dog was to accuse them of *anaideia*, a term usually translated as "shamelessness" but which in Greek had a somewhat wider sense.[12] It literally means "a lack of *aidōs*," that is, a lack of restraint, the moral curb responsible for inhibiting any behavior subject to ethical censure.[13]

The generality of *anaideia* has understandably not satisfied those modern commentators interested in specifying the key metaphor of the insult:[14] why should the dog represent immorality in general, unrestraint in all its possible manifestations?

What canine behavior is so shameless that it became emblematic of every manner of excess and impudence? On this crucial question anyone can speculate and express an opinion. But the fact remains that no single canine characteristic can account for all the uses of the insult found in ancient texts. To take just a Homeric example, when Achilles calls Agamemnon "dog-faced" this might allude specifically to the Achaean chieftain's greed, representing it offensively as canine voracity, but what greediness is involved when Hephaestus calls his mother Hera "dog-faced" for excluding him from Olympus on account of his lameness?[15]

Analysis of the offensive uses of *kyōn* and its derivatives clearly shows that the trope did not have one single key: the dog was not emblematic of one particular human attitude or behavior. The only certainty here is that the dog functioned as an insult in a wide range of contexts—and that it is not always easy to specify what precise property of *kyōn* the metaphor is meant to reference. In short, even given that the mechanism underlying the affront *dog* was the common one of antonomasia, it is still not clear what *kyon* was antonomastic for. In the *Odyssey*, the goatherd Melanthius accosts the swineherd Eumaeus with the insult "dog, skilled at tricks."[16] But to criticize falsehood and cunning malice, why did he not choose the wolf or the fox, the clever animal deceivers par excellence in Greek culture, instead of implicating the dog? Similar questions arise when a faithless woman is called a bitch: why is it only the dog that is enlisted to hurl the accusation of unbridled sexual lust when the animals that Greek figured as lascivious were the goat, the cow, and the horse?[17]

At this point we should ask whether the impasse to which the traditional explanations inevitably lead doesn't result from an error in posing the problem. Instead of trying to explain away the variety and complexity of disparaging uses of *kyōn* and its derivatives, we can simply take note of it and pose the question in these terms: why was the dog capable of serving as the term of censure for such a wide range of behaviors?

INSULTS AND ANIMAL CATEGORIES

Let us step back a bit from ancient Greece and turn to some considerations of a more general nature. Since the insult *dog* is by no means unique to Greek but is found in many languages ancient and modern, the problem of its multivalence deserves to be viewed from a wider perspective than the one adopted so far in historical studies.[18]

Many societies that use the word for dog as an insult do not by any means regard the animal with repugnance, and the various negative cultural elaborations that play on it coexist with the animal's conspicuous presence in daily life, even its extraordinary nearness to man: as a collaborator or even a vicarious surrogate in the work of its owner, an institutional frequenter of domestic domains, and a presence in public social spaces. The apparently contradictory situation in ancient Greece is not an exception but the norm. It is therefore likely that the reason for such a cultural model (and its common occurrence) may be found in some structural feature of the human-canine relationship.

This question, truly quite complex, fits into the wider anthropological topic of denigrating uses of animal terms. A first observation of interest here is that in the various languages with insults using animal names, there seems to be a certain tendency to put the names of domestic animals to such use. In 1964, the distinguished British anthropologist Edmund Leach wondered about this fact. By reflecting on English vocabulary and comparing it with usage in the Tibeto-Burmese Kachin culture, with which he was closely familiar, Leach tried to articulate a general theory of animal insults.[19] In a study of considerable interest, he claimed to find a correlation between the offensive use of an animal's name and its position in the cultural taxonomy: it is not so much the animal's negative characteristics as its position with respect to humans that determines the choice of zoonym for an insult. The reasons explaining the selection are thus to be found in the animal's nearness to or distance from cultural spaces (domestic/hunted/wild), its ease or difficulty of classification, its dietary position (edible/edible with restrictions/ taboo), and so on.

In Leach's analysis, it turned out that the insulting animal names come mainly from species that occupy an ambiguous position in the classification scheme, in a poorly defined space between one category and another: those animals closest to but not identical with humans and so not entirely friendly but not completely wild and hostile either. For being unclassifiable, such species are perceived with a certain anxiety and tension and are subject to taboo, whether explicit or unconscious. Because of this, the zoonyms most used for insults come from domestic animals regarded fondly—so-called pets—such as the dog, perceived as halfway between human and beast, or else from hunted species, toward which human feelings alternate between friendly nearness and aggressive impulses of hostility. These names' efficacy in giving offense and in cursing derives from the fact that in pronouncing them the speaker sets off the charge of tension inherent in their being subject to taboo.

This theory, summarized here in broad strokes, is in fact quite complicated and subject to several objections.[20] For instance, how does it explain an insult such as pig or swine? The pig is a domestic animal but certainly no pet. Nor can it be counted among hunted prey animals, nor is eating it taboo. Again, how to explain the use of rat, one of the most common animal insults in English? Still, Leach's study has the merit of having raised a problem that loses none of its importance for being unresolved. Although it is theoretically possible to construct a derogatory metaphor with any animal name—most people called an animal, of whatever sort, will be offended by the mere fact of being degraded to a category considered inferior—reality shows that in any culture only some species are suited to this, while others are employed in laudatory metaphors. For instance, the boar and the lion often appear in positive metaphors of courage and invincibility. But why are the positive aspects of these animals, so fierce and aggressive toward humans, their herds, and their crops, picked out instead of their negative aspects (even if still present) of bloodthirsty ferocity and wildness? Again, why is the fox, a harmful animal that is despised as a chicken killer, nevertheless stereotyped by its positive aspect of cleverness, such that one expresses appreciation for a sly person by calling them a fox? Conversely, the pejorative charge of an animal name cannot always be ascribed to an explicit hostility that a culture has toward that animal nor linked to a negative ethological trait in the animal. In English, for example, it is no compliment to call someone a horse, despite the notorious British passion and admiration for horses.

One theory worth testing would be to see whether an animal's position of strength or weakness relative to man determines the positive or negative valence of the metaphorical expressions using its name. This might explain not only why subordinate domestic animals lend themselves more than wild animals to pejorative uses but also why animals such as the dog, cow, donkey, pig, and sheep—subordinate and generally parasitically dependent—so often become objects of negative cultural expressions while animals no less domestic but more autonomous and independent, like the cat, more often give rise to positive expressions. Also consistent with this explanation is the contrast between insults such as *worm, fly,* and *rat*—taken from animals that are harmful but easily overcome—and the positive metaphors linked to the wolf and the fox, animals also harmful but considered man's worthy antagonists, disdainfully aloof and independent and difficult to capture and kill.[21] In northern Thailand, for instance, such an opposition seems to be expressly recognized, and all domestic animals are considered stupid in comparison with wild animals, which are always thought of as clever and wise.[22] To formulate a theory of such general scope, however, would require the study of a much wider sample of ethnographic data on the uses of animal names and would digress widely from my main focus. I will therefore limit myself to using a more general idea as a working hypothesis: a causal connection exists between the expressions, positive or negative, that a culture derives from an animal's name and the position that animal occupies with respect to the human community.

QUESTIONS OF POSITION

As in many places in the world, in the Thai village of Baan Phraan Muan (Village of the hunter Muan) the only domestic animals allowed to frequent the inside of houses, to come and go at will as humans do, are dogs and cats.[23] Other animals—pigs, buffalo, chickens—live strictly outdoors and shelter underneath the family house at night, among the pillars on which the structure is raised. They are not crowded in at random, however, but occupy spaces assigned with great precision and in relation to the arrangement of rooms in the house above. In this way, at night every species resides on a part of the ground on which the pillars rest, and each "stable" that these columns mark out matches one type of animal: one in the sub-bedroom, another in the sub–living room, and so forth. Very rigid norms govern the distribution of living spaces, including those outside, and even require, in the case of an animal trespassing outside its assigned area, the performance of apotropaic rituals, designed to ward off possible negative consequences. For example, if an ox or a buffalo accidentally lies down in the subatrium, an area considered dirty that is meant to remain empty, a ceremony is required that expels the bad luck from the house.

The inhabitants of Baan Phraan Muan thus pay close attention and attach great importance to the boundaries and distribution of spaces and appear particularly unsettled when an animal disrupts the order that regulates traffic in domestic spaces. But to dogs and cats, tradition grants almost complete freedom of movement, and community members recognize this exceptional privilege: everyone knows that dogs and cats are special animals, and among domestic animals they constitute a specific subcategory.

Although they share this prerogative, dogs and cats are nonetheless not treated the same. Cats enjoy free access to all rooms in the house, without restriction; dogs are kept out of bedrooms and seem in general to possess a negative symbolic relation to ideas about sex and marriage. Cats are considered useful and beneficial: it's said that they have the power to keep the house cool, that they are efficacious in rituals to summon rain, and that Buddha himself created them to catch mice. Dogs, on the other hand, are explicitly defined as animals of low rank and are used in one of the worst insults you can hurl at someone: "A dog mated with your ancestors!" Why all the distrust, reservations, and bad judgments regarding dogs?

Here we are lucky to have the answer from the villagers themselves, who say it is because dogs eat excrement and couple with their parents and relatives.[24] Let's examine these two reasons. The first, the tendency toward coprophagy, is certainly one of the animal's characteristics and, though not unique to it, at least distinguishes it from the cat, in which the phenomenon is not seen with such frequency. In this case, then, the canine behavior seems to furnish a distinctive trait that makes negative cultural elaborations of this sort possible. In other words, it provides an "affordance,"[25] an ethological fact that offers the symbolic imagination a good foothold for constructing metaphors, figures, and stereotypes in which the dog plays the role of a negative referent, not least the use of its name as an insult.[26] But a hint of pretext in the second reason offered somewhat darkens the clear evidence of native explanation: the dog, they say, is incestuous. Generally speaking, no animal considers kinship an impediment to copulation, and dogs as well as cats are no exception to this rule. Why, then, is this behavior noticed and censured only in dogs?[27]

The prejudice underlying the explicit reasons offered by informants is not exclusive to the traditions of this Thai village but rather seems to be a regular feature in many folk theories about the lowly position of dogs. Here we can cite another case, this time from ancient Greece. In a passage discussing why in Rome the priest of Jupiter, the *flamen dialis*, was not allowed to touch or even speak the name of the dog or the goat, Plutarch notes that in Greece as well the dog endured ritual exclusions:

> Some argue that the dog is not allowed in the Acropolis of Athens or on the island of Delos because they copulate openly—as though cattle, pigs, and horses copulate in bedrooms and not shamelessly in the open![28]

This brilliant critical observation has not received the attention it deserves. Most classical scholars have been content to repeat the traditional explanation, that the dog was despised in Greece because it explicitly displays its sexuality—no matter that Plutarch had already pointed out the absurd pretext of this claim that imputes to dogs alone sexual conduct that is in fact common to all animal species. To bolster the "objective" validity of this traditional Greek explanation in modern times, appeals are made to the authority of Sigmund Freud, who argued that "man's best friend" has lent its name to disparaging uses because dogs pay no heed to the two strongest taboos imposed by civilization: that linked to sexual behavior and that associated with the handling of excrement.[29] Rebellious against the cultural imperative to repress the organic, like an eternal infant incapable of feeling disgust for its excrement or shame for its sexuality, the dog arouses an unconscious reaction of rejection and contempt in man, expressed in the various cultural forms of a negative stamp—insults, proverbs, traditional stories—that concern it.

It's hardly necessary to emphasize that the Freudian explanation still leaves open the important question that Plutarch's incisive critique raises: since no animal shares with man the sense of shame for its sexuality or revulsion for its excrement, why do dogs alone attract such heavy human contempt in these areas?

When Plutarch notes the strange bias of his compatriots who are shocked by canine sexuality but not at all upset by the sexual exhibitions of other domestic animals, he identifies a crucial node for interpreting the cultural representation of the dog, and not only in ancient Greece. Let us look more closely, then, at what position dogs may occupy in the cultural spaces organized by man.

A METONYMIC SUBJECT

A famous study by Claude Lévi-Strauss, focused on the problem of the relationship between categories of proper names given to individuals of various species—humans, animals, plants—and the classification systems of the cultures that produce them, has some useful pages on the specific position of dogs within the human community.[30] Starting from an analysis of the typologies of proper names reserved for different categories of domestic animals, Lévi-Strauss notes that until recently in France, dog names were normally either abstract or derived from theatrical and mythic sources, with an implicit prohibition on the use of personal names. In fact, in Italy also until not very long ago, names such as Giorgio and Pietro were not given to house animals. So the fact that a recent trend has introduced such usage among pet owners is thus a good subject of study for anthropologists of modern urban society.[31] But Lévi-Strauss's finding about customary naming practices no doubt still holds good for most traditional rural cultures, and the probability of encountering dogs named Pierre-Georges or Christine in mountain villages and the countryside is presumably quite low in France, as elsewhere.

In this naming taboo, Lévi-Strauss identified an unconscious cultural response to a profound discomfort. In essence, the dog is in such a promiscuous position, such an intimate participant in human social life, that giving it a human name would cause an excessive identification. It may live in the house, in the bedroom, be present at its master's meals, "dialogue" with people in the house—but at least in its name it must be clear that a dog is a dog and a human is something else. This concern for distinction thus falls upon the dog, and only the dog, precisely because of its special position with respect to the community. In other words, this position is distinguished by a marked metonymy—that is, by the animal's full participation in the ranks of the social organization. Other domestic animals, such as cattle and pigs, also participate in the human community in which they live. But their metonymic relation is weaker, since, although close to man, they are always perceived as nonhuman or instruments of labor or even objects of our action, there for our use and consumption. Dogs, on the other hand, not just are constantly and intensely present in cultural spaces but also collaborate and communicate in ways that make them social subjects within the human community. By contrast, with animals such as horses and birds, the relation with humans may be so much less participative that it becomes at most metaphorical: such animals, clearly distinct and distant, are perceived as decidedly other, beings different from humans that can be represented only through an act of transference.

In summary, then, some animals are felt to be decisively different and other and thus can be thought of at most as metaphors for humanity; others instead are "metonymic," having their own part in the theater of social life, but only as objects of human action; and finally there is the dog, which is not only implicated metonymically in the spaces of human action but also participates as a subject. This is why, according to Lévi-Strauss, only the dog must be held apart from man in the naming system: participation at the level of individual names as well would provoke intolerable aggravation at the dog's extraordinary "humanity" by placing a disturbing emphasis on the fact that it is perceived as a metonymic subject, a member of the human community and a social actor in its own right.

Although they relate to data from a society quite different from ancient Greece, Lévi-Strauss's reflections offer an ideal analytical tool, one worth testing in a different cultural context. The distinctions it introduces permit one to think about the relationship between humans and dogs in categories more refined than those generally evoked. Labels such as *proximate* and *domestic,* so often employed in discussions of the dog, are altogether too vague and lacking in explanatory power. Just consider the fact that they apply equally well to other animals—such as cats and farmyard animals—which elicit cultural formations clearly different from and even the opposite of those regarding dogs.[32] With the dual definition of *metonymic subject* we are instead able to reflect on the position of the animal and on the structural constants of the human-dog relationship, taking into account both their unique and specific traits and how these were imagined in ancient culture.

2

The Dog in Greece

Quid immerentis hospites vexas, canis
*   ignavus adversum lupos?*
Quin huc inanis, si potes, vertis minas
*   et me remorsurum petis?*
Nam qualis aut Molossus aut fulvus Lacon,
*   amica vis pastoribus,*
agam per altas aure sublata nives
*   quaecumque praecedet fera;*
tu cum timenda voce complesti nemus,
*   proiectum odoraris cibum.*

Why needlessly torment guests, you cowardly dog among wolves?
Why not turn, if you can, your empty threats here and chase me, who'll
    bite back?
For like a Molossian or golden Laconian, the friendly force of shepherds,
I'll head through deep snows, ears straight up, to hunt down any beast—
while you fill the woods with your frightful voice
and sniff at food that is thrown you.

—HORACE, EPODES 6.1–10

HOMERIC DOGS

We will begin to track the salient traits of the Greek representation of dogs with Homer, not because the *Iliad* and the *Odyssey* are somehow privileged sources for our argument but rather because this will allow us to dispel the notion that one finds in these poems a "Homeric" dog, one different from the animal of later centuries. In chapter 1 I noted the view, common in many studies on this topic, that the epics provide evidence that in protohistorical Greece the dog was not yet fully domesticated, that it was perceived as a still partly wild animal and, for this reason, occupied a lower place in the cultural taxonomy. The following reflections will thus do double duty, both furnishing a first set of data on the cultural figure of the dog and demonstrating that Homeric dogs do not differ from those that Greeks in later periods talked about—nor indeed from those we know today.

We begin by noting the formal consistency of most of the canine images that recur in the poems. Indeed, the *Iliad* and the *Odyssey* contain a rich cluster of passages that speak of the dog in the same manner, and that clearly indicate, by the way it appears in the narrative, the dog's position in the cultural imagination of the rhapsodes and their audiences.

As is well known, the *Iliad*'s heroic battles beneath the walls of Troy are often described in hunting terms. In such cases the hero pursuing an enemy is equated, by means of simile, with a wild beast that, trusting its strength and its unconquered courage, attacks or chases its prey. Within this hunting imagery the animals most often used to represent the hero are *thēres*, wild and untamable beasts of the forest, chief among them lions and boars. A wild beast is the term of comparison most frequently used to describe the conquering warrior, he who best embodies the heroic virtues of a fighter: courage, contempt for danger, force, and indomitable violence.[1]

In the simile, the opponent of the hero-beast sometimes takes the form of hunters trying to catch it or herdsmen trying to protect their animals from its attack. And always—coherent with the realism of the simile—by the side of the hunters and the herdsmen are their dogs. This combined presence in the image of the hero-beast's collective antagonist is conveyed by a typical expression that, when variable features are removed, can be summarized with the schema "dogs and men." The intervention of the enemies opposing the hero is represented each time by the arrival on the scene of "dogs and strong young men," or "dogs and men of the country," or again "dogs and herdsmen," or, in the simplest variant, "dogs and men."[2] The very fact that the concerted action of hunters and herdsmen against the beast is imagined poetically as cooperation between dogs and men is an important indicator. An analysis of several of these passages will clarify how the formulaic nexus "dogs and men" allows us to trace an enduring conception of the relation between man and dog that serves as the basis for the poetic convention.[3]

When Odysseus, in battle, finds himself surrounded by Trojans, he is described as a boar beset by "dogs and strong young men" leaping around him; although the beast, by sharpening its tusks, displays in full its wild and frightening force, the latter don't back down but stand strong and await the attack:

> As when around a wild boar dogs and strong young men
> are rushing, and it comes out of the deep bush
> sharpening the white tusk in its curved jaws,
> and they leap all round it; and its gnashing of teeth
> rises up, but they wait for it, although it is terrifying;
> so then around Odysseus dear to Zeus leaped
> the Trojans.[4]

We can see how in the balance of the Homeric simile the hunter-Trojans confront the hero-beast Odysseus, but this group of hunters, presented as a homogenous bloc opposing the solitary hero, is made up of "dogs and strong young men." The dogs and young hunters compose in the image a united set, compact and indistinct. They are the collective subject of a common verbal action and an identical behavioral stance. This is not an isolated case. In another simile, the Trojans, attempting to capture the corpse of Patroclus, are "dogs and strong young men" whom the boar-Ajax scatters with the dreadful ferocity of his gaze.[5]

The collaborative relationship linking men and dogs binds them in a harmonious and homogenous collective and, moreover, places them in the same position with respect to the creature of the wild.[6] When the Danaans are hot in pursuit of the Trojans, Hector, to whom Apollo has appeared and promised protection, gathers strength and courage and descends to the field to urge his comrades to fight back. The sequence of events is described through a simile that compares the pressing Greek army to a group of "dogs and men of the country" hunting a deer or goat, while Hector is a lion that suddenly appears on their path and scares them all to flight:

> Like an antlered deer or wild goat
> that dogs and men of the country assault . . .
> but at their shouting a fair-maned lion appears
> on their path, abruptly sets all to flight, although they were eager.[7]

This common weakness of "dogs and men" in the face of a wild beast appears in several Homeric similes. An image of the hunting dog and hunters at times serves to describe the hero's assault as he pursues the routed enemy. At that moment he is in a position of strength, like hunters chasing wounded prey whose only hope for salvation is in speed of flight. So, for example, Achilles pursuing Hector is like a dog chasing a baby deer, Odysseus and Diomedes pursue Dolon as dogs would a hare or doe, and Antilochus leaps on the fleeing Trojans like a dog on a wounded stag.[8] But when, instead, the enemy is a strong lion or boar that wheels to fight head on, the position of the hunters and dogs reverses: they become weak, uncertain, and the "dogs and men" are afraid. Hence the episode in which Hector attacks the Achaeans "like a dog sometimes attacks a wild boar or lion from behind," biting at its flanks and its legs but "watching out for it wheeling around" in fear of it suddenly getting in front. In several episodes a single hero simply needs to turn around and confront his enemies head on in order to scatter them en masse, as a wild beast might do when chased by hunters and dogs.[9]

The nexus "dogs and men" also appears in similes depicting scenes of guarding flocks and herds. In these cases, too, men and dogs compose a unified front against the wild beast, with varying results but parallel action. The best example of this is when Menelaus has just killed Euphorbus and is about to strip his armor as spoils. None of the Trojans dares to go against him: he is like a lion "raised in the mountains" that steals a cow from the herd and devours it unperturbed while

around it dogs and herdsmen
cry out, but at a distance, and are not willing
to go up against it, being gripped by livid terror.[10]

A final example of this close participation of man and dog comes in a rather complex simile involving Antilochus. On orders from Menelaus, the young warrior rushes out against the Trojans and at first is compared to a hunting dog pouncing on a wounded stag. But then, when Hector comes out against him, his position of strength falters, and he begins to retreat. However, this change of stance is not expressed, as we might expect, by the figure of a dog retreating. Instead of developing the first simile, the poet decides to introduce a new one: the scenario shifts suddenly, and now Antilochus, frightened by Hector's advance, is likened to a beast, but one trembling with fear because it has just committed a misdeed and is about to flee before it is surrounded by a crowd of men and punished.[11] What misdeed could the beast have committed? It has slain, Homer says, "a dog or cowherd," an expression that can be seen as a variation on the phrase "dogs and men" in which the idea of a union between man and dog becomes simple equivalence: "dog or man," indifferently. This form of the phrase also provides clear evidence that the conceptual model of the man-dog relationship underpinning the various formulaic instances was based on a notion of full participation, an interpenetration of the two categories. The dog doesn't just help the herdsman work and get exposed to the same risks; he is himself a herdsman, posted as a cowherd to defend the cattle, and whether the man or the dog dies, the lion or wolf of the simile has committed a crime that deserves equal punishment.

So we see that in Homer, collaboration between man and dog is always a harmonious synergy, whether the job is to guard or to hunt. For whatever function they are used, dogs appear as part of the human group and are integrated members of the community. The text therefore does not support the notion that one can trace in it a not yet fully domesticated Homeric dog any more than it confirms the theory that hunting dogs enjoyed a privileged status in Greece and were considered more civilized than guard and herd dogs and therefore closer to man than other types of dog. It has been proposed that Homer presents a variety of dogs, differing in degree of domestication: the hunting dog, fully domesticated; the guard dog, semiwild and aggressive; and finally, further down the list, semistray or feral dogs, wild and vicious, given to anthropophagy and scavenging carrion.[12] Leaving aside for now the corpse-eating dogs, to which we'll return later, suffice it to say that such a list of degrees of domestication is not evident in the similes, which use the phrase "dogs and men" equally for hunting dogs and for guard and herd dogs; in fact, this hypothesis rests on one episode in the poems, which thus deserves further discussion.

Odysseus has just arrived on Ithaca. Athena has given him the unrecognizable appearance of an old beggar so the hero can enter town and his palace without arousing suspicion among his wife's suitors or those of his household who have not remained faithful throughout his long absence. But first, on the goddess's advice, Odysseus heads to the hut of his swineherd Eumaeus, one of the old servants still devoted to his memory. As he approaches the hut, Odysseus is suddenly attacked by the swineherd's dogs, four big brutes—says the poem—"just like beasts," that run out at him with threatening barks; Odysseus can't do anything except sit down and stay still, waiting for help from Eumaeus, who arrives and saves him, scattering the dogs with stones.[13]

Now, Eumaeus's dogs are guard dogs. Raised by the swineherd, they sleep with the pigs, and their job is obviously to guard the pigs, the pigsties, and the farm. So it's not strange that they are threatening "beasts" that behave aggressively toward a stranger; we should be surprised if it were otherwise. That Homer says they are "just like beasts" at the start of the scene should thus be interpreted simply as emphasis—hardly superfluous, given the unfolding scene—on their imposing figures: even to see Eumaeus's dogs sleeping is scary, because their size and demeanor show clearly for what purpose the swineherd reared and raised them.

Instead, this phrase has given rise to a series of ruminations on the presumed peculiarity of the Homeric dog. As already noted, some scholars have proposed a unique status for the guard dog, half-wild and situated on a lower rung of the domesticity scale than the tame and submissive hunting and companion dogs.[14] Others have even wanted to consider the dogs of Eumaeus as ancestors of an infamous Balkan breed common until modern times and known for its extraordinary ferocity.[15] As so often happens, an already forced interpretation gives rise to others still more far-fetched, each layer of exegesis building on the previous ones until the text is completely lost from view. Hence the bizarre proposal that the peculiar ferocity of Eumaeus's dogs would explain why, in a later scene, the swineherd is threatened with being mauled to death by his own dogs[16]—an interpretation that, as we'll see in the next chapter, fails to recognize the traditional and stereotyped nature of this kind of threat.

Returning, then, to the episode where Odysseus is attacked at the farmstead of Eumaeus, we see that the swineherd's dogs are not constitutionally more savage than others. Simply put, as guard dogs they are doing their job when they unleash their aggression against strangers. By attacking Odysseus they are behaving exactly as their master wants and presumably as he himself has trained them to behave. Ultimately, one can conclude that, so far as we can tell, the dog represented in the poems was exactly the animal we are familiar with today, and further, we can be certain that already in the protohistorical period the Greeks saw the dog as not only a fully domesticated animal but one so involved in human activity and so constantly present in social life that it was a creature uniquely homologous to man.

On closer inspection, the fact that the dog sometimes shows a wild side and acts "like a beast" is clearly just another aspect of this homology. In fact, Homer uses the same expression both to describe Eumaeus's dogs and in connection with one of the most prominent heroes of the Trojan War, Menelaus, who in the hot fury of battle becomes "like a beast." And just as the hero's savage ferocity is only one of his personality traits, a temporary psychological disposition and not the characteristic of a species or a cultural marker for the institution of a race of "half-wild" warriors, so the ferocity of Eumaeus's dogs is but one transitory and functional aspect of their being dogs, not a sign of their belonging to a particular species or of their special position on a presumed scale of domestication. In fact, the dogs that were so aggressive with Odysseus are the same lovable creatures that in a later episode run out quite tamely and fawn on Telemachus in welcome.[17]

Interestingly enough, ancient readers interpreted the episode where these dogs attack Odysseus in a manner diametrically opposed to that of modern interpreters who see Eumaeus's "mongrels" as examples of a wild and fierce canine breed. As it happens, the Greeks loved to cite this episode, not to show how poorly tamed guard dogs were during the heroic age but, on the contrary, to illustrate an extraordinary characteristic of canine psychology that clearly distinguishes dogs from "beasts" and other carnivores and makes them closer to man: their gentleness and submissiveness. The behavior of Eumaeus's dogs was taken as an example of the virtuous tendency, common to dogs and men, of allaying one's wrath and anger when the person against whom one's aggression is turned makes postures of submission. So it is that, according to Plutarch, by refraining from sinking their teeth into poor Odysseus, Eumaeus's dogs give evidence of their nature "at once mild and proud," because they refuse to attack an adversary who is unarmed and submissive.[18] Notably, Plutarch here uses the term *hēmeros*, an adjective that has much to do not only with gentleness but also with domesticity and civilization. Thus Eumaeus's dogs, contrary to what some modern readers maintain, are a typical example of how "civil" an animal the dog is, endowed with the sense of moderation usually considered an exclusively human privilege. But if the opinion of Plutarch, a passionate champion of the virtue of animals, might be suspected of some tendentiousness,[19] one would hardly say the same of Aristotle, who explained how the reaction of dogs before someone sitting down was the clearest evidence of the principle of human psychology as well, wherein anger tends to abate before those who humble themselves and concede their inferiority.[20]

Eumaeus's dogs, which acted "just like beasts," therefore are not normal guard dogs but rather, in the eyes of philosophers reading Homer, appeared to be particularly wise and temperate guard dogs, able to limit their aggression and thereby demonstrate that they share with man an aptitude for not raging against one who willingly submits to them.[21] The Homeric dog is no different from the domesticated, collaborative animal of later periods. Homer's dogs are dogs like all the rest: some more gentle, some more fierce; some more domesticated (if one wants to call it that), if only because they have an owner and live indoors, others more wild

because they are strays—and each of these is gentler or fiercer according to circumstances and contexts. That humans are social animals is not thrown into doubt
by the existence of misanthropes and hermits, and no person is at every moment
of their life a proponent of being social. In the same way, even if from a zoological
and ethological perspective, it makes sense to speak of "domesticated animals,"
from an anthropological perspective no species is wholly and by definition domesticated, and a dog can always show its wild side without being excluded for that
reason from the class of *Canis familiaris*.[22]

To conclude this foray into the Homeric poems, let's add one final proof of the
basic fellowship between man and dog in heroic society. In this case, again, it is
formulaic diction that offers the clue. Two passages in the *Odyssey* use the same
expression to describe Telemachus as he leaves the house accompanied by his
dogs, saying he exited the hall "and together with him his two swift dogs went
behind."[23] The phrase "together with him [*hama tōi*]" seems to indicate the sort of
companionship that exists between the young prince and his dogs, a relation like
that of a master and his servants or of a hero and his troops.[24] A third passage,
which slightly extends the expression, is even clearer. Telemachus sets out for the
assembly "not alone, but with him [*ouk oios, hama tōi ge*] his swift-footed dogs
went behind."[25] Significantly, the same sort of expression recurs in entirely human
contexts; for example, when Nausicaa leaves her father's palace, having prepared
the mule cart, she heads for the river "not alone, but with her [*ouk oiēn, hama tēi
ge*] her nursemaids went also."[26] The use of this expression for Telemachus's departure from the palace with his dogs would be unthinkable if the dog were not
regarded as having a position of metonymic contiguity with humans, enabling
them to be considered similar to traveling companions or attendants, such as Nausicaa's nursemaids, whose presence renders a person "not alone."[27]

From the passages discussed, which represent a large percentage of the places
where Homer mentions dogs, we can confidently affirm, therefore, that these texts
present neither a negative representation of the dog nor any sign of its peculiar
ferocity nor again any codified difference of status for different types of dog. Not at
all wild but instead a perfectly collaborative animal, the dog in Homer can be said
to possess a marked metonymic character: that is, it participates in human life so
closely that it is placed alongside human beings and in opposition to wild beasts in
many everyday functions, such as companionship and protection of property.

THE TABLE COMPANION

Having cleared the field of evolutionistic theories about the domestication of the
Greek dog, we can now consider the terms of the human-dog relationship and the
specific traits that ancient culture attributed to the animal, in order to better
understand what the dog's metonymic position involved, on what levels the

animal participated in human life, and how its similarity and difference, nearness and distance, were articulated in each of these areas.

Homer once again provides the first testimony on one of the most important aspects of the dog's representation in Greece, namely, its feeding habits. The poems give the first evidence of the habit of allowing dogs access to the table during the owner's meals, a fact so culturally significant that some dogs were even bred to become table animals, just as how today some are bred and reared as lapdogs. The most interesting hint of the dog's presence at its owner's table is in the *Odyssey,* in the well-known episode where the hero encounters his dog Argus. Having returned to Ithaca in disguise and now nearing his palace, Odysseus sees his old dog lying sad and neglected on a pile of manure. Famously, the animal senses Odysseus's presence but can only muster the energy to wag its tail and lower its ears, without running up to greet its old master. The one and only creature on the island to recognize the hero despite his disguise and his long years away, Argus moves Odysseus to tears. But lest the dog's reaction and Odysseus's own emotions raise the suspicion of Eumaeus, still unaware of his lord's true identity, the wily king stages a diversion: pretending not to know the creature, he says to the swineherd that at one time it must have been a fine animal, but now one cannot tell whether it was a quick runner or whether it was like "the dogs of the table [*trapezēes*] that their masters breed for elegance."[28]

The passage is important, for it attests to the fact that in the Homeric world, the dog could be an ornamental animal, serving a function other than as part of the workforce in daily labors and playing instead a voluptuary role somewhat comparable to that of today's companion animals. Already in archaic Greece, then, the dog could be accepted into an eminently social space—in this case, where food was eaten—and even more, could perform a social function: conferring prestige on his master's table. Table dogs were not raised to provide a service, such as hunting or guarding, and were selected not for their strength or ability but exclusively for their beauty: mere decorative elements, these animals attest by their presence to the richness of a laden table, the abundance of food able to feed many useless mouths, and presumably, the more dogs at the table, the more splendid was the effect of the display.[29] Not even during war expeditions did noble Achaeans give up surrounding themselves with dogs: in Patroclus's tent at Troy, as many as nine dogs loitered.[30]

From the polemical tone of Odysseus's question to Eumaeus, however, we can infer that not all aristocrats considered the practice of raising dogs for beauty respectable and that some nobility with more austere views saw table dogs as useless creatures, a waste of food, a luxury equivalent to the worst debauchery. Another hint of this moral censure is found in idiomatic usage later than Homer, when the term *trapezeus* was used for a parasite, the proverbial man "of the table," whose only thought is to find a loaded table where he can get a free meal.[31] To some, then, table dogs were despicable freeloaders, which makes sense since one of the most common paradigms of the relationship between man and domestic animal was based, as we will see later, on the debt the animal was thought to owe man in return for being fed. Dogs, like raised animals more generally, were expected to return the favor of feeding and care by providing useful service and benefits.

So not all Greek dogs lived the comfortable life enjoyed by the dogs of Trojan and Mycenaean kings. Even in Homer, the tendency of dogs to want and look for human food appears to be judged in various ways. If table dogs were a luxury item in some aristocratic circles, in other cases the presence of dogs in dining spaces was not particularly appreciated. From a passage in the *Odyssey* we learn, for example, that during meals some servants were posted at the edges of Ithaca's palace hall to repel any attempts of intrusion by dogs and pigs.[32] So, clearly, dogs were not always—or not all dogs were—allowed in the dining room; in some cases they endured the same exclusion from social spaces for eating traditionally imposed on pigs.

Still, the presence of dogs at human tables is amply attested in later periods as well. Post-Homeric sources offer a wealth of evidence for this participation, permitting us to document just how the animal took part in the rituals of human eating. From a great number of references and allusions in ancient texts, we learn that dogs were certainly eating companions, but of the lowest class, and they attended their master's tables to perform the humiliating task of eating table scraps. Not unlike what often enough still happens in our own kitchens and dining rooms, Greeks at the table would throw to dogs the bones and less edible pieces of meat, that is, the waste from human meals.[33] To the dogs also went the so-called *apomagdaliai,* napkins of a sort, made of soft dough, with which, during the meal, one wiped grease and fat off one's hands and then threw on the ground. In this case, we are dealing with not even leftovers but garbage plain and simple, refuse that dogs took away like "trash collectors" for the dining room.[34]

It also happened, however, that an owner might take the trouble when dining away from home to collect morsels to take back to his dog. This occurred quite often, it seems, to judge from the fact that Homer uses it as an example in a simile during the Circe episode in the *Odyssey.* As Odysseus's men approach the sorceress's house, they see a truly astounding spectacle: wolves and lions, bewitched by the goddess's potions, run up to them tamely, Homer says, "like dogs greet their master when he comes home from a meal, because he always brings them some morsels that please their heart [*meiligmata thymou*]."[35]

In an amusing fable of Aesop, this practice is explicitly and significantly interpreted as a privilege reserved for dogs, and not other domestic animals, on account of their unique bond of affection with their masters. In the fable is a little dog, a Maltese with long hair, which in Greece typically served as a companion animal.[36] Its master pampered it and had a habit of bringing back leftovers from dinners and throwing them to it as soon as it ran up to greet him. This made the master's poor donkey jealous, since it did not enjoy the same attention. So one day the donkey decided to try to imitate the little dog: when it saw the master returning from a dinner, it ran up and fawned on him in greeting, hoping to get some morsel. But in its misguided attempt to jump up to the master, it kicked him and wound up getting, instead of a tasty treat, a sound beating. This goes to show—as the final moral suggests—that not everyone is born to do everything: greeting the master is a canine specialty, and it's better for other animals to leave it to the dogs. To try to be the dogs' equals and aspire to their privileges is futile, if not counterproductive.

It is thus in the arena of food that one of the most important aspects of the symbiosis between humans and dogs plays out. This division of foodstuffs naturally gives scope for representations of various sorts, according to the different judgments that each social context and each individual brings to it. The dog can figure at different times as a welcome guest and a mark of luxury at the table, as an annoying parasite, as simply an eater of refuse, or as a beloved pet for which leftovers are saved. In each case, the dog is still the animal nearest to man from the point of view of eating habits. All the other domestic animals get their food from man, but they eat nonhuman food: horses, donkeys, goats, and cows, for instance, all eat grass, hay, and raw barley.[37] But the dog figures as a real and true dining companion, the animal with which people divide their own food and often share even the time and place of its consumption. Still, this fellowship does not create a situation of equality: the parts that belong to the dog are mostly predetermined—bones, gristle, fat unwanted by people—and constitute the waste products of human eating. As such, the banquet is the space that both unites men and dogs and distinguishes them, by fixing a definite hierarchy.

The hierarchy of the table places dogs definitively below humans and above the other animals. They therefore occupy an intermediate position and have, so to speak, two faces: when seen as included in the human ranks of honor, they sit on the lowest rung of the eating scale, the seat of the miserable lowly, but if we picture them in a ranking of animals, they are the favorite, the best nourished, as the Aesop fable clearly indicates, with its insistence on the dietary ease the dog enjoys because of its cozy relationship with humans. Last among men at the dinner table but first among house animals, the dog sits in the border zone that divides human from animal diets, a gray area without sharp lines where one reality blurs into the other.

The intimate relation between man and dog with respect to food, as we have said, consists not solely in their sharing the same diet but in the fact that they eat it in the same places and at the same times. The dining room, the table, the kitchen are the cultural spaces where the dog, unique among animals, is allowed to enter and to eat: its metonymic character on this point is clear. The peculiarity of this coincidence of the dog's and man's dietary practices emerges in a passage of Theophrastus's *Char-*

acters, where one sees how, by contrast, the common cultural norm posits a radical distance between human eating and that of the other domestic animals.[38] Among the amusing collection of human types compiled by Aristotle's pupil is the country yokel (*agroikos*), a bumpkin whose uncouth ways are manifested in a range of improper manners, such as wearing big shoes, talking loudly, seeking advice from slaves, and sitting in a sloppy manner. One of his boorish habits is eating while he's feeding the beasts of burden; this shows that, contrary to the dog's presence at his master's table, the coincidence of human food with that of cattle, donkeys, and horses[39] constituted an incongruous situation, counter to good manners and absolutely unthinkable for a well-mannered citizen. You may eat with dogs, and indeed the aristocrats do, but to eat with cows and horses is sheer savagery.

The dog thus enjoys an institutionalized privilege to attend its master's table, which sometimes (at least in the imaginary psychology that humans attribute to it) risks giving him a big head. In one funny Aesop's fable, a dog, seeing his master invite a friend to dinner, decides he'd like to invite a dog friend over too.[40] His attempt, as one can imagine, doesn't turn out well. The visiting dog, seen by the cook as it wanders around the kitchen sniffing the lavish banquet, gets thrown out the window. Here we have a case where the dog incorrectly interprets its role as its master's dining companion, on shamelessly equal terms: it acts like the double of its master, as though it can throw dinner parties, instead of doing what it should do, staying in its place as the disciplined subordinate that waits for leftovers under the table. Here, then, is a first instance of how the metonymic position of the dog—its being perceived as an element of the human community—could give rise to stories of transgressive intrusion, imaginative constructs that suspect the animal of wanting to take advantage of its privileged position to become an unwelcome competitor of man. A dog can be at the table, but it must stay in its place. This ethical and normative burden to which the dog was subjected as a member of cultural and social spaces is a constant that we will see recurring time and again.

"HUNGRY LIKE A WOLF" AND MENTAL DISTURBANCES

Whether they get tidbits under the table, leftovers given outdoors, or carcasses and scraps of offal kept for them by the cook, dogs eat a part—the residual part, let's say—of what their owners eat. One consequence of this practice is that their diet tends to be oriented toward the regime of the cooked, those processed foods—boiled, roasted, baked, or otherwise subjected to transformative procedures prior to being eaten—that are the almost exclusive prerogative of the human diet and that distinguish our dietary regime from those of other animals.

The dog eats cooked meat, cooked fish, baked goods such as bread and rolls, and cheeses, all eminently cultural foods, and displays a marked proclivity for this diet, as indicated by the many ancient sources that represent it as ever intent on stealing off with dishes from the kitchen. In a fragment of the comic poet Anaxandrides, for example, a dog steals from its master a dish called *to opson,* a term that indicates specifically cooked food, and in Aristophanes's comedies, the dog is the thief par excellence on account of its notorious habit of snatching cheeses, rolls, and other dishes from the kitchen and the spread table.[41] In Hesiod, the food that an owner gives his dog is called *sitos,* a word that means "grains" and more generally foods derived from cereals, those plants—as opposed to wild grasses—considered cooked because the work of cultivation makes them soft and pleasant. Cereal grains are indeed the fruit of the farmer's labor: he makes them grow in the heat of the sun, and by tilling and plowing the land he makes them soft to the palate, just as the kitchen's hearth does with raw foods. *Sitos* was such a part of culture and the cooked that to define the savage, brutal nature of the men of the Bronze Age, who did not yet practice agriculture, it was enough to say that "they did not eat *sitos,*" while human beings, in contrast to gods and beasts, could be described simply as "those who eat *sitos.*" The testimony of Hesiod is even more significant if one considers that in the same passage, when the poet speaks of the diet of cows and mules, he chooses instead from terms for uncultivated foods—wild plants, moist and "raw," such as hay and fodder.[42]

So the dog shares with humans a love for cooked foods, for grain and its products. But sharing does not mean identity: the dog's metonymy is based on alterity and difference as well as similarity and nearness. On closer look, this matter of diet puts the dog in an ambiguous position. On one hand, it prefers culture's cooked foods, but in other ways its diet is entirely antithetical to man's. For instance, dogs despise raw vegetables and only eat grass as an emetic, when they need to vomit.[43] At the same time, they enjoy meat raw, which humans find edible only when cooked or otherwise processed. The dog's rejection of raw vegetables and taste for bloody meats reveals its close kinship with other four-footed carnivores that the Greeks called "sharp-toothed" (*karcharodonta*), with which it was normally grouped, especially when it showed its radical distance from the herbivores.[44] So the dog consumes cooked food but at the same time is bloodthirsty and raw-eating, able to tear still-throbbing meat to pieces, a diet that puts it halfway between humans and wild carnivores such as wolves and lions.

Their tendency toward the wildness of a carnivore features in the way Greek culture represents dogs. In Aesop's fables, for example, the dog always appears at man's side, as defender of its master's flocks. But its wild side sometimes peeks out, as when, faced with the flattery of a wolf that calls him "brother" and promises to split the spoils with him, the dog gives in to the bribe and surrenders the sheep he's guarding in exchange for a portion of meat.[45] This fable passed into proverb: of a thief who offered a share of his spoils to placate the gods, it could be said that he acted like a wolf with a shepherd's dog, in the mistaken illusion that a portion of ill-gotten goods could bribe the divinity into complicity.⁴⁶ Aesop also tells of a dog that takes advantage of a sheep recently slaughtered by a wolf, willingly eating some morsels.⁴⁷ In such a case, the Greeks believed, by eating raw meat a herd dog may turn into a hunting hound.⁴⁸ Not to mention that the dog's kinship with predators such as wolves, foxes, tigers, and lions was thought to be so close that some breeds were believed to have originated in a cross with one of these animals: the dogs of Cyrene were said to be a cross between dog and wolf, and the prized hunting breed the Laconian a cross between dog and fox; from the coupling of dogs and tigers, it was said, the Indians got their large, fierce breed used for defense and in combat; finally, the Hyrcanian, also large, was believed to derive from crossing dogs and lions.⁴⁹

This kinship with raw-eating beasts, though close, manifests subtly in dogs, in the form of a latent tendency that reveals itself only in certain circumstances. As a rule, the dog is not a predator. The raw meat it eats generally comes from animals killed by others. Otherwise, man could not entrust to it the tasks of hunting and protecting flocks. In fact, even when it hunts, the dog is not trying to procure meat to eat but instead doing it for the pleasure of the chase, and it takes delight in the satisfaction of its master, who is the one directing the hunting. In his *Cynegeticus*—a precious resource for this research—Xenophon portrays the pleasure, which in his view is expressed with a conspicuous smile of joy, that a good hunting dog feels when it manages to find or sets off to follow a track.⁵⁰ The prey neither belongs to the dog nor is killed by it, except in rare cases such as during training, when the hunter may reward his helper animal for finding a rabbit by handing it over to be torn apart. Otherwise, the dog does nothing more than hold the prey, alive, until the hunter comes and decides what to do with it.⁵¹ Even in the two Aesop's fables about a dog bribed by a wolf, the guard dog waits until a sheep is killed and only then takes advantage of the opportunity to eat it. Similarly, entrails snatched from the kitchen are from animals already dead, as are those that a hunter tosses his dog from the prey killed during the chase.⁵²

This lack of natural predation is so much the case that when a dog's wild, predatory instinct gets the upper hand and it starts devouring live prey, it is thought to be suffering from a disease: it is a dog gone mad (*lyssētēr, lyssōdēs*), afflicted with a malady that in Greek was called *lyssa,* a term derived from the word for wolf (*lykos*).⁵³ The symptoms of lyssa are fits of pathological aggression during which a dog loses itself, becoming like its most ferocious wild ancestor and, so to speak, "turning wolf." In fact, the term indicates more a symptomatology than a pathology properly speaking and denotes behavior unnecessarily and indiscriminately wild, a blind fury that might be caused by a real pathogenic agent—especially canine rabies—or by a momentary lapse of control over aggressive impulses.⁵⁴

In other words, the dog's violent energy is normally unleashed with a certain order and control, and it is because of this that man is able to exploit it for his own ends. It is an aggression that distinguishes between the familiar and the foreign, the flock to protect and the predator to attack, the hunter to help and the prey to pursue. But when a dog is afflicted with lyssa, its mental clarity wavers and it tends not to make distinctions, becoming hostile to all, a savage wolf. In this sense, a dog differs from a wolf as a sane person from a psychopath. And if to suffer from lyssa is to become a wolf, it is clear that the main difference between the dog and its wild brother is located precisely in the sane dog's capacity to exercise judgment in using violent force. Nevertheless, the fact that lyssa is a typically canine illness—that the dog is thought to be particularly and constitutionally vulnerable to mental imbalance—shows how thin a line separates its aggression from the wolf's.

Some well-known myths and rituals seem to reflect the anxiety that the dog's congenital wavering between docility and fierce aggression might arouse in a culture like that of Greece, which relied on the animals for several important duties. At Argos, for example, they celebrated a festival called Arnēis, "Of the lambs," or Kynophontis, "Of the slaughter of dogs," during which the Argives killed any dog that happened to be nearby. The festival's foundation myth told of a child, Linos, the son of Apollo and a maiden, who was abandoned after birth and then raised by a shepherd, who brought him up among his lambs. But one day, the shepherd's dogs tore the boy apart. From that time, the Argives began to celebrate their annual ritual massacre of dogs, to punish them for their crime and to expiate the death of Linos by placating the wrath of his father, Apollo.[55] It seems reasonable to suppose that beneath this ritual and its etiological myth lay an understandable preoccupation with the reliability of herd dogs. The very name of the festival and the month in which it fell—Arneios, "month of lambs"—seem to indicate that the sacrificial expiation aimed to secure the safety of flocks by averting the danger of inappropriate behavior from the dogs posted to protect them. The worst and most shameful thing that can happen to a shepherd, Plato said, is to raise dogs that "through intemperance, hunger, or any other bad habit" behave like wolves and attack the flock.[56] As a rule, when a dog attacked livestock it was immediately put down.[57]

Greeks also harbored grave suspicions about hunting dogs, concern that the animal accompanying the hunt might at any moment turn into a fierce wolf and unleash indiscriminate aggression against the wrong prey. This is the situation illustrated, for instance, by the infamously cruel myth of Actaeon, in which hunting dogs end up dismembering their own master. In one version of the myth, this happened because Artemis transformed Actaeon into a stag, thus misleading his pack of dogs, who were convinced they were attacking a prey animal. In another version, the dogs' sudden blindness was due to an attack of lyssa that impaired their judgment. But in either version of this story of an unfortunate hunter, the dogs no longer recognize their master and their aggression fatally overflows in an improper direction.[58]

A dog might suffer a sudden and unexpected attack of lyssa at any moment and turn from a faithful companion and co-worker into the enemy, a wolf, the "butcher," for whom every living thing is nothing but meat to eat.[59] As said before, we are not just dealing with a particular predisposition of dogs to become rabid; although it may indicate the genuine pathology of canine rabies as well, the term lyssa had a more generic meaning and could refer to sudden and unexpected outbursts of indiscriminate aggression not necessarily caused by a disease. A dog might occasionally turn wolf only from irresistible hunger or rage.[60]

This worrisome aspect of dogs is also evident in Homer. In one episode, Teucer, seeing Hector raging with unchecked violence against the enemy line and unable to strike him, calls him a "*lyssētēr* dog."[61] This insult is not, as one might suppose, purely a metaphor, since lyssa, wolflike violence, was in fact a state into which human beings could also fall.[62] The term could also refer to a form of homicidal mania, an attack of blind and savage violence of the sort that overtakes the spirits of the strongest warriors—precisely those heroes, such as Hector and Achilles, who excel in hand-to-hand combat, advancing irresistibly into the enemy camp by force of arms and leaving the ground littered with corpses. So, for example, Odysseus describes to Achilles the unstoppable violence of Hector on the field of battle thus:

> He's so mad it's frightening, and, trusting in Zeus, he hasn't the least respect
> for men or gods; a powerful lyssa has come over him.[63]

This heroic excess, the unleashed fury that knows no rein of respect for anything, is one of the ambiguous virtues of the Homeric warrior. Intimately connected to martial valor, lyssa is nevertheless a form of insanity, of madness, as the start of the above quote clearly shows. Even of Achilles it is said that "a violent lyssa always possessed his heart," and regarding the constitutionally excessive character of the son of Peleus there can be few doubts.[64]

In sum, if the dog is liable to degenerate into a wolf, to unleash aggression without limits, the same thing can happen to man. Even here one cannot help but notice the extraordinary principle of metonymy that governs the representation of dogs in Greece. An animal subject to a disturbance consisting in impaired self-control and inability to direct aggression toward the proper objects is not all that far from participating in the typically human mental opposition between sanity and madness.

THE FACULTY OF DISCERNMENT
AND CONGENITAL DEFECTS

That dogs' mental stability might be an object of special attention makes sense when one realizes that the functions given to them—hunter, guardian of flocks—were based in large part on their ability to recognize, to correctly perceive and make distinctions. Already in Homer, the theme of cognitive faculties—having sharp senses and knowing the identity of perceived objects—plays a significant role in the appearance of some canine figures: thus, there is the dog that recognizes its master's friends, the one that recognizes its master even despite his absence of many years and his disguise, and the dogs that identify the invisible presence of a divinity.[65]

In short, the dog is ideally able to discern and distinguish individuals, leading it to adapt its behavior to different situations. This faculty, however, not only is subject to occasional pathological deviance, as seen above, but also has normal manifestations that are a bit different from those of typical human perception and discernment. For example, dogs can perceive and recognize things that people cannot, allowing them to track scents, flush out hidden prey, or detect presences in the dark of night. But in other cases, they are incapable of distinguishing what people can normally distinguish.

Unlike human beings, for example, a dog doesn't distinguish between strangers of (presumed) good and bad intent. Dogs treat everyone unknown to them as an enemy to attack, not a potential guest to be welcomed—as anyone well knows who has been invited to dinner at a house guarded by dogs! Obviously, the results of this congenital mental blindness are most frequently observed in guard dogs, on account of their function, but many dogs placed in a position to show it will reveal the same deficiency in this area.

On this point, then, the dog is quite far from culture and civility, one of whose most important imperatives is the correct practice of hospitality (*xenia*), of welcoming strangers in need. In Greece, hospitality to strangers was a duty no good person could avoid, on pain of terrible wrath from Zeus "of Strangers" (Xenios), who punished those who denied polite requests for aid from travelers in distress. Though endowed with discernment, dogs are simply unable to share with man this solidarity with unfamiliar travelers. And in their constitutional inability to recognize *xenia,* dogs expose their bestial nature and their proximity to those brutish men who populate the margins of the civilized world: aggressive, savage races such as the Cyclopes.[66] In short, guard dogs and strangers don't mix. Only an inexcusable oaf would not see that to introduce a guest just arrived to their mastiff, to show off how good it is at guarding, would be rather tactless, putting the stranger in the embarrassing situation of feeling threatened, and constantly watched, by that fierce guardian of its master's property.[67]

A remarkable piece of evidence for the dog's peculiar faculty of recognition occurs in Plato's *Republic,* which takes the dog as the model for specifying the faculty required in the guardians of the state.[68] The philosopher is being deliberately hyperbolic, but this allows us to observe how the more positively valued side of canine discernment could be presented, before illustrating the aspects liable to an opposite valuation. After establishing that the guardians ought to be individuals specially chosen for their *thymos,* Socrates asks how to prevent them from being a danger to their fellow citizens. For having *thymos* means being endowed with strong reactions and passionate energy, a dynamism that in some cases results in courage and effective resoluteness but can also manifest as a short temper and unwanted aggressiveness. Good guardians must know how to direct their aggression against enemies and, on the contrary, always be gentle among their own citizens. How can gentleness and aggression, antithetical to each other and seemingly irreconcilable, be found in the same individual? The world of nature provides the answer: it is possible, because there is an animal whose nature contains these two contraries. The entire passage is worth quoting:

> "You're familiar, I think, with dogs of good breeding, and you know that their natural behavior is thus: they are very gentle with those they are familiar with and recognize, but against those they do not know they are entirely the opposite."
>
> "Indeed I know."
>
> "Then," I said, "this is possible, and it is not against nature that we are seeking a guardian with this characteristic."
>
> "So it seems."
>
> "And does it seem to you also that the future guardian must have this additional characteristic, that besides being spirited, he must also be by nature a lover of wisdom [*philosophos*]?"
>
> "How is this?" he said. "I don't understand."
>
> "This too," I said, "you have noticed about dogs, something truly surprising for an animal."
>
> "What?"
>
> "That when it sees someone unfamiliar it becomes aggressive, even if it has suffered nothing bad from them, but when it sees one it knows it greets them warmly, even if it has received no benefit from them. Haven't you ever marveled at this?"
>
> "No," he said. "I had not noticed that before. But that is certainly how they behave."
>
> "Well, this element of their nature seems a fine one, something truly wisdom-loving [*philosophos*]."
>
> "In what sense?"
>
> "In the sense," I said, "that it has no other criterion for distinguishing friend from enemy than that it knows the one and doesn't know the other. And how could any being not have a love of learning that defines the familiar and foreign by knowledge and ignorance?"

As a model of the perfect defender of the state, the guard dog becomes, in Socrates's argument, a "lover of wisdom," a "philosopher," precisely because it makes distinctions and discerns according to the sole criterion of knowledge. What is required of it is to distinguish the known from the unknown and to direct its naturally spirited aggression only against the latter. In his duties, a guardian is asked not to practice hospitality but to defend what he knows from dangers of the unknown. For this, the dog is a perfect paradigm.

But however "philosophical" and disposed toward learning Socrates wants to define them as, there are problems in that dogs aren't capable of responding to other beings on any distinction other than known/unknown and that although the equation "unknown = enemy" is generally valid for dogs, it is not always so for men.[69] The obvious implication is that aggression against the unfamiliar is not always commendable, especially for those unfortunates who suffer it; also, this violence has a dark side, blind and disquieting. In the dead of night, for example, a guard dog jumps out of the shadows and attacks any intruder, whether they are a thief and scoundrel or not; someone coming home at night—like Theophrastus's "scatterbrained" man—has to be careful not to be bitten by the neighbor's dog.[70] A common figure of blind and combative aggression, then, was a bitch that has just given birth, an image found already in a famous simile in the *Odyssey*. On seeing his palace's maids obeying the suitors, Odysseus is overtaken by uncontrollable rage to which he cannot give vent and feels his heart barking furiously in his chest like a bitch protecting her puppies, rabidly keeping everybody far away, without distinction, even her own master.[71] So not all dogs are good dogs or, in the word of Plato's Socrates, *philosophers*. As we will often have occasion to note, the Greeks were well aware—more so than we are—that a dog can bite unexpectedly, without apparent reason, even its own master, suddenly revealing a flaw, a worrisome lapse in that capacity for discernment considered typical of the species.

By nature, dogs are irascible and impetuous.[72] Plato himself emphasizes, in the passage on the perfect guardian, the dog's characteristic tendency to sudden and violent reaction. An intriguing indirect sign of how important the trait of aggressive biting was in the cultural representation of dogs comes from evidence regarding species that had a significant onomastic link with dogs. In Greek zoology there were several animals known as dogs (*kynes*). First of all there were sea dogs (*kynes thalattioi*), today known as dogfish, and "dogheaded" monkeys (*kynokephaloi*), which we call baboons. Consider the "dog" fish. Aelian hastens to say that such fish are so called because they are "similar to dogs."[73] But what kind of similarity is he talking about? What fish is similar to a dog in appearance? One suspects he means some other sort of similarity. Dogfish are in fact sharks and thus carnivorous and aggressive fish. It's likely they were called dogs simply because they bite. Significantly, the fiercest species of dogfish was called *karcharias*, a term that recalls the name "sharp-toothed" (*karcharodonta*), used for the family of terrestrial carnivores to which dogs belonged.[74]

Eloquent confirmation of how this naming reflex rested on just this analogical trait comes from a common tale that features a rabbit as its protagonist and illustrates the situation described in the common English saying "Out of the frying pan and into the fire." One day, it's said, an unlucky rabbit was running like mad to escape the jaws of a hunting dog chasing it. Having no choice but to jump into the sea, it leapt in, but—what terrible luck—went right into the mouth of a sea dog, the aquatic double of the biting *kyōn* on land. Out of the frying pan and into the fire—or rather, out of a dog's jaws and into those of a dogfish.[75]

The case of baboons (*kynokephaloi*) is slightly different. Unlike other monkeys, which have a flat muzzle more human in appearance, baboons have a markedly projecting muzzle that looks more like a dog's. Thus a morphological likeness is operative in this case. Aristotle adds that the muzzle of the *kynokephaloi* is also like a dog's in the shape of its teeth: "Baboons look like a chimpanzee, except they are larger and have a muzzle more like a dog's; also their nature is more fierce, their teeth are more like a dog's, and they are stronger."[76] So it is possible that baboons were also given the position of "dogs among monkeys" for being more aggressive and biting than other anthropomorphic animals too.

Other indications of the regular association between dogs and aggressiveness are found in botanical classification. Here as well, nomenclature seems to provide evidence that any biting trait might find expression in popular taxonomy by recourse to the category of dog. In fact, two plants have *dog* in their name: the *kynosbatos* (or *kynospastos*), the "dogbush," probably a dog rose or wild rose, and the *pankynion*, an aquatic species of algae. We can say at once that the common feature of these plants was that they both had a poison capable of killing on first contact. Etiological accounts elaborated the onomastic links between plant and dog in various ways. The name *pankynion*, for instance, might have derived from the Dog Star, Kyōn, also known as Sirius, inasmuch as it was the star thought to be conducive to the development of the deadly poison in the algae. But according to other accounts, both plants may derive their name from the fact that in order to harvest them without harm, people must use an animal intermediary; unable to touch the living plants, harvesters resort to a "sea dog" to obtain the pankynion's drug, and to a real dog to get at the kynosbatos's curative power without risking injury. Dog and dogfish are led to tear out the plant. They die at first contact, but by absorbing the toxic dose they make it possible for people to handle the plant safely and to use the poison as a drug.[77]

These fabulous stories of how to harvest these two *pharmaka*—transmitted by Aelian, the Roman sophist whose passion for the animal world preserved for us many precious fragments of the ancient zoological "encyclopedia"—elaborate different associations than those we are focused on here; from these, it would seem that the naming of the plants had nothing to do with the dog's bite. But another story, fortunately handed down to us through other routes of transmission, shows that the dog's bite was not foreign to the metaphorical move that led the kynosbatos plant to be called the dogbush. It is a foundation myth found in its fullest form in Plutarch, who probably read it in Aristotle's writings on political history.[78] This account linked the mythic foundation of the cities of Ozolian Locris to the memory of a "wooden bitch [*xylinē kyōn*]," a mysterious oracular sign given to the eponymous hero Locrus:

Having been told by the god to found a city on the spot where he happened to be bitten by a wooden bitch, as he was making his way toward the other sea [the gulf of Corinth] he stepped on a kynosbatos; suffering from the injury, he spent many days exploring the area and founded Physkos, Aianteia, and all the other cities inhabited by the Ozolian Locrians.

Locrus understood that the cut he received from the kynosbatos was what the oracle, in its twisted figurative language, had called a bite from a wooden bitch, and thus he founded cities where he'd been wounded. The dog rose is in fact a bush whose branches are covered with sharp thorns, in some cases looking very much like canine incisors. We can't be certain that the poisonous kynosbatos and pan-kynion mentioned by Aelian got their names from their dangerous nature, that they contained the *kyn-* root because they were biting plants, the dogs of the veg-etable kingdom, as it were. But the myth related by Plutarch at least testifies that the connection between the aggressiveness of a plant and the dog from which it got its name was an active association, one that the Greek imagination had, in at least one case, explored and exploited.[79]

It seems clear at this point that it was not only the dog's susceptibility to rabies that made it subject to sudden attacks of aggressiveness; its congenital mental blindness—its inability to distinguish between strangers of good and bad intent, its temporary lapses in judgment—and its tendency to lie in wait to bite caused it be seen as an animal that easily falls prey to lyssa. A passage in Xenophon, on the excitability of hunting dogs and its consequence, well illustrates this condition. In the presence of prey, says Xenophon, dogs tend to get wildly agitated, so the hunter has to calm them down. But he must not make the mistake of trying to calm them by shouting, since this only excites them more, and they'll end up "out of their minds [*ekphrones*]" and will lose track of the rabbit's scent.[80] The most interesting part of this passage is the choice of adjective, *ekphrones,* a common term in Greek that indicates altered mental states in humans, cases of madness and loss of self-control. That this term is used here to describe an agitated dog pack is unequivocal evidence that the dog's impulsiveness was perceived as a sign of its congenital psy-chic instability. In this way, the dog was co-opted into the cultural dialectic of health/illness, sanity/madness. It is no accident that the consequence of the pack's insane excitement on spotting prey was, according to Xenophon, altered cognitive faculties, an inability to recognize what in normal conditions they could identify with ease.[81]

To conclude, then, the dog is normally capable of close solidarity with man in its ability to direct its aggression against its master's enemies and prey; it is subject, however, to some potential deviations from this model of behavior. This deviance, thought of as altered faculties of recognition, is a source of anxiety for the master, who needs to be able to rely on the dog's judgment in its role as helper and co-worker. This is likely the main reason that the language and cultural models of madness, and conversely, as we will see below, of mental health and self-control, enter into the representation of dogs. As the lone domesticated carnivore, the dog is the only "sharp-toothed" beast, the only eater of raw meat, that is required to control its wild aggression and restrain its predatory instincts. The wolf and the lion are never mad, because their blind violence is a proper part of their identity as wild animals. They are sane—and indeed truly themselves—when they are uncontrollably ferocious. But dogs live among and with humans by virtue of their ability to be "wise" and to direct their aggression with judgment—with the result that when they don't behave according to this paradigm, when they show the wild side in their nature, they are labeled as crazy, as dogs denatured into wolves (the *lyssētēr* dog).

The fact that dogs are often represented as subject to psychosis can be attributed to their ambiguous metonymic position, the "sharp-toothed" animal included in the human sphere and invested with cultural models for behavior and psychology. According to a notice in Pollux, a Hellenistic poet named Nicander drew a connection between Indian dogs—a breed of hunting dogs known for ferocity and said in other sources to be a cross of a dog and a tiger[82]—and a pack of dogs that went suddenly mad and were unable to recognize their master, whom they attacked as prey and tore apart: "Nicander of Colophon says that Indian dogs are descended from Actaeon's dogs, which, having recovered from lyssa, crossed the Euphrates and wandered all the way to India."[83] Here we see that Nicander's etiological connection is based on a close tie between lyssa and the natural aptitudes of dogs. Only if we posit a common belief in the dog's congenital predisposition to wild aggression does it makes sense that Nicander could imagine and represent the Indian dog, the wildest dog breed, as nearer than others to the threshold of disease, or, in the terms of genealogical *aetion,* as the breed "descended" from mythical dogs gone wild that killed their own master.

HOW TO BIND, AND BOND WITH, A DOG

Let us return to the scene featuring Odysseus's old dog Argus. Still in disguise, the hero arrives at the walls of his palace and stops to speak with the swineherd Eumaeus. At the sound of his voice,

> a dog lying there lifted its nose and ears,
> Argus, of long-suffering Odysseus—he had raised the dog
> but could not enjoy him, since he left for sacred Ilium beforehand.[84]

These first verses dedicated to Argus strongly emphasize the dog's belonging to the hero. The master's name, in the genitive case, determines the animal's identity like a high-sounding patronymic: he is "Argus of long-suffering Odysseus."[85] But the following words are still more interesting, as they reveal what framework of relations was believed to bind a dog to its master. The poet says that Odysseus raised or nursed Argus personally (*autos threpse*) and would have derived satisfaction from this, something he wasn't able to realize because of his sudden departure for Troy. In other words, Odysseus never had the time to enjoy the pleasures reserved to a breeder, such as seeing the dog obey orders, follow tracks, or welcome one home.

The text stresses the king of Ithaca's direct participation in raising the pup, hardly by chance, since it is through food that an exclusive bond of reciprocal belonging is established between dog and man. Argus is the dog of Odysseus, and reciprocally, Odysseus is the master of Argus, recognized as such even after twenty years away because the dog does not forget who has nourished it. A rather obvious point in itself: the main means that people use to create a relation of dependence with domestic animals is to feed them. Only in this way do animals come to recognize our leading role and to respond to our calls.[86] Much of the language of domestication in Greek involves terms relating to nutrition and nourishing: a breeder was *tropheus* (nourisher) or *tithaseutēs,* formed from the root *tithēnē,* the "nurse" who suckles and takes care of the house's children. Reciprocally, the domestic animal, gentle and tamed, is *tithasos* (nursed, raised).

The paradigm of nutrition/nurturing, however, seems to depict the dog in a distinctive way. For other domesticated animal co-workers, such as horses, donkeys, and cows, the relationship is defined differently. Cattle, mules, and horses are included in the class of animals "under the yoke" (*hypozygia*), a category that patently underscores how the collaborative relationship results necessarily from an imposition of human force, whether in the domestication phase—the "breaking" of the animal—or in activities of cooperation, using bits, bridles, yokes, and saddles.[87] The imposed violence was one usual connotation, among others, of all these instruments of domination, which made them available as well for significant figurative uses. The yoke, bit, and bridle were fertile ground indeed for metaphors expressing situations of submission, constraint, and control. To take one example, fate's inevitable destiny was called the yoke of necessity. Self-control—domination of oneself—was represented as an internal charioteer with the task of keeping on course the otherwise runaway horse of the passions and emotions. And any constraining or coercive action could be figured in terms of a bit in the mouth. One cannot forget, besides, that the Greek lexicon for taming (words with the root *dama-/dmā-*) was for the most part fashioned on the Indo-European root **domā-,* which means "to do violence, exert constraint."[88]

Nothing like this occurs with dogs. First of all, unlike horses, dogs do not need to be broken. When Hesiod advises the good farmer on the fourth day of the midmonth "to calm the flocks and the curve-horned, shambling cattle and sharp-toothed dog and labor-bearing mules, laying on your hand," he is surely speaking not of breaking but of a ritual appeasement of domestic animals.[89] There is no need to break a dog, any more than goats or sheep, although it's easy to imagine that folk belief understood this act of laying on hands as a way to render the animals prone to obey, submissive and disposed to provide the required labors. Still, these lines are of great interest as evidence of how in a rural society, where the relationship with animals focuses on the exploitation of their resources and labor force, anxiety in the face of the "bestiality" of these collaborators—domesticated yet always animals—could be quite high. The more one relies on animals for one's needs, the more urgent becomes the worry that they might disappoint one's expectations.

But to return to the thread of argument, besides not needing to be broken, dogs are peculiar in another way when compared to the other collaborative animals. In fact, the collars and leashes that are put on them do not function in exploiting the animal's activities. In the tasks of guarding, hunting, and herding, the dog must have freedom of movement to fulfill its duties. On a rabbit hunt, for example, dogs are leashed in the initial stages but unleashed as soon as the pursuit begins. And if, at first, the hunter guides the dogs to the hunting ground—the hunter is, in fact, called he who leads dogs (*kynēgetēs*)—during the hunt it is the dogs who lead the hunter on the trail of scent. As for herd dogs, clearly their role as guide and protector of flocks requires full liberty of movement; moreover, one can even say that here the dog serves as a tool for controlling the movement of other domestic animals.[90] Guard dogs have to attack intruders and therefore, even at night, must be unleashed. Essentially, while cows, donkeys, and horses are unleashed when they are not serving, dogs, even if tied up the rest of the time, are unleashed when they serve. This is probably why the dog leash does not appear in the metaphorical lexicon for constraint and slavery, which borrowed instead from terms for forced labor among beasts of burden and of the yoke, nor in the lexicon for control, which drew from the technical vocabulary of horsemanship.[91]

If the necessity of free movement is obvious for hunting and herd dogs, perhaps it is less so for guard dogs. But on this exact point an extremely interesting example comes to the rescue, which we have thanks again to Aelian and his passion for animal stories:

> I have heard the following method has been devised to keep guard dogs from running away: cut a cane to the length of their tail, then smear it with butter and give it to the dogs to lick. They will then, so it's said, stay put as though they were tied up.[92]

This performance of practical magic was probably understood as a symbolic way of having the dog lick its own tail, analogically substituted by a cane of the same length. If so, the ritual perhaps intended to produce a representation of circular movement by the animal that would "bind" it and keep it fixed in place. A dog that licks its tail goes in circles and thus remains in the same place. Moreover, elsewhere in practical magic, animal tails themselves were considered a good bond. Comparable to a rope, they could be used in sympathetic magic to bind and hold movements, the voice, or impulses, and they could be knotted and, in turn, cause the knotting up of another body part. To moderate the sexual excesses of rams, for example, one would tie up their tails at night; to bind the voice of dogs one used a weasel's tail, while to silence a donkey one tied a stone to its tail.[93]

But most important in Aelian's prescription for magically binding guard dogs is the fact that it must have been devised as a symbolic substitute for a real leash, which could not be used because this would have impeded the job the dogs are called on to perform. A dog can be chained up only when not performing some task; unlike with horses, donkeys, and cows, which are made to obey through implements that control their movement, coercive measures cannot obtain a dog's obedience and effectiveness. On the contrary, a tied-up dog tends to get desperate and to unleash dangerous, uncontrollable aggression. It's a commonplace that it's best to stand clear of dogs just freed from the leash, because they're so furious that they'll bite the first person they meet.[94]

On what, then, is collaboration between dog and man based? By what means does man bind the dog to himself? According to a widespread and well-attested paradigm, the man-dog relationship is built on and maintained exclusively through food.

Let's consider a significant piece of evidence. In his treatise on hunting, Xenophon speaks of both raising and training dogs. After weaning, which must be gradual, young dogs are taken hunting and habituated to tracking prey, following one specific rule: training effectively consists in a regimentation of the natural instinct to track, habituating the dogs to hunt on command and not at other times. One also needs a way to make them return to their master after hunting. This end is achieved like so:

> While they are young, feed them near the nets as you take them down, so that if through inexperience they get lost in the hunt they will return to their post safe and sound. . . . Also it should for the most part be the master himself who gives hungry dogs what they need, for when they are not hungry they do not know who provides for them, but when they are hungry they have affection for the one who feeds them.[95]

A dog's master is not necessarily the one who owns it, the one who keeps it tied up and subdued, but the one it recognizes as such, and that is the person who feeds it. This is why Odysseus, the king of Ithaca, nourished his dog Argus with his own hands; if feeding had been relegated to a servant, the dog would have recognized the servant, not Odysseus, as the authority to whom it owed obedience.

THE PACT OF FOOD

In sum, a dog is tied by affection to whoever feeds it and considers its master whoever personally gives it food. More generally, one can say that the relationship between dog and master is not based on force but is a kind of alliance, a pact of food.[96] That there is a "contract" based on food is an ancient idea that continues to prove fruitful in the form of scientific theories on the beginnings of canine domestication.[97] Konrad Lorenz devoted some striking pages to reconstructing this process, imagining a suggestive prehistoric scene: In a wilderness teeming with ferocious animals, a tribe of hunters who have fled their land can't find a safe place to sleep because there are no jackals nearby. Jackals used to linger around their settlement, aiming to garner scraps from human meals. Their howls were clues, allowing the hunters to guess at the presence of other wild animals approaching the village. After abandoning their settlement, these people have been roaming for days—without jackals to raise the alarm, no place is safe enough for them to settle down. Running out of strength, the fleeing band hears a howl in the distance— jackals are nearby! At that point, a young tribal chief has an intuition. Acting "from the heart," he leaves a bit of his food on the ground, to the shocked looks of his hungry companions. Why give food to these scavengers? But lo and behold, the pack of canids, attracted to the meat, closes in on the new camp and lurks just at its edges. They form a guard, and the tribe will sleep peacefully at last, for the first night in a long time. After that, nobody disperses the jackals with stones, and after generations, they become gentle and fully domesticated guard dogs.[98]

But let us return to ancient Greece. Because of the contractual notion of their relationship, man expects the dog to recognize a debt: in exchange for being raised and fed—one and the same in Greek, since the verb *trephein* means both "to nourish" and "to raise"—a dog must show gratitude. We will see below how two concurrent models figured such gratitude: the first we can call familial, with an affectionate dog repaying its nourisher with attachment and obedience; the second has a more business cast, with a wage-earning dog working in exchange for food. But first let's illustrate in general terms the implications of the "pact of food" model in ancient representations.

One of the oldest and most explicit testimonies to the fundamental importance of food in the economy of relations between man and dog occurs in Hesiod. Listing chores good to do during hot summer months, the poet advises reserving for these sultry days less-tiresome tasks, things that can be done in the shade or indoors. After storing the grain in jars, one should hire for help a male servant without home or family and a female servant without children. Then one needs to tend to the guard dog:

> And look after a sharp-toothed dog, and don't be sparing of food,
> so that the "day-sleeper" won't carry off your goods.[99]

The "day-sleeper" is obviously a thief who does nothing by day and works by night, when the safekeeping of the farm is entrusted to a dog. For Hesiod, then, the guard dog's effectiveness depends on how much food its master gives it. And if it's true, as Xenophon says, that a hungry dog identifies the one who feeds it as its master, it's clearly important to keep a guard dog well fed—a hungry one might gladly take food from a thief, then let him go about his crimes undisturbed. So it has happened—and happens sometimes still—that burglars brings scraps to throw to guard dogs as a way to buy their silence and their acquiescence, exploiting the mechanism of the food pact on which the animal's help is based. With vivid brevity, an Italian proverb recalls two methods of defense against potential aggressors, violence and bribery: "Whoever walks among dogs brings either bread or rocks [*Chi va tra i cani, porti sassi o porti pani*]."[100] This expedient was not foolproof, however, since dogs may take food from a stranger's hand without feeling obliged to reciprocate with goodwill. Isocrates, warning against helping bad people, makes this comparison:

> If you do services to bad men, you will be in the position of those who feed other men's dogs, for just as they bark at those who give them food as loudly as at anyone else, so bad men injure their benefactors just as much as those who do them harm.[101]

Likewise, in antiquity there was a famous story about a heroic watchdog in the sanctuary of Asclepius at Athens: some sacrilegious thieves first tried to subdue it with stones, then by giving it pieces of bread they had brought as bait, but to no avail; for not giving in to the malefactors' lures, the Athenian dog was given the honor of being maintained at state expense. Other times, however, the food-bait technique worked, and as the case of the Capitoline geese taught the Romans, dogs are not the best guardians, because they'll be silent when thrown food, whereas geese start squawking when tossed feed.[102] So too, herd dogs must be well fed if one doesn't want them to unleash a wolflike hunger; if the herdsman doesn't feed them enough, the dogs might attack the flock rather than protect it.[103]

Another aspect of the dog's food to consider, besides the portion size, was the place where it was served. Homer, according to an account in one of his legendary biographies, referred to this in advice to a shepherd named Glaucus, who had kindly invited him to dinner. Glaucus allowed his guard dogs to surround the full table, begging for food and barking, and the poet made this comment:

> Dear Glaucus, I tell you something to keep well in mind:
> first give the dogs their food at the gates of the hall;
> such is best, for a dog is the first to sense when
> a man approaches and an animal comes in the yard.[104]

It was apparently considered a good rule not only to feed dogs before sitting down to the table—to prevent them from greedily begging food from the diners, creating a nuisance with barking, and being distracted from their guard duty—but also to feed them at the courtyard gate. Presumably the reason for this habit was a belief that food both binds a dog to the one who gives it and chains the animal to the place where it is fed. Giving a dog food in a specific place induces it to stay there. So if it regularly sates its hunger near the outside gate, it will tend to hold to that spot, best for keeping watch against thieves and predators. That a guard dog should stay by the door seems confirmed, among other things, by the proverbial saying that calls a person who takes charge of a situation "a dog in the hallway [*kyon en prothyrōi*]"; that is to say, she is free to act and set the rules within her realm of responsibility, just as a dog that monitors the entrance is the master of the space around the door.[105]

In any case, a dog's collaboration is gained only by means of an exchange. One persuades it to cooperate by forging a pact: in return for food, the dog is obliged to render its services to man. Force is neither necessary nor possible. The dog's duties require a freedom of action not found with any other animal helper. Myth reflects this peculiarity. As already noted, breaking, bridles, bits, and yokes are central elements in the representation of man's relationships with domestic animals such as horses and cattle. As the means to control and subjugate these animals, they were among the devices and instruments that humankind received as gifts from the gods. When Prometheus inventories the endless series of technical discoveries that he handed over to humans and that gave rise to civilization—from bricks to carpentry, from counting to writing, from astronomy to divination and seafaring—at the center of the list stand the techniques of domestication and exploitation of animals:

> I was first to put in harness the wild beasts
> that under the yoke's collar do service, to replace
> the bodies of men in the most difficult labors,
> and with the bridle I tied to the chariot
> docile horses, a token of richest luxury.[106]

In other mythic traditions, it is the goddess Athena who oversees these techniques of control, as can be readily inferred from some of her cult epithets: Athenas Ox-Binder (Boudeia) and Ox-Harnesser (Bouarmia) were called on in Thessaly and Boeotia, respectively, while in Corinth she was invoked as Athena Horse-Riding (Hippia) and Of the Bit (Chalinitis).[107]

In the face of all these examples containing yokes, bridles, and bits, it seems significant that no mythic account or cult epithet mentions the dog collar or leash. An eloquent silence, especially since canine cooperation had a myth of origin quite different from those for other domestic animals. There are, in fact, a whole group of stories in which the gods invent or construct not the tools to control and master the dog but the dog itself. Xenophon begins his treatise on hunting by relating that "hunting and dogs were a discovery of Apollo and Artemis; they gave them to Chiron as a reward for his justice."[108] No other animal boasts this strange status of divine invention. How to interpret it? One key to finding sense in the myth might be in a traditional story that attributed to Hephaestus the construction of certain extraordinary dogs. The works of the divine craftsman included, for example, the dogs that stood beside Alcinous's gates:

> To either side were dogs of gold and silver
> that Hephaestus had built with expert wisdom
> to guard the house of great-hearted Alcinous,
> immortal they were, not growing old forever.[109]

A tireless craftsman of automatons, marvelous self-propelled statues, Hephaestus had forged in his fires another mythic dog: from his hands came the famous golden dog that guarded baby Zeus in the Cretan cave where his mother, Rhea, had hidden him from the savagery of Cronus.[110]

Bear in mind that Hephaestus crafted infallible instruments and tireless robots: instruments of death, like the arms of Achilles, or of seduction, like the necklace of Harmonia, as well as mechanical servants of perfect and everlasting efficiency—untiring as machines—chief among them the astonishing golden handmaidens who worked in his forge.[111] We can also recall here in passing that among the god's wondrous works was woman, Pandora, the marvelous automaton and efficient instrument of Zeus's vengeance. Accordingly, the Greeks likely classified the dog in one of these two categories, or perhaps both: a living instrument, the dog is at the same time a servant of man, which man employs to his own advantage. When the dog is thought of as an automaton of Hephaestus or as an invention of Apollo and Artemis, collars and leashes are not needed: it is in itself a perfect instrument of collaboration, and the relationship between man and dog is direct, with no need for mediating artifacts.

Let us resume our thread of argument. As I have tried to demonstrate, one main consequence of the regime of vicarious labors performed by the dog is that it gets configured, in a common cultural model, as an active subject of a social contract. It is a tool, yes, but alive and endowed with autonomy; not to be bridled or put under the yoke, it offers its service only when it feels bound by a duty of gratitude, the only bond that a master can attempt to impose. The dog is bound to abide by an agreement, with the chief consequence that man tends to project models and expectations of an ethical-normative sort onto its actions. The dog "must" behave well. Not only must it do its job well—one can expect something of this sort even from a horse, a cow, or a donkey—but it must autonomously recognize what it owes to the one who feeds it and act accordingly. Like a good servant, a good dog must feel grateful to its master, be faithful to him, and earn the food he provides.

Although nearly always considered the lowest subordinate and dependent, the dog for this reason has been fully included in the human community and participates in social dynamics as an active subject of a contract of cooperation. A set of cultural elaborations, various moralizing discourses that center on the dog and play on the theme of feeding, declare this unique status. As already noted, we find two types of representation for this theme. On one side are stories that understand the food pact on a contractual model: the good dog is one that, in exchange for food received, recognizes its subordination and performs services like a slave or a wage laborer. On the other side, the food pact conforms to an ethical model of duty in which a reared dog is more like a member of the circle of loved ones (*philoi*)—parents, friends, and protégés—from whom the master of the house expects not just occasional services but a primary and constant solidarity founded on an attachment both mindful and grateful.

To begin with examples of the first sort: a commonplace playing on the contractual model contrasted the dog that earns its meals to the dog that eats without paying. This trope already occurs in Odysseus's question to Eumaeus about Argus, whether it was a hunting dog or one of those idle creatures fed at men's tables for their beauty alone. Eumaeus assures the hero that the old dog was not just fine looking but remarkable in the work it did, no mere table dog, a parasite, but a skilled hunter.[112] The contrast between dogs worthy and unworthy of the feeding they receive also appears in an Aesop's fable, where a hunting dog complains that the watchdog stays indoors and doesn't work like he does yet gets an equal portion of food. The duties of hunting were evidently considered the most laborious, and therefore, those who performed them were thought to deserve of better dietary treatment.[113] Also in Aesop, the difference between dog and wolf consists in how they assess the price of a good, plentiful diet: the dog chooses to be man's servant in return for food, whereas the wolf proclaims its freedom and unwillingness to subscribe to a pact of this sort, even at the cost of dying of hunger.[114] Another fable features a dog trained to fight bears and lions; tired of paying for the luxuries it enjoys in its master's home by risking its life, the dog decides to renounce its "salary" and go live in poverty like a mendicant.[115]

Aelian has a detailed description that shows how this contractual model could be elaborated further.[116] The account is not about dogs but another animal, and not even a domestic one, since it involves a fish, the mackerel. The episode is nonetheless quite compelling, since it shows what imaginary models were available for telling a story of collaboration between man and an untamable animal. And that model, as we will see, is the food pact. The service this fish provides in exchange for food involves hunting, so it seems fairly likely that the relationship between fishermen and mackerel follows the pattern underlying that between hunter and dogs.

It's told that in the Ionian Sea, around Epidamnus, was an island of fishermen called Athena's Isle. In a lagoon, they raised—or nourished (*trephontai*)—domesticated mackerel. But in what sense were these fish domesticated? The description goes on:

The fishermen throw them food, and they have a pact with them: they are free and are not to be caught, and so they live a long time, and some mackerels there reach a very old age. But they don't eat for nothing and are not ungrateful to those who feed them: after the fishermen have fed them at dawn, they themselves go out hunting, and so they repay the price for their feeding [*tropheia ektinontes*].[117]

The food pact could not be more explicitly presented. When man employs an animal as a "free" worker—inasmuch as it performs its cooperative activity without being subject to material restrictions—its condition is thought of in contractual terms. Food and security are the benefits conferred, and the animal renders services to man to pay its debt of gratitude. Most interesting here, however, is that Aelian chooses to describe the binding force of this contract by invoking one of most inviolable of ethical-normative precepts in ancient Greece: *tropheia ektinein* (repayment for nurturing), that is, the obligation of children to maintain their elderly parents in return for being raised and nurtured as infants.[118] And indeed, this contractual bond is so strong that it makes the mackerel comrades and allies of men against individuals of their own species:

Leaving the harbor they move against foreign [*xenous*] mackerel, and forming themselves into a squadron or phalanx they go up against those who are of their own kind and nature, who don't flee or avoid them but rather join up with them. Then the tamed fish surround the outsiders, and by encircling them and closing their ranks they manage to isolate a large number in the middle, and preventing the escape of these fish, they wait for their feeders: and so in exchange for being fully fed, they invite the fishermen to dine in turn. When the fishermen come, they catch and kill a great number of fish. The tamed mackerel then rush back into the harbor, and returning to their lairs they wait for their evening meal. And the fishermen have to bring it to them if they want to keep them as hunting partners and loyal friends.

Here we see how a hunting story, involving not dogs but domesticated fish, can be imaginatively embellished. The cooperative relationship between the cohunting animals and men is based on a food pact that establishes a strong bond of solidarity and attachment, expressed in terms of two of the highest ethical-social duties: the repayment of nurturing and of dinner hospitality.[119] The mackerel discharge their debt to the fishermen like children with aging parents or like those who repay an invitation to dinner: they procure food for those who fed them. The basic elements of the relationship between the fishermen and their mackerel are the same as those of the man-dog relationship.[120]

With the model of filial gratitude, however, we have already slipped into the second pattern for the food pact, the ethical model of affection for a nurturer. Aelian, at pains to prove that animals, though lacking reason, possess many natural virtues, is full of stories about the extraordinary loyalty that dogs have for their masters. In these also, as we will see, terms linked to feeding are so frequent as to leave little doubt about their structural value in how ancient peoples conceived man-dog relations. It's said, for example, that when Darius, the last king of the Persians, died, everyone abandoned his body; only his dog would not betray him by leaving even though he would no longer feed it. Instead, it remained at the side of its nurturer's dead body as though he were still alive.[121]

Roman history records similar tales. In a section devoted to stories illustrating dogs' unbreakable affection for the one who cares for them, Aelian relates that when Galba was murdered, his assassins could not cut off his head without also killing his dog, which stubbornly defended its master's corpse even at the cost of its own life.[122] Another remarkable account in the same passage tells how Pyrrhus, the king of Epirus, once ran across the body of a slain man whose dog was standing guard over it; for three days the dog had been there without food. Pyrrhus wanted to strip the body of spoils, so he devised the following way to deal with the dog:

> He ordered special treatment for the dog and with his own hand gave it the food one gives dogs, of the sort and enough to rouse its feelings of affection and goodwill [philian te kai eunoian] toward those around it, luring it [hypagōn] little by little.

Later we will return to this verb hypagein—"to attract, lure," but also "to subdue"—chosen to describe the way that Pyrrhus tried to earn the dog's goodwill. Here it suffices to note that despite the progressive "retraining" that Pyrrhus undertakes, the dog still did not forget its old master or the faces of his murderers. Some time later, in fact, it recognized the evildoers and attacked them, thus revealing their guilt and delivering them to justice.[123] Similarly, it was said that the poet Hesiod's dog revealed the identity of its master's murderers.[124] The comic poet Eupolis also had a dog, which he had gotten when it was a puppy and which, "blandished with food and lured by long habituation," loved its master very much. So much so that when Eupolis died, the dog died howling in grief at his master's grave on the island of Aegina. For this reason the place was called Dog's Lament (Kynos Thrēnos).[125] Another famous dog was that of Xanthippus, the father of Pericles, who tried to follow its master by swimming all the way from Athens to Salamis; it made it there but died from exhaustion on the beach, and Xanthippus erected a funeral monument to it.[126] The dog of Gelo, the tyrant of Syracuse—a dog that "he raised himself"—jumped onto the bed of its "nurturer [tropheus]" when it heard him cry out in his sleep; thinking that its "friend and companion [philos kai syntrophos]" was in danger, it started barking to defend him and woke him up from his nightmare.[127] According to this model, then, the dog tends to have expectations projected upon it that are similar to those of parents for their children. The sources never make this parallel explicit, yet we will see later that in some circumstances, a dog could be enlisted to metaphorically represent a perfect child or, on the contrary, a child that has dashed the expectations of those who brought it up.

IN THE CIRCLE OF *PHILOI*?

The examples collected so far show clearly enough that the bond between dog and master is founded mainly on the sense of attachment the animal is capable of feeling toward the one who cares for it. Through a gradual effort of enticement, of seduction, by means of food, the dog is induced to feel, says Aelian, a sense of community, of *philia:* little by little, the animal constitutes itself as a loyal ally (*philos*) of the one who feeds it by hand.

At this point, before drawing any further conclusions, a clarification is necessary. The term *philia* is commonly translated as "friendship," but this is liable to create misconceptions in the case of canine philia. It is quite clear that the relation between dog and master did not—and still usually does not—involve either an equality of status or, as a consequence, perfect reciprocity. The model of philia to which the man-dog relationship could conform was certainly not the ideal of friendship among equals, the perfectly symmetrical bond that Aristotle theorized in his ethical works.[128] Despite dozens of examples of dogs honored for sacrificing themselves for their masters, not one ancient testimony ever cites an example of human heroism consisting in a master sacrificing himself for his dog. Someone who behaved in such a way would probably have been considered a fool. To tell the truth, it is not at all common in ancient sources that a dog, however devoted and loyal, is honored with the title *philos*.[129] For us to say that the dog is "a friend" presents no problem, on account of the stereotypical notion that dogs are man's best friend. But were things the same for the Greeks? It's difficult to say. To judge from the reticence of our sources and the categorical assertions of Aristotle—who said that philia could not exist between a human being and an animal, given the enormous divide of inequality that makes impossible the reciprocity on which friendship is based—it would seem that the dog had a status excluding this kind of relationship.[130]

In Greece, however, as Aristotle himself says, not only a "friend [*philos*]" but any "dear" person was bound by feelings of affection and a bond of community. Therefore not just an ideal friend—an adult citizen, male, free, affluent, and of the same rank—but all of one's family and relations, including wife and children, were *philoi*. But with the dear ones, the head of a family maintained not an equal but rather a hierarchical relationship. In the family, a type of asymmetrical philia was expressed between husband and wife, father and son, master and servant, an affection that knew a superior and an inferior and bound the inferior to love more than she could hope to be loved, prove devoted and supportive without expecting the same, and bridge with full subordination and obedience the divide separating her from father, husband, or master.[131] Although Aristotle does not admit that philia could exist between human and animal in theory, it is possible that in practice—and well before Aelian had the courage to state it explicitly—someone might have been tempted to consider a dog *philos:* certainly, by expecting much more affection and devotion from the creature than they were disposed to give but nonetheless including it among the loved ones of the house, on whom they counted. In our culture as well, we can easily say that the dog is man's friend, but we couldn't say with equal lightheartedness that man is a dog's best friend.[132]

Besides, there are traces in the sources, however faint, of circumstances that should not be underestimated. The first example that comes to mind on this subject is obviously the emotion of Odysseus when he sees his old dog Argus again, a reaction comparable only to what he feels in his reunions with his son and wife. So there are indications that in some cases, a dog might be thought of as an active part of the family, although a member of the lowest rank. For instance, we find a dog named in sequence after wife, children, and slaves—but before pigs—in a list of the members of a nuclear family; we see one explicitly invited, along with family members, to a birthday dinner at a friend's house; and when, in a famous comedy of Aristophanes, old Philocleon, a fanatic for legal trials, has to pick someone in his family on whom to vent his obsession with judicial proceedings, it's the dog who winds up in the dock.[133] Nor can we forget that some owners were so fond of their dogs that they not only suffered at the animals' deaths but even felt a duty to honor them with graves, just as they would a relative.[134]

So, even if they were asymmetrical, the attachment and affection between man and dog are undeniable. Whether or not perfectly classifiable in terms of philia, this relationship was nevertheless configured such that the human social sphere of ethical bonds co-opted the animal. Thus, the position of the dog in ancient Greece seems to match surprisingly well the model that Claude Lévi-Strauss proposed for it in modern French culture. The dog was not only implicated in the human sphere through metonymy but also considered a subject: subject to an ethical norm, a participant in a dynamics of duty imposed by the debt of nourishment and by recognition of the social contract.

In a fable of Aesop mentioned above in connection with the dog's inclination toward manifesting the wildness of the raw-eating beasts, some wolves try to persuade herd dogs to hand over their flock with the promise of sharing the spoils. But consider how the story concludes:

> The dogs yielded to their proposals. But once the wolves got into the pen, the first thing they did was to kill the dogs.
> Such is the reward for those who betray their homeland.[135]

The social contract that the wolves propose is really a trick, and it proves ruinous for the dogs. This interspecies friendship cannot exist, because the wolves know cooperation only within their species. But the moral of the fable is most interesting, interpreting the story as a parable about traitors to their native land. Beyond their naïveté, the dogs deserved their sad fate for their betrayal of their contract with the human community, which is, for the dog, what the homeland is for the citizen. Only someone who is party to a contract can commit treason.[136] If a dog can be represented as a traitor to its society, this is only because it is thought of as a member of the herders' community, an active subject included in the culture's ethical order, which requires respect for the rule of social cohesion and loyalty to the alliance based on recognition of the debt of nourishment. Wolves, foxes, lions are outside the human system, forever enemies and adversaries, representing an alternative world to man's. The dog, on the other hand, is the animal insider, the heterogeneous but assimilated element involved in the ethical mechanisms of duty and even in the emotional dynamics of affection.

A final consideration may help confirm the uniqueness of the dog's classification. There are a group of related stories in Greece that illustrate the inevitable consequences of trying to extend to other animals the same food pact that establishes the dog's cooperation with man. The general scheme of these stories is the following: a person decides to raise a wild animal cub—a wolf or a lion—thinking he can make it into a domestic and allied animal. But once grown up, the beast cannot but reveal its true nature and ends up destroying the people that raised it along with their belongings. Aesop has various versions of this story, all featuring a wolf cub that a herdsman raises like a tame puppy dog, which ends up slaughtering rather than protecting the flock.[137] But the tragedian Aeschylus provides the most interesting example of this plot. In the *Agamemnon*, the chorus reflects on the sad ruins of Troy—which the Greeks destroyed on account of Helen and Paris's fatal adultery—comparing it to a house in which a lion cub has been raised:

> A man raised in his house
> a lion cub
> deprived of mother's milk and longing for a teat;
> early in life
> docile, playful with the children,
> a joy for the old;
> often held in the arms
> like a newborn child,
> smiling and fawning [*sainōn*] over caresses,
> spurred on by its belly.

> But in time it revealed the nature
> of its parents, repaying the favor
> of those who nurtured it
> with raging slaughter of flocks.
> It prepared, uninvited, a banquet:
> the house was soaked in blood,
> unconquerable sorrow for the family,
> great loss of many murders.

By a god's will, a priest of Ate [Ruin]
was welcomed and raised in the house.[138]

The story is invoked to illustrate the dreadful effects of Helen on the Trojan palace: through a fatal error, she was welcomed into the family of Priam like a harmless puppy but then revealed to be a devastating beast, a bringer of death and destruction. In the first part of the image, the young lion behaves like a dog, playing with the children, pampered by adults, held in the arms like a newborn. The reference's paradigm is unmistakably seen in the participle *sainōn*, which refers to the typical behavior of a dog when it wags its tail and fawns on someone in greeting: the cub licks the hand of the person who feeds it, "spurred on by its belly." The whole passage clearly exemplifies the mechanisms of the food pact. The animal gets the food it wants by fawning, thus displaying its gentle submissiveness to the master and his family. This is how the dog is assimilated into the house, by becoming a trusted element expected to repay "the favor of those who nurtured it."[139]

This is precisely what the lion cub, once raised, cannot do. The repayment that the grown lion gives its caretakers is ungrateful, since the beast takes for food what belongs to the house; instead of protecting and defending the master's property and constituents, it lays them waste. The nature of the species admits no compromise. The family banquet, in which a dog takes part by waiting for its portion, transforms, with the lion, into an alter-banquet, antagonistic to the human, becoming a dinner the beast prepares for itself and participates in "uninvited."

One of the Aesopic versions of this story type is also of interest here. It tells how a wolf cub was raised alongside herd dogs and describes the different results of such upbringing for the wolf and the dogs. When an outside wolf carries off sheep from the herd, the raised wolf rushes in pursuit along with the dog pack, but

while the dogs, unable to catch the [wild] wolf, turned back, the [other] wolf kept in pursuit, until catching up it got its share of the prey as a wolf, then it too returned. And if no wolf came from outside to plunder a head of livestock, he would sacrifice one himself in secret and throw a feast for the dogs.[140]

Although raised and cared for just like the dogs, unlike them, the wolf doesn't recognize any social contract except perhaps the one that binds it to its own species. The wolf does not accept the food pact with humans, will not tolerate becoming part of the human community as a slave, and prefers to endure the risks of its independence. Wolf society, irreconcilable and eternally at odds with that of humans, is an alternative one, with its own rituals and laws of internal cohesion, in which no outsider can participate.[141] By contrast, dogs know no intraspecies solidarity. They do not constitute a society of their own but live in symbiosis with human society. They are individuals within the community of men.

AN INDIVIDUALIST ANIMAL

As the end of the fable indicates, however, dogs are not perfect collaborators. They lean toward raw-eating wildness and prove corruptible in the face of food offered by the wolf. This renders their loyalty uncertain, making their position, so intimately implicated in human normative paradigms, a source of perplexity and concern. With this we have arrived at a crucial point. As a subject and internal member of the human circle of comrades, the dog is an animal that man puts trust in. The unique relationship that one can form with a dog is of a fiduciary sort. But for this reason, the dog is able to betray the trust placed in it, violate the pact, not recognize itself as bound by the debt of nourishment, give in to the enticements of other providers of food, lose its capacity of discernment, and lapse into the savagery of a wolf. Invested with a number of ethical expectations aimed at subordinates, the dog excites great hopes as well as great anxiety about its credibility.

In relation to this, another fundamental fact needs to be kept in mind, one that often recurs in the symbolic complexes constructed on the image of the dog. A dog's submissiveness is not something won once and for all, nor does it hold for all people who approach the animal. A tamed horse will carry any rider, even if it might act more gently with its master; anyone can use a yoked cow or a pack mule as a helper. A dog's cooperation, however, is achieved personally. A dog is not gentle with everyone but only those it recognizes as familiar. It is neither domesticated nor wild *tout court* but is simultaneously and always between the two. Tame with those it identifies as familiar and friends, fierce with strangers, a dog knows how to draw distinctions and enjoys relationships with humans that are eminently intersubjective. This obviously constitutes a further cause for anxiety. The dog does not have an immutable species trait of cooperation and cannot be considered harmless to humans in general. It is trustworthy not as a species but only as an individual. A dog is always a subject whose collaboration is won from time to time and whose loyalty depends exclusively on its willingness to regard itself as bound by a pact. If a dog doesn't recognize you or no longer sees you as its master, there's nothing to give you certainty that you won't wind up between its teeth, just as sharp and pointed as those of a wolf or a lion.

Consistent with this peculiar ethological dimension, the dog in ancient sources presents not a species identity, like other animals, but rather an individual identity. The wolf is always vicious, the lion fierce, the fox a trickster, the pig stupid—and all wolves, lions, foxes, and pigs are such. But the dog can be gentle or fierce, good or bad, loyal or treacherous, a work partner or a parasite and thief. To fill out this individualism, one must add the fact that dogs differ greatly in bodily traits by breed: size, color, quality of fur, type of muzzle, and tail all vary greatly.

An Aesop's fable illustrates in a surprisingly clear and effective manner how this variety of appearance could provide material for imaginary elaborations of the individualistic dog little interested in species-based solidarity. One day, the story goes, dogs and wolves went to war. The dogs chose as their commander a Greek dog. Arrayed for battle, the army of dogs would never decide to attack, and the wolves began to grow impatient. Then the dog commander took the trouble to explain to their adversaries the reason for their indecision:

> You are all of the same race and the same color. We, on the other hand, have many different characters and are all proud of where we come from. There is not one color equal for all, but some are black, others golden, still others white and gray. How can I lead them into battle, so discordant and diverse in every way?[142]

Quot canes, tot sententiae. In other words, for dogs, the general laws that Prometheus established at the beginning of time do not apply: each other animal type possesses a singular nature—just one per species—whereas each human has an individual personality distinct from those of its conspecifics. A wolf is like all other wolves; a human is different from all other humans.[143] But dogs don't fit the taxonomy. Residing in an interstitial niche, the dog straddles the line that separates humans from other animals. Dogs have neither a species life nor features common to all members of the species, and a society of dogs does not exist, just as there cannot be an army of dogs. Only single dogs exist, each one living a promiscuous life among individuals of the human species.

3

Food for Dogs

The true limit of our relationship with our dog lies not in finding an animal we can treat like a person but in the impossibility of having a dog truly treat us like a person.
—GIOVANNI JERVIS, *PRESENZA E IDENTITÀ: LEZIONI DI PSICOLOGIA*

CANINE NECROPHAGY AND "THE CORPSE-EATING DOG"

After all that's been said about the preeminence of the theme of nourishing—"upbringing"—in Greek cultural representations of man-dog relations, there are good reasons to hypothesize that the canine trait of attraction to carrion and corpses triggers a series of reactions in the symbolic imagination that other animals, however fervent their scavenging, would not set off. But before we analyze passages about the dog's necrophagy and propose an interpretation, a glance at how the question has been addressed so far will help bring the argument into sharper focus.

We have already noted that historical studies have often assumed necrophagy to be the disturbing trait par excellence in Greek representations of the dog (see chapter 1). According to some scholars, in fact, the desire for corpse meat explains the Greek's presumed negative view of dogs, the animals' no less presumed impurity, and the origin of the offensive use of *kyōn* and its derivatives. These suppositions turn out to be unsatisfactory, for reasons explained above. To those observations we now can add another: scavenging was not at all salient in the construction of the "Greek" dog, whereas of recurring importance were mentions of its desire for cooked food, its capacity for discernment, and its vulnerability to psychic imbalance.

Still left to explain, then, is the prevalent image of the dog as a devourer of corpses in the Homeric poems. Previous formulations of the question can be summarized as follows. The often repeated image of the necrophagous dog in Homer inexplicably contradicts the positive representations of the animal in other passages of the poems. If Homer represents corpse-eating dogs so often, it is argued, clearly the dog was repulsive in the society that the epic describes. But what then justifies the touching episode with Argus and the fact that dogs feature as positive comparanda for the bravest heroes in many similes? Some scholars have even asked whether the poems' partiality to the image of corpse-eating dogs is a sign that Homer was not fond of the animal. Or perhaps the poet was an ardent dog lover but, despite this, could not avoid recording the existence of other dogs, not yet domesticated, that roamed the land around communities in Greece and Anatolia searching for corpses to scavenge. Still others want to identify distinct conceptions of the dog in the *Iliad,* which abounds in images of canine necrophagy, and the *Odyssey,* where this is notably less frequent, and even summon this difference as proof that the poems are not the work of the same author.[1]

It's not my aim here to settle this question. Rather, the fact that scholars have framed the discussion in these terms provides an opportunity for opening remarks on my divergent approach to the subject. That Greek culture, not just Homer, noted the dog's scavenging tendency is something that requires no justification, inasmuch as this is a normal part of the animal's dietary behavior. One should ask instead why modern cultures in the West have eliminated from the dominant canine image certain traits such as the tendency to eat carrion and excrement. It could be because these behaviors are observed less frequently, since our urbanized dogs have less need and occasion to display their scatophilia and necrophagy. But it is also likely that the progressive reduction of its functions to those of a companion animal has also Disneyfied the dog, flattening out its representation according to standards for animated cartoon characters, resulting in a predominantly anthropomorphized image that excludes undesired bestial traits.[2]

What is more worth investigating, then, is not why ancient sources transmit images of necrophagy in dogs but the ways this trait fits into the complex of opinions, ideas, and beliefs that the Greeks compiled under the word *kyōn* in their cultural encyclopedia. The questions to ask concern how Homer and other Greeks conceived of canine necrophagy and why, when epic heroes threaten to throw their enemies' corpses away as meals for beasts, they speak more often of dogs' jaws than vultures' beaks. The aim will therefore be to understand what resonances, associations, and symbolic implications an ancient poet might trigger in presenting a hero's corpse being dismembered by dogs rather than crows or other necrophagous animals.

From this perspective, the differing views of the dog within the epics offer riches to be exploited, not a difficulty to overcome. They simply result from the variety of man-dog relationships in the cultural context that produced the *Iliad* and the *Odyssey*—so the fact that contradictory traits were present poses no problem at all. To understand the absurdity of presuming that the Greek category of *kyōn* should be homogeneous, it is enough to realize that our culture also classifies as "dog" specific animals with widely divergent physical and behavioral traits, to which we relate in very different ways. Nobody would make a problem out of reconciling the view of their little house dog with that of the neighbor's fierce Doberman; nobody would see a contradiction in the fact that both are classified as dogs. So, too, in the case of dietary habits, none of us would dream of throwing our dog out of the house in disgust or refusing to consider it domesticated and a welcome dinner companion because it was caught at scavenging or scatophagy in a public park, or because other dogs were seen behaving this way. These aspects are part of the dog's nature and can be present with its other traits in its cultural representations without their having to be reconciled. The differing views can be stored simply as distinct pieces of information or else classified in pairs or clusters as ambivalences and oppositions.

More generally, each culture may associate a variety of traits with one class of animal without problems of incompatibility arising. The contents united within each independent field—"dog," "cow," "horse"—are in fact concepts in an encyclopedic knowledge, and under each term a heterogeneous group of opinions and beliefs can coalesce, however divergent and conflicting.[3] There is nothing to stop the spider, for example, from being portrayed as a malicious weaver but then in other cases being considered a lucky talisman that protects the house. Nor are the two conceptions necessarily polar opposites of a single representation of the animal.

One may wonder further whether Homeric dogs have caused such a stir due to an inadvertent projection onto the epic world of modern and Western cultural models of the dog.[4] At least one gets the impression—from the complete silence on this point in ancient texts—that the frequent allusions to corpse-eating dogs in the *Iliad* have disturbed modern commentators far more than they surprised ancient audiences. One suspects that the reason for such amazement at the contradictory elements in the Homeric representation of dogs is an unconscious resistance among scholars to admitting that necrophagy and man-eating ferocity might slip back into their image of the dog.[5] And thus the proposed solutions seek to repel the horror of necrophagy from the normal representation of the dog by attributing it to a peculiar type of dog: a "protohistoric" dog is posited, or a dog "imported" into Greek epic from a different cultural tradition, so that one winds up with chapters devoted to "scavenger dogs" that treat dogs portrayed in their aspect of corpse eaters as another species entirely, having nothing to do with the gentle house dogs and noble hunting dogs that other parts of the poems describe.[6]

Against such views one can object first of all that if Homer wanted to distinguish between two kinds of dogs—one domesticated, the other wild and feral—he could have done so easily, by giving them different names or by simply modifying *kyōn* with the adjective *agrios* (wild), as he does to distinguish the wild boar (*hys*

agrios) from the domestic pig (*hys*). But this is only a minor objection. More decisive is that the presence of dogs scavenging on a field of battle and during a siege—
the conditions in which the *Iliad*'s events unfold—requires no particular justification. Dogs' tendency toward necrophagy mainly appears in situations when there
is a scarcity of food—when people have nothing to feed their domestic animals—
and an availability of abandoned, unburied corpses.[7] Here we can recall a telling
passage in Thucydides. During the plague that struck Athens in 430 B.C.E., the
historian records, neither birds nor "four-footed beasts that eat human flesh"
would come near the corpses, even though a great number were left unburied. This
was because the bodies were so infectious that an animal that ate any at all would
die. Proof of this was that in those days, no more scavenger birds were seen around,
but even clearer evidence of what was happening, according to Thucydides, was
the behavior of dogs, more easily observed "because they live together with people."[8] The dogs that the Athenian historian counts, without astonishment, among
the potential devourers of human flesh are thus domestic dogs—which live among
people—and not semiwild dogs that live far from human society.

All dogs, given the right conditions, may reveal their tendency toward necrophagy, and there is no evidence for us to assume that in Greece, necrophagy was a
distinguishing trait of a class of feral dogs, different from those raised in the home.[9]
"The corpse-eating dog" does not exist. Instead, we may speak of the dog's corpse-
eating behavior as one aspect that the Greeks included in their encyclopedic definition of *kyōn*, and it is this that deserves further scrutiny.[10]

CANNIBALISM BY ANIMAL PROXIES

Undoubtedly among the greatest fears for the Greeks was dying far from home and
going without burial or funeral rites. Jean-Paul Vernant has clearly traced the system of beliefs that cultivated this fear: a dead person uncremated, left to decay or
be eaten by animals, could not attain the status of deceased. The unburied thus
remain hybrid beings, neither alive nor dead, consigned to oblivion, without a
place either in the world's memory or in the sort of shadowy, otherworld society
that was the kingdom of the deceased.[11] Animals credited with corpse-eating habits, and thus capable of causing this wretched fate, included birds (*oiōnoi*)—sometimes further specified as vultures and ravens—the large wild carnivores (*thēres*),
eels and fish, worms and flies, pigs, and dogs.[12] The two Homeric poems, which
often invoke the image of a corpse given as a meal to beasts, describe the devouring of a corpse—by eels and fish[13]—only once, while in the majority of cases the
image is used to threaten enemies and adversaries ("I will feed you to beasts") or
comrades-in-arms ("Whoever doesn't fight valiantly will wind up food for beasts");
it also appears in frequent expressions of fear connected with the horrible prospect
of one's body—or those of one's relatives or comrades—not receiving proper

burial.[14] In more than three out of four cases, dogs are named as the animals to profit from the corpse, most often alone but sometimes together with birds.[15] Why do dogs predominate in these images of threat and fear?

I propose that the dog, as opposed to other corpse-eating animals, adds a symbolic value, a surplus meaning directly connected to the unique elements in the Greek representation of the man-dog relationship. Before evaluating this theory, however, we should briefly recall the general context in which the image of corpse-eating dogs appears—in other words, consider the key symbolic implications of the act of feeding a corpse to animals.

One must remember first of all that leaving a body as food for beasts constituted one of the possible forms of ritual annihilation called *aeikia,* which consisted in outrageously defacing the corpse and rendering the person unrecognizable. The verb for such an action was *aeikizein,* "to disfigure" a body, by making it "dissimilar" (*a-eikos*) to its original appearance. In this way, one aimed to destroy in an enemy what had made their body distinct, what had made them a person. The cadaver caked in dirt and blood, mangled by beasts or abandoned to decay, constitutes the annihilation of the dead's personal identity through the dissolution of their appearance beyond recognition.

Such aeikia aimed to achieve a result diametrically opposite to that of funerary practices, which work to eternalize the identity of the dead: the laying out of the corpse, whole and in full dignity, to be mourned by friends and relatives; the cremation of the body, which removes it from view at the height of its grandeur, avoiding the disfigurement of decay; the insertion of recollections into the collective memory through the raising of a funeral monument and the undying fame in song assured by poets.[16] To deface the corpse of an enemy is to negate all of this, negate the antidote for the horror of dissolution that the funeral rite effects. But we can go further and identify some more specific implications of that exact form of aeikia that consisted in feeding a corpse to beasts.

When a Homeric hero threatens his enemy, he is emphatically forecasting his triumph as an act of cannibalism, expressing the peak of superiority in the image of eating the body of the slain warrior. So, for example, Achilles triumphs over dying Hector, who has just supplicated Achilles to not violate his body and to allow him to receive funeral honors from his loved ones:

> No, you dog, don't supplicate me, not by my knees nor my parents!
> My fury and my heart urge me to devour you
> Raw and torn to pieces, for what you've done to me.[17]

Doomed by his radically heroic status to the excesses of total action, the Homeric warrior at the peak of his martial fury crosses over into bestiality and becomes an eater of raw flesh. His unleashed rage makes it so that he no longer knows any duty, any cultural curb, no "restraint [*aidōs*]" of any form.[18] At the conceivable limit of his exploit, the corpse of his enemy now becomes for him, as for a wild beast, meat on which to feed. The force of his bellicose fury obliterates the warrior's ability to recognize his enemy's body as that of a person, which in normal conditions would trigger the curb of a taboo against cannibalism.[19]

Although this threatened cannibalism never occurs, the Homeric warrior nevertheless has good reasons to invoke it. To foresee an end of this sort for a dying enemy means to humiliate and annihilate him in the most violent way imaginable. It tells him that in the victor's hands, he is virtually no longer a person and cannot hope to obtain the glory that would save his identity from the oblivion of dissolution. It also means to make the enemy know that he is prey with no escape, just a carcass of meat. The offensive intention of radical depersonalization that the threat implies is thus fully realized at the moment when the hero presents his beaten enemy with the idea of ending up torn to pieces in his jaws.

But even if the image of heroic anthropophagy is useful and effective on a symbolic level, cannibalism is nevertheless not the solution that Iliadic warriors adopt in practice. Not even Achilles, the most extreme of Homeric heroes, goes so far as to eat an enemy's body. And yet there exists a viable alternative, heard as the exchange of Achilles and Hector continues:

> Nobody will be able to keep your head from the dogs,
> Not even if ten or twenty times they bring here
> Endless ransom and promise again still more,
> Not even if Dardan Priam bids me take your weight in gold as ransom,
> Not even thus will your noble mother mourn you
> Laid out on your bier, the woman who gave you birth,
> But dogs and birds will tear you utterly to pieces.[20]

To disfigure the corpse—to disintegrate that unitary aspect that makes an individual recognizable and reduce him to pieces of meat—is the job of beasts. The cannibalism taboo that stops Achilles from tearing his enemy to bits does not exist for the animals, and they will be the authors of the ultimate outrage.[21]

This sort of cannibalism by animal proxies emerges elsewhere in the poems also, if more covertly.[22] In another case, Glaucus of Lycia rebukes Hector, blaming him for failing to recover the body of their comrade Sarpedon:

> You wretch, since Sarpedon, your guest-friend and comrade,
> You left behind as prey and spoil for the Argives,
> A man very useful to the city and to you
> While alive, but now you lacked the courage to defend him from the dogs.[23]

To leave the body of a fallen comrade on the battlefield thus means to abandon it to the mercy of both the enemy and their dogs. The degree of symmetry here is best discerned in the expression Glaucus uses to describe his friend's body—"prey and spoil [helōr kai kyrma]" of the Greeks—the same one the poems use many times for corpses given over to corpse-eating beasts.[24] The idea that the enemy wreaks havoc on opponents' bodies is therefore made explicit through the image of dogs devouring a carcass, but in such a way that to be "prey and spoil" of the enemy becomes homologous to being devoured by dogs.

This homology between the two situations—or, better, the interchangeability of the two representations of a corpse's fate, to become enemy spoil or food for necrophagous animals—also helps explain the meaning of a curious formula. It often happens that the beasts, especially the dogs, that are predicted or feared will inflict the corpse's fate are specified with an exact belonging that is perhaps less casual than it may seem at first sight. Notice, for example, that Hector foresees Ajax's imminent death by saying that he will soon be food for "dogs and birds of the Trojans," and that again, in Ajax's helpless observation, "dogs and birds of the Trojans" will sate themselves on the corpse of Patroclus.[25] So, too, Hector wants to decapitate Patroclus's lifeless body and throw it to "a Trojan bitch," Menelaus exhorts his comrades to be outraged at the idea that Patroclus will become a plaything "for Trojan bitches," even Zeus cannot stand that Patroclus's corpse will be prey "for the bitches of his enemy, the Trojans," and Iris convinces Achilles to return to battle to prevent Patroclus from becoming a "plaything for Trojan bitches."[26] In his intense final exchange of words with Achilles, Hector prays that his body will not be devoured near the ships by "dogs of the Achaeans," and when Priam asks Hermes for news of his son's body, what he wants to know is whether it is still intact or whether Achilles has already torn it to pieces and thrown it "to his bitches."[27] Particularly the last two passages in this list seem to show that outraging the enemy's corpse did not simply consist in abandoning it on the field to the mercy of any scavenging animal but rather, at least in some cases, in a formalized ritual that probably had a precise symbolic value: it's one thing to leave a body unburied and another to cut it into pieces and feed it to one's dogs.[28] We will return later to these specific cases. For now, let's stick with the situation in which a corpse is simply abandoned on the field.

Note, first of all, that these passages always specify their dogs as belonging to someone (this includes two that characterize both dogs and birds this way); only of dogs do the poems say every time that those of the enemies will devour the hero's body. How should we understand this strange habit of identification? The easiest hypothesis—but perhaps also the most superficial—is that the formula conveys merely a spatial emphasis, indicating that the body will be dragged into the enemy's sphere and abandoned there, and thus the animals living in that area will eat it. Dogs or birds, in this view, would be "of the Trojans" because they eat the body in Trojan territory.[29] This interpretation, however, does not seem to explain the formula's persistent appearance. It is therefore legitimate to explore a "thicker" meaning and propose that this type of expression responds to a deeper, more hidden cultural scenario.[30]

If we accept, for example, that the underlying idea in these menacing expressions is symbolic cannibalistic consumption, then the specification that the dogs and birds are of the enemy takes on a decidedly sinister shading and the threat a more violent tone. The scavenging animals about to ravage the dead body, expressly defined as belonging to the enemy's community, clearly assume the symbolic role of enemy devourers. In this interpretation, the epic formula loses its apparent redundancy. Instead, when seen in this light, the preference for dogs as opposed to other scavengers in the formulaic language for outraging an enemy's corpse can be traced to the position of the dog, that is, to its close participation in the human community. The solidarity that joins a dog to its human owner makes it the enemy of his enemy and thus, in this case, a sort of natural substitute for the master in consuming the enemy's corpse. If the hero does not eat the slain enemy's body, who better to do so than his own dogs, the animals that are his table companions? But this is just a first assessment. In the image of a body becoming food for the enemy's dogs there may be more specific things in play and still further implications to be traced.

MONSTROUS BANQUETS

As we saw in the previous chapter, the dog's dietary regimen makes it, uniquely and in various ways, man's dining companion: in a concrete sense because it frequents the dining room and the kitchen, where it waits for—or craftily steals—its share of food; in a more abstract sense because it tends to consume the same type of food that humans eat. This commensality in itself already gives a good reason to prefer dogs to vultures or hyenas in the imagery of defiling corpses. If one wants to imagine the greatest horror, ending up as food for an enemy's dogs, animals that eat with the enemy, is worse than being left for the jaws and beaks of wild animals.

But the dog's status as fellow diner also entails something else. From the point of view of potential victims of canine anthropophagy, being devoured by a dog also implies a monstrous inversion of the order of sharing at table and a radical reduction of the hierarchic distance that governs the presence of dogs in human dining spaces. Generally allowed at human tables as a subordinate diner and given a residual portion of food, the dog becomes in the act of necrophagy a consumer of man instead. Obviously, such an inversion of the model of commensality gives the threat of aeikia a greater force than it would have with other corpse-eating scavengers.

This observation finds support in a well-known scene of Aeschylus's *Prometheus Bound,* whose horrific violence seems significantly enhanced by the presence of a canine element. Prometheus, the philanthropic Titan who dared to challenge Zeus by favoring humankind, has for some time been chained at the world's end by the will of the king of the gods. He could mitigate his sentence by telling Zeus an important secret about the future, but he doesn't want to give in to extortion. Hermes comes to him, bringing an ultimatum: give up his stubborn resistance or thunder and lightning will crash down on him and a massive landslide will bury him. When he returns to the light at last, an eagle sent by Zeus will thrust its sharp beak into his flesh and feast on his liver as eternal torment.[31]

In depicting this dreadful prospect, Hermes calls the devouring eagle "Zeus's winged dog." Why this description? No doubt it expresses, in the first place, the particular relationship of allied subordination that ties the raptor to Zeus. The gods often have wild animals as their "dogs." Their supernatural power is in fact capable of dominating any natural force, so they can hold at the ready, like gentle pups eager to follow any command, lions and wolves, fierce beasts impossible for humans to domesticate.[32] Above all, then, the idea of the eagle as dog alludes to the grandeur of Zeus's power. In the second place, the image probably also refers to a particular doggedness that will characterize the animal's inescapability. The eagle will behave like a dog sicced on its master's enemy, a living weapon with unstoppable momentum. As we will see later, attack dogs were in fact a good model for representing acts of blind vengeance.

But there is more. With regard to this passage, some commentators have argued that Aeschylus has overlain on the eagle the image of the dog as an allusion to the Homeric–type scene of the dog scavenging.[33] But in what sense does this image make this allusion? The body of Prometheus devoured by an eagle is not, after all, a genuine corpse. If the Aeschylean passage and the Homeric image of necrophagy are related, it is in the amplification produced by the figure of the dog in the scene of anthropophagy. Aeschylus's text signals this connection when it points unequivocally to a salient associative link:

> . . . But Zeus's
> Winged dog, an eagle blood-colored, rapaciously
> Will tear your body to shreds;
> A daily dinner companion that sneaks in uninvited
> Will dine to the utmost on the black meal of your liver.

Overlaying the image of dog on that of eagle allows the poet to hone the scene's hallucinatory effect, by orchestrating a successive montage of anthropophagy with the cultural imaginary of the table and the feast. Every day at table, Prometheus will encounter the "dog" of Zeus, who will be "uninvited [*aklētos*]" because its dining will not accord with normal canine food sharing, in which the animal is allowed at the table only at the dinner provider's discretion.[34] The beast's food will consist not of humbly awaited thrown scraps but instead of the monstrously parasitic meal of a vampiric, man-eating animal. Zeus's dog will not be at Prometheus's table but will make a meal of Prometheus himself. It will have a human meal in the most horrifying possible sense.

The same effect of symbolic accumulation is at work in the *Agamemnon* passage discussed in the previous chapter, which uses a canine image in the story of a lion cub. Recall that the little lion, raised indoors like a dog, nurtured and pampered by old and young, becomes, once it grows up, a monstrous table companion that, in accord with its wild nature, devours everything it can eat: "It prepared for itself a banquet," says Aeschylus, "and the house was soaked in blood."[35] The *Prometheus* portrays the eagle at table in the same way, as a monstrous dog—or, rather, as a dog in reverse, preparing a table with human flesh for itself instead of waiting patiently for leftovers from human hands.

Note also that the *Prometheus* scene, just like Homer, uses the image of canine anthropophagy in a threat intended to terrorize its recipient. It is clear enough that we are dealing with a cultural model active in situations of intense conflict and verbal violence, where it certainly plays a specific role. To predict that a person will end up, alive or dead, as food for dogs is to project an image of destructive violence in which the subject foresees his dignity obliterated in a reversal of the table's hierarchy: he is forced to imagine himself no longer a giver of food to dogs but as food at a dog's feast. This image of overturned commensality thus intensified the theme of the disintegration of identity already present in the idea of dismembering and disfiguring the corpse. These were central elements of aeikia, whose victim would suffer disfigurement often predicted in an eloquent vocabulary of butchery that represented the body abandoned to animals' jaws as a piece of meat—"shreds," says Aeschylus—or an unformed mass of "fat and flesh."[36]

But as noted above, beyond simple images of a human body abandoned to the jaws of dogs, we also find in Homer more detailed and specific situations. There is, for example, the image of a man's body becoming food for his own dogs. First consider the threat that the violent, arrogant suitors hurl at the swineherd Eumaeus in the palace on Ithaca. When they realize that he intends to hand the bow to Odysseus, who can then take part in the test of strength that Penelope has arranged, they assail him with these words:

> Where are you taking the curved bow, wretched swineherd—
> Are you insane? The time is near when out there, among the pigs,
> Alone, far from all, they'll tear you apart, the dogs that you have raised,
> If Apollo and the other gods prove favorable.[37]

Terrified by this awful threat, Eumaeus puts down the bow. The punishment that the suitors forecast is one of extraordinary violence: an anonymous death, without witnesses, far from everyone, in the midst of pigs; Eumaeus's corpse abandoned to be eaten by the very dogs he has raised.[38] It's not clear whether the suitors are threatening to kill the swineherd and throw his body to dogs or predicting that dogs driven by a divine force will kill him. In any case, this is not just any body made food for any dog: the suitors summon up in Eumaeus's mind the prospect of being devoured by dogs that—the text is emphatic—he has raised himself.

If one recalls the importance attributed to raising and nurturing—the founding principle of solidarity between dog and master—in the man-dog relationship, it becomes clear that the violence of this image, too, is based on a reversal of the model. Only this time, the subverted scheme is the food pact. Consider the several possible implications of the curse hurled at Eumaeus: it entails the ideas that his dogs do not recognize the debt they owe their master for raising them, or, cruder still, they will not recognize him as their master and will unleash on him the aggression they normally direct at his enemies, or they will no longer be able to identify their master when he's just a body, which will be an anonymous piece of meat in their eyes. A vision of the world turned upside down, in other words: complete annihilation of identity by the very animals that normally are required to recognize their master and acknowledge his authority. It is no accident that this threat of unspeakable violence comes from the suitors, the arrogant usurpers of Ithaca's royal house and the poem's antiheroes.[39]

"I am I because my little dog knows me," Gertrude Stein wrote, provocatively reflecting on the vertiginous play of mirrors in which every attempt to determine one's identity tends to go astray.[40] We cannot rule out the possibility that in some cases in ancient Greece as well, the human-dog relationship was liable to meet up with the delicate dynamics of self-perception. Another famous passage in the *Iliad* seems to invite close attention to the complicated symbolic configuration brought into play by the image of a man torn apart by his dogs.

Hector is about to take the field against Achilles. It will be his final duel. His aged father, King Priam, begs him not to go. So many strong sons of Troy have already died in battle, and the death of Hector, the city's last bulwark, would prove its ultimate downfall. Priam tries to dissuade his son by summoning up a dreadful vision of the fallen city: Troy left without defenders, easy prey to the enemy, her stronghold invaded by Achaeans, his other sons all slain, his daughters and daughters-in-law carted off as slaves, bridal bedrooms looted, babies massacred. All this, says Priam, I'll have to see before dying myself the saddest death a man can have foretold to him:

> And finally me too, before the palace gates, dogs
> That eat raw flesh will haul me off—once someone with sharp bronze
> Has struck and wounded me, tearing life from limbs—
> Those dogs I raised in the house, table companions and guards at the door,
> They'll drink my blood with hearts racing
> And lie down in the doorway. For a young man it's fitting
> To be slain in battle; cut down by sharp bronze
> He's laid low; though dead, all is fine and noble for him,
> Whatever his appearance. . . .

But when a white head and white beard
And the genitals of an old man slain are defiled by dogs,
This is the most miserable thing for unfortunate mortals.[41]

As Jean-Pierre Vernant has observed, Priam's speech is important testimony on the Homeric conception of a "beautiful death."[42] For a young man, the beautiful death is the one met in battle, because it confers immortality, fixing in eternal glory the figure of the hero in his youthful splendor. A young warrior's dead body arouses admiration always and everywhere, even if covered with wounds. Scars and injuries sustained in fighting do not mar but rather enhance the fighter's appearance, because they attest to his virtue.[43] Priam contrasts this figure of the young hero laid low while battling the enemy with the image of an unarmed old man slain in his home. This is not a death that gives dignity to an elderly man. For an old father, a beautiful death consists in expiring in tranquil serenity in the privacy of home, surrounded by the loving attention of children, daughters-in-law, and grandchildren. The bloody wounds that add beauty to the young body struck in battle become disfiguring marks on a body already whitened with age.

The fear of losing Hector and the foreboding of his own end suggest to Priam the specter of an inglorious death. And to render the scene even more spine chilling, it involves the corpse being mangled by house dogs, who become the authors of a dreadful domestic aeikia, the violence of which is monstrous and unacceptable. The home is supposed to be a place of solidarity and cohesion, a space institutionally incompatible with the ideas of conflict and violence. On the battlefield, the place outside the city where the fury of Ares rages, violence has an order of its own, which is culturally codified: the beastly and the savage are paradigms of heroic valor, and the best warriors present themselves positively as wild lions and rampaging boars. Within the civic and domestic sphere, on the other hand, this force is not glorious, neither for the man-beasts nor for their unarmed victims. The violence that consumes them is pure horror, not a duel or a fight between equals but a sheer massacre of the weak, and inglorious for both its perpetrators and sufferers alike. This is why the domestic aeikia is "the most miserable thing for unfortunate mortals," as Priam says.

Priam's insistence that the dogs belong to the palace—specifying that he raised them, emphasizing their role as protectors of domestic boundaries ("guards at the door") and their regular presence at the table—leaves little doubt about the image's intended effect of reversal and self-consuming endophagy. At the moment of plunder, the house of Priam becomes a trap, an engulfing tomb. Everything unfolds in the entryway. There his own dogs will tear him apart, on the threshold that they formerly protected from strangers. It is also there that the dogs will turn and lie back down, having finished their horrible meal. Once violated by the devastating intrusion of the enemy, the domestic space of the Trojan palace is destroyed, and the house's threshold becomes a tombstone. The dogs close it again from inside, reversing the direction of their guardian function. The enemy's intrusion subverts the entire domestic equilibrium and tears down its ordered hierarchy, and the dogs, with their behavior, provide the most bloodcurdling sign of the inversion. Always recognizing the existing order before, now they not only do not recognize it but even become active agents of its dissolution. Faced with the dead body of their master, the dogs turn wolf, and Priam is nothing but meat to tear at. In this way they represent the unleashing of wildness, the transformation of cultural space into a chaotic and brutal scene of slaughter.[44]

If, for a young warrior, the threat of being defiled by the enemy's dogs covers a series of terrible implications—such as the idea of a cannibalistic meal, the omission of funeral rites that perpetuate identity, and, with this, the loss of human and cultural dignity for the dead—for Priam, to end up as a meal for his own dogs means becoming food for his former dining companions, nourishment for those he himself nourished, and seeing the annihilation of his identity in the gaze of the dogs that no longer recognize him. In such a situation the dog is thus called on to play a symbolic role diametrically opposite to that given in the *Odyssey* to Argus, who alone among the house's members recognizes the master, Odysseus, despite his long years of absence and the clothing that alters his appearance. The episode owes part of its appeal to the function it plays in the poem's narrative. The dog's recognition, after all, prefigures Odysseus's imminent recovery of his lost identity, for it is from precisely that moment that the king of Ithaca begins slowly to reconstruct his public personality and gradually regain his visibility and credit within the palace, by revealing himself step by step to his son, his wife, and his faithful servants. From that moment on, he also begins to glimpse the possibility of restoring order, the legitimate kingship, and the norms subverted by the suitors' occupation. In sharp contrast, the dogs of Priam that suddenly fail to recognize their master not only represent the annihilation of the identity and social dignity of the king but also prefigure the impending total destruction of his house and the entire Trojan kingdom.[45]

Commensality, the debt of nurturing, recognition of the master as a person and an authority: these three bases—on which, we have seen, the cultural representation of the man-dog relationship rests—serve as the principle axes for developments of the trait of anthropophagy. The dog's readiness to eat human flesh, a typical feature in the animal's ethology, is capable of activating a dense series of symbolic reflexes precisely because it contradicts other patterns in the encyclopedia definition of *kyōn*.[46] By coming into contact and opposition with the ideas from which the cultural image of the man-dog relationship is constructed, anthropophagy and necrophagy engender images of reversal, scenes of degradation, and intimations of mutiny.

At this point we must consider whether, and to what degree, these dynamics traced through Homeric examples may also provide valid keys to reading the most

famous and emblematic story of dogs devouring their master: the myth of Actaeon. Indeed, some versions of the story show how symbolic developments of
anthropophagy tend to be organized along the lines identified above. As seen in
the previous chapter, for example, the behavior of Actaeon's dogs could be
described in terms of failed recognition. It was delusion brought on by lyssa, some
sources say, that made the pack mistake their master for prey and attack him.[47]
Euripides prefers to emphasize the theme of nurturing: Actaeon had given food to
and personally raised the dogs now tearing him apart, and thus, the gratitude they
owe their nurturer is monstrously distorted.[48] Callimachus opts for the third possibility for symbolic effect and sketches the horror in terms of a feast: the dogs,
animal dinner companions, "made a meal of their master."[49]

More than all other animals with scavenging tendencies, the dog offered opportunities to elaborate images of terror with a broad spectrum of symbolic implications. This explains the preference of the Homeric poems for the dog in threats of
aeikia. By virtue of distinctive traits that characterized the animal's cultural image,
canine necrophagy allowed for reflections on the loss of both identity and being-
in-the-world, which constituted both the most terrifying aspect of death and the
horrible effect of ritualized outrage to the corpse.

CORPSES AS REFUSE

One further aspect remains to be considered. In speaking of the symbolic potential at the intersection of the images of canine dinner companion and man-eater,
we have not yet taken into account the relevant detail that dogs normally eat leftover food, the refuse from human tables. It's worth the trouble, therefore, to ask
whether this also sets off reactions in the symbolic chemistry of the image of a dog
intent on devouring a human body.

The previous chapter mentioned the pieces of soft dough called apomagdaliai,
which the Greeks used as napkins and then threw to the dogs under the table.
We've also already referred to the fact that dogs normally wait for leftovers, the bits
least appetizing to people and inedible parts such as bones. But further examples
give a more exact idea of how the Greeks conceived of "food for dogs"—"dog
food"—and what connotations it could have.

Ancient sources often depict dogs as dying of hunger. They wander around the
house constantly looking for things to eat, ever waiting for scraps and ready to take
food furtively at every opportunity. In Aristophanes's comedy *Wasps*, a satire of
the litigiousness of Athenians in the last decades of the fifth century B.C.E., the dog
Labes—whose name, roughly meaning Snatcher, conveys his trademark vice—is
accused of stealing and eating an entire Sicilian cheese and is hauled into court.
Old Philocleon, who has an uncontrollable passion for exemplary punishments,
relishes the chance to convict him. But luckily, Labes has a strong advocate, young

Bdelycleon, who pleads for mercy: he is just a poor dog (so goes the defense) who works every day and in return is content to eat paltry fish heads and bones.[50] Like all good dogs, in other words, Labes works hard and survives on meager leftovers.

The fact that dogs must settle for such a sorry diet leads people to attribute to them a secret aspiration to eat better and a chronic voraciousness similar to the traditional characteristic of the parasite, the sort of perpetually famished beggar who makes the rounds of wealthy dining rooms in hopes of being invited to dinner.[51] One of the dog's known specialties, for instance, was licking the pots in secret, by sneaking into the unguarded kitchen, preferably at night.[52] No less proverbial was the mangy ravenousness with which a pack of dogs will attack a single piece of meat, fighting over it with teeth bared and snarling, like people who haven't eaten for days.[53]

The poor quality of canine fare makes the image of dog food available as an antonomastic trope for discourses on the inequality of distributions, as when someone feels slighted by receiving a less appetizing portion of available dishes.[54] If someone saw a dinner host saving them the reject portions of a dish, they would feel treated "like a dog" and react with indignation. It is absurd—argued the comic poet Pherecrates, among others—that humans did not realize how offended the gods must be at every sacrifice, when they saw the priest setting aside the fleshy parts of the victims for himself and his friends while leaving on the altar only the least desirable remains, as one does for dogs.[55] The same comically polemical argument is found in an anonymous poetic fragment that asks who could be such a gullible fool as to think that the gods enjoy watching sacrifices of stripped bones and a burned-up gallbladder, "stuff not even starving dogs would eat."[56] Even a parasite, that marginal creature disposed by definition to adapt himself to any situation just to gain access to a richly spread table, was offended by the treatment he received in Corinth, where the rude symposiasts, little inclined to liberality and ignorant of refined Athenian manners, threw into a corner for him shin and ankle bones "fit for dogs."[57]

Among the most eloquent examples of how the idea of dog food could give scope for expressions of disrespect is a scene in Aristophanes's *Clouds,* the biting satire of the Socratic school and its sophistical ways. Strepsiades, ruined by his son's debts, decides to become a student of Socrates, who convinces him that he can learn to dupe his creditors by force of subtle discourse. Arriving at the philosopher's "Thinkery," he seeks to have a conversation with the master himself. At one point, Socrates says that he will toss down a piece of wisdom from on high:

> *Socrates:* Come, see that you catch some in the air [*hypharpasei*] when I throw you
>   [*probalō*] some piece of knowledge about celestial realities.
> *Strepsiades:* What is that? Am I to eat wisdom in tidbits, like a dog?[58]

The verbs that Socrates uses, *proballein* (throw before) and *hypharpazein* (snatch from below), are enough for the aspiring student to discern an offensive note of disparagement in the master's proposal: the philosopher intends to save only a residual part of his wisdom for Strepsiades, a "tidbit" or morsel, if not indeed a scrap or leftover, which Strepsiades has to catch in the air, if he can, like a dog under the table.

What goes to the dogs is table refuse, and thus the idea of eating greasy crumbs, the apomagdaliai, was in some sense equivalent to the idea of eating filthy garbage.[59] In fact, it seems that the Hellenistic term *skybalon,* which means "refuse, filth, excrement," derived from food for dogs, being a nominalization of the expression *Skynbale!,* a shortened popular form of "Throw it to the dogs [es kynas bale]!"[60] It must be remembered, however, that the contiguity of canine feeding was what made it activate such a strong cultural reflection on dog food: if the dog incarnated the lowest grade on the scale of human eating, this was only because it was indeed ranked in that class. As already observed, in the scale of animals, the dog enjoyed a privileged position with respect to nutrition; being closer than other beasts to man, it was imagined as the animal that eats better than all. Only when it is thought of as inside the human community, a participant in the social consumption of food, does the dog become the disadvantaged par excellence, the derelict, the last to dine, the "poor dog"—the underdog—lower than beggars and parasites (at least in the eyes of beggars and parasites).

If we turn now to consider the Homeric passages with threats or fears that a dead man's body will end up as dog food, we can add another inferential path that the symbolism of aeikia traces: the association of the corpse with the idea of refuse, of the remains of a meal. Two passages in the *Iliad* in particular, both regarding the fate of Hector's corpse, make it possible to deduce that the practices—or at least one of the possible practices—followed by Homeric warriors in the treatment of the enemy's corpse consisted in dragging it back to their own camp, mutilating it, cutting it in pieces, and throwing it bit by bit to their dogs, as one would at dinner with table scraps.[61] In this sort of aeikia the enemy corpse not only is butchered and served in a ritually codified cannibalistic feast but further plays in this meal the role of refuse, of undesirable leftover—something that undoubtedly adds a greater offensive charge to the symbolic act.

To evaluate the likelihood of this interpretation, however, it is well to ask first whether the ancient imaginary had available an idea of a correlation between a corpse and a leftover, potentially present, for example, in the different senses of the Italian word *resti,* which can mean "leftovers," the remains of a meal, but also the mortal "remains" of the deceased. A brief foray into Greek vocabulary suffices for an affirmative response. One term used for a dead body or for the ashes gathered in a funerary urn was *leipsana*—sometimes in the singular *leipsanon*—literally "remains," "residue."[62] Meanwhile, to judge from a verse of Euripides, it seems that *leipsana* could also be used of leftover food that is thrown out (*ekballein*) to dogs.[63] The verb *ekballein* has the sense, among others, of throwing out something unwanted; in this fragment, feeding dogs is configured explicitly as throwing out the trash from dinner. The same root (*bal-/blē-*) occurs significantly in a polemical fragment of Heraclitus where the philosopher states that the dead are "more to be thrown out [*ekblētoteroi*] than excrement."[64]

The idea that throwing to dogs, and in particular to one's own dogs, a corpse to eat is to reduce it to refuse, to unsavory leftovers from the table—in a word, to dog food—therefore seems probable. The cannibalistic gesture of eating one's enemy is in this way bypassed by means of another gesture, still more disgraceful, which, to paraphrase it, could be conveyed in the insult "I won't eat you, but my dogs will, since at my table you're nothing but trash."[65] When in Sophocles's *Ajax* the hero-protagonist is about to fall on his sword in suicide, he prays that a friend will find his body, "lest I, spotted by one of my enemies, get thrown as a meal [*problētos*] for dogs and prey [*helōr*] for birds."[66] The distinction between the two predicates may be quite significant. While *helōr*, indicating what his body will become for birds, is a traditional Homeric term, *problētos* is a Sophoclean coinage derived from the verb *proballein*, with the common meaning of "throwing out" scraps of food to dogs.[67] If this interpretation is correct, the verse can be more precisely translated: "lest I get thrown out as dog food and prey for birds."

A further observation may support this reading. The *Odyssey* gives us detailed testimony of how the aeikia of an enemy could be carried out, even if the case involved a personal adversary and not an enemy slain in battle. At the last moment of Odysseus's revenge, the unfaithful goatherd Melanthius, who had spent the years of the king's absence serving the suitors, suffers the most heinous punishment. First he is bound, with legs and arms tied together, and hung from a rafter in a locked room, where he is left to agonize while Odysseus carries out his great slaughter of the suitors. Then finally he is dragged outside and suffers horrific mutilation:

> And they cut off with pitiless bronze his nose and ears,
> And tore off his genitals to give them bleeding to the dogs,
> And severed his hands and feet, with heart raging.[68]

It's not clear whether this terrible butchery—depriving a body of every functional organ and reducing it to a formless trunk—was committed on the living Melanthius or on his corpse.[69] What seems certain is that this disfigurement has the same defamatory aim as other cases of aeikia, not to mention that to make someone die by mutilation is a particularly brutal way to carry out capital punishment and to outrage a corpse at one and the same time. But the most notable thing about this bloody act is that the dogs are not simply left the corpse but rather expressly saved a picked portion: the genitals. Treated like raw offal, red, bloody, and loathsome but loved by dogs, the genitals of the executed end up like the remains that a cook throws to the dogs when it butchers an animal before cooking it.[70]

This episode is not an exceptional case. A prior book of the *Odyssey* has a nearly identical passage, in which Antinous threatens Irus, the arrogant wandering beggar and parasite at the suitors' banquets, who is about to fight Odysseus: Irus better be careful not to yield, or Antinous will send him to the mainland, to that butcher of men King Echetus, who will cut off his nose and ears, tear off his genitals, and feed them raw to dogs.[71] Here the mutilation would clearly be done to a live man and not a corpse. A form of humiliation quite similar to this was a frequent punishment—or at least a frequent threat—and the final outcome of the dreadful process was the victim's reduction to slavery. First, one was tied up like a sack, hands and feet above the rest (as Odysseus does to Melanthius), then sold to traders after having, in the best cases, just one's ears lopped off.[72]

Tortures of this sort were not unknown among the Persians. Herodotus recounts how Amestris, the jealous wife of Xerxes, wanted to punish the wife of the king's brother Masistes, her sister-in-law, who was responsible, so she thought, for plotting to give her own daughter as a lover to the king. To fulfill her vengeance, Amestris waited for a grand feast celebrating Xerxes's birthday, when by tradition he couldn't refuse anybody anything, whatever they might ask. Amestris asked him to hand over her sister-in-law, whom, when she was brought into Amestris's presence, the queen destroyed this way:

> Cutting off her breasts she cast them [*proebale*] to dogs to eat, and lopped off her nose
> and ears and lips and tongue, then sent her home completely disfigured.[73]

Once again the verb *proballein* (throw forth) takes on the specialized meaning of throwing food to dogs. And here, as well, it is sex organs—the breasts in this case, for a woman—that become food for dogs. The symbolic significance of this particular mutilation seems quite clear. If one implication of the act of feeding something to dogs is treating it like a piece of refuse, then it's fairly evident that throwing the genital organs to dogs amounts to a symbolic degradation of the person, carried out first and foremost on the level of their sexual identity.

In conclusion, we can thus affirm that given their metonymic standing, and especially their dietary participation, in human society, dogs are carriers of a vast spectrum of symbolic potential, which is particularly potent when it illuminates a discrepant feature of theirs: anthropophagy and the attraction to raw meat, bloody offal, and innards. The ambiguity of the canine diet—at once human and wild—nonetheless neither makes the dog an "impure" animal nor excludes it from the dining room and other cultural spaces. Rather, this renders it a good subject for symbolic reflections on cannibalistic aggression, the taboo against eating human flesh, the relationship between bodily integrity and a person's recognizability, and the loss of individual identity. For this reason it is necessary not to forget that the dog is not an indiscriminate man-eater but only devours those it does not know and recognize.

THE DOG AT THE TOMB OF ITS MASTER

To the negative side of the portrait, where the dog functions as an active element in personal disintegration after death and the reduction of the human body to food of the lowest grade, we now add a positive side: the dog can also appear as an agent that confirms, or even defends to the utmost, the identity of the deceased.[74]

Homer once again offers a good introduction to this theme. At the end of the *Iliad* Hector is dead, and the disgraceful fate that Achilles intends to inflict on his corpse is presented as the exact opposite of the end that Achilles has prepared for the body of his friend Patroclus:

> Rejoice with me, Patroclus, even from the house of Hades,
> For I will accomplish everything I promised you.
> I have hauled Hector here to give him raw to the dogs,
> And twelve splendid Trojan sons to decapitate
> Before your pyre, enraged as I am at your death.[75]

Hector will wind up torn apart as a meal for dogs; Patroclus, on the other hand, will be consumed by fire on the funeral pyre and removed from the eyes of the world in the glorious fullness of his body's integrity.

The sense of this opposition, giving Patroclus the greatest honor while condemning Hector to the greatest infamy, emerges even more clearly in the speech Achilles gives after the pyre has been lit and his friend's body enveloped by flames:

> Rejoice with me, Patroclus, even from the house of Hades,
> For I will accomplish everything I promised you.
> Twelve noble sons of great-hearted Trojans
> Are all, along with you, being devoured by fire. But Hector,
> The son of Priam, I will not give the fire to gnaw, but to the dogs![76]

While "jaws" of funeral fire will perform the work of dissolution for Patroclus's body, for Hector's it will be the jaws of dogs. Two devouring agents will work to opposite ends.[77]

But Patroclus's glory is fulfilled not only by the miserable fate of his slayer. On the hero's funeral pyre, his friend also heaps a series of slaughtered victims:

> . . . And four long-necked stallions
> He hurried to throw on the pyre, greatly groaning;
> Of nine table dogs that the master had
> Two he slit the throats of and cast on the fire,
> And twelve noble sons of great-hearted Teucrians
> He slaughtered with bronze.[78]

Thus the body of Patroclus does not go alone onto the pyre; with it are burned, in order, four horses, two table dogs, and twelve Trojan youths. How should these sacrifices be interpreted? Probably they constitute an exaggeration of the model, quite common in many cultures, of sending the dead into the afterlife with the attributes of their rank and accoutrements that signaled their identity while alive.[79] The sacrifice of Trojan youths may be interpreted as a posthumous awarding to Patroclus of his part of the war spoils: if he had lived to see Troy's capture, he would have taken home youths as slaves. Thus, the victims Achilles places by him on the pyre are slaves following their master into death, and thereby Patroclus descends to Hades as a victorious hero. The same principle applies to the horses and dogs: they will continue in death as the attributes of his person that they were in life.[80]

Horse, dog, and servant are in fact the elements used to identify a person of free status, a master of an *oikos*, on funerary steles in later periods.[81] The dead man is often portrayed as a traveler with his dog or as a horseman accompanied by his dog and perhaps a servant. In each case, the dog acts as a mark of his master's character. To own a dog—especially a fine hunting dog—was a badge of distinction, while on the contrary, the sayings "He didn't even have a dog" and "He couldn't even raise a dog" referred to a person's utter indigence.[82] Horse and dog were, in other words, indispensable accessories for a man of rank, as well-known verses of the poet and legislator Solon imply: "Happy is he who has dear children and solid-hoofed horses / And hunting dogs and a foreign guest-friend."[83] But the dog did not always function simply as a status symbol. It does not seem to have this purpose, for example, when portrayed with women and children on funeral stele. Given the importance of the faculty of recognition in the human-dog relationship, it is likely that this depiction of the animal served to render the figure of the dead more complete, by acting as a mirror that reflected their identity. It is thus no accident that many of these reliefs show the dog with its head turned back toward its master, expressing the strong bond of belonging that joined dog to person by portraying the gaze of recognition. If we add that in some cases the stele depicts the master extending to his dog a bone or a piece of food, the impression is that the figurative mode was intended to emphasize specifically the exclusive and intimate nature of the bond: dog and master form an ideally indivisible dyad, so whoever wants to portray a whole person has to include their dog in the picture and show them in the act that founds and consolidates their bond with the animal.[84] The same intent may also lie behind the presence on a stele of a servant, who remained—in iconographic imagination, at least—an essential attribute of the master even after the latter's death. Dog and servant are supplements to the master's identity, characterizing attributes, because they recognize and regard their master as such.

The positive value of a dog for the deceased goes even further when it guards the tomb. Some statues of dogs in cemeteries are portrayed with this function.[85] Many stories also tell of dogs staying to guard their master's body and preserve its integrity, or trying to signal to passersby that their master is dead and thus help the body obtain burial, or lying down and dying at the side of their master's corpse.[86] In other words, these dogs perform the opposite function with respect to a corpse as the dogs involved in aeikia. In other stories, a dog is even entrusted with the task of restoring its slain master's honor, by identifying his killers and making sure they get the punishment they deserve.[87] It's not by chance that the Erinyes, the goddess of retribution, can assume—as we will see in the next chapter—the appearance of bitches, inasmuch as they are faithful avengers of murder victims.

The honor that Achilles bestows on Patroclus therefore consists in committing him to the fire that immortalizes him in a form of hyperbolic fullness of identity. Not only will his body be whole and decorously arranged on the pyre, but he will also descend to Hades surrounded by dogs, horses, and slaves, the same retinue he would have had if he had lived to enjoy the glory of a conquering hero. Evidence from many centuries later shows how the model of Patroclus's funeral could still be an effective paradigm in traditional Greek culture. The lexicographer Julius Pollux quoted this distich about a dead man:

> The man's name was Hippaimōn, his horse's Podargos,
> His dog's Lēthargos, and his servant's Babēs.[88]

This Hippaimōn, as we know from sources that preserve his entire funerary epigram, died as a hero in the front ranks of battle.[89] The formula listing the distinctive traits of this warrior's personality was probably intended to note the person along with his satellite attributes—his horse, his dog, his servant—as a sort of supplemental index of the deceased's identity and status at once. This does not imply that the servant and the animals were slain at the tomb and buried with the dead; rather, their names simply stand in their master's epigraph as would their images on his funerary stele, surrounding his figure as they did when he was alive. And yet, the lexicographer's note associates the dog Lēthargos with a genuine sacrificial burial: "Not even the Magnesian hound," Pollux says, "Hippaimōn's dog called Lēthargos remained without fame: in fact he was buried along with his master." In this account of Hippaimōn's life, the warrior gains the same honor that Patroclus did beneath the walls of Troy: he did not descend to the grave alone.[90]

4

Sad Fates, Low Morals, and Heinous Behaviors

After reconstructing the salient traits of the human-dog relationship and the dog's cultural physiognomy, after analyzing the rationale behind representations of canine necrophagy, we can now turn to the initial question of insults and place the problem on a more solid footing. We need to test whether and how the dog's unique metonymic position—its being perceived as a member of the human community, with the ambiguity this entails—might explain the fact that *dog* (*kyōn*) and its derivatives were used as terms of insult in Greek. In other words, can we affirm that the dog was chosen for insults not despite its familiarity and practical links with man but rather in virtue of its extraordinary closeness and solidarity?

Let's begin by considering the set of insults that use *kyōn* as metaphor but have no easy literal substitute. When Achilles, at the climax of the epic of his rage, has Hector at his feet, having sworn that he wanted to bring Hector down to avenge Patroclus and reaffirm his own superiority in battle, the two protagonists share an emotionally pitched exchange of words. Hector lies fatally wounded on the ground and begs his triumphing enemy not to outrage his corpse, to be content with victory and satisfied vengeance, and to return him to his parents, who will pay a worthy ransom. Achilles's reply, which leaves his dying foe without hope, begins with an insult: "No, you dog, don't supplicate me, not my knees nor by my parents!"[1] If we wanted to identify the key to this animal metaphor, we would have to ask what particular canine behavior Achilles is attributing to his enemy by labeling him *kyon*. But none of the negative traits in the dog's cultural representation—greediness, tendencies toward necrophagy and scatophagy, "rabid" aggressiveness or psychic instability—seem able to be the basis for the expression's outrageous quality in this context.

We can thus try to view the matter from another angle, by focusing attention on the pragmatic aspects of Achilles's abuse of Hector. We can analyze the performative aspect of the utterance, that is, its use as a linguistic act meant not so much to communicate propositional content as to express convictions, wills, and intentions and to produce in the hearer reactions of various kinds. From this perspective, we need to ask not what the insult means but what is its intent. This is because the main objective when we insult someone is not to describe the facts of a situation that exists prior to the words denoting it but to produce a state of fact: the humiliation of the addressee through the degradation of his or her dignity and the public proclamation of one's contempt. The insult is an act of denunciation and aggression.

Insults that use animal terms are really conventional metaphors—*Pig!* in Italian stands for "Greedy!" or "Dirty!"—but their offensive efficacy, we might say their communicative force, does not coincide exactly with the content of their substituted term. If *greedy* is a charge that can be disputed, *pig* is an outrage that must be avenged. When, to use the present example, one calls someone a dog, this is not saying "You are like a dog"—that is, "You are shaggy" or "You are shit-eating" or you have some other canine trait depending on context—but more precisely "You are a dog." The force of the expression is illocutionary: it's not the proposition's descriptive value that matters so much as the intention to denigrate with which it is spoken, seen here in the offense conveyed by the term *dog,* a conventionally recognized term of abuse. As a linguistic act that produces real consequences and effects in the hearer, modifying the state of things and inciting reactions from the interlocutor ranging from submission to violence in return, an insult has a perlocutionary force as well. Even more precisely, adopting criteria proposed by John Searle, we could say that insults are among those complex illocutionary acts that imply the affirmation of a conviction while also having to do with the interests of the speaker and the hearer, and that possess, moreover, a directive character like commands, and finally—at least in cases that occur in the presence of third parties—carry the effect of a proclamation.[2] Indeed, insults have a more offensive, degrading effect by being voiced in public. Like threats or commands, they are powerful, authoritative words, marked speech acts that aim to impose a superior will. As such, they are one type of utterance that in archaic Greece was called a *mythos,* distinguishing it from less authoritative and demanding discourses (*epos, logos*).[3]

Voicing an insult, then, unleashes first of all a charge of offensive aggression that aims to deprecate the antagonist as an inferior and to provoke either submission or acceptance of a challenge. The basic intent to denigrate may be accompanied by explanations of motivation, such as explicit accusations that justify the verbal aggression ("You are a dog because . . ."), but offensive degradation remains the main message, which can seem to lack specific justification or even to be completely unmotivated, at least on the level of the chosen metaphor's descriptive coherence. The injury in the animal metaphor *kyon*, as we will see, is distinctive in that it occurs in all these possible forms. It was not employed as a trope of specialized substitution—standing in for a single negative term as, for example, the Italian *asino* (ass) can for "stubborn" or "ignorant"—but could refer to one or more canine traits according to context or be used to denigrate and degrade the addressee entirely to the lowest level, for which canine animality was the privileged indicator.[4]

It remains to be explored here, therefore, why *kyōn* performed the task of denigrating better than names of other animals also subordinate to humans and considered low. Let's take another example. Two other times in the *Iliad* Hector is insulted with *kyōn*, first by Diomedes, then Achilles, both just having failed to wound him and now venting their disappointment at losing a good chance to kill him. They use the same verses:

> You've escaped death yet again, dog! And yet
> your downfall is at hand. Phoebus Apollo saved you once again,
> whom no doubt you prayed to when entering the fray,
> but I will finish you if I run into you again
> if I too have any god as my defender![5]

Rather than wondering whether Hector is called *dog* because it shows him as a coward for withdrawing from battle,[6] instead, let us ask what effect the insult *kyon* aims at in this context of face-to-face confrontations between heroes.[7] It seems quite clear that the end sought for the slight is the enemy's submission. Not for nothing does a threat follow an insult in these passages: to call someone a dog is to assert that he is about to die, that he is at the total mercy of an enemy professing superiority and his own imminent victory. Hector expresses himself in analogous fashion when he says of his foes that they are "dogs devoted to the Kēres," that is, destined to die.[8] In this case, too, the insult *dog* accompanies a threat or, better, an assertion of overwhelming supremacy that has doomed an enemy. The main message the insult conveys in these cases, then, turns out to be something like our expression "I'm going to kill you like a dog." Perhaps it is not by chance that *kyneios thanatos*, "a dog's death," was as proverbial in Greece as our saying "die like a dog" is today.[9]

The warrior who calls his foe a dog declares his power over life and death, his complete freedom to do with his enemy as he sees fit, without scruple and without the other being able to rebel or escape aggression. It seems likely that this meaning conveyed by the *dog* insult correlates to the animal's unique position with respect to the human community. As shown earlier, the dog is metonymically involved in social spaces and is classed within the human hierarchy but occupies the lowest rung: it eats table waste, it is beaten or killed without scruple whenever it does something humans don't like, it is allowed into cultural spaces but can be driven out of them just as easily. This is why many traditional Greek expressions use *dog* to denote the conditions of the last and the least, the most miserable, those who are despised and defenseless in society. It is enough to mention the variations on the theme of "food for dogs," equivalent to "wretched food" beneath the threshold of edibility. Or take the proverb "Even dogs have their Erinyes," meaning that any wicked deed will sooner or later be punished and thus one should respect even the most lowly of persons.[10] We can add to this list the verb *kynokopein*, "to beat like a dog," from which we can easily gather—even if we had no other sources to confirm it—that the Greeks did not hesitate to treat their dogs with a heavy hand,[11] not to mention that the lowest-scoring throw in dice, the unlucky throw, was called *kyōn*.[12] In all such expressions, the dog plainly plays the role of marker of lowest grade, of sorry subhuman condition, consistent with the place in society assigned to it. Here, too, one can't forget that the philosophical Cynics took the dog to symbolize their anticonformist program, on account of the fact that dogs embodied the miserable, the beggarly life of hardships that the philosopher "dogs" held up in provocation to their contemporaries as the condition for a life of blessed autarky.[13]

That the dog provides the denigrating image for insult-threats is thus not attributable to a lack of esteem for the animal as such. To put it in paradoxical terms, as an animal, the dog is highly prized; as a human being, its condition is despised.[14] When you insult someone by calling them a dog, you are asserting that they stand in your consideration *in loco canis,* at the very bottom of the scale of honor. It is an intimidation and a demand for subordination. It is a claim to treat the insulted person as one would a dog, toward which superiority is taken for granted and exercised in constant commands and regular calls for subjection.[15] To treat someone "like a dog" is to deny the minimum respect owed to a human being.

So the dog is in the position of someone with the lowest social status, who has to show more respect and obeisance than anyone else and, conversely, cannot expect to receive much. The dialectic of dominance/subordination and superiority/inferiority implicit in the offensive use of the term *dog* appears in an infamous marriage quarrel between Zeus and Hera in the *Iliad,* when the father of the gods, fed up with his wife's willful unruliness, cuts off discussion with a string of insults:

> ". . . I don't care one bit [*ouk alegizō*] if you
> fall in a rage, not even if you go to the farthest edges
> of earth and sea, where Iapetus and Cronus
> sit, enjoying no rays of Helius Hyperion
> nor any winds, deep in the depths of Tartarus—
> not even if you wander there and arrive, not even then
> would I give any thought to your rage, since you're no more than a dog to me!"
> So he spoke, and white-armed Hera made no reply.[16]

In this way, Zeus tells his rebellious wife that all the fury she can muster will have no effect on his command that she and Athena not aid the Greeks; she can shift seas and mountains, but it won't change the master of the gods' decree. Hera's anger will thus be without effect. Zeus will give her no more thought or consideration than he would an angry dog trying to oppose his designs. And the father of the gods' "I don't care one bit" will turn up again in this sort of intimidation, as we will see. The verbal quarrel between the two divinities is thus settled by Zeus's peremptory assertion of his superiority, expressed in exasperated terms of a hierarchy of power in which the highest authority opposes the lowest on the scale of dignity: the dog. At this, Hera falls silent.

Once again, the insult *dog* aims to achieve a humiliating effect: to recall the addressee into respecting hierarchical order and recognizing his or her inferior position. When Zeus says Hera is the "most doggish" thing he knows, it is not to communicate a descriptive fact but to define a relation of force. *Doggish* does not describe insubordination, as though the dog were an insubordinate animal; it serves to impose subordination to power, because the dog, by normative definition, must be subordinate. But most of all, the *dog* insult is able to convey a demand for submission because the animal responds to commands and recognizes demands for subordination. It knows, when threatened, that the time has come to retreat in good order, which is to say again that the insult exercises a mainly perlocutionary force.

To the passages considered so far can be added, in conclusion, one from the *Odyssey,* in which Melanthius, the unfaithful goatherd who takes the suitors' side, addresses faithful Eumaeus, who is guilty of having prayed that the gods will bring Odysseus home:

> Aha, so speaks the dog well versed in tricks!
> But soon enough on a well-benched black ship
> I'll take you far from Ithaca, and get a good price for you![17]

The specialized metaphorical content of *dog*—the slyness that Melanthius attributes to Eumaeus—carries little weight in context, while the priority of the insult's illocutionary force, *dog* as threat, is conspicuously confirmed by what follows: Melanthius declares that he will do with Eumaeus whatever he wants, such as put him on a ship and sell him as a slave far from Ithaca. If Eumaeus does not keep silent and dares to speak again in such a devious way, he will get the fate he deserves, the fate of a dog.

BEHAVING LIKE DOGS

That the dog is included in the human hierarchy as the member of lowest status does not mean that it can be used as the preferred marker only of an extreme condition of misery and subjection. Granting that the predominant effect of the word *dog* is to humble and intimidate, the insult can in fact arise from a more strictly punitive aggression. In such cases, the dog becomes a sign for moral baseness deserving punishment. Thus, it expresses not only intimidation but also the idea that the insulted person has degraded to "dog" by their own behavior. They have behaved "like a dog," and for this, they merit humiliation and the severest penalty.

Here we confront another problem: why does the dog provide the negative model for a wide range of improper behaviors, and what are they? We begin with the observation that if humans have no respect for dogs, the flip side is that they demand from dogs absolute respect. The dog must recognize its condition of subjection. By virtue of this situation, the animal finds itself enmeshed in the human system of moral expectations. It's not necessary to repeat that this singular fate affects the dog and not other animals because of the particular collaborative relationship that binds it to man. The dog acts within a regime of free movement. If it is bound, this is to neutralize its dangerousness, just as with human beings who are unable to respect the rules of social life.[18] In hunting, guarding, and herding activities, it is configured as a vicarious extension of the master, who does not directly control the dog by coercive means such as the yoke and the bridle. Dog and man share a fiduciary relationship, founded on the food pact and on the dog's capacity to respect it and to recognize itself bound by a debt of gratitude to the master. The concession of a benefit has conquered the dog's cooperation, the conditions of whose maintenance depend exclusively on the animal's will not to transgress its duty of grateful recognition.[19]

As a direct consequence of this participation in cultural rituals and the human sphere of ethics, humans tend to project onto dogs their whole complex of socially enforced rules of etiquette. Dogs thereby tend to be subjected to categories of ethical judgment, to charges of bad manners, transgressions, and moral censures. Seen from this perspective it is not quite so strange that people regard some behaviors as scandalous and unwanted in dogs but not in other animals—and without sensing any incongruity in this. The traditional charge of indecent sexual behavior, for example—which, as chapter 1 notes, Greeks used to justify the exclusion of dogs from some sacred spaces and is said to motivate the use of *dog* as an insult in other cultures—is restricted to dogs because unlike other domestic animals, they live inside human spaces as active subjects in cultural dynamics, where the human rules of behavior are in force. Thus, unlike horses, cattle, or sheep, when dogs copulate or show their genitals, they are effectively doing so in front of everyone. The same can be said about incest. The single assumption that dogs are perceived as subjects within social spheres and invested with ethical precepts makes sense of why this animal alone must abide by cultural orthodoxy, respecting sexual taboos and rules of good taste.[20] Even in our culture, "to behave like a dog" means to behave badly, but generically and independent of a specific type of transgressed social norm. The phrase can be used to describe—and criticize—the behavior of a rude person who has caused scandal by a breach of etiquette but also the behavior of someone who has betrayed another's trust or has failed expectations, and so forth. The generic nature of the insult arises from the dog's peculiar position. It is the animal in society, and for this it can become the emblem of the irksome intruder, the boor, the transgressor.[21]

If, in the human community, the dog plays the role of lowest member, this is because it manages to satisfy society's requirements only partially. Above all, it lacks restraint (aidōs), the sense of shame that most effectively regulates social equilibrium.[22] In fact, having aidōs means both caring about preserving one's dignity and knowing how to respect that of others; dogs seem not to measure up in either situation.[23] About their dignity dogs don't seem to be particularly troubled. The lack of restraint in exhibiting their sexuality, in begging or stealing food and accepting table scraps, makes them similar to the kakoi, those persons of low rank, such as parasites, peddlers, and pimps, in whom material and moral poverty go hand in hand.[24] And with regard to respecting others' dignity, it is understandable that people expect a lot from dogs; being at the bottom of the hierarchy of honor and power, dogs are required to have the virtue of subalterns, to exercise aidōs as the respect that inferiors owe superiors.[25]

Yet this expectation does not always pay off, since if, on the one hand, it is founded on a sensible trust, on the other hand, it constitutes an unjustified pretense doomed to failure for structural reasons. What I will attempt to demonstrate is that at the base of the negative elaborations on the dog, all the numerous figures of doggishness that Greek culture developed, must lie this tension of moral concern and expectation. It is because humans expect so much from dogs that dogs may disappoint, and from this disappointment spring the reflections on canine nature as emblematic of moral poverty and the specter of uncontrollability, infidelity, and betrayal. In other words, if the dog is able to turn into a typical figure for a loss of aidōs, in every sense of the concept, this is because it is perceived as a subject that, since it lives in society, should possess restraint. And when it doesn't display aidōs, it causes scandal and is a "bad dog," a "bitch," an odious transgressor, a subject to be punished.[26]

In the following pages, therefore, we will treat the series of dog insults that a person earns as a result of behavior deemed improper and transgressive. At the same time, we will analyze some figures of the Greek imagination whose doggishness or bitchiness (in Italian cagneria) seems to be constructed on premises quite close to those identified for the abusive uses of kyōn and its derivatives. For purposes of analysis, we will separate out several distinct themes that we will call masks, a term suggested by the common Greek insult kynōpēs/kynōpis (dog/bitch-face), which appears to provide a felicitous ethnographic relevance to the metaphor of a canine mask. It is understood, however, that the distribution of these occurrences is purely practical and should not be taken as a rigid classification. The insult dog may be read in more than one direction in a single context, so it must be kept in mind that each occurrence might also be treated under a different mask than the one assigned to it here. Despite this limitation, the masks of dog-gishness seem useful to represent a gallery of transgressions that the Greeks imag-ined as having a dog's aspect and visage. They are gazes of subjects that, called on to recognize their master's identity and attest his natural superiority, show them-selves capable of unexpected refusals and reckless challenges. But they are also shifting faces that the anxious human drive for reflection has projected onto dogs, to fill with meaning the unsettling interstices of a promiscuous animal alterity, dif-ficult to classify and distinguish. We will also seek to trace little by little the psy-chological dynamics of expectation and disappointment that, like generative seeds, lie at the origin of the traditional flowering of these canine masks; to under-stand why the figure of the dog afforded the Greeks an effective means of thinking about the infidelity of inferiors and subordinates; and finally, to determine the effects on the ancient imaginary of this illusory perception of specularity that the dog was able to produce with its recognizing gaze.

FIRST MASK: THE HEEDLESS

Zeus has realized that his wife and his daughter are away from Olympus, bringing aid to the Achaeans against his will. Enraged by the insubordination of the women of his house, he instructs Iris to go and stop them. The swift messenger intercepts the two goddesses and relates the order of their husband and father: cease from their undertaking, or he will come and break their horses' legs, hurl them from their chariots, and strike them with lightning. Zeus's rage is huge, not only against his wife—to whose unruliness he is accustomed and to which he claims he pays no heed—but also against Athena, his favorite child. He cannot tolerate that she would dare go against him:

> For Hera he doesn't bear much wrath and is not so angry—
> it's her habit to obstruct him always, whatever he might say.
> But you, heedless dog [kyon adees], are truly most dreadful if indeed
> you dare to raise your massive spear against Zeus![27]

A brief note is necessary here before I comment on this passage. When the insult kyon is used of a female character, Italian usage requires the translation cagna, "bitch." Thus, Iris's insult of Athena would be rendered as the equivalent of the English "heedless bitch." But this would be misleading, since the Greek kyōn means "dog" in general, whether male or female, whereas the usual gendered translation would make the insult refer to a female dog—a "bitch"—rather than to a dog generically speaking. [The same caveat also obviously applies to English, and perhaps even more so, with the strong, categorical differences in connotation between dog and bitch.—Trans.] I will discuss the importance of this point, and the reasons for translating *kyon* as *dog* even when the insult is directed at a female, in greater depth as we proceed. For now it's enough to note the problem.

We saw before how Zeus used *kyon* in a denigrating fashion against his wife, to contemptuously express his superiority. Iris's words confirm his attitude, plainly emphasizing how Hera's "doggishness" is connected with her vain ambition and the scarce relevance of her rebelliousness, which Zeus no longer deigns to notice. For a husband so powerful, a wife's protests are empty barking, irritations of a mangy mutt unworthy of rebuttal. But with his daughter, the situation is different. Zeus cannot endure the trespassing of his paternal authority, the fact that Athena is not recognizing his complete supremacy and has no fear of him.

The adjective *adeēs* modifying the insult *dog* here expresses a lack of *deos*, the proper fear that should act as an inhibiting factor and healthy deterrent to excessively bold actions, to unfortunate daring that consists in opposing someone of superior rank or superior strength and power.[28] Its translation here as "heedless" is perhaps less elegant, but unlike more-generic translations, such as "bold or brazen," it emphasizes the essential element in this sort of wicked courage: a censurable absence of the proper limits that should rouse fear of punishment. Before her omnipotent father, Athena is a dog, an inferior force, or rather—since insults gain efficacy through hyperbole—the lowest force, from whom subordination is required. If she dares to oppose him, she will be a bad dog, not recognizing her subaltern status or staying in her place, and for this she will be punished.

Why the Greeks chose the dog to criticize a lack of deos seems clear enough at this point. It is certainly not because they perceived the animal as incapable of fearing punishment. Instead, the dog was obviously used as an emblem of the heedless insubordinate because the Greeks assumed that it must not be so. When dogs act contrary to human wishes and don't display fear, they are creatures in need of correction. To put someone back in their place—which is to say, underneath—nothing works better than calling them a dog and promising certain punishment, assuring them that they will soon regret their behavior. It seems evident here once again, moreover, that far from originating in disgust at canine scavengers or in anxiety caused by an alleged semiwild dog in the heroic age, the insult *kyon* arises instead from the image of the domestic dog, from which respect and obedience are expected. Nor is it by accident that the great majority of Homeric scenes that use the insult are situations either of family tension and conflict or of rivalry within a faction.[29]

Another example: the endless struggle that divides the Olympian gods in support of one or the other army fighting at Troy finally erupts into an all-out brawl. Pro-Achaean and pro-Trojan gods square off against one another with no holds barred. At one point, Artemis tries to get her brother to defend the Trojans and react to the taunts of Poseidon. But Hera, who heads the pro-Achaean faction, cannot stand that a young goddess, her stepdaughter, would be so bold as to face her wrath. And so, before thumping her or stripping her bow from her hands, Hera uses these words:

> What mad frenzy has possessed you, heedless dog, to face off against me?
> It is hard to compete with me in force,
> even for you, who carry a bow, since Zeus made you a lion
> against women, granting you to kill whomever you like.
> But far better to slaughter beasts in the mountains
> and wild deer than to strive with the stronger.
> But if you want to learn of war, then you will know well
> how much stronger I am than you, since you compete with me in force.[30]

Hera has no difficulty reducing Artemis to size, forcibly disarming her and sending her fleeing in tears to her father's arms, like a naughty girl just spanked by her stepmother. Here again, it is clear that *dog* is used as a message whose principal aim is to put someone in their place, bring them down within their limits and reassert their inferior condition. Hera's speech leaves no doubt about specifics: it is in a contest of force, a hierarchical conflict, that the insult *dog* is effective, precisely because of the position—lowest—that it is able to evoke. In contrast, the same passage uses the metaphor of the lion to express a position of power: Artemis's superiority with respect to mortal women, over whose lives she exercises full power.

Lack of fear also characterizes the insult *kyon* in a passage of the *Odyssey*. Odysseus has just begun slaughtering the suitors. After killing Antinous, the hero wheels on the others, who have yet to realize that they are shouting threats at the Ithacan king, disguised as a beggar, and facing his revenge. Odysseus silences them with these words, revealing at last his true identity and declaring his vengeance:

> Dogs! You never thought I would come back home
> from the Trojans' land! And so you laid waste to my house,
> took my maidservants to bed by force,
> and courted my wife while I was still alive,
> without fearing [*oute . . . deisantes*] the gods, who hold broad heaven,
> nor that any human retribution would come later.[31]

The key note of this menacing speech is the suitors' foolish confidence in remaining unpunished. They have behaved this way because they had no fear of suffering retaliation, no fear of divine justice nor the possibility of human vengeance. But now the moment has come for them to reckon with reality: faced with the power and stature of Odysseus, they are nothing but reckless dogs, and bad dogs can only expect the worst.

If a dog's courage has come to symbolize temerity, it is because the dog, the lowest member of the community, is the one who least of all should be daring. A dog must never challenge a man, since it cannot win a fight that is unequal by definition. Thus, a dog challenging man becomes emblematic of a lack of restraint (*anai-*

deia). "No one who fears," says Aristotle, "lacks respect," and inferiors, when they admit they are so, do fear.[32] To show reverential fear before superiors is ethically good, according to the common Greek concept of morality as a sense of proper limits, tersely expressed in the famous Delphic maxim "Know thyself."[33] Conversely, to not show fear, to overestimate one's powers, is a moral fault, an attitude ripe with negative consequences.

This is the prohibition dogs must respect. Any transgression of this ethical precept—which is as good as adopting the position of the lowest subordinate—is bound to be punished: driven off with rocks, beaten or killed without pity, a dog cannot and must not expect to get off scot-free nor hope to challenge human superiority with impunity.

It needs emphasizing, however, that the dog symbolizes lack of deos only when thought of as inside the human community; only in relations with men is reverential fear a virtue and challenge a transgression. With other animals, by contrast, the dog in fact needs reckless daring: before a wolf, a boar, a lion—clearly superior in force as well—a dog must not show any fear at all but instead be combative and attack, even at the risk of its life. Such reckless courage and contempt for danger were what, for instance, the Indian breed of dog was prized for. They were such intrepid warriors that they spurned easy fights and would attack only lions and other fierce beasts.[34]

A dog's courage was therefore subject to a double assessment, which, as we will see in other situations as well, constituted one of the contradictory aspects of the animal's cultural representation. Being perceived as part of the community and included in the workings of its ethical system, dogs were required to adapt their behavior to various circumstances and to possess a sense of discernment that they were not always able or willing to display. One wanted a dog with courage, but it should show this only in certain cases. This duality in the evaluation of canine courage is well captured in the Greek term *thrasos* (or *tharsos*), which denotes courage in both senses: the good and desirable sort, boldness that is productive and virtuous, but also the bad sort, reckless daring.[35] It is no accident that the dog was often depicted as *thrasys* (full of thrasos).[36]

The divergent valuations of thrasos depend on the situations in which it occurs. Specifically, positive courage is what drives one to confront a foe of the same rank, to take on battles on a level field; it is the courage that in the human world is the essence of manliness, to the point that the word for it (*andreia*) derives from the word for an adult male (*anēr*). A good fight is one in which a contestant can hold his own. Bad courage, by contrast, drives one into untenable contests, whether because one dares to put oneself on par with someone of higher rank and strength or because one dares to challenge the observance of a higher moral norm. Then, thrasos is no longer valued as courage but maligned as impudence and a lack of aidōs (*anaideia*).[37] It is quite clear that for subalterns—women, slaves, young children, and all those subordinate to the paradigmatic adult male, including domestic animals—good courage, the most virile andreia, was a difficult virtue to practice. From the moment that the chief talent expected of them was obedience, they were inevitably excluded from the moral realm of competition and conflict; any initiative in this arena would necessarily be chalked up to bad thrasos and impudence.[38]

So although a dog was expected to show courage in its collaborative functions—hunting, guarding, protecting herds—in which cases it was considered virtuous,[39] the same courage was perceived as reckless daring when revealed in a contest with man, the dog's superior by definition. The mask of the "heedless [adees]" dog therefore arose from the relationship between dog and man and from the resulting cultural construction that turned the dog into a subject occupying the position of lowest subordinate in the social hierarchy. Viewed in that light, a dog's chief virtue is submissiveness, obedience, reverential fear. With regard to man, a dog's courage cannot but be bad thrasos and despicable insolence.

SECOND MASK: THE BRAZEN-FACED

One of the images that best represents a dog brazenly challenging a man gave rise to one of the most common forms of insult since Homer. The epithet kynōpes ("dog-faced"), with its corresponding feminine form, kynōpis, is a term of abuse that probably evoked the demeanor of a dog daring to look a man in the eyes even when it has gotten in some trouble and should lower its gaze in shame.

In the brazen-faced dog, the temerity of a direct gaze may be associated with an expression of feigned innocence that conceals in shameless arrogance a consciousness of guilt. This interpretation of the kynōpes trope seems suggested in particular by the famous passage in the Iliad in which Achilles insults Agamemnon with a string of less-than-flattering epithets, including dog-faced. Following the Achaean commander's decision to repair his loss of the beautiful prisoner Chryseis by taking one of the other heroes' prizes, Achilles charges Agamemnon with shamelessness and greed: the Achaeans have come to Troy merely to satisfy his desire, and he, "dog-faced [kynōpa]," has the nerve to dishonor those who are risking their lives only for his benefit.[40] Agamemnon, Achilles says, is so brazen-faced as to steal from someone who has agreed to fight for him. As the violent exchange escalates, their irreconcilable claims emerge: Agamemnon assumes that Achilles should bow to his will and his rank, while Achilles believes he can speak freely as an equal. The text explicitly evokes the image of two men standing eye to eye without lowering their heads: it is a contest of words, but also of gazes that refuse to flinch.[41] This contest enlists dog eyes to represent the provocative gaze of a person who should refrain from looking down on someone of equal or even superior rank—and Achilles certainly has good reasons to consider himself a better warrior than Agamemnon.

Although terribly enraged, Achilles obeys Athena, opting to stay his weapon and instead venting his anger toward Agamemnon with insults: "Drunkard, you have a dog's eyes and a deer's heart!"[42] While a charge of cowardice lodges in the image of the heart of a deer, a weak and fearful animal, the dog's eyes express shamelessness. For the Greeks, the sense of shame and proper measure (aidōs) resided in the gaze rather than the tongue.[43] The eyes are the preferred site in the body for the nonverbal communication of power. The gesture of a direct gaze or a lowered gaze is a conspicuous signal of challenge or submission, respectively. Possessors of aidōs know when to look their interlocutors in the eyes and challenge them or when to avert their gaze instead and avoid confrontation.[44] Dogs, pitiful and lowest in the hierarchy of power, must always lower their eyes before a man. When one does not, it's intemperate and shameless.

Yet "dog-faced" Agamemnon does not show himself devoid of aidōs only in this respect. He also combines deception with his reckless arrogance, as Achilles observes on a later occasion.[45] In this new context, insisting on the motive of deception, the gaze of a dog is evoked for a third time. The first test of strength between Achilles and Agamemnon ended in a stalemate: neither chief backed down, and their unsettled quarrel led to a broken war alliance; Achilles retired from battle in disgust and refused to listen to any appeals. Later, when Agamemnon is convinced that he needs Achilles and sends word that he is willing to compensate the latter if he will only return to battle, Achilles refuses yet again. His speech to the ambassadors sent to bring Agamemnon's offer and to urge Achilles to return to his post in the Achaean army is adamant that the offense is irreparable: Agamemnon has cheated him, is a lying deceiver, and can never be trusted again. The specific reason that Achilles cannot give in to Agamemnon's appeal, the precise motivation for his flat and final refusal, is that his arrogant adversary "won't have the courage, doggish though he be [*kyneos per eōn*], to look me in the face anymore."[46]

If Achilles were to give in, it would mean that he has in some sense agreed, even if only partially, to bow before the challenge to his power that has been leveled at him. His not yielding to these new supplications means instead that Agamemnon will be forced to lower his head, recognize his inferiority, and abandon once and for all his reckless—canine—haughtiness. Agamemnon is so shameless and underhanded that the only way to get him to lower his gaze is to humiliate him in the most brusque and violent manner. Force alone can manage someone who lacks proper aidōs; he can be put in his place only by being treated like a dog.

THIRD MASK: THE INTRUDER

Greek literature abounds in images of rash and shameless dogs. One term of abuse, perhaps coined by the tragedian Aeschylus, combines in a single word temerity and a dog's wicked boldness: the adjective *kynothrasēs*, which could brand someone as lacking prudence and moderation, roughly means "of doggish courage."[47] As seen above, ancient authors regularly associated anaideia, often connected with bad courage (thrasos), with the insult *dog*. But an interesting piece of evidence allows us to expand the horizon of reference for the insult and identify another aspect of reckless canine daring.

In fact, another animal shares the dog's tendency toward shameless temerity and the association with thrasos and anaideia. Ancient sources often explicitly connect the dog with the fly (*myia*): "Animals that are brazen and difficult to get rid of," Aelian says, for instance, "are flies and dogs." The fly is a weak animal with little power of self-defense but that nevertheless has the courage to invade human spaces with surprising persistence. With a parasite's casual impudence, it lands on human food, on corpses and wounds, on excrement, and anywhere else it pleases. In short, it's a creature that dares to frequent human bodies and spaces without asking permission. Lucian of Samosata chose the praise of the fly as the theme of a rhetorical exercise to demonstrate, in the best sophistical tradition, his ability to weave with subtle argumentation even the most absurdly improbable of discourses.[48]

Some stories about the fly are framed by its characteristic intrusiveness, particularly felt during occasions such as sacrifices, when the blood and flesh of the victim stood exposed on the altar and attracted swarms of insects. At Leucas, for example, a sort of preliminary sacrifice for flies was held to keep them away from the festival of Apollo; in advance of the festival a cow was slaughtered and left for the flies, so that once they glutted themselves on its blood they would stop circling and leave the celebrants in peace. Meanwhile, the flies at the Olympian Games at Pisa, in Elis, seem to have given miraculous respite to the people by dispersing of their own will; these were obviously extraordinary flies, endowed with exceptional temperance for their species.[49] Not everyone, however, interpreted this marvelous occurrence as proof of the special virtue of these flies; according to others, the insects did not appear at the sacrifice only because it had been placed under the protection of Zeus Fly-Shooer (Apomyios).[50]

In its shameless daring, the fly has something in common with the dog. Dogs also take liberties that they shouldn't and often don't stay in their places. But unlike dogs, who are allowed some legitimate overlap with human spaces and actions, flies are always unwanted. These insects have no collaborative role, no place assigned in the social order, and thus, when they are present they are always out of place. In this regard, a myth recounted by Lucian seems significant. In this story, Myia was once a pretty girl but a terrible and annoying chatterbox; she fell in love with Endymion and did nothing but bother him with her chatter, including disturbing his sleep. Then Selene, jealous and irritated by the impertinent girl's behavior, transformed Myia into an insect that kept her old name and, moreover, never lost her habit of bothering people who are trying to sleep.[51]

In other words, the fly is something like a dog that is always bad, possessing the characteristic intrusive side of doggishness. This manifests, for example, when a dog steals food instead of waiting for a human to select a portion for it. In these cases, the dog's ordinary participation at the human table becomes an unwarranted invasion and its metonymic presence runs the danger of trespassing. A dog that aspires to human food is thought of as a wretch meant to receive only scraps who cannot look forward to getting the main dish. And sometimes it dares to do just that.[52]

The most surprising intersection between the dog and the fly in ancient sources is undoubtedly the Homeric insult *kynamyia,* a compound noun that can be translated as "dog-fly." It appears twice during the great family brawl that breaks out on Olympus between the pro-Argive and the pro-Trojan factions. The first time is in an insult that Ares directs at Athena:

> Why, dog-fly, do you incite the gods to contention
> with boundless daring [tharsos]?[53]

This sets up Ares's physical assault on Athena in return for a prior slight. Intended to belittle and aimed at asserting the aggressor's superiority, the insult does not intimidate as Ares had hoped: Athena dodges his spear and, far from being finished off like a pesky fly, pummels him with a stone, turning his mockery back on him. A little later, Aphrodite, rushing to Ares's aid, is called *dog-fly* by Hera, and in this case as well, the insult is prelude to physical conflict: in the duel, Aphrodite comes off worse than Athena, who beats her and calls her rash and arrogant.[54]

Ancient scholiasts explained *kynamyia* as a Homeric coinage, a compound created to make an insult combining the dog's impudence with the fly's rash daring. And indeed, the invasiveness and audacity that dogs and flies display in defying humans and barging into their space uninvited are sufficiently explanatory facets of the shameless courage of inferiors that the insult *kynamyia* criticizes. But the scholia also suggest another reading, one that shifts our inquiry to another mask— even more unsettling—of the dog's shameless daring.

FOURTH MASK: THE PARTISAN AVENGER

Apparently, the insult *kynamyia* may conceal a reference to vampirism by a certain kind of insect. According to this scholiastic interpretation, the term is not an imaginative Homeric coinage but rather means "fly of the dogs" and is a name for the tick, the distressing insect that the same Homeric commentators describe as "a drinker of blood."[55] Indeed, in his collection of animal stories Aelian mentions an insect called *kynomyia* but unfortunately does not say much about it except that it is smaller than a fly, so we can't be sure whether it is some harmless gnat or a kind of tick, or even whether it's a biting insect.[56]

Although references to the kynamyia are scant and contradictory, we know much more about the aggressiveness of the myia, which ancients describe as biting, and especially prone to biting humans, like mosquitoes and horseflies. Thus it is not clear whether this is the familiar housefly with wrongly attributed vampiric behavior or whether, as seems more likely, the Greeks used *myia* to refer to a wide range of insects, some of which were biting.[57] The fact remains that in at least one Homeric passage, the myia's brazen temerity is exemplified by its clinging to human skin to suck the blood and resisting every attempt to swat it away. The image occurs in a simile that compares the strength that the goddess Athena inspires in Menelaus to the boldness (tharsos) of a fly "that, though swatted away, stays stuck to a man's skin to bite him, and sweet to it is human blood."[58] In Aelian, too, the myia is a biting, carnivorous insect: flies feast on animal corpses or, more precisely, gorge on blood; once the corpse is drained, they vanish.[59] Lucian is particularly eloquent on this point:

> They [sc. flies] do their fighting not with the back part of their body like wasps or bees but with their mouth or, better, with their trunk, an organ of theirs like that of an elephant that they use for their thieving; when it carries something off, it holds it tightly with its trunk, whose tip is very much like a suction cup. From this a tooth comes out, with which it pricks and then drinks the blood—it is true that it drinks milk, but it does not dislike blood also—yet without causing much pain to the person it bites.[60]

If Greek culture traditionally attributed biting and a love of blood to the myia, it's not necessary to identify the kynamyia as a tick to see an allusion to a more malicious and worrying sort of recklessness than just an unwanted but harmless intrusion. The Homeric compound alludes to a bloodthirsty attack.

On this head as well, the figures of fly and dog may well be connected, inasmuch as dogs were also credited with a marked propensity for blood, human blood included, as already noted. In the two instances of the Homeric insult *kynamyia* just related, an allusion of this sort seems pertinent in the case of Ares insulting Athena, accused of inciting the gods to internecine conflict; it is less well suited to Hera's insult of Aphrodite. But to assess the relevance of this connotation it is not really necessary to prove that the insult is meant to convey a specifically bloodthirsty image nor that the possible allusion to insect vampirism is plausible for the context. To work, an insult does not need to be plausible, and indeed, it is all the more effective if more hyperbolic and overblown. So it is part of the rhetoric of injury to express loathsome aggression in terms of the nasty bitingness of an insect that sticks to the skin and sucks blood. But most important, given the perlocutionary force of insults, *kynamyia* contains an implicit threat: the behavior criticized with this term of abuse will lead to a bad end because the insulter will disgracefully swat down the kynamyia-person like a pesky fly.

This point leads us to reconsider ambiguous canine courage, a theme that reflects one of the most problematic aspects of the human-dog relationship and thus constitutes a principal generative nexus for the image of doggishness. A dog's courage, as we have said, is problematic for several reasons intimately connected with the animal's ability or inability to distinguish and recognize and to behave differently according to context. The faculty of recognition, as we have seen, unites dogs and humans and enables the cooperation between a dog and its master. But still there are discrepancies, which deserve some focused attention.

First and foremost, a dog is not always willing to use its discriminating powers to satisfy human demands. In such cases, it gets branded with the label *anaideia* and is punished like a wretched and impulsive criminal: all is put back in its place. But in one particular situation, canine courage is not so clearly judged or so easy for humans to handle. Let's consider this case.

Canine aggression is not always undesired. Rather, the capacity to attack and intimidate is something humans take advantage of and, in specific cases, is the main characteristic a master demands in his dog. With guard dogs, one human uses impulsive belligerence against other humans. In these cases, the animal's aggression, which at the level of interspecies relations is constructed as undesirable—dog is inferior to man and thus should not dare oppose him—is not only tolerated but even requested and appreciated. This situation produces a certain schizophrenia of imagination, which is liable to represent the courage of guard and attack dogs in two contrary modes: one positive, if it is one's own dog attacking an intruder, and another negative, if a stranger's dog attacks you to defend its master and his property.

This double valuation is obviously not without consequences: the ambiguity feeds into symbolic developments. We'll begin to disentangle the knot with a concrete case found in our sources. Sometimes a master is forced to conceal his satisfaction with the prompt service of his guard dog and, out of politeness, show his regret to the stranger who has just suffered its aggression. As though it is solely responsible for the embarrassment, he fingers the dog and doesn't hesitate to blame it: behavior like this shows the dog's inferior mind; the beast (he says) does its guard duty too zealously; it attacks everyone it doesn't know—which just shows the limits of its powers of discernment.

An epyllion attributed to Theocritus contains just such a scene, which shows well the psychological dynamics at play here and seems to indicate how this circumstance could be a generative matrix for the figure of doggishness. The poem narrates the arrival of Heracles in the land of the Epeians, in Elis, where he has to perform one of the labors imposed on him by Eurystheus, cleaning out the vast stables of King Augeas. On the way there, Heracles meets an old cowherd, who offers to accompany him. They then come across some dogs, which run up to attack Heracles while barking furiously, with clearly aggressive intent, and surround the cowherd, still barking but fawning on him too. The old man scatters them with the simple gesture of picking up a rock and some harsh shouts, but in his heart—so says the text—he was pleased with their performance, apparently happy to see them so ready to defend his property from strangers. Then he delivers an apology to his guest that has obvious importance to our argument:

> Ah, what a race of beasts the gods above have made
> for us humans, how impulsive they are!
> If they had in them a mind as prone to reasoning
> and knew who and who not to be aggressive toward,
> no beast could vie with them in honor.
> As it is, they are too irascible and snarling.[61]

Dogs' inability to distinguish between well- and ill-intentioned strangers mars human esteem for them, an esteem that is otherwise manifestly quite high.[62] A good guard dog must attack strangers. Yet in fulfilling this valued function it manifests a propensity for excessive, blind violence. To attack a human without discerning status and dignity, intentions and needs, is behavior lacking measure, unreflective and intemperate.[63] In this case, a dog is *anaidēs* due to a structural flaw, not because of a momentary yielding to passions or some misguided attempt to usurp human privilege. The sense of respect for strangers who come seeking hospitality, friendship, or aid is simply not a trait the animal possesses; this is a "defect" of the entire species, which guard dogs reveal more clearly only because they act within the liminal space that divides their master and his property from the outside world.[64]

The lack of a sense of hospitality (*xenia*) is one of the salient aspects dividing dogs from human beings. It is part of the animal's congenital blindness and, as can be expected, is an ethological trait that stands at the base of insulting uses of *kyōn* and its derivatives. "Everybody everywhere, even the most doggish man, observes and respects the laws of Zeus Xenios," Apollonius of Rhodes says, implying that no human being is so wretched as not to be above a dog at least in having a sense of hospitality.[65] Moreover, in the realm of xenia, dogs generally seem to lack a sense of measure, since they also tend to misbehave in reverse situations, when they are to be the guest. In such cases, as we have seen, the animal displays all the insolence of a greedy parasite and obnoxious intruder, demanding more and better food than its human host is inclined to give. But, if as a brazen parasite, the dog transgresses only the rules of good manners, as an angry gatekeeper, it dares to challenge the divine laws of Zeus Xenios, protector of strangers, and betrays a lack of measure, a structural intemperance even more disturbing: a blind thrasos lashing out indiscriminately with rage that knows no rein of circumstance.

Still, those who own dogs appreciate how promptly they jump to defend, how they snap to obey commands, and the courage they display in resisting any intruder and in hunting prey. In this regard, the Theocritus passage above is remarkably subtle in expressing the cowherd's double disposition: he apologizes to Heracles for his dogs' rudeness and scolds them but at the same time—to himself—is pleased with their fiery dispatch, a clear sign of their fidelity as personal assistants.[66] Without a doubt, a dog's courage is indispensable to its master and a warrant of trust, whether in guarding or in hunting. A good hunting dog must be aggressive and pursue prey without fear or faltering.[67] Mythical dogs such as Cerberus, the dog of Hades that watches the gates of the underworld, and Orthros, the imposing beast that guards the herds of the giant Geryon, are examples of infallible guardians. They are full of thrasos and merciless, not because they are defective; on the contrary, they are perfect dogs, exact copies of their ruthless and invincible masters. Thus Cerberus is strong, invincible, ravenous for raw meat, and knows neither aidōs nor pity, just like his master, Hades, the lord of death's kingdom. For the same reason, Orthros is sometimes represented as a many-headed dog, a worthy companion of the three-headed Geryon.[68] Proud of their masters, these mythic dogs appear as detestable monsters of blind, inhuman aggression in the eyes of strangers who approach them. Nothing can elude their surveillance. They can be killed or gotten rid of only by someone with immense strength, such as Heracles, a hero able to strangle lions and dragons and decapitate gigantic, many-headed monsters.

From a master's point of view, however, the courage of a dog before strangers is a virtue, and its blind obedience and utmost solidarity are proper behaviors. It's no accident that dogs feature as executors of justice and as avengers in several exemplary stories. One reads, for example, that the dog of the poet Eupolis, a Molossian named Augeas, mauled to death someone who tried to steal some of its master's comedies. Or again, the guard dog of the sanctuary of Asclepius in Athens pursued and stopped a thief who had entered the temple to steal votive offerings. Pantacles of Sparta, who forbade some theatrical artists from entering the city, paid a high price for his outrage against their patron god, Dionysus: he was executed by a pack of furious dogs, unleashed against him by Dikē (Justice) herself.[69]

Consistent with such representations, the expression *to be someone's dog* was a positive metaphor implying solidarity, fidelity, and attentiveness to commands on the part of a servile figure. To say that someone was "the dog of X" was to claim that he or she was a faithful executor of X's orders and a zealous defender against any opposition to X. The formula was used, for instance, to indicate a faithful servant within the divine sphere. Pan, a minor deity, is called the dog of the Great Goddess, while the divine messenger Iris is portrayed as Hera's dog because she swiftly executes her orders.[70] Then there were the demagogues, the inflammatory leaders of the popular party in democratic Athens during the fifth century B.C.E., men of humble origins and plebeian manners who called themselves the "dogs of the people [*dēmou kynes*]" to assert their role as faithful servants and guardians of the *dēmos* against the abuses of the nobility. In truth, this nickname wasn't particularly well chosen, since it inadvertently exposed them to ridicule by their opponents, who could take advantage of the traditionally abusive charge of *kyōn* and derisively hurl back at them the badge they wore with pride. So one finds frequently in Aristophanes's comedies, for example, the poet exercising his biting sarcasm by attributing to popular leaders the various negative aspects of doggishness—gluttony, corruptibility, the tendency toward fawning, and so forth—and thus scoring comedic insults all the more effective because the demagogues, by calling themselves *kynes,* seemed to be denouncing their own, questionable morality.[71]

Certainly contributing to the expression's ambiguity is the partisan character of canine cooperation and the consequent partiality of justice it readily serves. Even the dreadful punitive monsters that gods or the dead sent against mortals could be described as praiseworthy "dogs," insofar as they were disposed to blindly execute their master's orders. Take, for example, the Erinyes, frightful vampire goddesses that pursue wrongdoers without respite, to the point of driving them mad: to those who summon them for aid, they are faithful and heaven-sent avenging dogs. The bacchantes, dreadful and divinely possessed executioners of anyone who resists the power of Dionysus, are described as the god's trusty kynes. Likewise, the loathsome Harpies are portrayed as the faithful "kynes of mighty Zeus."[72]

As is so often the case in paradoxical situations, the structural contradictions of canine justice offer good material for reflecting on certain ambiguous realities and provide an ideal model for representing some conundrums of classification.[73] Take, for example, Aeschylus's extraordinary creation of the Erinyes-dogs in the *Oresteia.* The Erinyes take the stage after Orestes who, to avenge his father, Agamemnon, has killed his mother, Clytemnestra. Just before dying at her son's hand, Clytemnestra invoked these furious goddesses of vengeance, unleashing them against Orestes, who now finds himself hounded on account of his mother's curse. Drenched in matricidal blood, he is chased without respite, like a wounded hare, by a pack of monstrous ghouls who sniff out his red tracks on the ground. The poet represents these frightening creatures, figures of implacable punishment, as she-dogs spurred on by the huntress-Clytemnestra in pursuit of the prey-Orestes.[74] But as anyone familiar with the symbolic density of Aeschylean tragedy can imagine, this is no simple and superficial simile. The Erinyes in the *Oresteia* are she-dogs not only because they hunt prey by tracking the scent of blood but also because they stand for a certain type of justice—the law of vengeance, the lex talionis, of "an eye for an eye"—which canine behavior is particularly well suited to portray. Let us consider why this is.

The Erinyes purport to punish Orestes on behalf of Clytemnestra. But can what these goddesses plan to do be called justice in all respects? After all, Clytemnestra was slain by her son because she had murdered her husband, Agamemnon. By killing his mother, Orestes had exacted "just" vengeance for his father. If he had not done so, his father's Erinyes would have pursued him, just as his mother's Erinyes do now. What sort of justice is it, then, that short-circuits the vengeance a son owes his father and sends goddesses of vengeance to pursue him? A blind and partial justice of endless blood feuds, rough and primitive, that the gods will redress at the end of the trilogy. Thus, in a fundamental sense, the Erinyes are monsters of dogged persistence, doggedness: they act like dogs, for which the only conceivable justice is that of their master. When its master sets it on an enemy, a good dog snaps to pursuit, in blind allegiance to the mandate of cooperation that binds it to the one who feeds it; all the prey can do is flee or die. Likewise, Clytemnestra's Furies, loyal ministers of the law of vengeance, snap to the call of their mistress and are completely at the service of her justice. They acknowledge no other reason, and no one can stop them but the one who set them loose.[75] But the Erinyes would have done the same thing if Agamemnon had unleashed them against his son and Orestes had not avenged him by killing Clytemnestra. Retributive justice, the partial justice of personal vendetta, can therefore be portrayed as a situation in which everyone has a pack of avenging dogs—their own Erinyes— which they can unleash against an offender by means of a ritual curse. This is the archaic model of justice that Athena, at the end of the *Oresteia*, denounces as a dysfunctional source of endless internal discord, inviting the city to embrace and practice procedural justice instead, which settles differences through arbitration and the judgment of an external jury equidistant from the parties at suit.

This is the general framework. But the semiotic richness of the homology between Erinyes and dogs is conspicuous even in the details. The courage of the Erinyes, for instance, is like the dog's ambiguous thrasos, praiseworthy and virtuous for its master but monstrously excessive for its human victim. In the eyes of their victim, Aeschylus's Furies are horrid vampires that gain their dreadful courage by drinking human blood—a characterization that may well be a subtle allusion to the practice, attested in ancient sources, of giving hunting dogs the blood of prey to drink, to sharpen their desire to hunt.[76] Also, like dogs, the Erinyes don't distinguish stranger-enemy from inviolable suppliant. Once set on their blind pursuit, they are inexorable as machines and the curses of which they are the divine executors, and when Orestes takes refuge in the temple of Apollo at Delphi, they neither respect the suppliant's inviolability nor recognize the temple's sanctity, since their action is *anaidēs*, knowing neither curb nor moderation of piety.[77] Euripides also calls the divine persecutors of Orestes "dog-faced [*kynōpides*]"—in this case, the Erinyes are identified with the Keres, odious specters of death for those who suffer their attack but at the same time implacable avengers and faithful agents of the will of Hades, their divine master. The epithet, applied to the Keres by the Dioscuri, betrays its insulting charge and reflects the dread that even gods feel for the faithful servants of the lord of the dead.[78]

The Erinyes are therefore dogs in many senses. They are dogs that defend the dead who claim vendettas, as well as watchdogs of Justice (Dikē), of the sanctity of oaths, and of all sacred, inviolable boundaries.[79] In this last function, they display above all the aggressiveness of a canine *phylax* (guardian) that attacks someone who crosses a property boundary or trespasses some off-limits barrier.[80] But they are also hideous hunting dogs set loose against human prey. As such, to the hunted they are monstrous images of reversal: furious dogs unleashing aggression against a human instead of their usual animal prey. Representing the Erinyes as she-dogs thus allows Aeschylus to exploit the awful ambiguity of canine courage.

This is perhaps why dogs have sometimes assumed the role of demonic beasts, dreadful creatures of the night. In fact, many cultural traditions imagine demonic guardians and protectors as malicious beings. Apparently, the guardian function renders them susceptible to being thought of from two perspectives: benign protectors on one side, demons of incredible cruelty on the other. In the latter capacity they are believed to wander the earth, committing the worst atrocities, bringing death and diseases and persecuting evildoers by stalking them everywhere.[81] This is how Greek tradition imagined the Erinyes. They were often considered protective figures—they were called on as, among other things, tomb guardians—but at the same time they were thought to be responsible for particularly horrible events, such as the death of infants or of women in labor.[82] The dogs of Hecate, the goddess of crossroads, were similarly envisaged. She wandered cemeteries by night with a torch of infernal fire, surrounded by dogs whose barking announced her passage. Popular superstition made these dogs the source of certain nocturnal disturbances, such as nightmares and panic attacks.[83]

To conclude this description of the avenging dog, let us allow another ancient source to speak, which better than anything else evokes with striking vividness the complex of interrelated ideas and the web of associations underlying the figure of the phylax, at once benevolent protector and perilous agent of vengeance, attentive watchdog and inescapable hound. It is an explanation that Plutarch gives regarding the nature and function of the Lares Praestites, Roman deities charged with overseeing the house; the passage allows us to verify what came to mind when a Greek saw the image of a dog at the side of these spirit guardians:

> Why is there a dog placed next to the Lares that are called Praestites, and why do the Lares wear dog skins? Perhaps it is because—since the Praestites are those who "stand in front" and their task is to stand in front of the house as its protectors—like a dog, they are frightening to strangers but gentle and good-natured to those who live there? Or, as some Romans say, the truth is rather that, according to those who follow Chrysippus—who think that there are malevolent demons that wander here and there observing, demons that serve the gods as avengers and punishers of criminals and the impious—the Lares are also this sort of punishing demon, like the Erinyes, watching over the lives and houses of men? For this, then, they wear dog

skins and have a dog as assistant, since it is believed that they are good at following tracks and hunting down evildoers.[84]

FIFTH MASK: THE BLOODTHIRSTY PSYCHOPATH

The unleashed fury of Aeschylus's Erinyes is that of a dog set loose on enemies or prey by its master: it is blind, unbridled, biased, and definitely dogged aggression. In this aggressive rush, the dog doesn't distinguish objects. It goes after whomever its master marks as the foe to attack, including strangers, whom its master has taught it to keep off the property. From the point of view of weighing its discerning faculties, this ambiguous courage reveals the dog's latent madness. We've already seen how even the best hunting dog must be treated with caution lest the animal's tendency to excess, in the heat of the chase, drive it "crazy" and "out of its mind" (*ekphrōn*). We've also seen how *lyssa* signified not only a typical canine malady—the disease of "rabies"—but also the dog's more general tendency toward mental disturbance, a lurking madness due to a congenital weakness in the species, ever perilously imbalanced toward the wolf's indiscriminate ferocity.[85] It ought to be clear, then, that we have focused at length on the guard dog's aggressiveness because this trait of antihuman violence, functionally present in the activities of guard dogs and avenging personal security dogs, is of fundamental relevance to the complex of ideas relating to the dog's congenital mental instability.[86] Indeed, when used in these capacities, dogs exhibit a limited ability to recognize—not distinguishing guest from hostile stranger—a temperament given to excess, and, not least, no scruple in attacking humans. But these are not exclusive traits of guard dogs; they are common to the species, present in latent form in all dogs, including hunting dogs and gentle house pets.

This furious characteristic (*lyssōdes*), composed of dogged vehemence, failed recognition, and boldness in resisting man, produces disturbing images of crazed hunting dogs that mistakenly exchange prey for man. Aeschylus's image of dog-Erinyes exploits in multiple directions the ambiguous complex of elements that make up doggishness in ancient Greek culture, but undoubtedly the most salient component of their being dogs is the unleashed and biased fury of their action. It's no accident that from their earliest occurrences in Homer, the Erinyes are divine agents of madness and mental blindness.[87] And, as often happens with the Greek pantheon, their control of madness could also be expressed as a divine essence: the Erinyes *are* madness—they are *mainades,* or "raving" goddesses, just like the possessed women in the revels of Dionysus.[88]

By this point, it should come as no surprise that the maenads of Dionysiac ritual lent themselves to being portrayed as driven to the heights of madness by swift "dogs of Lyssa."[89] This is what happens in Euripides's tragedy *The Bacchae,* which relates the myth of Dionysus at Thebes. The story is familiar: Dionysus is the son

of Zeus and Semele, who is a daughter of King Cadmus of Thebes. Her sisters—
Agave, Autonoë, and Ino—deny that her baby is the son of the father of the gods.
So, to punish his aunts and prove to all of Thebes his divine power, Dionysus, once
grown up, returns to the city and drives all the Theban women, raving, from their
houses and onto the wooded mountain of Cithaeron to celebrate his Bacchic rites.
For Pentheus, the ruler who doesn't acknowledge the god and opposes the spread
of his mystic frenzy, Dionysus plans a cruel vengeance: he imbues the king with
irrepressible curiosity to spy on the women's revels, inducing him to cross-dress in
women's clothes and infiltrate the bacchantes. But the women, hallucinating under
the intoxicating god's force, take Pentheus for a prey animal, chase him down,
catch him, and tear him to pieces, with his mother, Agave, leading the way; after
killing him, she sticks his severed head on a stake and carries her macabre hunting
trophy into the city. Only when the divine possession subsides does Agave regain
her senses and recognize in the severed head the beloved features of her son.

In their hunting cry as they begin to chase Pentheus, the bacchantes invoke the
swift "dogs of Lyssa," blind canine fury, rabid raving personified and deified as a
hunter of human prey: Lyssa will turn them into implacable pursuers of the unbe-
liever, the true she-dogs of Dionysus, their master, whose terrible vengeance they
will execute. Lyssa will make Agave's eyes see her son deformed into a mountain
lion. Yet again, then, we have a poet choosing to exploit the duality of the dog's
cultural model to construct disturbing figures of ambiguity. He crosses the divide
in the schizophrenic imaginary whereby dogs are at once faithful companions to
their masters and hideous man-eaters to strangers. In its master's eyes, the dog is
not a monster at all, but in the eyes of a stranger, it becomes a wild animal seized
with stark raving madness. And this is not the only such instance in the tragedy.

Another passage explicitly highlights the ambiguity of Dionysiac madness with
an image of the maenads as hunting dogs of the wise Dionysus.[90] As they pursue
Pentheus in Dionysiac ecstasy, Agave and her companions feel "wisely [*sophōs*]"
set loose by their god—the "wise hunter [*kynāgetās sophos*]"—against their prey.
As victims of delusion, the bacchantes effectively see everything from the point of
view of their master, the divine Bacchus, who has mastered their minds, and their
cooperation with him is blind and total, like that of a dog with its master. Thus,
while they viciously hunt their son and nephew, the women feel like good ministers of the cult of Bacchus, his trusty allies, justly set loose against a worthy hostile
prey to punish it for not willingly acknowledging the god's great power. But the
partiality of their justice, the blind bias of their "wise" action, is at the same time
clear proof of their insanity, the unrestrained and visionary fury that drives them
to their ruin. Set loose on a human, they don't distinguish him from a prey animal;
set loose on their relative, they treat him no differently than a fawn or a lion.
Dionysus thus takes vengeance on his mother's sisters with a perfidy truly worthy
of a powerful deity, by making them enthusiastic, joyous executors of their own

punishment. They are their own Erinyes, a pack of raving she-dogs deluded by lyssa. The moment they admit the divinity of their nephew, whom they had earlier denied was a son of Zeus, the bacchantes become good kynes, the god's personal guard dogs, defending his honor and power as relentless avengers. But through the cruelty of this same god, first they become hunting dogs spurred on against human prey, rabid animals that, like Actaeon's pack, no longer recognize what is familiar, and then, after wising up again, they understand at great cost how limited is the vision of the human mind before the impenetrable mysteries of the gods.[91]

The doggish nature that the poets attribute to the Erinyes and to the maenads no doubt evokes the traditionally insulting charge of kyon. If they are dogs or dog-faced, this is because, in the eyes of those who don't enjoy their cooperation, they are hideous figures of bloodthirsty audacity, man-eating vampirism, and ruthless aggression. With this, let us turn back to insults—and the theme of the vicious brutality of canine courage, from which this excursus into the mythic bitch figure began—and once again to Homer. Let's reconsider the passage in the *Iliad* where Teucer, a son of Telamon, wounds several Trojans with his arrows but fails to hit Hector, whom he dubs a "rabid dog [*lyssētēr*]" wreaking havoc on the battlefield.[92] Teucer's insult asserts that Hector ought to be put down without pity, exactly as one does with dogs gone mad.[93] In this case, again, a dog's aggressiveness is suited to represent the detested side of courage—as viewed by those who suffer it. To his companions, a warrior who rages is, of course, a glorious hero, an invincible lion or a valiant boar; but in his enemy's eyes, the same warrior takes on the semblance of a rabid dog, a vicious, raving beast deserving of a speedy death.[94]

SIXTH MASK: THE TRAITOR

As stated above, a dog is bound to its master by a pact of alliance that the animal has to honor, by recognizing itself as a trusty companion (*philos*) to the person who feeds it, to whom it owes respect and gratitude. A situation like this cannot but elicit anxiety about treason, and indeed, another figure of canine anaideia is the traitor.[95]

To begin with Homer once more, note that the *Odyssey* uses kynes several times, directing its abusive sense at the unfaithful maidservants who have gone over to the suitors during Odysseus's absence.[96] Among these, Melantho stands out. As we will see, her masters have rather more reason to call her *dog* than her anonymous colleagues. The first confrontation between the king of Ithaca and his maids comes when Odysseus, still disguised as a begging stranger, intervenes in palace affairs by offering to tend the fire for the suitors and urging the girls to go keep Penelope company in her rooms. The maidservants laugh at this proposal and mock the apparent naïveté of the stranger, who feigns ignorance of their complicity with the suitors. In fact, Odysseus is subtly putting them to the test, and their fate will depend on their reaction to his proposal. If they prove, as they will, loyal to the suitors instead of to Telemachus and Penelope, they will seal their doom. Here, Melantho takes the stage, with a dismissive response of abuse to Odysseus, telling him not to meddle in the affairs of the house and to keep silent if he doesn't want to be driven off with sticks. At this, Odysseus glares at her and says:

> Now I'll go and tell Telemachus—dog—what you've said,
> so that he can cut you to pieces right here and now![97]

The intimidating effect of the insult *dog*, accompanying a promise of ruthless punishment, needs no further emphasis; it is a typical part of the expression's illocutionary value, seen so often before. In the king's absence, it falls to the master of the house, Prince Telemachus, to punish his kynes. But Melantho merits the name for other reasons as well. To be rude to a foreign guest, for instance, is a typically dog-like action. In themselves, the violation of xenia and lack of respect for the beggar earn her the label *kyōn*. To these we can add her insolent verbal outburst, another typical trait attributed to dogs in Greece.[98] On closer look, Odysseus's insult of Melantho evokes yet another behavior of a bad dog. When Odysseus asks the maids to leave the hall and join Penelope, in effect he is saying that they should go back to their proper post, beside the queen, and stop tending to the usurping suitors. Although, in a subtle and indirect manner, Odysseus alludes to the fact that among the suitors, the maids are not in their place, betraying their role of servants of Odysseus's palace.

But if the maidservants' betrayal in serving the suitors as their new masters is a grave enough transgression to earn the title of *kynes*, Melantho's case is even worse. Her position is different from that of the other girls in Penelope's service. To show this, just before her rude reply to Odysseus, the poet lingers to describe the maidservant, stating, quite significantly, that the queen had raised the pretty maid "like a daughter":

> Dolius had sired her, but Penelope raised her,
> bringing her up like a daughter and giving her pleasant toys.
> But she had no grief in her heart for Penelope
> and instead mingled with Eurymachus and was endeared to him [*phileesken*].[99]

Melantho's betrayal—after being raised by Penelope as a daughter and thus owing her a crucial debt of gratitude—lends itself quite well to being criticized as dog-gish. The betrayal of a dog, whose master has both raised and nurtured it, is an emblem of heinous ingratitude. When Odysseus, unable to reveal his identity and punish the maid with his own hands, calls her *kyon* and promises to tell Telemachus about her behavior, he is reminding her of the gravity of her situation. Her true, legitimate masters are Penelope, in whose debt she is for her upbringing, and

Telemachus, the legitimate head of the house. To them, and for her behavior toward them, Melantho must give account. These should be her philoi, companions to her as "dog," not the suitors. From her legitimate, betrayed masters she will receive, in due time, the treatment a runaway dog deserves.[100]

It's not surprising, then, that on another occasion Penelope also expresses her disappointment with Melantho in terms of doggishness. The maidservant again offends the guest with insulting words, and again Odysseus threatens her by recalling her duty to recognize that she is Telemachus's slave. At this point, Penelope intervenes and reproaches her foster child:

> Not at all, you rash [*tharsaleē*], heedless dog [*kyon adees*], has your grave deed
> escaped me, which you will have to pay for,
> since you know well, and heard it straight from me,
> that I wanted the stranger here in my halls
> to ask him about my husband, since my grief sits heavy on me.[101]

Melantho had spoken ill to the guest—Odysseus—whom Penelope had expressly said she wanted to meet with in her palace. The servant was therefore not just rude and heedless of the norms of xenia but also insubordinate to her mistress and foster mother. This is a "grave deed," for which, sooner or later, she will have to render account. As seen above with the canine mask of recklessness, the insult here censures insubordination driven by a lack of fear of punishment, which it is believed can be escaped, and by wicked audacity ("tharsaleē, kyon adees"). But if the maidservants behave thus, it is because they have changed masters. Their obedience has gone over to the suitors, whom they now consider their companions and protectors. Their entry into a new alliance took place through a genuine act of treacherous informing, also denounced as doggishness: it was they, "heedless kynes," who told the suitors about Penelope's trick with the shroud.[102] Among these shameless and disrespectful kynes, Melantho stands out, since her betrayal of the queen who lovingly raised her is even more severe: she is a wicked foster child who refuses to pay the debt she owes her adoptive mother.

Sometimes, the dog is evoked in connection with a different sort of betrayal: violated bonds of marital fidelity. In every instance, doggishness is used to censure the oath-breaking behavior of a wife. Let's stick with Homer for the moment. Poor Hephaestus is infamous for the humiliation he had to suffer in seeing his wife, Aphrodite, betray him with her lover Ares. Informed of her treachery by the spying sun god, Hephaestus the lame smith sets a trap, surrounding his bed with invisible and unbreakable chains designed to net the two lovers as soon as they lie down again to enjoy their illicit embraces. With the trap sprung and the adulterers immobilized, Hephaestus calls the other gods to witness, crying aloud his charges and his demand for damages: because he is lame, Aphrodite humiliates him and dares to make love with another in his own bed,

But the trap of chains will hold them both bound
until her father gives me back the whole bride-price,
as much as I gave in pledge for this dog-faced girl [*kynōpidos . . . kourēs*],
since his daughter is beautiful but can't control her passions.[103]

"Dog-faced" Aphrodite has broken the rule of marital fidelity, according to which a wife must prove *philē* to her husband alone: for this, Hephaestus can demand that her father take her back and that he be reimbursed the price he had paid to take her in marriage. A good wife knows to restrain her impulses in order to comply with the dictates of marital fidelity. That a wife is beautiful may be important, surely, but more important still is that she has timid respect (aidōs) for her husband and is wise and sensible (possessing the virtue called *sōphrosynē*): she must know how to keep her exclusive companionship with her husband firm and unwavering and repress deviant desires.[104]

It needs to be recalled at this point that the model of companionship between dog and master foresees two possibilities. One is that mentioned in connection with Melantho: the dog has been raised and nurtured by a human being and for this remains bound by a debt of gratitude. This analogy is oriented toward the relationship between parent—natural or adopted—and child, who must be grateful to those who've raised her or him.[105] But another possibility is that one may acquire a full-grown dog. In this case, how does one induce the required senses of cooperation and obedience? We already know the answer: one seduces the dog. As seen in chapter 2, to encourage a dog's goodwill, one must entice and bribe it with food. Not only those who want to adopt a dog do this, but also thieves who want to neutralize a guard dog and, in Aesop's fables, wolves that bribe herd dogs.[106]

The models for matrimony and for dog acquisition, on closer inspection, present some surprising analogies. Like a bride, a dog is taken from a former guardian. Just as a husband-to-be sometimes pays his future father-in-law a price for the girl he will marry, so a future master may pay the dog's former master.[107] One can imagine that in both cases, the giver assures the buyer of the good nature and training of the purchased property and that even with a dog, "divorces" and demands for repayment occur, much like the one that Hephaestus makes to his father-in-law, Zeus. But this is not the main point. What matters more is that a dog, like a wife, must go from being philos to its nurturer to being philos to its new owner-guardian. It must identify itself as the companion and ally of another man. Obviously such fidelity cannot be directly bought; it has to be won. So just as it is crucial that a wife be led to feel devotion to her husband, so it is essential that a dog be induced, with treats of food, to affectionately attach itself to its new master.[108]

At the same time, however, it is fundamentally important that woman and dog not be too enticeable: they must be able to be seduced one time only, and just by the one with the legitimate right to obtain them. It is thus hardly far-fetched that the anxiety a husband has about his wife's fidelity would tend to line up, in the imagination's analogical web, with the figures of doggishness dictated by anxieties about the dog's fidelity. If a scene of seduction obtains the companionship of bride or dog, this means that either might be won by anyone.[109] The danger is that another might take advantage of this ever-lurking availability. For this reason, women and dogs must be continent, know how to keep their desires in check, and resist flatteries from outside tempters.

It's not surprising that adulterous wives earned the title of *kynes,* and chief among them is the prime symbol of feminine seducibility: Helen of Sparta. But her association with doggishness has a surprising side in Homer. Contrary to what one might expect, it is not Menelaus, the abandoned husband, who calls his adulterous wife *kyōn.* In fact, this is what Helen calls herself. She does it the first time while sitting in a tower of the Trojan wall, speaking with Priam, the father of her second husband, Paris.[110] In this heartfelt talk with her second father-in-law, who calls her "my child," to which she replies that he is "worthy of respect and awe"—the exact sense of the two adjectives *aidoios* and *deinos*[111]—Helen expresses grief for the war she has caused. She would have preferred that things not turn out thus; better that she'd been killed at the very idea of leaving her husband, child, and old friends to follow Paris to Troy. But she was not. So now she finds herself in the dramatic situation of having to identify for Priam her former husband's allies, arrayed in arms to reconquer her and cleanse Menelaus's honor with Trojan blood—the blood of her new relatives. In this context, Helen speaks of Agamemnon as "brother-in-law of me, the dog-faced one [*kynōpidos*]."[112] In what follows, she calls herself *dog* twice more in succession: first, she addresses Hector as "brother-in-law of me, a dreadful, evil-devising dog [*kyōn*]"; then, again expressing her regret for causing so much grief, she tells Hector that if he must endure so much pain, it is the fault of her, the *kyōn,* and the ruinous folly of Paris.[113] This is not all. In the *Odyssey* as well, the Spartan queen accuses herself of causing so much trouble and calls herself—needless to say—*kynōpis.* But in this case, Helen is back at Sparta, having returned to her old home with Menelaus, the conqueror. The regret she expresses here is thus for the pain her behavior caused the Achaeans, not the Trojans. It was for her, "dog-faced," that they undertook the bloody war.[114]

As the paradigmatically seducible figure—the wife who abandons her husband and gives her companionship to another man—Helen is well suited to don the mask of traitorous dog. And indeed, as we will see shortly, doggishness is a personality trait of hers in tragedy as well. That Homer's Helen and not others heaps these insults on herself raises an interpretive problem about her role in the poems that cannot be addressed in detail here. Homeric Helen is an elusive figure, difficult to pin down: the cause of the Trojan War, the main source of all the events that epos narrates, she seems surrounded by an aura of mysterious ambivalence that many scholars have tried to shed light on.[115] I will simply add the suggestion that certain characteristics of the position of the adulterous woman in Greece might resolve the problem of Homeric Helen's self-definition of *kyōn*.[116] Greek legislation on adultery, as far as we can tell, adopted the principle of the guilt of the seducer—whom the injured husband was allowed to put to immediate death—but did not pay equal attention to outlining juridical sanctions for the woman who cheated.[117] At the public level, the woman tended to be treated as an object, not a subject, of adultery. She was considered a passive party, "the seduced." The public contention that adultery roused was thus configured as a conflict between men and not a dispute between husband and wife. The adulterer is a thief, whom the legitimate owner must punish to fully recoup his stolen property. By contrast, a husband's treatment of his seduced wife is a private matter, something that the law has no concern for.[118]

One can therefore theorize that Helen's self-definition as a *kyōn* might find justification in the exclusively private character of her responsibility. In other words, at the level of public and political disputes, within the realm of the armed conflict provoked by the adultery, Helen could not be called as an official defendant—and for this reason, the male protagonists in the story never insult her—inasmuch as her responsibility carries no weight. She is not the party summoned to answer publicly for what happened; Paris and his companions are the officially responsible persons deserving prosecution and punishment. Supporting this interpretation is the fact that Menelaus, who never publicly condemns his unfaithful wife, instead openly accuses her seducer, Paris, and all the Trojans as his accomplices, calling them—needless to say—"miserable kynes," thieves and violators of the laws of xenia, as the Spartan king puts it in Euripides's *Trojan Women*: "I came to Troy not, as they think, for a woman, but to confront the man, traitor to hospitality, who carried off the bride from my house."[119]

By having Helen claim responsibility, the Homeric version of the myth manages above all to reconcile two conflicting requirements. On the one hand, the story of the Trojan affair needs to preserve her as a figure of divine beauty, one worth fighting and dying for. As a precious object of contention and divine prize for victory—at the level of the heroes' public dispute—Helen must remain clear of the charge of being a miserable *kyōn*.[120] But on the other hand, she remains the woman who has changed husbands, a model of incontinent feminine volatility that is morally unacceptable, like adulterous Aphrodite, an intemperate "dog-face" in Hephaestus's resentful speech. Therefore, at least at the private level, Helen is responsible for betrayal, and it is at this level that her admission of guilt takes place, in the form of self-reproach. Only she, and not those who are fighting over her, can express her responsibility for the adultery by calling herself a *kyōn* and imagining herself as the guilty wife whom Menelaus, if he succeeds in getting her, will bring back "despised [*stygerē*]" inside the walls of his house.[121] She's like a traitorous dog that its master has come to reclaim and that, once back home, will get the severe punishment it deserves. The solution the two poems adopt, if this reading is correct, is to make Helen an object in the public and political conflict and a subject in her private transgression—exploiting, perhaps, the opportunity given by the double register of the woman's role in the Greek conception of adultery.[122]

So much for Helen's self-defined doggishness in Homer. But as for the exemplary nature of her canine traits, an argument that more closely concerns us here, what matters is that, as with other adulterous figures in Homer, a marked seducibility associates her with the dog and is, indeed, her most prominent personality trait in the compass of events in which she features. Whether she feels like a *kyōn* or others refer to her thus, as happens in other contexts, Helen has changed allegiance, done what no woman or dog is supposed to do: switched her companionship on her own initiative from a man who legitimately possessed her to a stranger who did not receive her through a legitimate exchange with her prior, male master.[123]

From the ambiguity of Homer's Helen and her doggishness we pass to the brilliant reworkings of the classical Athenian poets. The Helen-*kyōn* theme also appears in Aeschylus's *Oresteia*, although completely transformed. The most beautiful woman, who has caused so much loss and devastation, is no longer a treasonous dog but something yet worse: a savage beast raised in the Trojan palace like a dog but in reality a bloodthirsty lion. This is the famous metaphor of the lion cub discussed in chapter 2.[124] In Euripides, Helen is once again a dog, the treacherous *kyōn* that Menelaus should have left at Troy or killed instead of taking her back to Sparta with endless coaxing.[125] Moreover, the term Euripides employs for Menelaus's coaxing is *aikallein,* a verb also used of a dog's fawning.[126] If it is right to see an intentional allusion in this word choice, then Euripides's version of events doubles the canine image: Menelaus, the betrayed husband, also takes on the shape of a dog—a pathetic dog devoid of dignity, fawning over the bitch that abandoned him. The charge that Peleus levels at him thus translates into a double insult: Helen is a bitch, but Menelaus, who takes her back into his bed as soon as she bares her breast, has well earned the title *kyōn.*[127] Variations on the theme are potentially infinite, with the masks of doggishness multiplying and unfolding the entire spectrum of symbolic refractions: the beast that wags its tail like a gentle puppy, the traitorous dog, the moral baseness of a dog without pride that licks the hand of the one who beats it, and so on.

Yet the mask of the dog traitor represents not only faithless feminine seducibility, the problematic and unwanted mutability of a woman who enters and exits at her pleasure the house of the man, father or husband, who has her in his power. It can also serve to portray a truly bloody mutiny, the mauling to death of her master by a dog-woman. The consummate performer of this act in the Greek canine imaginary is the vindictive wife of Agamemnon.[128] In Aeschylus's trilogy about the house of Atreus, Clytemnestra is not only the treacherous dog that in its master's absence takes food from a stranger (i.e., her lover Aegisthus). She is also a dog that goes so far as to premeditate her rebellion and dares to maul her master to become autonomous, take his power, and upset the iron hierarchical law of canine subordination, intolerably perverting the natural order. A dog mauling its master, as seen many times before, is an image of monstrous reversal. Clytemnestra, who murders her husband, is the paradigm of this monstrousness, the extreme perversion of the "female who kills the male."[129]

Aeschylus's use of another mythical woman-*kyōn* figure in relation to Clytemnestra's crime seems to confirm the connection between her doggishness and her homicidal mutiny. In this case, it is not a wife but a daughter, who also kills her master, her father. When the libation-bearing chorus in the *Choephori* searches for words to describe Clytemnestra's crime, they come up with the name of Scylla. What can compare to such a woman, they ask, what monstrous beast of land or sea, what destructive storms in the sky? No natural comparison suffices, since in nature there may be appalling violence, but no perversion. To find monstrosity, one must look to human stories, particularly those of women who went so far as to kill their blood relatives: Althea, for example, who killed her son Meleager, or Scylla, the "dog-hearted [*kynophrōn*]" daughter who dared to kill her father. Giving in to her desire for a gold necklace offered by Minos, who was besieging her city, Scylla betrayed father and fatherland at once. She cut from her father's head a purple lock, on which his life magically depended, thus handing the city over to the enemy.[130] Here again, then, we have a seduced woman earning a canine epithet. Notably, moreover, other versions of the myth of Scylla have erotic overtones: she betrays and kills her father not from a desire for gold but for love of Minos.[131] In Scylla there are potentially many models of doggish betrayal: the corrupted dog that changes hands without its master's consent, seduced by a stranger, like Aphrodite and Helen; the mutinous dog that treacherously kills its master, like Clytemnestra; and finally, the dog raised in the house that betrays and mauls to death the one who reared it.

Whatever the means by which the woman is seduced—whether love or riches or power—the mask of the dog traitor is a specter of uncontrolled feminine mobility: spontaneous, autonomous movement of an element that, due to its subordinate condition, should not move itself but should only be moved. This element is thought of as an object of property but is actually such only when and if it decides to be. Since women and dogs are in reality subjects, their subaltern status, though presented as a natural fact, is the result of a normative model and not some binding physical law. In light of these initial conclusions, we should now begin to trace the outlines within which we will attempt to answer the questions posed at the outset. The hypothesis that I seek to develop and demonstrate, with the aid of ancient sources, is the following: the masks of doggishness were especially adapted to female figures, because there was a structural analogy between the positions of woman and dog in Greece that was susceptible to producing some overlaps within the male imagination. In other words, the parallel flowering of negative representations of bad dogs and unfaithful women shared an identical root of anxiety. As I will show in the last paragraphs of this section on the dog traitor, a profound structural reason determines the exclusive link between this canine trait and figures of unfaithful women. The parallel between the positions of women and dogs, with the various consequences this had in the ancient Greek imaginary, is also the central line of inquiry in the next, concluding chapter.

Now is an opportune moment, however, for an observation relevant to the mask being analyzed here but also important to the argument that follows. If a dog's treachery well portrayed a woman's treachery, this was not because the bitch, the female dog, was considered a lustful and treasonous creature toward the male of its kind.[132] Instead, if anything, it was because the dog—understood as a neuter animal—stood in a position relative to man that well suited it for analogies to women. In other words, it wasn't the she-dog's betrayal of the dog but the dog's betrayal of man that informed the metaphor. Therefore, although they may be linked (via relevant domains of experience, such as trust and betrayal), female fidelity and canine fidelity nevertheless clearly operate in entirely different spheres. For women, the prevailing anxiety involves sexuality, while for dogs, most of the worry relates to food. Seen from this perspective, the greater prevalence of the theme of the dog's ravenous hunger than that of its lasciviousness is no surprise.[133] In fact, the figure of the hungry dog probably originated in an anxiety over seducibility quite similar to that which generated misogynist discourse on the voracity of women—whether in sexual appetite, gluttony, or lust for jewels and riches.[134] Ancient sources frequently accuse dogs of insatiable hunger because the alliance between dog and master is based entirely on food, which is therefore the realm in which it can break down. So even when doggishness is employed to portray feminine submission to erotic temptation, one should think of the dog's greed for food, not the sexuality of she-dogs. Reciprocally, women of immoderate sexuality often correspond to figures of canine greediness because the male imagination pinned most of its anxiety about seduction on female chastity (i.e., self-denial).[135]

It should now be clear why throughout this chapter I've deliberately avoided translating as *bitch* and *bitch-faced* insults and epithets that refer to female characters. Translating the insult *kyon* with gendered terms, *dog* or *bitch,* would be misleading, since Greek *kyōn* is a noun of common gender, so even when the insult is used for a feminine figure, it does not refer to a female dog but rather to the species in general. Indeed, the "bitchiness" of the various characters examined so far always refers to negative characteristics of the neuter animal: neither audacity nor brazenness, that is blind and partial persistence, nor betrayal specifically has to do with a female dog, not even when the mask is applied to female figures, but rather always points to canine species traits. The Erinyes, the bacchantes, Helen, and Odysseus's nursemaids should only be called "bitch" or "bitch-faced [*kynopis*]" to accord with English usage.[136] It would be in error to suppose that the metaphorical coupling of woman and dog rests on properties that ancient Greek people assigned to the she-dog. The distinction of gender involves the *comparandum,* not the *comparatum.* Only in English usage is Agamemnon a dog and Helen a bitch. In Greek, they are both simply kynes.

SEVENTH MASK: THE FURIOUS MOTHER

As one may guess from the name chosen for the seventh canine mask, the rule just formulated, that the insult *dog* relates to generic species traits, nevertheless has at least one exception. In fact, in one case the doggish figure must refer to the behavior of a specifically female dog. It is a she-dog protecting her puppies, whose comportment provided material for metaphors of irascibility.

Semonides says that the hotheaded woman is like a sea storm that swells up and lets loose its violent rage. She often becomes unapproachable, like a she-dog that has given birth. In fact, the mother dog is so driven to protect her puppies that if anyone comes near, she turns hostile and no longer recognizes even her friends:

> But other times she [the sealike woman] is
> impossible to look in the eyes
> or even get near: then she rages
> unapproachably, like a she-dog around her litter;
> ruthless to all and disagreeable
> she becomes, with foe and friend alike.[137]

Postpartum behavior is thus another area where a dog reveals its inclination to lose its discerning faculties and unleash its aggression indiscriminately—another case of its congenital tendency toward lyssa. Only this time it occurs not randomly but in a regular and recurring situation, when a female dog nurses her pups. The image must be proverbial, and it occurs in Homer as well, in the simile of the she-dog with puppies used to describe Odysseus's raging heart (*kradiē*), barking in his chest at the sight of his unfaithful nursemaids.[138] The fact that Odysseus not only reproaches his bitch-heart but also gives it a thrashing by pounding his chest shows that this figure symbolized blind rage, a hostility perhaps not unjustified but certainly uncontrolled.[139]

There is a mythic figure, a true wrathful mother, who so violently experiences the rabid reaction of a she-dog whose puppies have been taken away that she even ends up looking like one. This is the metamorphosis of Hecuba that Euripides relates in one of his tragedies. After the fall of Troy, Queen Hecuba and her daughters are put on board Achaean ships bound for Greece, where they are to be slaves of their conquerors. But misfortune has other, greater sorrows in store for them. During a stop on the Thracian coast, Hecuba's young daughter Polyxena is sacrificed to favor the return voyage, slaughtered in Achilles's honor; a little later, the queen finds on the shore's edge the body of her son Polydorus, who had been sent to Thrace as a baby to be raised in safety, far from the war, by a family friend, King Polymestor. But as soon as he learned of Troy's fall, Polymestor murdered the boy and took the gold that King Priam had entrusted to him. Hecuba is devastated and cannot allow this heinous betrayal to go unavenged; Polymestor, a friend who'd visited the Trojan palace many times, will pay for his treachery. The queen plots her revenge: she has Polymestor come to the Achaeans' tents, and with the other Trojan prisoners' help she kills his children and blinds him, stabbing his eyes with a brooch pin. The Thracian king, bloody-eyed and groping, makes a prophecy: Hecuba will not be a slave in Greece but will fall from the Achaean ship and become "a bitch with a gaze of fire." Her tomb will be a signal for sailors called "the Sēma of the wretched she-dog."[140]

In a valuable study, Anne Pippin Burnett shows how Euripides uses this prophesied transformation to link his heroine to a specific locus of memory: the lighthouse on the promontory of the Thracian Hellespont, whose beacon fires guided sailors heading for the Black Sea. This promontory was called Sēma of the Dog (Kynossēma), and the poet decided to tie it to Hecuba's fate by means of a literal metamorphosis: in the lighthouse fire, sailors would have seen, from then on, the flashing gaze of the most miserable of mothers, the mother dog buried on the Thracian promontory. According to Burnett, the association arose in the tragic poet's imagination through a series of analogical steps: Greek tradition regularly associated the dog with women, and the she-dog in particular was a symbol of fertility and maternal care; to this must be added that the story of Hecuba is a model of bad fate, what the Greeks would have called a fate "most dog [kyntatos, on which see the last section of this chapter]." With these implicit connotations of the tradition active, Euripides then developed Hecuba's canine potentials, to which he added punishing cruelty. Through an intersection with the dogs of Hecate, a goddess associated with motherhood, and the vindictive, bitchlike fury of the Erinyes-dogs, Hecuba—the mother who avenges her child's death with a bloody retaliation against her enemy's child—thus ends up transmuting into the dog torchbearer of Kynossēma, and from the traditional mother of the destructive firebrand that burned Troy—as she had dreamed herself when giving birth to Paris— the Trojan queen transforms at the end of Euripides's drama into the positive lighthouse fire for sailors. Such are the terms, in brief, of Burnett's interpretation.[141]

Although for the most part the arguments made in this study of Euripides's *Hecuba* garner ready assent, two points deserve comment: the first regards the connection between Hecuba and the model of dog-mother, and the second specifically concerns the "gaze of fire" attributed to the Kynossēma. First of all, the Greek model of the dog-mother is not, as Burnett maintains, wholly positive. Even the positive testimonies of canine motherhood focus more on the fecundity of she-dogs than their care and concern for the puppies.[142] By contrast, examples of maternal bitchiness also exist. A well-known proverb, for example, warns against overhasty action by recalling that in her hurry to give birth, a she-dog brings her babies into the world blind. Hephaestus in Homer would thus not call Hera, his mother, "dog-faced"—because she delivered him crippled and did not hesitate to get rid of him—if the dog-mother did not also model, at the least, slightly hasty maternal behavior.[143]

As for the trope of the she-dog fiercely defending her puppies, it is not a praiseworthy likeness for model mothers but an image—unsettling at the very least—of uncontrollable wrath. Indeed, the proverbial bitch-mother is represented from the perspective not of the puppies she protects but of the men who approach her, in accordance with a principle at play in the development of all the masks of doggishness and attributable to the dog's metonymic position. The reckless, the brazenfaced, the intruder, the avenger, the bloodthirsty psychopath, and the traitor are all masks developed from the dynamics of the human-dog relationship, not based on ethological traits of the species as such. This is due to the fact that dogs, perceived as included in society, almost always tend to be configured as individuals in the human community rather than as part of a secluded species with a metaphorically alternative society apart from man's. For this same reason, the she-dog of the simile is not, in fact, a caring mother but a combative one in the grip of a blind fury.[144]

It therefore seems more likely that the traditional image of the angry bitchmother rather than a model of a good mother plays some role in Euripides's portrayal of Hecuba and that the association between the vengeful queen and the Erinyes comes straight from this specific image of maternal rage. It should also be noted that the Erinyes often serve mothers enraged against their own children—like Clytemnestra with Orestes—and can thus represent she-dogs set loose by a mother seeking vengeance. This further confirms that the link between she-dog and motherhood produced depictions not of motherly care and love for offspring but of raving mothers acting furious and dreadful even to their own children.[145] In other words, the she-dog offered material mainly for elaborations on the dangerous and blind aggression that an enraged mother was capable of unleashing—against whoever tried to touch her children, but possibly also against her children themselves, if they happened to oppose her.

A mother dog, in short, is a mother raging to excess, whether fighting for or enraged against her child.[146] We may recall that in the iambics of Semonides about the different kinds of women—the same iambics containing the comparison between the sea-woman and the she-dog that rages to defend her pups—the dogwoman also possesses maternal overtones, and here again, the contact between she-dog and mother produces a negative image:

> The woman who comes from a dog, she's wicked, just like a mother [autométora],
> she wants to hear everything, wants to know everything,
> sticks her nose everywhere and wanders here and there
> barking, even if she doesn't see a living soul.[147]

Whatever the exact meaning of the mysterious epithet *autométora* (just like a mother, all mother, a true mother) that Semonides applies to the dog-woman, he undoubtedly intended it as an insult: this passage therefore confirms that the connection between she-dogs and motherhood mainly pointed the imagination toward figures of unexemplary women.[148] Note that Phocylides, who imitated Semonides's poem, sums up the character of this dog-woman by emphasizing her penchant for aggression: she is "troublesome and savage."[149] If this female type's behavior, as it seems, is indiscriminately aggressive, stubborn, and relentless, a mother dog is the perfect model for it: like the guard dog, the bitch with her pups represents a typical situation in which the dog's latent lyssa, its blind aggressiveness, reveals itself with abhorrent clarity.

Let us attempt, then, to reconsider the question of the unfortunate Trojan queen's metamorphosis. Notice first of all that in the epic tradition, Hecuba is a fiercely protective mother capable of pondering cruel revenge; after the death of her son Hector, she expresses her bitterness at his killer thus:

> Would that I could seize upon his liver
> and devour it—that would be an act of vengeance
> for my son![150]

So already in the *Iliad*, Hecuba is a vindictive mother. But further, with her desire to maul Hector's killer to pieces, the fertile queen of Troy shows her affinity to the cultural paradigm of the raving she-dog ready to do anything to protect her pups. The two stereotypes, of mother grieving for the loss of a child and of she-dog raving around her pups, were probably perceived as contiguous long before Euripides associated Hecuba with the dog of Kynossēma.

Vindictive fury falls within the realm of the Erinyes. So, too, maternal rage at the loss of a child, with the accompanying desire for revenge, summons the goddesses of vengeance into the picture. Even the great goddess Demeter, when she wandered through Arcadia in search of her daughter Persephone, whom Hades had abducted, was a "furious" mother, and her worshippers in Arcadia even invoked her as Erinys.[151] The *Homeric Hymn to Demeter* describes the desperate, raving goddess as a mother gripped by "unapproachable [*aplēton*] . . . rage" and by a "grief all the more dreadful and more dog [*kynteron*]" the more the other gods try to soothe her.[152] These expressions recall, with significant lexical overlap, the hotheaded woman in Semonides, relentless and "unapproachable [*aplēton*]" like a she-dog around her puppies. The doggish feature characterizing these mother figures is the Fury-like lyssa of a bitch protecting her pups, blind rage unleashed without distinction against any and all, not the reassuring protectiveness of a gentle creature. One cannot forget that Demeter, in her rabid grief at losing her child, inflicted the world with sterility. The *Homeric Hymn* describes the terrible year of famine that her ire caused as "most dog [*kyntaton*]."[153]

As for the "gaze of fire" that Hecuba-turned-dog will shoot from Kynossēma according to Polymestor's prophecy, this extraordinary detail in Euripides's image offers a further hint of the canine fury that the heroine embodies, as I will show. It reappears in an anonymous lyric fragment where the Erinyes, as it happens, transform Hecuba into a "she-dog with gleaming eyes [*charopān kyna*]" that emits sounds of brass from foaming jaws.[154] In other words, the Erinyes transform Hecuba into a rabidly barking dog with eyes of burning coals.

Burnett interprets this gaze of fire as the result of associations between Hecuba, a fecund mother figure, and Hecate, the *phōsphoros* (light bearing) goddess of childbirth and a sort of "mistress of dogs."[155] To this effect, in a fragment of one of Euripides's lost works, one character delivers the following prophecy to another: "You will be a dog, a semblance of Hecate Phōsphoros."[156] Provided that the Hecate-like dog here is Hecuba, the passage proves, if nothing else, the close symbolic affinity between the goddess and the tragic figure of the Trojan heroine.[157] However, supposing this contact between Hecuba and Hecate exists, on what is it based? According to Burnett, the two intersect mainly in the sphere of motherhood and childbirth. But how did it happen that the idea of fertile and happy motherhood and a figure of a light-bearing, benevolent mother changed into that of a dog with menacing eyes of flame, if not through the transformation of the luminous progenitor into the raging mother dog whose sinister glare of lyssa flashes from her eyes?

DOGS OF FIRE

There are good reasons to believe that the figure of Hecuba of Kynossēma was constructed on the model of the raging mother dog even with regard to the detail of the gaze of fire. In fact, in ancient Greek tradition, the dog's hotheaded aggression, its tendency toward rabid attack, manifested precisely as flashes of flame that shot from the eyes. Let us look at some examples.

To begin with, the Greeks called the brightest star in the sky the Dog (Kyōn), the parching star that signaled the height of the summer season. In popular opinion it was the Dog Star that caused drought and the withering of crops. In a significant passage of the *Iliad,* from atop the citadel, Priam sees Achilles running on the plain below, approaching the walls to confront Hector in their final duel. At that moment Achilles gleams like a star: the rays that flash from the warrior are baleful like those of the Dog, the brightest but also the most destructive star, since it brings scorching heat to the earth.[158]

As is well known, the star that dried up mortals with its burning rays was also called Sirius, the name of the impetuous dog of the equally impetuous and gigantic hunter Orion. In myth, both master and dog were transformed into stars and placed in the heavens.[159] Achilles is compared to Sirius the Dog Star on account of the gleaming light that flashes from his wondrous bronze armor, forged in the fires of Hephaestus, blazing on the field like a star in heaven, but also because he burns with the same flame as the fiery and invincible hunting dog of Orion. A warrior possessed by battle lyssa is, in Homer's words, "like a flame." And for the Greeks, one "burns" with lyssa.[160] We saw in the foregoing section how the case of the mother dog is a particular manifestation, an example proving the rule, of canine lyssa, the fiery excess always ready to flare up. Just this sort of hot fervor characterized the star that the Greeks called Kyōn. The dog days were those burning days of raging assault by the Dog Star.[161]

As it happens, another myth has it that the heavenly dog was once a she-dog in mourning. In this version, the Dog Star was not Sirius transformed but Maira, the she-dog of the gentle farmer Icarius. Once upon a time, the young god Dionysus began visiting mortals to bring them the gift of his new beverage, wine. Arriving in Attica, he received generous hospitality from the farmer Icarius and so decided to entrust wine and the vine to him, instructing him to spread them among humankind. But Icarius soon had to pay the price for the ambiguous gifts of Dionysus: the shepherds whom he had sample the new drink got drunk and, believing he had poisoned them, killed him in revenge. Icarius's loyal she-dog, Maira, was so grief stricken at losing her master that the gods were moved to pity; they carried her aloft to the heavens and transformed her into the blazing Dog Star, which returns each year to pour out its vengeful wrath.[162] Curiously enough, a late Greek poet applied the name Maira to Hecuba, the she-dog desperate with grief over her lost son: "Your body will turn into a dark-tailed Maira."[163] The path leading from Hecuba to the Dog Star thus seems to have come full circle.

But let us examine the series of associations one more time. The Greeks imagined a close connection between canine lyssa and blazing flame. More precisely, the dog's gaze reveals this spark of latent madness that dwells within. This gaze is a sinister gleam, an ambiguous and troubling glare. On the one hand, the fire in a dog's eyes is one of the animal's chief endowments. It is so bright that it lights up the night, and by this means, dogs can see us in the dark. Guard dogs are *charopoi* (bright-eyed); their eyes flicker like flame, just like an owl's.[164] The dog is well adapted to guarding because its shining eyes are fire enough in themselves to overcome the darkness.[165] Not for nothing, then, as we saw, were the perfect guard dogs forged by Hephaestus, the god of fire.

Yet in their fiery gaze, dogs also reveal their kinship with carnivorous beasts—lions, eagles, dragons, and above all wolves—that is, their constant imbalance toward wild and man-eating ferocity, the aggression which, when unleashed, turns them into wolves (*lyssētēres*).[166] For its victim—whether attacked or hunted as prey—this canine gaze is an unquenchable fire, a keenly raging heat. The same ambivalence we saw at play with regard to canine courage is thus active as well in representations of the dog's perceptive faculties. Due to this ambivalence, the dog appears as an animal with, on the one hand, perfect vision, filled with a fire that enables it to see what humans cannot, making it a valuable tool for surveillance, but on the other hand, with easily excitable senses, as seen by those who suffer the consequences, and in its gaze flashes a flame of potentially uncontrollable, aggressive madness. Acute vision and blind rage—between these two poles oscillates the appraisal of the dog's gaze of fire.

Let's now go back to the eyes of Hecuba-turned-dog in Euripides and consider some scenes that precede the final prophecy. The motif of the dog with eyes of fire creeps into the imagery of the work well before Polymestor's prophecy of the heroine's impending transformation into the Kynossēma lighthouse. At the moment when the Trojan women blind Polymestor (who calls them, among other things, "murderous bitches"[167] and wants to get hold of them and tear them to pieces) he lets out a desperate cry of raging grief that anticipates the theme of nocturnal fire. What will happen to me?, the Thracian king asks. So horridly mutilated, where will I end up? Significantly, he imagines that his despair will take him not to the gloomy, underground abode of Hades, where common mortals go, but into the celestial realm, reserved for the elect, to shoot from the sky his flashing fires of rage:

> Will I reach the highest peak
> of the heavenly vault,
> where Orion and Sirius flash their flaming rays of fire
> from their eyes?[168]

Deprived of sight and gripped by raging sorrow, Polymestor imagines himself transformed into a shining star, a nocturnal fire like Orion and his dog Sirius, who illumine the sky's blind darkness with the sinister gleam of their impetuous gazes.[169] The passage seems to foreshadow the end of the tragedy. The gleam that Polymestor connects to his blinded gaze is the same fire in the darkness, the same ray of blind fury, into which Hecuba will be transformed: the she-dog Hecuba of the Kynossēma lighthouse, the Hecuba-Maira Dog Star in the tradition of Hellenistic *katasterismos*. The eyes of a dog that shine in the dark thus furnish a model for representing a nocturnal glow, whether of a star or a of signal fire for sailors.

Through the motif of nocturnal fire, the metamorphosis of Hecuba into a dog with a fiery gaze can also readily enlist the goddess Hecate. But rather than thinking of Hecate as a goddess of childbirth and happy, fertile motherhood, which are hard to reconcile with this image of a fiery, Fury-like she-dog, one can think of another of her aspects, outside the maternal sphere and having to do with the inviolability of boundaries and thresholds. The Trojan queen is a bitch inasmuch as she is a wild and implacable huntress but also because she is a zealous guardian of a partisan justice, that of a mother who, with her child's murder, has had the inviolable norms of *dikē* trespassed.[170] In the latter domain, the avenging dog intersects with Hecate the Guardian (Phylax) and the Gatekeeper (Prothyraia or Propylaia).[171] It is perhaps no accident that both the Erinyes and Hecate are deities associated with dogs and madness, are divine guardians of boundaries and inviolable thresholds, and are hunters and bearers of torches, lamps for the darkness. The figures overlap at many points, not least in being underworld deities particularly inclined to display the vindictive side of their excitable natures.[172]

If a fiery gaze is a common canine trait, representing both the instrument of dogs' keen perception and a symptom of their tendency toward lyssa, it seems plausible enough that the guard dog, and perhaps the dog of Hecate Prothyraia, could inspire variations on the theme of nocturnal fire. Like infernal torches blazing in the darkness, a guard dog's eyes are both a sign of peril and a threat of ruthless, raging punishment for those who don't respect boundaries and thresholds. The marvelous guard dogs of Alcinous's palace, for example, made of precious metal and forged in Hephaestus's fire, protected the royal threshold with perfect vigilance, sleepless and missing nothing.[173] So too, as the perfect guardian and as watchdog in Hades's murky kingdom, Cerberus was, naturally, forged in fire, which hardened his thundering voice and flashing eyes.[174] His gaze was blinding, impetuous and penetrating, like armor forged in a blaze of heat, to the point that it took a man endowed with equally fiery eyes to overcome it; thus, it's no accident that Heracles, the only one ever to dare descend into the underworld and haul back the ferocious infernal hound, was venerated with the title Charops (with flashing eyes) at the site where he ascended from Hades with Cerberus.[175] No accident, either, that Heracles was the hero destined to experience a most wild and devastating lyssa, the cruel madness that made him not recognize his children, whom he killed like a murderous wolf.[176]

At this point, we can advance a more precise theory. It seems possible that the name of the Thracian promontory first meant "Signal [Sēma] of the Dog [Kynos]," with reference to the nocturnal eye of the lighthouse that warned of danger. Then Euripides—exploiting the double valence of the word sēma—identified it as the tomb (sēma) of the she-dog (kynos) Hecuba. Indeed, he does not fail to emphasize the signaling function that the lighthouse performed on the waterway leading to the Black Sea, and in so complex a fashion that it makes one suspect that the verses contain a resemanticization of the term sēma in the toponym:

Polymestor: You will die, and your tomb will be given a name.

Hecuba: Will it mirror my form, or some other?

Polymestor: A miserable dog's [Kynos talainēs] tomb [sēma], a signal [tekmar] for sailors.[177]

To judge from the care with which the poet breaks apart the toponym, cutting between its two elements to insert the feminine adjective talainēs, it seems that he wanted to transform the sense of the name, shifting the original Sēma of the Dog into Sēma of the (Miserable) She-Dog and, by mentioning the tomb first and then the signal (*tekmar*), playing on the double sense of *sēma*: "signal" in the original toponym and "tomb" in the tragedy's etiological story. Of course, this does not exclude the possibility that sailors perceived the lighthouse's nighttime flashing, its torchlight placed on the coastal cliff to signal a dangerous passage and a narrow strait between two seas, as the shining eye of a guard dog and thus gave it a name that recalls the fiery gaze of Hecate's dog, which signaled by night thresholds dangerous to cross.[178] Moreover, there was another, equally famous promontory in Greece with the name Kynossēma. It was a coastal rise on the island of Salamis, at the site where the faithful dog of Xanthippus, the father of Pericles, was said to have reached land and died. The poor creature had swum far in a desperate attempt to reach its master, who had sailed to the island from Athens on a trireme. It died from exhaustion and was buried on the promontory that ever after was called Sēma of the Dog.[179] One wonders whether in this case, as well, the place-name originally referred to a signal of danger for sailors, which a mythic tale of a dog raving in grief then resemanticized into a tomb.

Perhaps the association between lighthouses and the dog's fiery gaze was based on the animal's important function as a pointer, a giver of signs, capable of seeing and gesturing toward what is invisible to men. When hunting, a dog can detect prey by following its scent, which humans can't discern: it signals to the hunter what is invisible by day.[180] But a guard dog also signals, by barking and flashing with the beam of its eye of fire, revealing presences hidden from man, signaling what is invisible by night. Dogs even perceive the presence of gods, even when the latter are wandering invisible. Only Hermes, the god of movement who can trespass any boundary, can get past dogs without detection and without them barking. This is probably why he was the patron god of thieves and was invoked by scoundrels as Hermes Dog-Choker (Kynanchās)—that is, able to keep guard dogs quiet.[181]

Dogs were thought to have tremendous power over the invisible. Notable in this regard is the *kyneē*, the helmet of Hades, the king of the dead, which was a magic dog-skin cap that made its wearer invisible. Because of their ability to detect what cannot be seen, dogs were also regarded as having divinatory powers: the bark of dogs, especially at night, was an omen or even a direct indication that Hecate was near.[182] Their close link with the invisible dimension of reality must have been one of the reasons for their close association with graves and the afterlife. Statues of dogs were fairly common in cemeteries, where they marked the inviolability of the grave, which was entrusted to the invisible supervision of the Erinyes—guard dogs and punitive hunters—and to chthonic Hecate and her dogs.[183]

If this reconstruction is correct, the fiery gaze of Hecuba at Kynossēma arose from a rich symbolic texture in which are interwoven the extreme sorrow of maternal grief, the vindictive rage of a she-dog, danger, a light signal, and nocturnal fires of both the Dog Star and guardian Hecate's torch. Turning now to folkloric beliefs, we find two surprising stories with a web of motifs that should sound, at this point, quite familiar. Only this time, everything is transposed to the realm of plants.

Aelian offers us a glimpse of dogs of fire in ancient botanical lore, with two stories about a pair of toxic plants with derivatives of *kyōn* in their names: the *kynospastos,* or "dogbush," and the alga *pankynion,* described in chapter 2 as the dogs of the plant kingdom on account of their dangerous bitingness. As it turns out, these plants had another peculiar trait: both were luminescent. Like the torches of Hecate Phōsphoros (Light-bearer), they were visible even at night, due to phosphorescence. The one was found in meadows; the other could be seen in submarine darkness.[184] The pankynion happened to reach its greatest toxicity when Sirius rose, and thus got its name from the Dog Star. Fishermen waited for its glow to attract the dogs of the sea, dogfish, which then ingested it and were killed by its venom. The fishermen gathered their floating bodies and extracted the *pharmakon* of the algae, which was rendered harmless by the animals' mediation and could be used for cures.

A nearly identical sequence was followed to collect poison from the kynospastos, a plant also called *aglaophōtis,* "of shining light." The dogbush appeared only at night, "like a star," Aelian says, and "flaming like a fire." By day it was just like surrounding plants in every way, making it invisible. Therefore, gatherers found it at night and left a sign (*sēmeion*) by its roots to mark it for daytime. They wouldn't pull it out, because that would prove lethal. The next day they returned, bringing along a young, hungry dog, which they tied with a rope to the plant's stalk, and then placed a nice bunch of meat, carefully roasted on a fire, just beyond where the dog could reach without tugging on the rope. The poor dog, purposely deprived of food for days, burned with hunger. Lured by the smell, it bolted at the meat and pulled the rope, which uprooted the plant. But it paid dearly for this coveted meal: as soon as the sun looked on the kynospastos's roots with its rays of light, the dog dropped dead. At that point, the gatherers buried the dog on that spot and paid tribute to its body with secret rites, thanking it for being sacrificed for them. The kynospastos was now safe, due to the dog's mediation, and they took it home to make a potent drug that was effective, apparently, against moon sickness and an eye disease that deprived one of sight.[185]

Such is the skill with which narrative imagination could modulate a melody into a botanical key by varying ad lib the motif of the dog of fire: just as its flashing gaze is benign and malignant at once, so, too, is the pharmakon extracted from the pankynion and the kynospastos; the blazing fire of the Dog Star, the heavens' nocturnal sign, transfers to flowers that glow in the dark; and further, on the sign of fire a grave appears, of dogs from sea and land that with their deaths allow men to obtain a medicine to restore sight, rekindling the fire in the eyes of those who, having lost it, need a dog to lead them out of night's blindness.[186] The dog in plant form shines in the night, the nocturnal signal of a spot where, once it is uprooted, will rise another kynos sēma—a tomb and signal of a dog of fire.

MORE DOG THAN ANOTHER, MOST DOG OF ALL

A final item remains to be discussed to round out this chapter devoted to analyzing the insulting uses of *kyōn*, its derivatives, and other negative figures with canine traits. Here we are dealing with expressions that employ *kyōn* not to injure somebody but to describe an action or a situation. A situation dubbed *dog* was particularly detestable or undesirable, as might be imagined from analogous modern usage—in Italian, *un freddo cane* ("a dog cold," that is, cold as hell) or *un male cane* ("a dog hurt," that is, something that hurts like hell).[187] In these expressions, the appealed-to doggishness can be viewed—according to the two axes identified for the foregoing cases—as a symbol of either moral baseness or a pitiable condition of hardship. But it is not necessary to pinpoint in every case an exact reference to a single aspect of the canine imaginary. As is common with symbols, *dog* conveys a complex constellation of elements, difficult to analyze discursively; each case is a multidimensional design, so to speak, and reducing it to a single angle would be a mistake.

Let's look at some Homeric examples. After slaughtering many unarmed warriors in their sleep during a night raid into the Thracian camp, Diomedes ignores Odysseus's signal to retreat and stands pondering what "most dog [*kyntaton*]" deed he will commit.[188] The expression is surely chosen to describe Diomedes's unrestrained homicidal fury and the treachery of his actions: a gluttonous binge, like that of a dog that breaks into the kitchen at night and gobbles down food. But this is only one possible reading. The doggishness of Diomedes's actions coincides with fairly everything that the phrase *a dog action* conjures up, the whole set of possible associations that made up the derogatory use of *kyōn* in ancient Greek culture.

When Odysseus apologizes to the Phaeacians for having to ask for food while he is in such a sad state of distress, he says that nothing is "more dog [*kynteron*]" than the belly.[189] Here, one readily thinks of a dog's annoying demands to be fed, even at the least appropriate times; their irritating and embarrassing lack of manners makes one apologize to guests.[190] Likewise, Odysseus seems to beg the Phaeacians' pardon as though it were his dog that was pestering them: the famished belly is a ravenous dog that begs for food from within. Just as the heart seething with anger could be imagined in terms of a she-dog furiously barking in the chest, so the belly that wants to be fed and won't relent out of proper manners is a dog, the animal that best represents uninhibited impulses, the imperious press of desires, and the lack of measure, everything that is liable to make one lose control but must still be kept under control.[191] Yet one may also suppose that by apologizing for his dog belly, Odysseus alludes to his humiliating role as a parasite at the Phaeacians' table, undignified indeed for a valiant hero, a free man and a king, but one into which his uncurbed stomach forces him.[192]

On another occasion, Odysseus uses the term *kynteron* to recall his terrible experience in the cave of Polyphemus. As he tries to hold back his reaction to the ignoble spectacle of his nursemaids' defection to the suitors, the hero encourages his heart with these words: "Something still more dog [*kynteron*] you endured that day when that uncontrollable force, the Cyclops, devoured my stalwart companions."[193] The unstoppable violence of the monster, a violator of the laws of hospitality and the taboo against cannibalism, is a thing "more dog" than Odysseus's maids—whom he has already branded *kynes*.

The *Homeric Hymn to Demeter* describes the goddess's grief at losing her daughter as ever "more dog" the more the other gods try to placate her, and calls "dreadful and most dog" the year of famine she inflicts on the earth to vent her rage.[194] We've already discussed how much all this has to do with the sorrowful rage of a she-dog who has lost her puppies and of a grieving mother who has seen her child taken from her. But that was meant to show just one possible pathway of associations that the terms *kynteros* and *kyntatos* may have opened for the poet and his audience in connection with the deeds of Demeter. Like the insult *kyon*, its derivatives, whether comparative or superlative, can refer to multiple aspects of doggishness at the same time, the common denominator being a situation of the lowest level: either extreme moral baseness, comprising treacherous deeds or unrestrained aggression, or a condition of extreme misery or despair. In the case of the *Homeric Hymn*'s year of famine, the predominant sense of the term may be extreme deprivation: the year is most dog because the scarcity of food makes it the most miserable, worthy of a dog—that is, the most miserable being in the community, the preeminent symbol of starving to death.[195]

If the semantic content and connotations of *kynteros* and *kyntatos* have been sufficiently explained by now, there are still some interesting notes to add about their morphology. Both are modifications of degree—using the comparative and superlative suffixes, respectively—to the nominal root *kyn-*, and not, as one might expect, to the adjective *kyneos*. In other words, *kynteros* does not mean "more canine" or "more doggish" but exactly "more dog." So too *kyntatos* does not mean "most canine" but "most dog."

Pierre Chantraine defines the two terms as "expressive derivatives" of the nominal stem *kyn-* and compares them to Homeric forms such as *basileuteros* ("more king"), *basileutatos* ("most king"; both derived from the noun *basileus*), and *oresteros* (derived from *oros*, "mountain").[196] The last fits this classification quite well, since it works as a simple intensifier: referring to a serpent, a lion, or a wolf, *oresteros* means "mountain animal" and not "more mountain animal (compared to another)."[197] Its force is intensive rather than comparative. The same cannot be said about *basileuteros* or *basileutatos.* These terms appear in undeniably comparative and superlative expressions, where one person is "more king" than another or "the most king" among many. The reason for this is that the noun *basileus* is a title, conferred on a person in virtue of certain prerogatives he possessed, and because this position admitted distinctions of rank with respect to other subjects who, in their own domains, were equally kings. It's well known how in the *Iliad* the ability to distinguish different ranks of kingship is a cause of conflict between Agamemnon—the "king of kings"—and the other *basileis,* chief among them Achilles.[198]

If we reread the passages chosen above to illustrate the senses of *kynteros* and *kyntatos,* we can easily observe that both are always used as true comparatives and superlatives. When Odysseus says nothing is "more dog" than the belly, or Diomedes ponders what deed would be "most dog" among all those he could do, it is clear that *kynteros* and *kyntatos* are not intensifiers but indicators of degree. But the noun *kyōn,* in its primary sense as an animal name, does not allow for conceiving and expressing these gradations; a dog is a dog, period, and no dog can be said to be more dog than another (unlike a king, who can actually be called "more king" than another). On the other hand, when the noun *kyōn* is used as an insult—with the illocutionary force of *Dog!*—the possibility of varying degrees arises. Used as a personal epithet, *kyōn* becomes a title, just like *king,* though with a decidedly less flattering intention. Among those who might be disparaged with the epithet *kyōn,* whether pathetic or morally deplorable, differences of degree are conceivable. One can be called *more dog*—more at the bottom, more low-down—than another, or named the most dog among all those ever seen or thought of. Therefore it seems more correct to count *kynteros* and *kyntatos* among the so-called delocutive derivatives, those that stem not from a substantive noun but from a locution: as the Latin verb *salvere* derives from the exclamation *Salve!,* so *kynteros* and *kyntatos* would derive specifically from the insult *Kyon!* and not the substantive *kyōn.*[199]

These considerations are able to explain why *kynteros* and *kyntatos* were coined from the nominal stem and not the adjective.[200] They transpose into indirect discourse illocutionary expressions of an abusive nature. As attributes, they name an action or a situation that in a colloquial context or direct discourse one could address with the abusive *Kyon!,* just as one does in Italian by saying *Che male cane!* (It hurts like hell!) or *Che freddo cane!* (It's cold as hell!)

Return to Pandora

Nothing is more dog and more dreadful than a woman . . .
—ORPHIC FRAGMENT 234 KERN

THE SPECIES OF DOGS AND THE RACE OF WOMEN

By a long route of analysis we have traced out the probable reasons why the category "dog" has been used to insult. We can now advance and at last address the problem first posed, examining the causes that may have produced the marked feminine character of the negative elaborations on the dog theme in Greece. Indeed, scanning the pages dedicated to the masks of doggishness, one will notice that in the sources discussed, the epithet *kyōn* and its derivatives are frequently directed at female figures, and the disturbing characters with canine traits in myth—Erinyes, bacchantes, Hecuba—are all feminine. This leads one to suspect, as said before, that the doggish disposition—the *kyneos noos*—that Hesiod attributes to his ambiguous prototype of women, Pandora, should not be considered a malicious joke by a misogynous poet but rather reflects a stereotype widely diffused and deeply rooted in ancient Greek culture.

To begin with *Kyon!* and its denigrating derivatives, it seems clear that the common denominator in all the cases analyzed is their use in situations where speakers assert their superiority over, and demand the subordination of, those being insulted. The insult *Dog!* amounts to a command to obey and a threat of punishment for any insubordination. Now, it would be easy enough to claim that such a command was particularly suited to women, from whom the virtues of submission and obedience were expected. But it is no less evident that if this were all there was to it, the insult would be equally well suited to servants and slaves, whereas the examples we've seen also include speeches addressed to enemies in war and especially to nursemaids raised in one's house, daughters, wives, mothers, and so forth.

So if we want to discover the root cause of why the mask of the dog was so frequently called on to distort the features of a female face, it is best to search elsewhere.

We may therefore start to consider which of the animal's specific traits was important in this regard. First and foremost, as we've seen, the dog is the only animal collaborator whose activity cannot be forced by means of a coercive instrument. The dog works within a regime of autonomy: its effectiveness depends exclusively on its ability to recognize a human as a superior to whom it shows solidarity and obedience. In a word, one needs to trust a dog. We have also seen how this circumstance entails several consequences for how the animal's image is constructed, chief among them the fact that the dog, bound to man by the food pact, is metonymically included in the system of human ethical expectations: it is asked not only to respect the debt of gratitude it owes its caretaker but also to adapt its behavior to the complex norms of *aidōs*, including decorum, restraint, and the sense of reverence, which keep the system of social relations in balance by guaranteeing respect for hierarchy.

From Plutarch we learn that the chief endowments wanted in a dog were three: self-control and mastery of impulses (*enkrateia*), obedience (*peitharchia*), and mental alertness (*anchinoia*).[1] Clearly these are moral virtues, which then significantly become part of the dog's endowments, in value equal to if not greater than its physical traits. But even with these new particulars added to the dog's representation, we still have not gotten very far in explaining why feminine and canine virtues and defects came to be parallel in the ancient imagination. It is true, as many studies on the condition of women in Greece have established, that docile obedience and the ability to control one's impulses were the cornerstones of feminine "wisdom [*sōphrosynē*]," but self-control and obedience were also required of slaves.[2]

Alternatively, a characteristic of the relationship between dog and master seems to point in a more precise direction: the expectations of loyalty from the animal that man maintains, a theme highlighted by the mask of the traitor and worth exploring more deeply here. Indeed, we saw how the dog's cooperation is not thought of as simple acquiescence to the master's domineering will, some ready, mechanical response to his commands. It is conceived instead as a sentiment of grateful, acknowledging affection, of exclusive attachment and devotion that includes the dog in the circle of one's loved ones, companions, and family members (*philoi*). One of the most vivid descriptions of this bond in Greek sources can be read in Arrian's treatise *On Hunting*:

> For I have myself raised a hound whose eyes are the brightest of the bright, such a
> swift, hard-working, brave, and sound-footed dog that when she was in her prime,
> she was a match for no less than four hares. Moreover, she is . . . the most gentle and
> affectionate [*praotatē kai philanthrōpotatē*] dog I have ever seen: never before had

any dog shown such an intense yearning for me [*eme epothēsen*] and for my friend and fellow sportsman Megillos. In fact, since she was retired from the chase, she never steps away from us, or at least one of us: if I am indoors, she stays with me; she escorts me everywhere, accompanies me when I go to the gymnasium, and sits down by me while I am exercising; on our way back, she precedes me, looking back constantly to see whether I had turned anywhere out of the road, and when she catches sight of me, she smiles [*epimeidiasasa*] and starts trotting ahead again. Whenever I go out on any political business, she remains with my friend and behaves in the same way toward him. She never abandons either of us if we get sick. And if she sees us even after a short period of time, she jumps up nicely, as though she were warmly greeting us [*hōsper aspazomenē*], and adds to her welcoming gesture some sweet vocal expressions of love [*epiphtheggetai hoia philophronoumenē*]. When we have our meals, she stays by and pats us with one paw first and then with the other, to remind us that she too should be given her share of the food. She can utter an extraordinary variety of tones, more than I ever knew in any other dog: she knows how to vocally express her needs [*hosōn deitai tēi phonēi semainei*]. Since she was corrected with a whip during the training process as a puppy, still now if someone mentions a whip, she will come up to him cowering and begging and apply her mouth to his mouth as if to kiss him [*hōs philousa*] and jumping up she will hang from his neck and won't let him go until she has appeased his angry threats. Therefore I don't think I should feel ashamed to immortalize the name of this dog: that it may be left to posterity that Xenophon the Athenian[3] had a dog called Rush [*Hormē*], of the greatest speed and wisdom, almost a divine creature [*hierotatē*].[4]

As we saw in chapter 2, when the master raises and cares for the dog, the ethical model that regulates their relationship tends to appear, through the language of duty and debt for care received, quite parallel to that of parent-child relationships; when, instead, the dog is acquired as an adult, and the new master attracts it by offering food to induce its affection for him, the model approaches that of matrimonial acquisition. In each case, something more than mere cold obedience is expected from the dog: one wants it to demonstrate that it is *philos*. The dog is supposed to display the same devotion that one claims from a nursemaid or a servant born and raised in one's house or from a child or a wife: an exclusive solidarity, unconditional and permanent.[5]

Ancient stories that celebrate the virtue of exemplary dogs offer a good example of what we are talking about. These narratives nearly always portray dogs fondly attached to their masters to the point of refusing to abandon them, even after death. The food pact for the dog is not a simple *do ut des* without memory but a chain of grateful recognition that endures even when the master can no longer, because of death or absence, feed it: the reaction of old Argus on Ithaca—the literary champion of canine recognition—shows this, as do the many stories of devoted dogs preferring to die of starvation rather than take food from a stranger's hand and thus be tempted to change allegiance.[6] There are even stories of dogs committing suicide in order to die beside their masters or howling in grief at their masters' tombs until they die.[7] We saw before in this regard as well how dogs played an important role in the complex of postmortem survival strategies codified in funeral ritual: the dog participated in this work to perpetuate symbolically the identity of the deceased, being an element that with its capacity for recognition constituted an integral part of its master's personality, a significant attribute for the persistence of his identity.[8]

Now, this capacity for extreme devotion, capable of effecting a solidarity unto death, composed part of the ideological baggage of womanly *sōphrosynē* as well. We could cite the figure of Alcestis, who agreed to die for her husband and gained immortal glory not only for herself but for all wives to come: in other words, the paradigm of the perfect bride.[9] But the sources direct us toward another exemplary woman: Evadne, the wife who killed herself by leaping onto her husband Capaneus's funeral pyre, unable to endure the thought of outliving him. In his treatise on animals, Aelian mentions this heroine right at the start of the paragraph devoted to the extraordinary love (*philostorgia*) that dogs can demonstrate for their masters: "Poets pay homage to the daughter of Iphis, [Evadne,] and the theaters pack with spectators applauding this heroine, who surpassed all other women in *sōphrosynē* when she valued her husband more than her own life, yet animals too have not failed to prove an extraordinary capacity for love."[10] The examples of canine love follow this opening. The term Aelian uses for Evadne's paradigmatic love for her husband and of dogs for man is *philostorgia,* which generally denotes love of family members and parental affection. Evadne, the heroine of feminine *sōphrosynē,* of "wisdom" composed of altruistic self-sacrifice, voluntary and loving subordination, is thus a model for the ideal dog.

This instance of analogy between feminine and canine devotion is not isolated. According to one version of the story of Icarius—the Athenian farmer encountered in the previous chapter—his daughter Erigone, having learned of the miserable end of her murdered father, decided to follow him into death and hanged herself, and his she-dog, Maira, preferred to end her days also and committed suicide beside her master's dead body. The ideal daughter and she-dog do not survive their father and master but immolate themselves on his corpse, closing the circle of family solidarity: both Erigone and Maira are carried up to the heavens—as the constellation Virgo and the star Prokyōn, respectively—and continue for cosmic eternity as the satellites of their greater star, their father and master Icarius, himself transformed into the constellation Boōtēs. In this case, a daughter's devoted love is paralleled with a dog's, but once again it is the love of a family member, and a female one, for the man who is her guardian and has virtually absolute power over her.

In essence, a dog could apparently raise its master's expectations for an attachment rather greater than what was expected of a slave or a servant. Aelian, a sharp observer of human-animal relations and a praiseworthy annotator of cultural traditions that pass down ancient models, here transmits a precious piece of information: no human servant ever passed into history or the glories of myth for voluntarily dying with his or her master, something that can, however, be said of many a dog.[11] So although conceivable in terms of a servant or a slave, a dog was nevertheless something different: it was viewed as a subordinate of the philos sort, expected to prove affectionate and deemed capable of extreme acts of love for its master.

Another example of a wife called to play the role of implicit referent for the model of canine devotion comes in an episode of the *Life of Aesop*, a collection of mythic anecdotes about the wise fabulist that comes down to us in a rather late redaction, though its contents probably go back to a much earlier period.[12] One day, Aesop, who at that time was the servant to a certain Xanthus, accompanied his master to a dinner with friends. During the meal, Xanthus passed him some tasty morsels and told him to take them home: "Take these to my darling," he said. Aesop obeyed at once, but his diligence wasn't exactly motivated by good intentions. The clever servant glimpsed a chance to play a nasty joke on his mistress, with whom he had a score to settle. Evidently, Xanthus meant to send the food to his wife and by *my darling* meant his spouse. But when he got to Xanthus's house, Aesop put down the bundle and showed his mistress the helpings, and when the woman asked him if the tidbits were for her, Aesop said no, since his master had sent them for "his darling." "And who," retorted the lady, "might be his darling?" Aesop said, "Wait a second and you'll see." The anecdote concludes, "Spotting a well-bred she-dog raised in the house, he called to it and said, 'Come and get it, Wolfy!' and the dog ran up to him. Aesop fed her, and once the animal had devoured it all, he went back to the dinner and resumed his post at Xanthus's feet."[13]

The importance of this passage for our discussion is fairly obvious. Fundamentally relevant is the implicit parallel between a house dog's affection and a wife's love for her husband, an analogy that Aesop exploits for his ironic prank in the bitch's favor. The anecdote is intriguing as well for the way in which the clever servant takes advantage of the context by playing on the paradigm of "tasty morsels for the dog": we saw before how masters, when dining away from home, used to save pieces of food to take home to their dogs, and dogs enjoyed this privilege in virtue of their ability to show love for the master.[14]

Can we assume that such an intersection between the models of exemplary dog and ideal wife or daughter was already active in the classical period or, to judge from the age of the sources mentioned so far, should we think this is a more recent development in Greek cultural history that appeared only in the Hellenistic age? On closer look, at least one source attests that the idea of a dog-woman might have served as a positive model already in the fifth century B.C.E., and it specifically regards the role of wife. In Aeschylus's *Agamemnon*, Clytemnestra sends a messenger out to greet her husband on his return from Troy, who relays to Agamemnon his wife's words of joy. Among the various coaxing expressions of affection that Clytemnestra's ambiguous rhetoric manages to devise are some that present her to her husband as a faithful house *kyōn:*

> And on your return you'll find your faithful wife
> just as you left her, dog of the house
> devoted to you, foe to those you wish ill.[15]

Clearly, Clytemnestra—actually behaving as a real "bitch" to her husband, as the audience knows—could not have maintained her ruse with the image of the "dog of the house" if the cultural paradigm of guard dog were not available for positive portrayals of the faithful wife. And in fact, Agamemnon doesn't detect any ambiguity in his wife's words but instead, a few lines later—naïvely picking up on the image suggested by Clytemnestra—calls her "guardian of my house."[16]

In any case, that a house dog might be a positive metaphor for a wife is obvious enough if one considers that a good spouse was required to be an attentive and trusty guardian of the marriage home and a protector of her husband's goods. The entire semantic sphere of *oikouria* (safeguarding the house) was reserved for the guard dog and the wife,[17] both elements expected to act inside the domestic sphere, to represent the steady permanence and enclosed integrity of the *oikos,* their movement constrained to a circumscribed space: their task was to stay and preserve, their living quarters defined by the limits of the house's walls.[18]

So, apparently, there was no lack of positive intersections between the figures of dog and woman, and they all played out on the field of *philia,* of family attachments and solidarity. But why then, in all the evidence of symbolic connections between dogs and women, do the negative elaborations largely predominate? Or we might also ask: why, whether of women or of dogs, do the Greeks tend exclusively to speak ill?

To answer this question, let's begin with a general principle from sociology: people tend to speak about subordinates only when they disappoint expectations. In ancient Greece, women were consigned to silence, and not only because they were not supposed to speak: even more important was that others were not supposed to speak about them. To paraphrase Pericles's infamous words, the greatest fame for a virtuous woman was to not have any fame.[19] The subordinate's virtue consists in doing their duty without fuss. No striking deeds or prestigious victories but moderation and self-control while carrying out their entrusted tasks.[20] If a woman behaves with excellence, that is no reason to speak about it, except maybe at the very end of the story: on her inscribed gravestone. Otherwise, women are spoken of when they do not comply with their duties, when they transgress the norm of obedience, when they delude the system of expectations that masculine culture has constructed. Only then do women emerge from the anonymity in which the veil of modesty envelops them and gain fame—or rather, infamy. With a few exceptions—among them the stories of wives who give their lives for their husbands, such as Alcestis and Evadne; the *Odyssey*, which celebrates womanly glory in Penelope and the good fame of a faithful dog in Argus; and Arrian's praise of the dog Hormē quoted above—it seems that Greek literary sources hide the lives of women and exemplary dogs alike behind a veil of hushed secrecy. If a dog behaves well, it's not talked about: obedience, affection, and unconditional solidarity are the norm, and what is normal holds little interest. It's when it behaves badly that a dog, like a woman, becomes an object of discussion and, in particular, presents a good occasion to belabor anxious speculations on the untrustworthiness of the species.

All of this may seem less strange if one considers, in light of the reconstructed image of the dog that we have tried to outline, how ancient culture constructed an intensely codified representation of this animal. It bears repeating that *kyōn* was not just—besides being a flesh-and-blood animal—a rhetorical figure, a metaphor used to represent certain human behaviors, but moreover a social figure, endowed with its own physiognomy and its own proper role in the human communal order. Thus, it is not so farfetched to think that people tended to build up around the dog's actions and behaviors an ideology comparable on many fronts to the one to which other subordinate figures, such as women, were subject. Yet since the likelihood of ideologically conditioning the race of dogs was—obviously—practically nil, the animal was better poised to become a symbol of subordinates' natural inferiority and tendency to transgress than women were, since the systematic pressure of cultural expectations functioned presumably somewhat better on the latter, producing their normalizing effects through educational processes and the various types of subliminal conditioning that every effective cultural strategy is capable of, not least among them what is achieved through the "politics of reputation."[21]

Most likely, a dog doesn't care much about its reputation. The normative pressures of cultural models are inevitably doomed to failure in the case of a nonhuman animal. Nevertheless, it is verifiably the case that dog behavior was invested with a series of prescriptions and norms both moral and hygienic—that of *aidōs*, for instance, as well as self-control and mental health (*sōphrosynē*)[22]—besides a long list of popular beliefs and superstitions (such as their seducibility, discussed in chapter 4, their uncontrollable bloodlust, their boundless voracity, impulsiveness, and fiery impetuosity, and their ambiguous courage), such that it is no risky venture to compare these with the equally imposing accumulation of codes to which the figure of woman was subject.

The best soil in which to crossbreed these two cultural stereotypes would seem to be none other than the common horizon of expectations of guardian and master, the citizen male founder of the governing ideology. Dogs, like women, must behave well, but behaving well means just one thing: stay in one's "proper" place, act submissively, docilely allow oneself to be guided and commanded, obey, do not dare.[23] The founding justification for this subordination was therefore entrusted to a cultural strategy that made both women and dogs into figures of natural excess, overflowing, intrusive, constitutionally lacking restraint, and for this reason needing corrections and restrictions of every sort.[24]

Both woman and dog were burdened with a heavy system of expectations: both were required to make their behavior live up to the normative ideal that wanted them obedient, affectionate, readily disposed to acknowledge the superiority and authority of their male guardian or master, and bound to him by exclusive and unwavering solidarity. Both were expected to demonstrate in all circumstances their faithful and loving allegiance, just as one's closest relatives should do. But as with all cultural constructions, the one for dogs and the one for women could not be unwavering, and a dog or a woman who behaved badly roused resentment, bringing down on the whole "race"—on their cultural image—the hatred and distrust of men. Thus, the dog could go from perfect companion to hateful mask of doggishness and figure for insults, while the reaction of misogyny could transform woman from irreplaceable companion—guardian of the house and indispensable link in the reproductive chain—into treacherous, destructive presence.

What dogs and women share in the male imagination is the suspicion that neither will behave as expected, as the cultural model wants them to be. Men always fear that at any moment or other, women and dogs might reveal their "true" faces: both bear the doubt that their "true" nature might burst the banks so laboriously erected by cultural strategies and their overwhelming otherness would deluge everything. From indispensable elements, symbiotic and fully embedded in the social order, dogs and women may transform into disturbing intruders, detested inferiors daring to rebel, aspiring to autonomy and power, spontaneously changing allegiance. This anxiety found expression in the various masks of doggishness but especially, as is obvious by this point, in those of female "doggishness" or "bitchiness": at once fearful fantasies and warnings to wariness, engendered by profound doubts about the binding force of the cultural models of the ideal dog and woman.

This may be, in broad strokes, the principal reason that the foundational discourses of Greek misogyny were at the same time discourses about the doggishness of women. We mentioned Pandora and her doggish nature at the beginning, and we'll have more to say about her. For now, let's take the other infamous prototype of dog-woman: Clytemnestra. The unfaithful wife and murderer is invoked in Homer by the shade of her dead husband Agamemnon, who tells Odysseus, who has descended to Hades, the story of his miserable end. Slain by a wife who in his absence transferred her love and devotion to another man, Agamemnon points to Clytemnestra as the archetype of faithless feminine nature and definitive example of the doggishness of women:

> . . . And I struck the earth with my hands
> Dying, pierced with a spear, but that dog-face [*kynōpis*]

Turned away, didn't even have the heart, when I was heading down to Hades,
To shut my eyes with her hands and close my mouth.
Ah! There is nothing more dreadful and more dog [*kynteron*] than a woman
Who holds such thoughts in her mind . . .

. . . What a monster of perfidy
She covers herself in infamy and all women to come
Hereafter, even if one of them might behave herself well.[25]

And this is not enough. To Odysseus's reply, which recalls how many men died in the Trojan War on account of another woman—ruinous Helen, with her equally doggish nature—Agamemnon ups the ante against women:

So you too, don't ever be kind, even if it's your wife.
Don't reveal everything you know,
But say one thing and keep another hidden.
. . .
And I'll tell you another thing, and keep it well in mind:
In secret, not openly, to your native country
Bring your ship, since there is no longer any faith in women.[26]

It is Odysseus, the lucky husband of Penelope, the most faithful wife ever, who is the recipient of this speech on the untrustworthiness of women, one of the most vehement in all of Greek literature. An invective aimed at "dog-faced" Clytemnestra snowballs into a resentful indictment against all of womankind: the queen's behavior has revealed an immutable truth, that—in the words of Da Ponte's Figaro— "trusting a woman is always madness."

Deluded hopes, the failed reflex of an ideal paradigm, generate doubts about the trustworthiness of the species: this seems to be the deep root of the troubled Greek ruminations on the race of women and the species of dogs.[27] A dog's solidarity, like a woman's, is individual: no law of nature makes women and dogs into two races devoted to and fond of men; there is only a cultural construct that wants this to be so. The good disposition they show is uncertain, contingent, dependent on the subjective will to acknowledge time and again their allegiance and obedience to the man who requires it. This is why the two most famous archetypes of Greek misogyny, the Hesiodic myth of Pandora and the Homeric account of Clytemnestra's crime, are discourses on the doggishness of women, on their natural untrustworthiness and, at the very same time, on the dog's natural untrustworthiness.

A DOG'S MISCHIEF

The case of Hesiod's Pandora prompts us to consider another aspect that needs to be added to the list of canine traits prone to representing a disturbing feminine characteristic. We'll therefore turn back now to the myth recounted in the first pages of this journey into how the ancients imagined the dog and doggish women.

When he describes the orders that Zeus gives the other gods to construct the first woman, Hesiod says the almighty father delegated to Hermes the task of endowing Pandora with "a dog's mind and a wily nature [*kyneon te noon kai epiklopon ēthos*]." But a bit further on, when Hermes carries out the command, what he instead puts in Pandora's still lifeless body are "lies, seductive speeches, and a wily nature [*pseudea th' haimylious te logous kai epiklopon ēthos*]."[28] So in the second instance, the wily nature of Zeus's order remains, but the *kyneos noos,* the dog's mind, has been substituted with falsehoods and ambiguous rhetorical skills. Does this mean that Hermes has modified Zeus's plan in the course of his work? The narrative logic suggests that if the substitution were significant, the text would signal this in some way: for example, by stating the consequences of the divine messenger's change of design. Since this does not occur, we should take the two expressions—of Zeus's command and the execution of the order—as equivalent. The poet may have varied the phrase for any number of reasons, but the fact remains that when Hermes's "gift" to Pandora recurs, the *kyneos noos* from the first instance is replaced with "lies and seductive speeches." So, it seems at least permissible to ask whether this tendency toward deception, and deception through seduction, does not perhaps form part of the trousseau of doggishness for this progenitor of womankind.[29]

The question to tackle at this point will at first sound a bit bizarre: why do "seductive speeches" figure in the trousseau of ambiguous canine abilities? Let's take it step by step. First we can verify a connection between dogs and the idea of deception. One example is in the *Odyssey,* where, as already discussed, Melanthius insults Eumaeus with "dog well skilled in tricks [*kyōn olophōia eidōs*]," a pejorative and menacing phrase that ties the insult *dog* to an accusation of dishonest behavior.[30] Especially significant here is that the cunning ascribed to dog-Eumaeus uses the same term that describes the shape-shifting Old Man of the Sea, Proteus, one of the most famous models of metamorphic intelligence; the term *olophōia* also occurs elsewhere in the poem with regard to the sorceress Circe's cunning.[31] This confirms that from the time of Homer, the dog readily fell within the sphere of tricks and ruses. However, the ancient bestiary characterized other animals with extraordinary shrewdness and credited them as inventors of cunning deeds and malicious tricks far more often than they did the dog: the fox, for instance, or even the octopus and the wolf.[32] Why, then, should the dog sometimes be enlisted to represent the trickster? How does the dog's cunning differ from that of other animals?

As we know by now, the dog was considered quite close to both wolves and foxes, to the point that some dog breeds were considered the result of crosses with these species. But the dog, while possessing as latent potentials the same talents as these two wild animals, acts in an entirely different environment from them, and its cunning lends itself to different sorts of exhibitions and a different valuation by humans. A certain sort of cunning can be attributed only to dogs, which also might in some sense correspond to the "seducing speeches" that Hesiod gives Pandora as one of her characteristically doggish traits. This is the capacity to *sainein,* the verb indicating the typical canine way of displaying restlessness that consists in wagging its tail and ears and jumping up and down around a person—that distinctive canine behavior that is called "fawning."[33]

The Greeks interpreted this behavior as a form of intentional communication by the animal, and in fact, despite all the caveats by ethologists about the groundlessness of traditional interpretations, it's not easy even for us to banish the idea that the frenetic tail wagging, the yelps, and the leaps are actually cheerful signs of recognition, enthusiastic expressions of friendship that our dog gives us with the specific intention of returning our love and satisfying our need for affection.[34] But the Greeks were much less gullible than we are and did not put so much trust in the dog's uncontrollable effusiveness; on the contrary, they regarded it with a measure of suspicion.

The reasons for this distrust can probably be traced to the fact that sainein, along with barking, was one of the two means dogs could use to provide signals; in other words, it was one of the aptitudes that allowed the animal to be employed as collaborator, and so it is understandable that this gesturing was more important than it tends to be for us modern urbanites, who regard the dog mainly as a companion animal.[35] The notion that dogs could make a distorted use of communication must have been a more widespread concern than we, who don't rely as much on the dog for signaling, are inclined to believe. To give an example, when Xenophon explains how to interpret the signals of hunting dogs intent on the hunt, he thus warns the aspiring hunter: some dogs "cheat" and point out wrong tracks or "try to make the false appear true," or again, only "pretendingly" set off in pursuit.[36] Throughout the paragraph dedicated to dog signaling, Xenophon significantly employs the language of trickery (*apatē*).

Second, since this is the conduct of dogs—the subordinate animal, the creature of inferior status—sainein presumably carries a connotation of subaltern effusiveness, a fawning deference that is both self-effacing and self-serving. Undignified and often self-interested, the gesture of sainein is something the lowly do and for this very reason is a bit suspect.[37] In fact, dogs do not fawn only to signal the presence of someone they know or to show that they've found a hunting trail. They also use the gesture in a typically seductive way: for example, to get food or fond attention. Fawning is how dogs procure the privileges other domestic animals don't get because they don't have this effective instrument for coaxing. A fable of Aesop mentioned in chapter 2 is quite eloquent with regard to the dietary luxuries that dogs enjoy compared to the other animals: the donkey, jealous of the attention the master gives his little dog, decides one fine day to try to mimic its sainein, but in trying to fawn on its master, it instead clumsily kicks him.[38] The moral of the story? Don't do what doesn't accord with your natural inclinations.

So we see that the question posed a bit timidly at the start of this exploration of canine mischief no longer appears so farfetched. Seduction is not an art unknown to the dog; on the contrary, it is a typical talent. Through the irresistible effusiveness of sainein, a dog tries to charm its master and secure privileged treatment from him. But fawning is also a potent and dangerous weapon: it's an instrument of flattery that, while conveying its user's submission and devotion, can be used to disguise a self-interested motive or even hostility ready to strike a treacherous blow. In this case as well, as we will see, it is a highly codified aspect of the dog's cultural image, one that provided material for a number of anxious reflections: fawning might reveal illusory and deceptive signals, collapse the ideal construction that codifies it as a sign of a dog's affectionate recognition, and give rise to yet another mask of doggishness, one engendered by the suspicion that the true meaning of canine sainein does not in fact always correspond to what the cultural norm assigns it. We will therefore see how the Greeks took up sainein as a way to reflect on the perils of dissembling and, in particular, what types of dissimulation came to be associated with the image of the fawning dog.

At the end of *Pythian* 2, an ode dedicated to Hiero, the tyrant of Syracuse, Pindar encodes his message in a complex symbolic texture composed of animal images. The message the poet wants to transmit, the *gnōmē* conveyed in a complex of animalistic metaphors, is an invitation to wisdom, the Delphic precept of "Know thyself," the virtue of coherence that consists in acting in accord with one's abilities, in accord with that harmony of natural qualities and acquired knowledge that makes a man into a model of moderation and balance.[39] The series of animal figures serve to illustrate the various outcomes, positive and negative, of behaviors that comport or fail to comport with this precept. Appearing in order are, first, the monkey, offered as emblematic of merely external and superficial learning that leads to vain exhibitions of skills for their own sake, and then the fox, symbol of the slanderer, one who intentionally deceives for personal gain: this is an example of concealed action, which the poet contrasts with "staying on the surface," like the cork on a fishing net, that is, acting frank and in the open, with loyalty. But at this point, the theme of contrasts between cloaked, deceptive action and action that is open, direct, and remote from hateful ruses shifts to another animal image and metaphorical opposition:

> It is impossible that a strong word be cast against the nobles
> By a cheating townsman, yet he fawns [*sainōn*] on all, weaving ruin.
> With the rashly bold [*thraseos*] I have no share.[40]

The slandering fox of the preceding strophe thus gives way to the image of a fawning dog, indicated by the choice of the participle *sainōn*. It is perhaps no accident that this occurs at the moment when Pindar moves from speaking of slander, represented by the fox, to that which paves the slanderer's way: flattery.

Pindar alludes here to the behavior of a man who flatters all his fellow citizens with the adulation of sainein in order to inflict treacherous harm on those against whom he nurses secret hostility. Being the typical way a dog shows that it distinguishes familiar from stranger, as well as a potent means to monopolize its master's attentions and benefits, sainein also lends itself to a distorted use: to fawn "on everyone" instead of just on one's master and familiars is to blur boundaries and seek benefits from all by flattering with claims of solidarity that can't be backed up by true commitment. The dog's prized capacity to distinguish between *philoi* (friends) and *echthroi* (enemies) and to signal clearly this distinction can transform, if the dog decides to fawn for personal gain, into an insidious weapon of deceit. This is a dog's typical deceit, and it forms part of its *thrasos,* "rash boldness," which the text promptly recalls.

The dog's cunning, therefore, is an inside job. Wild animals excluded from the human community, such as the fox or the wolf—certainly no less sneaky than the dog—could never, despite their cunning, perform this act of betrayal: the tactic of flattery, for which the dog is, in fact, the symbol in most ancient sources, relies on a grant of trust that strangers cannot receive. But since it is included in human society, a dog can exploit its effective power of seduction in sainein to prepare the field and strike unexpected: it is trusted as philos and then "bites" in betrayal.[41] For confirmation of this it suffices to continue on in Pindar, where the metaphor of a fawning dog is followed by another animal metaphor:

> With the rashly bold [*thraseos*] I have no share. A friend to friends,
> But on foes as a foe I'll pounce like a wolf,
> Ranging here and there on crooked pathways.[42]

Against the flatterer's reasoning, Pindar sets his own moral code, that of confrontation: the reckless dog's plots are answered by the savage wolf's assaults. But how are we meant to construe this opposition? After all, the wolf also, as the text makes explicit, adopts a technique of trickery, "ranging here and there on crooked pathways," confounding his tracks. The difference lies in the fact that the wolf doesn't wag its tail, doesn't want to make anyone believe it's a friend; it deceives, but not with the particular form of deceit that confounds the distinction between friend and enemy, familiar and stranger. The wolf is always the enemy, and an open, declared one; its ruses play out in external spaces, in places designated for conflict with foreign foes. The dog's plots are internal, domestic, woven into the social fabric, where solidarity and true friendship, not hostility, is expected.

The wolf's morality is the famous Greek precept "Friend to friends, enemy to enemies," a norm dear to archaic aristocratic ethics that imposed on the nobility the greatest transparency and clarity in determining alliances and enmities, and while this ethic required absolute loyalty to and solidarity with friends, it also sanctioned the use of any means against declared enemies, including "crooked pathways" of trickery and cunning. Considerate and faithful to his philoi, the nobleman knows how instead to be brutal and perfidious against his echthroi.[43] If the wolf does not fawn, it is because it is constitutionally unfamiliar with any logic of bargaining with humankind; it is forever outside the system of alliances, forever an enemy, and for it, trickery is not treachery. The man who trusts a wolf is a fool.[44] The dog that deceives, on the other hand, is a dirty traitor, since its ruse is accomplished through an offer of philia, an immoral falsehood that violates the ethical precept that wants the philoi-echthroi distinction to remain ever sharp and truthfully stated.[45] The dog's deceit lies within the realm of *stasis,* of hateful internal strife, that arises among fellow citizens and within families, people who ought to be allied. The wolf's cunning is instead a praiseworthy tactic of *polemos,* war between foreigners, open conflict between declared enemies.

This model of the wolf as a symbol of coherence and sharply delineated positions—as opposed to the dog's faithless vacillation—reappears in iambics composed by Solon to defend his political actions. In these verses, Solon proudly takes credit for never having changed his allegiances nor muddied the waters with any fickle about-faces.[46] Steadfast and incorruptible—says Solon—I was able to prevent the city from falling into civil war; among the crowd of devious, self-interested agitators that surrounded me, trying to enlist me in their conspiracies, I remained a "wolf," above and in opposition to all: "Protecting myself from every party / I remained a wolf, looking around among many dogs [feminine in Greek]."

We will discuss this passage again a bit later in order to explain—and perhaps one may already start to guess—why Solon contrasts himself as a male "wolf" with the devious, plotting fellow-citizen female "dogs." For now, it's enough to observe that the wolf-dog opposition works once again as a metaphor for the oppositions between declared hostility and devious evildoing, open war and internecine strife, which constituted one of the most important ethical themes in the archaic period.[47]

In later periods, as the aristocratic ethos declined, the wolf lost its value as a positive model and became, like the dog, a negative figure. But significantly, the structural opposition between the two animals was maintained and played out in terms of the contrast between external and internal, between the action of an enemy of all—who is placed above and outside the scale of alliances—and the cloaked, devious action of an enemy infiltrator among allied friends. Let's take an example: when the sage Bias of Priene was asked which animals were the most frightful, he responded, "Among wild animals, the tyrant; among domestic, the flatterer." Plato provides the key to this riddle: the tyrant is the wolf, a brutal but declared enemy. It's fairly evident, then, that its domestic counterpart, the flatterer, is none other than the dog, the enemy disguised as philos, the traitor who strikes from within.[48]

The traditional inclination of dogs toward covert action is also apparent in other circumstances. For instance, the dog was often described with the epithet *laithargos,* an adjective probably connected with the root *lath-,* conveying the idea of a hidden action, of something escaping notice. Its exact derivation and thus its precise meaning are uncertain, and so is its connection with *lēthargos* (with which it tends to be confused), but the passages that define the dog as *laithargos* leave little doubt that the word has to do with traitorous conduct and the animal's ability to feign kindness in order to then strike suddenly.[49] Moreover, a gloss in Hesychius explicitly ties the adjective *lēthargos* to sainein and defines a dog with this quality as one "that fawns and then bites without one expecting it [*lathrāi*]."[50]

The earliest attestations of this typically doggish epithet appear in Hipponax, Sophocles, and Aristophanes. In a fragment—sadly very brief—of Hipponax, we find a laithargos dog that "then gnaws." Perhaps the passage echoed a common proverb that spoke of how dogs often have the bad habit of chewing through their leash to get free. In Aristophanes, on the other hand, the adjective is significantly applied to a "foxy dog" (*kynalōpēx*), a the metaphor that Aristophanes applies to the pimp Philostratus—a particular breed used in hunting that was thought to have derived from crossbreeding a dog and a fox: in other words, a type of dog that in both its genetics and the name that recorded it bore traces of a far-from-reassuring parentage. Lastly, in a fragment of Sophocles, a character addresses a woman, saying, "You fawn [*saineis*] while you bite, and you are a laithargos dog."[51] Knowing how to fawn allows a roguish dog to create a diversion that induces feelings of calm trust in the person watching it and thus permits it to strike unexpectedly, like the creature in Aristophanes that crouches under the table and fidgets in sainein, hoping to snag a meal.[52]

We can thus affirm with some certainty that in the ancient Greek cultural encyclopedia, one of the notions that appeared in the entry for *kyōn* was a specific mode of deception in which sainein played a prominent part: it was a demeanor ascribed to no other animal, least of all to wild beasts. Indeed, unless a powerful deity bewitched them, wolves, lions, and other wild animals did not fawn, since fawning is a manifestation of docile subservience, a declaration of submissive dependability that none of the "sharp-toothed" animals besides the dog is disposed to grant to humans. Goddesses such as Circe, Artemis, and Aphrodite may be able to tame savage carnivores and lead them around like a gentle pack of fawning puppies, but this is just one of the marvelous signs of their boundless power.[53]

A passage in Aeschylus's *Choephori* clarifies the exact nature of this canine behavior. It allows us, among other things, to observe once more how vividly the dog-wolf opposition was imagined in that period, especially with regard to having access (or being responsive) to the tactic of flattery; moreover, it enables us to make advances in deciphering this ambiguous technique of canine cajolery. In the middle of the tragedy, Electra gives voice to what she has suffered as a result of her mother's crime. By killing Electra's father, Clytemnestra has not only deprived her daughter of a loved one but also doomed her to the life of a wretched orphan, taking away the possibility of her becoming a bride to a prince of her rank. Electra's grief at this humiliation and her mother's betrayal is intense, but however painful, she must confront it, without succumbing to a temptation to ignore it or reduce its significance:

> One can try to soothe it [*sainein*], but it will not be beguiled [*outi thelgetai*],
> For like a savage wolf insensitive to flattery [*asantos*]
> Is the rage [*thymos*] that comes from my mother.[54]

The grief-stricken rage that Electra feels toward Clytemnestra is unyielding; her suffering cannot be soothed or beguiled with a fawning wag of the tail. She has no illusory hopes or misplaced trust. Electra's *thymos*—that is, her present emotional state, aroused by her mother's deeds but also by the proud nature she has inherited from Clytemnestra—is a fierce wolf that has nothing to do with the fawning of a dog: it is not sensitive to fawning and thus it cannot be charmed away.[55] Electra can neither forget nor endure her mother's attempts to appease her anger; instead, like a wolf, she reacts with rage to the situation, unresponsive to compromise or mediation. The grief that Clytemnestra has caused her is too violent to be mitigated; she'll never allow it to be appeased by consolatory gestures of any sort, no matter how enticing. Compliance does not suit Electra, just as it does not suit her mother, whose canine behavior only conceals her ferocious, wolflike nature.[56]

As the presence of the verb *thelgein* (charm, bewitch) in the Aeschylus passage clearly indicates, fawning possesses the dangerous and ambiguous power of an incantation.[57] For on one hand, it is a positive signal that can inspire trust and appease anger;[58] on the other hand, it is an illusion, a fiction that sets up painful disappointment and engenders expectations doomed to be frustrated.

The verb appears with this sense in a speech of Electra's earlier in the tragedy. Coming to visit her father's tomb, she finds a lock of hair placed on the grave. Such a sign of mourning could have been left by no one except a close relative of Agamemnon: the idea that the lock belongs to Orestes and that her brother has unexpectedly returned does creep into Electra's mind. But what to do? Give in to or resist the temptation to deceive oneself? Perhaps it would be better not to dare to imagine that Orestes could have come back to Argos, that it was he who laid the lock on their father's grave: "Yet," Electra says, "I am flattered [*sainomai*] by hope."[59] Doing the fawning here is hope itself, *elpis*, which in Hesiod's myth is one of Pandora's ambiguous contributions to humanity. Hope can, in fact, be positive and negative: it can be a force of optimistic foresight, a resource that favors confident action, but it can also turn out to be an empty and blind illusion heralding grievous disillusionments. With its strange, double status, elpis is the only thing that remains inside the jar of evils that Pandora opens. By uncovering the vessel,

Pandora let free to wander the world all the diseases and misfortunes that plague mankind like maleficent, invisible demons. But by closing the lid on elpis, she kept in custody something that—like Pandora herself—is not completely evil but has two faces, one negative and one positive.[60] And it is to exactly this ambiguous entity that Aeschylus attributes the no less ambiguous expressiveness of a fawning dog.

So if, as seen above in other contexts, the Greeks nursed anxieties about the dog's seducibility—since it might be seduced with food offered by a stranger—seemingly no less strong was their suspicion of its seductiveness: able to deceive and bewitch, the dog reveals yet another mask of ambiguity. In this sense, part of Pandora's doggish nature as well is the "lies and seductive speeches" of the dog: the bewitching seduction that sainein can represent. A codified signal of trustworthy benevolence offered in love and devotion, the dog's fawning fell under suspicion of crooked, self-serving uses, and the reassuring image of an effusive creature was substituted by the dog as flatterer and devious trickster.

At this point it needs recalling how one of the most famous dogs of myth used sainein for its own horrible ends. According to Hesiod, the faithful guard dog of Hades, Cerberus, possessed a truly diabolical technique. Diligently stationed at the threshold of the underworld, the dreadful mongrel wagged its tail at all who arrived there, enticing them to enter its master's abode—but then it did not let them out again.[61] A strange guard dog, indeed! Normally, a guard dog does not fawn at just anyone who approaches, inviting strangers to enter; on the contrary, it barks and keeps them at bay. Indeed, the typical defect of an "earthly" guard dog is that it won't let in even those its master wants to welcome. But this fawning guardian has good reason to behave in this reversed way: it's a dog worthy of its master, Hades, "who welcomes all," death that plays host to all and never lets anyone leave.[62] The frightful image of Cerberus is thus construed in Hesiod according to the same sort of reversal that makes Hades into the "generous" hotelier of all mortals; the easy descent of man into the kingdom of the dead is promoted by an inviting, and dreadfully sinister, canine sainein.

A WOMAN'S MISCHIEF

As a manifestation of attachment and an assertion of affection able to induce sentiments of faithful abandon, fawning is as ambiguous and suspect as seduction can be. To complete this line of inquiry into the dog's weapons of seduction, we will now bring Aristotle's zoology in for questioning.

In his description of characteristic tendencies and habitual behaviors that distinguish different animal species, Aristotle defines dogs as "impetuous [thymika], affectionate [philētika], and flattering [thōpeutika]."[63] This definition contains crucial information. The mention of the canine capacity for showing affection, for instance, confirms the centrality of philia among the dynamics at play in human relations with the animal. But most notable is that the tendency toward flattering cajolery is such a marked trait that it even found its way into this ethological definition of the dog. The adjective used for *flattering* derives from the verb *thōpeuein,* etymologically connected to a root denoting amazement. The original meaning of the verb must have been something like "to treat with enthusiasm/admiration," and it is not impossible that it was used to describe the dog's effusive gesturing as it fawns; the meaning "to flatter" would then be a secondary, transferred sense, just as seems to have happened with another verb of uncertain etymology, *aikallein*— perhaps a term in colloquial language for a dog's fawning that then came to designate metaphorically the act of coaxing and cajoling.[64]

If this is the case, then the two semantic spheres of *thōpeuein* and *aikallein* reaffirm the close association between canine behavior and flattery already attested in the uses of *sainein.* And the reason for all this must reside in the fact that canine fawning was burdened with the anxious suspicions noted above. Ancient sources bear clear witness to the coherence and vitality of the metaphor, associating, for example, *thōpeuein* with the low morals of a servile spirit, of someone who does not take direct action but, through cowardice and weakness of position, tries a less open path, avoiding exposure and trying to get what (s)he wants surreptitiously, such as inducing another, more powerful person to concede in exchange for a show of deference, or wearing down the other's resistance through flatteries.[65]

But what does all this have to do with Pandora, the first woman, and her doggish nature? As a matter of fact, if it is true that the dog's fawning lent itself to representing flattery in general, it seemed to have a particular affinity with the art of feminine seduction. An important passage in Aristophanes supports this supposition. In his comedy *Lysistrata,* the women of Athens and Sparta, rebellious and determined to make their men stop fighting and declare a peace, manage at last to achieve their end. The men, deprived of sex, are ready to capitulate; even the chorus of old men, up to that point unyielding in their hostility, start to give in to the myriad enticements that Lysistrata and her companions assault them with. Nearly hoodwinked, the angry old men burst out against evil feminine wiles, shouting, "To hell with you! You are born seductresses [*thōpikai*]!"[66]

And that is the point. The women are *thōpikai* by nature, just like dogs in Aristotle's definition. Dogs and women both possess the art of cajoling, and this aspect of their behavior is not at all reassuring. For their sweet talk may be pleasing, but at the same time it's an insidious weapon for attack: indirect attack that consists in disarming the adversary by inducing a credulous abandon to the force of kisses and caresses. Like a dog that jumps into your arms and fawns, women implement an irresistible lure of affection, but also as with a dog, feminine effusiveness can prove an illusory signal, can conceal mere self-interest and malicious intents and prepare the way for disillusionment and betrayal. Another passage in Aristophanes seems to confirm this parallelism, allowing us to glimpse how the interested—but seductive and pleasant—zeal with which women try to obtain certain concessions from the paterfamilias can easily be compared with the canine gesture. Old Philocleon loves serving as a juryman on trials, most of all because when he comes home from court with the pay, his wife and daughter are abnormally zealous in their attentions. It's a juicy scene that deserves reading in full:

> Oh, then there's one other thing, the most delicious of all, that I almost forgot:
> when I come home with the pay, when I get here,
> everyone greets me tenderly [aspazōntai]—for the money, you understand—and
>   first my daughter
> bathes and anoints my feet and bends down to give me hugs and kisses
> and calls me daddy and fishes with her tongue the money out of my mouth,
> and my little wife makes a lot of sweet talk [hypothōpeusan] and offers me a muffin
> and then comes and sits beside me and insists, "Eat this, and this, and this!"[67]

When the women of the house fawn on him, the master is overjoyed: the disenchanted old man knows well that all these feminine attentions have the money in view, but he enjoys the favorable treatment anyway and even considers it the greatest benefit of jury duty. In Philocleon's humorous description, both of the verbs he uses for the women's attitudes are also used of fawning dogs: aspazesthai (greet tenderly), which does not appear in the lexicon of canine ethology specifically but was used as a synonym of sainein, and the wives "make sweet talk," which is expressed with a compound of thōpeuein.[68]

It seems confirmed, therefore, that one item in Pandora's doggish equipment, as well as that of all the disturbing women in ancient Greek misogynist accounts, was this canine seductiveness: a capacity to engender trust by making the target of their sweet talk feel loved and by disarming in some manner his vigilant control, an ability to show attachment (philia) as well as to feign it. In light of these considerations, then, Helen's doggishness, treated as an emblem of seducibility in chapter 4, should be read from another angle as well: Helen is a "bitch" not just because she betrays by letting a stranger seduce her but also because she herself seduces and is able, with all her "venomous" skill,[69] to lead thousands of young heroes to destruction.

The dog's wily seductiveness—as we've seen—was such a prominent motif as to turn the animal into nothing less than a symbol of delusion: in the Greek imagination, misplaced hope, the bad form of elpis, could assume the physiognomy of a fawning little dog that charms the heart with a ruinous optimism.[70] Is this projection of a canine image onto the feminine entity elpis just a coincidental case? Is it a coincidence as well that elpis is the only thing Pandora leaves in the jar of evils? Or is Pandora herself an ambiguous and insidious hope, a seductive little bitch ready to beguile and deceive the man who welcomes her into his house?

INTIMATE ENEMIES

It is foolish, Father, to lead unwilling hounds to hunt:
The man that's given an unwilling wife marries an enemy.
—PLAUTUS, *STICHUS* 139–40

Canine fawning behavior offered links to feminine behavior not only because it constituted a display of affections, of womanly sweet talk, but also because it was a culturally codified signal of philia. And as a codified sign, sainein was prone to distorted uses. Let us look closer at how this typical dog trick furnished the model for the backstabbing plan of one of myth's most deadly wives: Clytemnestra, the woman who conspired with her lover, Aegisthus, to murder her husband.

In order to eliminate Agamemnon, Clytemnestra resorted to lies rather than open conflict. Like a dog, a woman can't be a wolf or lion, at least not without distorting her nature. Direct confrontation isn't among her prerogatives. The feminine asset par excellence is subterfuge, and woman, like dog, works by stealth.[71] In a subversive plot, her role is not that of warrior but of infiltrator, confounding the adversary by luring him in. So in the two lovers' murderous plot, Clytemnestra's job was to set the trap, since, as Aegisthus says, to deceive is "clearly woman's work." Only she could act without arousing suspicion, as presumed philē to Agamemnon, while Aegisthus, a longtime sworn enemy of the king of Argos, could never have done the same.[72]

Excluded from the heroic ethos of direct conflict, disqualified from the masculine virtue of courage,[73] women engage in warfare which is never that of a declared enemy. Woman, a being deprived of political autonomy, whose social identity coincides with being "the woman of" someone—father or husband—is never a foreign outsider; combat for her is always that of philē against philos, always a domestic dispute, unexpected and traitorous. Exactly as it is with dogs. Therefore, like a dog's courage, the courage of a woman who dares to grapple with a man is configured as thrasos, the cursed boldness of an element that should never be daring but should only practice the virtues of patience and obedience, not self-confident aggression.[74]

The figure of Clytemnestra allows us to verify how this parallel between dog and woman, both being institutionalized philoi of the man-master, made the canine paradigm available to embody the feminine in representations of internal conflict and domestic strife. As is well known, Aeschylus's *Oresteia* reflects exactly this sort of family discord. Indeed, in the kingdom of Argos, those considered philoi, from whom supportive behavior is expected, are instead unexpectedly hostile: Agamemnon is a father who sacrificed his daughter Iphigeneia; Clytemnestra is a murderous wife who slays her children's father; Orestes and Electra are children who plot their mother's death. Clytemnestra's crime, in particular, creates a situation of impasse—murdering her husband forces the male heir to avenge his father's death through matricide, an even more horrendous crime—because it throws into crisis the categorical distinction between loved-familiars (philoi) and hated-foreigners (echthroi), a distinction that doesn't correspond with reality in Argos: those who should be called *philoi* (loved) by their children—such as Clytemnestra—are instead echthroi (hated), but they cannot be treated as echthroi (enemy-outsiders) without a violation of the sacred respect owed to philoi (relatives).[75]

As she schemes her criminal plot, Clytemnestra—whose doggishness the text often explicitly recalls—behaves toward Agamemnon just like a sly dog. She greets her husband with fawning, insisting that she is a "faithful spouse" and "house dog," but does this only to strike better, as soon as credulous abandon has disarmed him. Her trick is doggish because it works through the same type of mechanism that marks the acts of the traitorous dog: by distorting messages of philia. The only one to comprehend the true sense of Clytemnestra's words is Cassandra, the prophetess of Apollo who, with her nose for hints, is able to detect the hidden meaning of what the perfidious queen says. Of his wife's intentions, Cassandra says, Agamemnon has understood nothing:

> He doesn't know what her tongue—of that hateful bitch
> licking and cheerfully perking up her ears like
> some stealthy ruin [*atēs lathraiou*]—will do to work his wretched downfall.[76]

Only a prophetess with the prodigiously skilled nose of a hunting dog[77] could track the invisible scent of the truth to understand what the malicious bitch Clytemnestra has concealed in her cheerful fawning, which should, in dog language, express loving kindness. Clytemnestra's malice is that of a sneaky dog that happily greets its master, making him believe it is friendly, and then strikes out of the blue. It's perhaps no accident that the poet describes the "ruin [*atē*]" that Clytemnestra causes with the adjective *lathraios,* which is probably connected with the epithet *laithargos,* seen above as a typical attribute of the sly dog. Moreover, this image is closely echoed in another passage of Aeschylus, where Atē personified—a divine deception sent to wreak ruin on men—uses sainein like a she-dog plotting a dirty trick against those for whom she's wagging her tail.[78]

Woman, like dog, can thus use her displays of affection to confound the philoi-echthroi distinction and delude with her seductive weapon of wicked elpis, misplaced trust. Nothing illustrates this better than the passage in Aeschylus where Clytemnestra calls herself the "house dog" and orders the herald to take Agamemnon her twisted message of womanly solidarity:

> On your return you'll find your faithful wife
> just as you left her, dog of the house
> devoted to you, foe to those you wish ill.[79]

We've already cited these verses as an example of the positive model of the dog-woman, the wife who protects her husband's property like a good guard dog. But now we can add another important note, that what is expected from a good wife and a good dog are loyalty and constant and unassailable trustworthiness but also the ability and the will to take the husband-master's side completely. Women and dogs don't have friends and enemies of their own but hold—or at least should hold—the same friends and enemies as the man to whom they're bound. This is what Clytemnestra means by calling herself a loyal house dog: kindly to her husband and his friends, hostile to his enemies. Women and dogs don't have an independent place in the political dynamics of allegiances; they are first and foremost philoi of a male master, they belong to him, and he therefore demands that they abide by this exclusive solidarity, sharing entirely in the choices of the man on whom they're dependent.

With regard to the dog, the situation by now should be sufficiently demonstrated; with regard to women, we have the uncommon fortune of possessing an explicit statement in the form of a precept. In a moral treatise dedicated to a young married couple, Plutarch in fact makes the specific claim that "the woman should not make personal friends but should share her husband's."[80] Acting the bad wife, Clytemnestra also acted like a bad *kyōn* by changing allegiance and siding with Aegisthus, her husband's enemy. She transgressed the demand for exclusive and total solidarity that falls equally on women and dogs. And she employed the malicious weapons of canine *sainein*, concealing beneath seductive displays of affection an enmity all the more odious for being hidden, all the more insidious for being unexpected: domestic hostility, betrayal by the "house dog."

BITCH OR "DOG IN THE FEMININE"?

The cases analyzed so far relate to female figures that the Greek imagination assimilated to dogs, and the deeper reasons for this constant association seem much clearer by this point. But now we need to treat another specific phenomenon of the Greek cultural system that presents a further point of intersection between dogs and the feminine. The question that will occupy this study's final pages concerns cases where, with a mirroring motion, the dog is in some fashion assimilated to woman. Let's see what this means.

As noted often enough before, the substantive *kyōn* is a noun with common gender—that is, a noun that can be applied equally to male or female referents. So unlike in, for instance, the Italian usage, which refers to the male dog as *cane* and the female as *cagna*, the one term *kyōn* can designate either a male or a female dog, and any gender distinction is made only by syntactic means: either by adding the article (*ho kyōn*, "the dog [m.]," or *hē kyōn*, "the dog [f.]") or else through gender agreement with an attributive modifier. In other words, the Greek noun functioned something like *dog* in English, which can be used for both female and male animals of the species and needs to be qualified (through a pronoun: *he-dog* vs. *she-dog*) whenever knowing the sex of the animal is relevant.[81] This allows *kyōn* to denote, at different times, either "dog" or "she-dog" and the plural *kynes* to indicate either "dogs" or "she-dogs."

However, when the noun has a generic referent—that is, when *kyōn* points to an exemplar of the species *Canis familiaris* whose sex is unknown or irrelevant—it normally receives attributes in the masculine: when speaking of dogs in general or even a mixed pack of male and female dogs, *kyōn* and *kynes* are treated as masculine nouns. Generally speaking, then, a dog is *kyōn* (m.) and several dogs are *kynes* (m.). Explicit evidence that the unmarked form of *kyōn* was masculine is found in a passage of Aristophanes's *Clouds*. Asked by Socrates to state the names for male animals, Strepsiades mentions, besides *krios* (ram), *tragos* (billy goat), and *tauros* (bull)—all words specifically designating males of the respective species—two names of common gender, *alektryōn* ("rooster" as well as "hen") and *kyōn* ("dog" and "she-dog"). The masculinity of these two nouns is less strict than that of the preceding list, since it is determined neither by semantics (a *kyōn* is not necessarily a male dog) nor by morphology (*kyōn* has no corresponding feminine, as, for example, *lykos*, "wolf," has its opposite *lykaina*, "she-wolf"), yet they are masculine by virtue of the grammatical convention of the generic masculine,[82] the same convention that, despite warnings from proponents of gender-neutral language, would induce an English speaker to say that by pushing a "person," you may make "him" fall down. Consistent with this rule, in Homer *kyōn* is a masculine noun in the majority of cases that denote an animal of the species *Canis familiaris*. But there are exceptions, and it is exactly these that we will linger on, so as to trace, if possible, a definitive ethnographic description of the position the dog occupied in Greek culture.

Let's begin with the *Iliad*. At one point, Menelaus, with his foot propped on the body of a warrior he's just defeated, delivers a bitter tirade against his enemies: death is what the Trojans deserve, since only their blood will pay for the injury they inflicted when they took advantage of Menelaus's welcome to carry off Helen, his lawful wife. Menelaus ruthlessly insults the Trojans, and as we've seen so often before, the slur that comes out of his mouth to belittle the enemy is none other than *Dogs!* Yet he says not "Wicked [m.] *kynes!*," as we might expect, but "Wicked [f.] *kynes!*"[83] Why so? In this case, the sex of the *comparatum* isn't determining the choice of gender, since the enemies he targets are Paris and his comrades. Are we to think that Menelaus uses the feminine to imply that the Trojans' behavior is like that of bad bitches—that is, female dogs? But in what sense should a she-dog be more suited than a dog to assume the role of immoral creature, thief, violator of the laws of hospitality, intemperate, reckless, and responsible for the long list of villainy that Menelaus heaps on his enemies by insulting them? From what we've seen so far, except for the image of the she-dog protecting her puppies, none of the images of doggishness that can be traced back to the pejorative uses of *kyōn* and its derivatives or any other of the various doggish figures has to do with the she-dog but always just with the dog, the animal understood in a generic sense and sexually indeterminate. So there is no reason to suppose that the rule has changed for this case.

A few other examples confirm that a change to the general rule is not the way to go. In several Homeric passages that enlist the dog in the role of corpse-eating scavenger, the text again marks *kynes* as feminine. Hector wants to drag off Patroclus's corpse to feed it to "Trojan *kynes* [f.]," Menelaus exhorts his comrades to make sure that Patroclus doesn't become a plaything for "Trojan *kynes* [f.]," Zeus prevents Patroclus from becoming prey "for Trojan *kynes* [f.]," Iris urges Achilles to prevent his friend's body from going "to Trojan *kynes* [f.]," and finally, Priam inquires whether his son Hector's body is still whole or whether Achilles has already fed him "to his *kynes* [f.]."[84] Why should Homer here speak of she-dogs instead of dogs? In the realm of scavenging, it's doubtful that male and female dogs would manifest different behavior, or that the she-dog would thereby become more representative of dogs in general.

The problem is not easy to resolve, so it will be best to proceed by careful approximations. One way to explain this phenomenon would be to take into account the strongly illocutionary dimension of these passages. By calling the Trojans "wicked [f.] *kynes*," Menelaus is not only offending his enemies by calling them *Dogs!* and so degrading them to the lowest level of material and moral misery, nor only threatening that they'll get what a bad dog deserves; he is also calling them *Females!* and degrading them into inferior beings on the level of gender oppositions.[85]

In analogous fashion, the play on the male-female opposition would have a biting supplementary symbolic effect in the images of necrophagy as well. The image of a corpse thrown to dogs once again terrorizes with its reversal of the principles of canine subordination: it overturns the hierarchy of the dining table and the debt for nourishment. When the gender opposition is added to these inversions, the image becomes even more disturbing: not only will the hero end up as dog food—scraps from a human table—but he'll be eaten by a female animal as well; a masculine hero, whose glory depends entirely on a beautiful death on the battlefield and on funeral honors, instead ends his days ingloriously in the jaws of a "devouress" of leftovers. A similar effect of exaggerated monstrosity, achieved through the double inversion implied by ending up as food for dogs and as food for females, seems to be the aim in some versions of the Actaeon myth. Euripides, for instance, speaks of the mythic hunter as being the victim of "raw-eating [f.] puppies that he had raised himself," a formulation that turns hunting dogs into man-eating female dogs, lethal little feminine beasts.[86] Callimachus, as well, was perhaps similarly exploiting a gender opposition when he wrote that Actaeon became a meal for "his own [f.] *kynes.*"[87]

In other words, to call someone "a [f.] *kyōn*" or threaten them with becoming a meal "for the [f.] *kynes*"—or even worse, "for their own [f.] *kynes*"—is more terrible, offensive, and horrifying than to call one simply *Kyon!* or envisage one becoming "food for *kynes.*" But even in this case, it would seem that the aim is attained not by evoking a different *comparandum*—"she-dog" instead of "dog"—but rather through a feminization of the animal dog, an option that the indeterminate nature of *kyōn* makes possible; being undetermined, it allows one to use freely the grammatical markers of gender categories (masculine, feminine) in order to exploit the symbolic opportunities that the cultural opposition of male-female creates. There are, in fact, reasons to believe that this phenomenon of the feminization of the dog was fairly common in Greece and that it was one of the manifestations of the radical contiguity that engendered the many intersections between the two categories of woman and dog in the ancient imagination.

This explanation of the feminized dog in Homer warrants expanding into a more general framework, where we will see the male-female opposition exploited via the figure of the dog in a much wider anthropological context. This phenomenon is found not just in offensive or threatening illocutionary expressions or poetic images of monstrous hunting but in other, much more neutral contexts as well.

Xenophon offers the most conspicuous evidence in this regard. Despite the aforementioned rule whereby *kyōn* is treated as masculine when referring to dogs in general, throughout his treatise on hunting, Xenophon treats not only *kyōn* but also the term *skylax* (puppy) as feminine. He speaks of dogs and puppies, whether male or female and whatever the breed, as "the [f.] dogs [*hai kynes*]" and "the [f.] puppies [*hai skylakes*]." This does not involve only hunting dogs; for Xenophon, guard dogs are also *hai kynes.*[88] Apparently, then, there were cases when *kyōn* was used as a generic feminine. In light of this discovery, it appears even more likely that in the Homeric passages discussed above, "the [f.] *kynes*" are simply dogs— that is, members of the species *Canis familiaris* specified grammatically in the feminine, as if we were to refer to an unknown dog with feminine pronouns by default: "Look at the stray dog over there: isn't she skinny?" (not knowing whether the animal is male or female).[89]

We find other examples where *kyōn* is treated as feminine without there being any good reason to think the animal is meant as specifically female. In the Isocrates passage mentioned in chapter 2, the man who does services for bad people is doomed to suffer the same fate as those who feed "other men's dogs [*tas allotrias kynas* (f.)]."[90] A proverb used to illustrate the tenacity of vices and habits says, "*Hē kyōn* that has learned to chew on leather does not forget the art," which means that the dog that has learned to gnaw its leash to get free never loses this bad habit.[91]

The adage refers to a well-known habit of the entire canine species, and it's hard to see why the ancient saying should refer to she-dogs specifically rather than to dogs in general. Another proverbial saying raises the same doubt. To illustrate the situation of people always imagining in dreams what they most desire, the Greeks had a saying to the effect of "in dreams, *pāsa kyōn* always sees bread." This refers to a dog's inclination for bread, the human food par excellence: why then should the *kyōn* of the proverb be a she-dog and not just any dog? Another expression with a proverbial ring was used to describe a particularly bad woman, saying she is "so mean that *hē kyōn* refuses to take bread from her hand."[92] In this case, as well, it is hard to explain why the dog in question should be a she-dog.

From the available examples, we have notably selected ones with a proverbial character because these seem to attest more clearly than others that *hē kyōn* might have denoted dogs in general, thus allowing us perhaps to formulate a hypothesis on the original context for this phenomenon. The popular and gnomic character of these expressions suggests that despite the grammatical norm that would designate the generic dog in the masculine, in actual usage the Greek language tended to adopt the principle of contiguity between dogs and women whose prevalence in the poetic imagination we have established: that, in a word, folklore perceived the dog as such a feminine animal as to deserve being referred to as *hē kyōn*.

In fact, when the distribution of occurrences of *kyōn* in the feminine is considered, a pair of constants strikes the eye. The first is that dogs of the Laconian breed are always treated as feminine, something that might be thought of as a dialectical feature: perhaps at Sparta, dogs were called *hai kynes,* and it may be that, as opposed to Attic-Ionic, the Doric dialect used the feminine as the unmarked form of the substantive *kyōn*.[93] It is also possible that the use of the feminine reflected the actual prevalence of female dogs in hunting packs, since Aristotle notes that females were preferred to males for being more obedient and responsive.[94] The second constant is that non-Doric Greek tends instead to treat as feminine the house dog, that model of domestic guardian that we have so often seen overlapping with woman as the safeguard of family property and that is frequently evoked in the *sermo humilis* of comedy, scenes from everyday life, and proverbs.

Thus, besides those mentioned already, we can cite other proverbial expressions in which *kyōn* in the feminine certainly refers not to a she-dog but generically to house dogs. In a comic fragment, for instance, a character gives a tip to someone who wants to know the mood of a friend he is visiting: observe his dog's behavior—if she fawns at your approach, then that means her master is in good spirits, too. In another fragment, a character contrasts the Greek way of treating dogs with the Egyptian: "You venerate the [f.] dog," the Greek says to the Egyptian. "I beat her when I catch her filching my sauce." A proverb ridiculing a useless deed describes it as "flaying a flayed [f.] dog."[95] Another idiomatic expression, proverbially used to warn people against barking up the wrong tree, says that "dogs [f.] get angry at the stones with which they are pelted but stay away from the one who throws them."[96] In all these cases, the feminine *kyōn* and (plural) *kynes* seem to mean not female animals but rather generic dogs.

On the other hand, the passages in Aristophanes deserve their own treatment. In *Lysistrata,* the chorus of old men, staunchly opposed to the feminine insurrection spearheaded by the comedy's pugnacious female protagonist, carry wood up to the Acropolis, where the women have barricaded themselves, to stoke the bonfire meant to smoke them out. But the fire's acrid smoke nearly blinds the old men, who describe the smoke—referred to by the masculine noun *kapnos,* it should be noted—as "a [f.] rabid *kyōn*" biting their eyes. In this case, the gender of the *comparatum* does not require the feminine, so why does *kapnos* (m.) become *hē kyōn* (f.) in the chorus's metaphor? Likewise, at another point in the comedy, the typical warning *Cave canem* appears, as "Beware the *kyōn* [f.]!"[97] Considering the theme of the work—this is one of Aristophanes's "female" comedies, whose plots play on the social dynamics between the sexes—the question to ask here is probably this: why does Aristophanes, who elsewhere observes the rule of a generic masculine for *kyōn,* treat the noun as feminine so many times in *Lysistrata*?

Another passage in the comedy suggests one answer. When the old men threaten blows to the jaw to shut them up, the chorus of rebel women respond in defiance, "Well, do it! But watch out—no other *kyōn* [f.] will ever get you by the balls again!"[98] The chorus leader also expresses herself in this way, angry—and rightly so—at the chorus's just having been treated "like dogs." Indeed, to be precise, the old men had said they were going to give them what the dog-woman in Semonides gets, a good rap on the "muzzle" for her petulant chatter: a talkative bother, the dog-woman is the type of woman who won't stop ranting, even if you break her teeth.[99] Well, in *Lysistrata,* the women "dogs" not only will not be quiet; they also, as the chorus leader's joke lets on, are ready to go from verbal (metaphorical) "biting"[100] to biting in fact. One suspects, then, that the play's emphatic use of *kyōn* in the feminine was Aristophanes's way to turn the dog into a double for his subversive heroines, genuine antitypes of submissive and modest *sōphrosynē,* that ideal of womanly wisdom.[101] But perhaps to this (subtly malicious) end, Aristophanes exploited the possibility, suggested by common usage, of thinking—and speaking—of *kyōn* as feminine, allusively pointing out to his listeners the "true" meaning of this femininity: the doggishness of woman. Rather than saying explicitly that women are bitches, Aristophanes uses an indirect method to leave the impression that the dog—this bothersome, aggressive, noisy, obnoxiously reckless, and lowest-class creature—is a female animal.

But if specific dramatic reasons might have motivated the feminization of *kyōn* in *Lysistrata,* there are other places in Aristophanes's works where the same phenomenon doesn't seem explicable except as evidence of common usage. In the *Acharnians,* for example, the chorus wishes this ill on someone: that he will long for a fine cuttlefish, well cooked and set on the table, and just as he is going to take it, a (female) *kyōn* will pilfer it.[102] Here again, an unidentified dog is feminine, and moreover, there is no female character in the plot determining the word's gender. Even more significant is a passage in *Wealth*, where the god Hermes orders the servant Karion to call his master's whole family out of the house and lists, in order, "the master, his wife, children, servants, the dog [f.], you yourself, and the pig [f.]."[103] It's quite clear that poor Karion, though a lowly servant, must take some offense at hearing Hermes list him alongside the bitch (*hē kyōn*) and the sow (*hē hys*), not only because he's placed between two animals but because it's two female animals to boot. But are a bitch and a sow really meant, or do *hē kyōn* and *hē hys* indicate a generic house dog and house pig? Have these animals, being domesticated and metonymically perceived as the lowest and least valued among the humans of the *oikos,* come to be treated—not without some malicious irony—as feminine?[104]

GRAMMATICAL GENDER AND CULTURAL POLARITIES

Apparently, in Greek the dog as species was sometimes designated with the feminine (*hē kyōn*). Based on the last-mentioned Aristophanes example, one suspects that the same thing happened with the pig, which Hermes calls *hē hys*. A possible explanation for this phenomenon can be proposed here, one that draws on a principle developed in linguistics.

According to a hypothesis advanced by Romano Lazzeroni, the distribution of names into opposing categories of masculine and feminine in Indo-European languages may not be entirely arbitrary but instead may follow, at least in certain cases, a criterion that can be defined as "the principle of polarization." To take a concrete example, objects in the world that a culture perceives and categorizes as dichotomous pairs—such as sun and moon, earth and sky—will not be distributed into grammatical gender classes at random; if a given language identifies the word for the sun as masculine, its opposite, the moon, would thus tend to be assigned a feminine name, and vice versa. In other words, a language will tend to adapt grammatical categories of gender to the structural oppositions that exist in the cultural system, and the grammatical oppositions of masculine-feminine would therefore constitute in such cases "linguistic metaphors of polarization."[105] Obviously, this doesn't mean that the grammatical gender of every noun is similarly motivated, but rather, only the gender of certain nouns—in particular, of those denoting objects or entities susceptible to forming strong relationships of structural opposition with another element in the cultural encyclopedia.[106]

In ancient Greek, a quite similar phenomenon, whereby a noun's gender is (re)oriented under the influence of a consistent cultural polarity, can be verified in certain animal names. For instance, the noun *hys* just mentioned could denote a wild pig (*hys agrios*)—that is, a boar—or a domestic pig (simply *hys*). But while *hys* is normally masculine when it refers to a wild boar, *hys* for a domestic pig displays a tendency to be treated as feminine.[107] In the last Aristophanes passage cited, it is certainly possible that by using the feminine, Hermes means to speak of a she-dog and a sow, specifically female animals, but at least one other clear example makes this explanation far less definite. In a collection of bizarre and marvelous facts that was once attributed to Aristotle but dates (like much of this sort of paradoxography) to the Hellenistic period, the author at one point recounts how in the region of Thrace inhabited by the Maedians and Sintians, there is a place where a strange type of barley grows. Only humans eat it. Horses and cattle reject it, and even more surprising, "none [*oudemia* (f.)] of the pigs and dogs" will dare to eat even the excrement of people who have ingested bread made from this barley.[108] Is it possible that the author, intending to talk about the diet of different animal species in this strange place, is referring here to specifically female dogs and pigs and not to dogs and pigs in general, as seems more coherent with the previous mention of horses and cattle? Furthermore, the same thing is found in Aelian's treatise: *kyōn* is sometimes treated as feminine, and *hys* tends to be feminine when it refers to a domestic pig, while a boar is a *hys* in the masculine.[109]

Two hypotheses, not necessarily mutually exclusive, can be formulated to account for these facts. The first is that swine may have tended to be treated as feminine because farms kept many sows but only a few boars; therefore, overall, a pigsty was a stable more for sows than boars. But this does not exclude the possibility that in contrast to the wild pig—the boar so often taken, from Homer, on as a paradigm of manly courage, untamable ferocity in battle, and an independent animal and external rival—domesticated swine tended to be placed at the opposite pole and thus to slide into the realm of the grammatical feminine: sedentary, with parasitic dietary habits, an uncompetitive animal, the pig would come to oppose the boar as female to male.[110] A wisecrack in Aristophanes may involve this dynamic. The passage is also in *Lysistrata,* a comedy in which the women assert their right to act politically, to exercise the manly virtues of courage and the capacity to deliberate—and where the poet often makes the proud words of his "heroines" recoil back against them. To the umpteenth threatening provocation from the chorus of old men, the women fire back another threat: "If you provoke me, by the two goddesses, I'll unleash the [f.] *hys* that I have in me [*tēn emautēs hyn*]!" which is to say, "I will let loose my anger against you." The metaphoric animal in the usual proverbial phrase was the dog ("I'll unleash the dog in me!"), and the substitute swine here was certainly meant, in the women's minds, to refer to a boar, a savage and hostile beast that—no less than a fierce dog—provided a good model for exemplary portrayals of irrepressible rage. One might think, then, that the chorus of women wanted to use the image of an enraged boar but, forced to put *hys* in the feminine to make its gender agree with the sex of the *comparandum,* ended up inadvertently describing itself more as a domestic pig than a female wild boar.[111] Moreover, the term *hys* was used as a metaphor for the female sex organ.[112] But a translator is forced to neglect this idiom and choose between *she-boar* and *sow*, because English distinguishes boar from pig and pig from sow (a female pig) with different specific names, with the result that, if our hypothesis is correct, Aristophanes's subtle joke—a play on words with a misogynist dig ("I'll unleash the pig/vagina that I have in me!")—gets irremediably lost and the embarrassing slip by the chorus of women loses its comic point.[113]

Now, inquiring whether the same thing may apply to the dog, we need to identify the other member in the dichotomy, the animal to which the dog was opposed like female to male. It seems obvious enough that this should be the wolf. The perceived contiguity between the two animals in Greek culture has already been amply explored; we have seen how, with regard to the relationship with food, the debt of raising, and fawning, the typical behaviors of the dog were contrasted with those of its wild cousin, making of it a sort of urbanized and degraded wolf: a domesticated, parasitic subordinate to man, a miserable, subhuman creature that waits for leftovers and tries to win others over with womanly cajolery instead of fighting man in an open rivalry of equals, the dog is well suited to be configured, in contrast to its "brother" of manly virtue, as a being with a feminine nature.[114]

The passage most significant in this regard seems to be the fragment of Solon mentioned above in connection with the dog-wolf opposition on the level of aristocratic virtue. The good citizen, says Solon, refuses to attain his ends by provoking internal strife, confounding distinctions between friends and enemies, and cheating his allies. An honest man never calls his fellow citizens "dear [*philoi*]" only to stab them in the back, shifting alliances for reasons of expedience. Firm and independent, open in hostilities but no less open and loyal in friendships, the man of honor deliberately refuses the dog's tactics, which, as we have shown, constitute the typical, covert and treacherous tactics of a woman. This is what the Athenian poet and statesman says by depicting himself as "a wolf . . . among many *kynes* [f.]." He is a real man and therefore "wolf," independent and frank, among crafty and cunning fellow citizens who practice crooked feminine wiles. These citizens are unworthy of being called men; they're nothing but "wicked *kynes* [f.]," to use Menelaus's words in Homer to insult the Trojan traitors to hospitality. Not bitches, then, not she-dogs, but feminine animals: just as dogs are with respect to the wolf.[115]

In light of this hypothesis, the fact that dogs are charged with a host of defects that women are also reproached with no longer seems like some accidental and superficial convergence. To both dog and woman, for example, are attributed an excessive talkativeness, senseless and annoying, that constitutes a symptom of intrusive and impertinent aggression,[116] but also of an intrusive curiosity; an uncontrollable voraciousness, the habit of getting free meals; and a fiery impulsiveness and unwarranted aggression. In a word, the entire spectrum of feminine *anaideia* and thrasos.[117] No less significant, then, would be the availability of the dog for representing bodily organs that must be held in check, such as the angered *kradiē* (heart) and the famished *gastēr* (stomach), both "feminine" organs; add to this the loose *glōtta* (tongue), which can be silenced by calling it *Dog, dog!* as though it were a *kyōn* to be told, "Sit!" before it does something it shouldn't.[118] In the same fashion, there's the eloquent fact that the dog was chosen to portray the insidious seductions of hope—elpis—another deceivingly feminine entity, not to mention Atē, the demonic force of fatal error sent by the gods to lead men to ruin; Atē ensnares the mind of her victim by feigning friendship, fawning like a perfidious little bitch.[119] All these phenomena may well be so many clues to a polarity active at the structural level of the cultural system and reflected in linguistic usage, in which the dog, once regarded as the domestic and inferior correlative of wild "sharp-toothed" predators, necessarily took on the feminine role.

Let's consider other passages where our hypothesis seems to provide a good key to reading. In the dispute over the superiority of poets or philosophers, for example, poetry's supporters portray philosophy as "a [f.] *kyōn* that barks at her master," that is, an inferior being that should stay in its place but instead dares to howl against its superior: the master, representing poetry, is metaphorically masculine. The poets themselves define philosophers polemically as "*kynes* [f.] barking in vain."[120] The principle we have seen acting beneath the surface in the symbolic construction of so many masks with canine traits, the principle according to which doggishness—the dog in its disappointing aspects, in no way worthy to represent manly virtue—tends to be feminine ("bitchiness"), may therefore be active even on the linguistic level: a bad dog, or the dog when viewed as the domestic, weakling counterpart to the wolf, is *hē kyōn*, a female animal. If such is the case, a proverb like "As the mistress, so *hē kyōn*"—a warning to consider how servants can be just like their superiors—would be an ironic exaggeration of the principle that women and dogs occupy a cozily parallel position in the male imagination, to the point that the Greeks saw woman as a creature with a doggish nature and the dog as an animal with a feminine nature.[121]

This deep intersection perhaps allows us to understand better the meaning of certain religious prohibitions. At a sanctuary of Cronus, for example, an inscription forbade entry to women, dogs, and flies.[122] If one recalls the close contact verified by other means between the cultural representations of dogs and flies, this triple exclusion fully confirms the relevance of some of the associative pathways we have sought to trace in the course of this study. In a sanctuary at Lindos, the sacred space was off-limits to any man who had had recent contact with a woman, a dog, or a donkey (and it would be interesting to explore further the position of the donkey); another inscription denies access to a man returning from contact with a corpse, a new mother, or a dog giving birth: symbolic associations that seem to fit nicely in the complex of our report on the dog's cultural traits and the relationships between this animal figure and woman, which we have sometimes seen play out specifically in the sphere of fertility and birth.[123] Nor does the notice in Pausanias that men and male dogs were kept away from the rites for Demeter that the women of Pellene celebrated invalidate the outlines of our reconstruction;[124] if anything, it confirms another salient trait in the dog's cultural representation, its radical metonymic character: dogs are included in the human community to the point that they even participate in the social dynamics dividing the sexes and in the reciprocal exclusions enforced when masculine or feminine rituals are celebrated.

A good guardian of the house, a dog, as we've seen, can be a good example of womanly devotion. But more often, as the subaltern animal—uncompetitive, parasitic, and prone to deviance—the dog represents femininity as the negative imprint of masculinity, as lack of self-control, ineptitude for ruling and deliberation, an emblem of all the shortcomings that make woman into a being by definition excluded from masculine virtue, a creature barred from *andreia* and destined for odious, intrusive thrasos.[125] We will draw this line of argument to a close by turning one last time to folklore. Chapter 2 mentions that there was a common breed of dog in Greece with a robust build and remarkable courage, the Indian dog. These marvelous beasts were among the few adapted to hunting wild boar and were said to be so proud natured that they would attack only worthy foes, beasts at least as dangerous as lions. Because of this extraordinary characteristic, popular imagination held that the Indian breed of dogs derived from a cross with a tiger. The report is intriguing in itself. But it is further notable for the way that the Greeks, in imagining this fantastic and improbable coupling, made the tigers male, and thus the fathers, and the dogs female, and thus the mothers. This is how Aristotle recounts the event: "They also say that Indian dogs derive from a tiger [m.] and a dog, not all of a sudden but after the third pairing: the first litter born are in fact wild beasts. They carry the dogs [f.] to a deserted place and bind them; many of them are devoured when it happens that the fierce male is not inclined to mate with them."[126]

It is evident, after all that we've observed above, that in Greek mentality, the warrior ardor of Indian dogs could have come only from a fierce father. Thus, the tiger (*hē tigris* [f.]), as the prototype of masculine virtue, becomes *ho tigris* (m.) and takes on the paternal role; so too, in relation to the tiger, the dog cannot but be feminine and—when she doesn't end up being eaten—cannot but transmit to her litter the recessive trait of maternal softness, which is able with difficulty to pass into such a savage genetic makeup only after two generations. Not translating *kynes* as "she-dogs" or "bitches" is an attempt to not lose sight of the eminently cultural matrix of the dog's femininity here: these *kynes* that couple with the tiger (m.), it is well to recall, are not real she-dogs, animals of flesh and blood, but figments of popular fantasy, or better, they are products of the structural oppositions that underlie the Greek elaborations on the femininity of dogs.

Aelian's report is faithful to Aristotle's account but more colorful. After explaining that Indian hunters select female *kynes* of the breed that are good for hunting, then take them to a deserted place and leave them bound in the hope that tigers will pass by in the mood for mating, he goes on:

> When the tigers happen on the *kynes,* if they have not captured any prey and are hungry, they devour them; if instead they arrive in heat and sated with food, they mate with them: even they, when sated, think of love. From this union, they say, a tiger, not a dog pup, is born; from the latter and a female dog would once again come a tiger pup, but one that is born from this last one and a [f.] dog inclines toward the mother; the seed declines in the worse direction, and a dog is born from it.[127]

In short, to make an Indian dog, fierce but subordinate and useful to man, requires three successive degenerations of the masculine tiger seed in the feminine matrix of the dog.[128]

If such was the case, it is apparent that in the *kyneos noos,* the doggish nature of Hesiod's Pandora, we can rightly hear echoes of a deep cultural model. For several reasons that we have sought to clarify, the dog lent itself to playing the female part in imagination, to the point of becoming a sort of totem animal for the race of women and all its various tribes. It symbolized the faithful wife, ward of the house, the spouse who threw herself on her husband's funeral pyre, the devoted daughter ready to follow her father into death—but it also especially evoked various images of bitchiness, of ungrateful goddaughters, adulterous spouses, audacious and reckless women who dared to insinuate themselves into places of power, aspiring to autonomy and dominion, with the duplicitous weapons of a flattering dog.[129] On a linguistic level, this propensity of the culture to portray woman as a negative cast of man, as an excessive nature constitutionally excluded from manly virtue, manifested itself as a feminization of the entire canine species: the dog, as opposed to the wolf and other wild beasts emblematic of masculinity, became *hē kyōn,* the generically feminine dog.

Another portrayal passed down in ancient texts offers a final, evocative trace of this deep intersection between dogs and the feminine gender. According to a familiar legend, the Athenian tragic poet whom a long tradition called an enemy of women—brazen creatures "hateful to Euripides and to all the gods"[130]—died at the hand of those very ladies whom he had so often chastised and mistreated in his dramas. Well, as it happens, a variant of this apocryphal tale has Euripides torn to pieces not by furious women but by dogs.[131] With a substitution that is by this point hardly surprising, in this alternate version of Euripides's biography, the enemy of women winds up being punished by their totem animal. Whichever way this retaliation is portrayed, for the Greeks, the death of the misogynist poet must clearly have been the work of creatures with a bitchy nature.

Conclusion

The account has come full circle, and this foray into the Greek imagination, begun with Pandora, has returned in the end to woman and her "doggish" character—hopefully, with some increased understanding of the problem that initiated this research and, more generally, of the figure of the dog in ancient culture. All that remains is to retrace our path briefly and give a short, comprehensive view of the themes touched upon along the way.

The problem first posed can be summarized as follows: how did the dog, "man's best friend" in our contemporary culture—indeed, known as Fido (Trusty, Faithful)—in ancient Greece instead get implicated in so many elaborations of a negative sort, becoming a symbol for a hateful inclination to transgress and, above all, used to portray the deceitful and untrustworthy nature of woman? The first necessary step for tackling the argument was to review the state of the question and in particular, to discuss the current explanations of the use of the word *kyōn* as a pejorative term (chapter 1). The essential difficulty that these explanations face is this: if one supposes as a general rule that an animal name gets enlisted as a term of abuse when the animal so named is held in contempt, it is not at all clear how the name of the dog, an animal highly prized and active in the daily life of Greeks as a crucial collaborator and companion, could have turned into an insult. Nor is it clear exactly what *kyōn* meant as an insult, when an examination of its uses shows that it assumed quite different meanings at different times.

We have therefore tried to frame the problem by reversing the terms of the question: it's a matter not of asking how *dog* became an insult despite the animal's good reputation and its intimate closeness to man but of understanding whether perhaps *kyōn* afforded insults precisely because of the dog's nearness to the human community. This reversal of perspective came about through, among other things, an analysis of comparative evidence and, above all, the realization that the seemingly paradoxical situation of the Greek dog was in reality a sort of anthropological universal: in very many societies where the dog is considered an intelligent animal, communicative, an effective helper and trusted collaborator, where dogs are allowed to be present in the culture's ordered spaces and even inside human houses, the word *dog* is injurious and recurs in expressions of a derogatory nature.

The first step was to consult ancient sources to corroborate whether and in what specific ways the dog in Greece was considered close to humans. To this end, we have adopted the categories "metonymic"/"metaphorical" and "subject"/"object," proposed by Claude Lévi-Strauss to describe the position of different animal categories in the cultural taxonomy of modern France. We found (see chapter 2) that in ancient representations, from the most archaic periods down to the Roman Empire, dogs seem fully incorporated in society, not only because they participated as table companions in human rituals of eating but also because they came to be perceived as agents responsible for their own actions, capable of discernment and acknowledging their involvement in a collaborative contract with their owners: food in exchange for devotion and obedience. In Greece, therefore, as Lévi-Strauss determined for modern France, the dog was a metonymic animal subject.

Along with this extraordinary participation of dogs in human social life, however, we have also highlighted its gray areas and paradoxical consequences. A rather complex picture emerged, in which the traditional model of dog is also characterized, with respect to an ideal codification, by a series of defects and weaknesses, which sometimes problematize its inclusion in the human community and make it more akin to the wolf: it eats raw and bloody flesh; it attacks strangers, unable to distinguish guest from intruder; it shows a tendency to attacks of blind violence, sudden rampages of bloodthirsty madness (*lyssa*).

After this, it was necessary to look at the ways in which all the symbolic variations on dogs might be traced back to fundamental traits of their cultural physiognomy and, in particular, to determine whether the typically negative character of many portrayals might originate in the strict codification to which the dog was subject. To test this hermeneutic theory, we began with one of the ancient images of the dog most disconcerting for modern readers: Homeric scenes of necrophagy (chapter 3). We were able to establish how the presence of a canine image in threats of outrage to bodies had the precise function of creating a surplus symbolic effect that other corpse-eating beasts, such as vultures or other wild animals, could not generate. Indeed, the idea of a corpse being torn apart by dogs draws into the image of necrophagy a host of supplementary resonances, which play out primarily through reversal: a human corpse becoming food for dogs is a monstrous inversion of the model that makes the dog the lowest fellow diner at man's table or else his appreciative debtor for being fed and raised on human food. Canine necrophagy elicits a further possible inference. In this case, the model is not subject to inversion but is tapped for the transitive property of symbols: if the dog is the animal that eats refuse, then a human corpse fed to dogs is (treated as) garbage.

At the opposite pole stand figures of dogs called on to guard a tomb or accompany their master on his underworld journey: in these cases, the elaboration tends toward hyperbole, and the positive model of the grateful animal companion takes on its most idealized form. With respect to human mortality, the dog could play quite diverse functions, but in all cases, its unique position and specific traditional traits provide the building blocks: combined and recombined, exaggerated or distorted, the elements used by the imagination were always among that range of characteristics—commensality, the capacity for recognition rendered uncertain by the attraction to raw meat, the debt for care received—that made up the animal's cultural representation.

Then, armed with a greater trust in the relevance of our reconstruction of the dog in Greece—and the resulting possibility of following the tracks of the ancients' "canine" imagination—we tackled the problem involving the use of *kyōn* as a term of abuse while inspecting the cluster of doggish figures found in myth and other ancient literary sources (chapter 4). First of all, two fundamental questions needed to be addressed here: Why was the dog suited, more than all other animals, to serve as a marker of degradation? And why was doggishness able to serve as an emblem for a wide range of transgressions—from simple bad manners to blind violence, from slimy deference to treacherous deceit—identified with the term *anaideia*? Once the dog's position in the community had been detailed, answering the first question became fairly simple: if *kyōn* was taken as a marker of the lowest level and became the insult par excellence, this was because in Greek society, the dog was perceived as the last and least among humans. In this way, the inexplicable contradiction whereby the dog is simultaneously a much-prized animal and the source of a disparaging term is resolved, finding its reason in the paradoxical aspect of the dog's metonymic position: as an animal, the dog was quite esteemed, but when perceived as a member of the human community, the *kyōn* was instead typically placed at the lowest rung on the scale of honors.

However, with regard to the conspicuous quantity of transgressions, low morals, and undesirable behaviors to which the figures of doggishness could refer, the task was less simple. Nevertheless, we think we pinpointed the root of this phenomenon in the general principle by which the dog, as a subject included in social dynamics, was to some degree also co-opted into the ethical system. In effect, the dog symbolized a lack of restraint precisely because it was the only animal required to have it: only dogs were expected to stay true to a pact, to show their gratitude, to know how to distinguish friend from stranger and treat one differently from the other—in sum, to have that sense of *aidōs* that consists of knowing how to stay in one's proper place in all circumstances.

The wide gamut of typically canine transgressions thus corresponded to the range of expectations that burdened the culturally codified figure of the ideal dog. A dog was expected to be always gentle and obedient, faithful and friendly, grateful and collaborative, but sometimes, because of occasional inabilities to restrain its instincts and other times, because of structural flaws, a dog could not fully respond to this demand. Disappointment with this failure to adapt lay at the root of a great blossoming of negative stereotypes linked to dogs and to the "dog face": rebel, traitor, blind avenger, bloodthirsty psychopath—these are all figures born of anxiety about an animal in which great trust was placed.

This was also the point where the problematic connection between dogs and the feminine, or better yet, between doggishness and the many negative women figures with canine traits in myth, could finally be untangled (chapter 5). In describing the mask of the dog traitor, we had, in fact, already observed how the productive polysemy of the doggish woman figure was founded on a structural parallelism that made it easy for the male imagination to fuse the two figures of unfaithful wife and disloyal dog. Both woman, whether wife or daughter, and dog were burdened with a strong expectation of faithful solidarity: both were considered subordinate *philoi* and therefore expected to display for their male master an exclusive and steadfast attachment, strong enough to provoke self-sacrifice. For this reason, the good dog could serve as a positive paradigm of the ideal wife. But what proved even more effective was the opposite image, a bad dog used to symbolize feminine untrustworthiness. No doubt playing its part in this as well was the traditionally pejorative charge of the term *kyōn*. As we saw in the case of comedic jokes at the expense of demagogues, any canine image was liable to be easily twisted toward a negative connotation, precisely because it almost inevitably evoked the insult *kyon*.

But this was not the sole reason. Indeed, the dog image more generally provided a good subject for reflecting on feminine alterity and the metonymic position of woman in male society, or, better put, it was a precision instrument for reflecting on women as a race, distinct from male humans yet intrusively situated in the heart of humanity. Like the dog, an "other" creature co-opted into the community of men, woman is a subject in an ambiguous position, relied on, surely, but with the wariness that one instinctively maintains against anyone different. This similarity of position made it easy to assert the natural inferiority of women. Indeed, the dog-woman parallelism served remarkably well for reinforcing the assumption that woman was destined to her subordinate position due to her constitutional inability to control her impulses: feminine nature, being less endowed than masculine nature with rational control, required a guide to direct and contain it, or it would overflow in continual and disastrous excess. In other words, a woman, like a dog, does what she's supposed to only when she diligently follows the will of the man who is her guardian. Thus, one finds a parallel profusion of anecdotes about the lack of restraint and the consequent untrustworthiness that typify both women and dogs. Both are perceived and classified among the philoi of those who expect their cooperation in labor and affectionate gratitude, to be sure, but at the same time, they are dangerous elements—easily seducible by strangers' hands, subtly seductive and self-interested—that, due to their constitutional incapacity to exercise the perfect male human virtues, tend to deceptively evade what is expected from them, and so are kept constantly under control. With women as with dogs, it's always best to stay on guard. For as flighty and morally inconsistent as they are, one can never be sure if they'll agree to stay in their places.

The symbolic overlap between dog and woman turned out to be a perfect training ground for exercising ideological strategies that maintained feminine subordination. Thus, it is no accident that canine attributes formed part of Pandora's disposition: she was the first woman in the history of humanity, whose actions earned eternal scorn for the race of women from male humans. But this is not all. The parallel position of woman and dog offered at least one other opportunity that symbolic thinking could not pass up: exploiting the traditional dog-wolf opposition to represent the feminine-masculine opposition. Morphologically similar to the point of seeming like brothers, dog and wolf tended to be configured as an opposed pair, in which the dog was perceived—correctly, as it seems, even from the perspective of modern science—as a sort of domesticated and urbanized version of the wolf. Dog and wolf were therefore opposed as domestic is to wild, but also as subordinate to autonomous, parasite to predator, servant to competitor—in other words, as inferior to superior. Not surprisingly, this opposition readily lent itself to being declined on the axis of gender opposition, where the dog obviously came to represent feminine nature—weak, fickle, incapable of self-control and autonomy, excluded from the manly morality of open conflict and given instead to devious and treacherous action—as opposed to the strong, straightforward, independent, and steady nature of the hypermasculine wolf, a cunning animal but never a traitor. In this way, the symbolic intersection between two categories, woman and dog, was enriched with a further element and could produce an effect even on the linguistic level: the dog, seen as the negative of its wild, manly brother, was called *hē kyōn,* in the feminine. The circle is complete: if woman has a doggish nature, the dog is equally a "feminine" animal.

Appendix

Reflections on Theory and Method in Studying Animals in the Ancient World

This book is the result of research begun, as it happens, while I was working on something else entirely. I was rereading Hesiod's version of the Pandora myth and wondered what exactly the poet meant when he said that Hermes gave the first woman a "mind of a dog" (*kyneos noos*). Modern commentators, following ancient scholiasts, explained that the adjective *kyneos* (canine) was for the Greeks a synonym for *anaidēs* (without restraint). I began to ask myself why the dog would have seemed to the Greeks to be an animal lacking in moderation and a sense of shame (*aidōs*). It soon became clear that this question required answering a more general one: why did the word *dog* (*kyon*) and certain related compounds serve as rather common terms of insult in Greek already in the Homeric poems, despite a marked contiguity and cooperation between humans and dogs attested in a large number of sources, also including the Homeric poems? Given the importance of this phenomenon, I thought that surely I would find adequate answers in previous scholarship. So I started reading the available works, from the old dissertation of Herbert Scholz (1937) to Ferdinand Orth's article (1913) for the Pauly-Wissowa *Realencyclopädie* and studies by Denison B. Hull (1964), R. H. A. Merlen (1971), Saara Lilja (1976), and Carla Mainoldi (1984).

But these studies either did not address the question or else sought to explain the phenomenon by hypothesizing the presence in prehistoric Greece of semiwild "pariah" dogs, scavengers of carrion and corpses, which would have caused the cultural representation of the animal (even those completely domesticated and collaborative) to be aligned with spheres of impurity, lowness, and loathing.[1] Yet the existence of such dogs remained hypothetical, with no evidence found in the sources. The Homeric passages figuring corpses of heroes fed to dogs are not factual descriptions but imagined situations of hostility, and Homeric diction does not distinguish between domestic dogs and the presumed pariah. Moreover, the dog's alleged impurity did not seem to be sufficiently supported by statements in ancient authors.

With these valuable collections and commentaries on the relevant sources produced by earlier scholars at my disposal, I had plenty of literary and documentary evidence in which to seek more satisfying answers. The task was then to find the right questions to ask. A strong believer in the power of comparison, I began by reflecting on how in other cultures, including my own, the dog is at once the animal most markedly entrenched in human social space and the one that provides the greatest number of insults to our lexicon (along with the pig). So the problem needed to be addressed on a different level. It was no longer a matter of explaining something peculiarly Greek but of understanding a more general cultural mechanism, in order to account for why it is that in the society of the epic poems also, in Hesiod and Plato, Pindar and Aristophanes, the name of the animal most domesticated and situated in the human community was employed as a term of abuse. Instead of conjectures about the existence of a Greek protodog distinct from the domestic dog we all know, what was needed was a detailed investigation of how the animal's salient traits appeared to Greek eyes and in what ways the Greeks conceptualized their relationships with dogs.

Claude Lévi-Strauss's study on the names given to animals in modern France marked a turning point for my research.[2] In "The Individual as Species," he theorized that the names given to animals would fall into a typology that varied according to the position (metonymic/metaphoric, subject/object) that a given species occupied with respect to human society. I tried therefore to verify whether this general scheme could adequately explain the specificity of the Greek dog. Perhaps in Greece, *dog* was an insult precisely because the animal had been co-opted into the human social sphere in a metonymic-subject position. It seemed to me that this might well explain why certain behaviors exhibited no less by other species (the display of sexual acts, incest, coprophagy, necrophagy) were imputed as shameful only to domestic canines.

The importance of a given species-assigned position in determining the basic character of cultural representations elaborated around the animal seemed confirmed, moreover, by independent ethnographic observations showing the relevance of problematic positioning for some species within a cultural taxonomy, of the sort of relation a given species has with humans (competitive, collaborative, symbiotic) and of an animal's behaviors deemed out of place according to social expectations (studies by E. Leach, S. J. Tambiah, and G. Wijeyewardene). Basically, a single ethological tendency might be judged positive or negative not in itself but relative both to the type of relation between human society and the animal exhibiting it and to the places and times when it manifested itself. In ancient societies, for instance, an animal's positive or negative value as an omen does not seem to have been ontologically tied to a species's characteristics but rather depended at different times on certain actions or movements of an animal regarded as in place (positive) or out of place (negative): for the Romans, if a wolf was seen in the countryside crossing the road from the right with a full mouth, it was good luck, but if seen in the city, it portended disaster.[3] Similarly, in Greece the dog was often associated with Hecate, nighttime, and cemeteries, but despite this, it was not considered impure and inferior *tout court*. If it had been, it would not have been permitted in the most civilized and ritually bound human spaces: at the tables not only of humans but also, as in some visual depictions, of the gods.[4] And although there were sacred spaces that prohibited dogs, it was no less the case that others, such as the sanctuary of Asclepius, allowed and even welcomed them. Like any social group (men, women, children, slaves), dogs were subject to ritual restrictions in certain spheres of divine action and social interaction where they were perceived to be out of place.

Meanwhile, J. L. Austin's speech act theory and George Lakoff and Mark Johnson's study of the conceptual and cognitive value of metaphor confirmed for me that the strictly semantic approach to analyzing animal metaphors adopted by Manfred Faust (1969) was limited and, because of this, unable to account for a cultural phenomenon as complex as insults that use animal categories. It seemed clear to me that if the invective *kyon* was an effective metaphor that remained current and productive throughout the entire long history of the Greek language despite the generality of its semantic content ("lack of restraint"), this was because it constituted a metaphor of position that had an extraordinary illocutionary effect of degrading (putting the insulted person on a lower rung); because it had a structuring force, being able to articulate the conceptual field of moral baseness; and because it worked as a tool of social regulation, permitting normative uses (the insult *kyon* served to put a reckless "dog" back in its proper place).[5] At the same time, I noticed that defects and vices of doggishness were more often imputed to feminine characters and that the only figures in myth ascribed canine traits (from Scylla to the Erinyes, from Clytemnestra to Hecuba and Pandora) were female. Even in modern cultures, I thought, the insults *cagna* and *bitch* strike a more aggressive and vulgar tone than the corresponding masculine terms. This phenomenon, too, seemed accordingly more general and meriting anthropological reflection before being subjected to the fine-grained analysis of historical philology.

Unique among animals in having been required—and still today being required—to adapt its behavior to human standards, the dog thus turned out to be a perfect subject for the sort of comparative investigation that Marcel Detienne has engaged in for years: a good "comparable" that aids historians and anthropologists

alike in unmasking the self-evident character of their own or others' cultural constructions.[6] In fact, my hunch was that one problem in dealing with ancient Greek
representations of dogs was that modern scholars had not reflected sufficiently on
their own presuppositions about the animal: claims that hunting dogs were more
noble and fully domesticated, say, while guard dogs were semiwild or that the
insult *kyon* originated in disgust at canine necrophagy or in the hypersexuality of
she-dogs were not confirmed in the sources and seemed instead to derive from
idiosyncratic modern interpretations projected without warrant onto the ancient
world.

TEXTUAL INTERPRETATION AND RECOVERING
THE CULTURAL ENCYCLOPEDIA

For several decades now, disciplines such as semiotics, literary criticism, and
reception theory have called attention to the active role that each reader plays in
constituting the sense of a text. The meaning of a text is always the fruit of semiotic
work, and the reader cooperates in realizing it. But the professional reader and
critic wanting to avoid aberrant interpretations is obliged to stay within the limits
of readings "authorized" by the text, through both its code (language) and its encyclopedia, definable as the complex of cultural conventions that that language has
produced, along with the history of previous interpretations of many texts (in
addition to the text in question).[7] This model of the "ideal reader" proposed by
Umberto Eco seemed to me quite useful to describe the task of philology: to interpret an ancient text competently means to retrace all the possible authorized readings (not only according to the code but also according to textual coherence and
the encyclopedia of cross-references) while avoiding unwarranted inferences and
anachronisms. This was the kind of interpretation I wanted to conduct, being
more interested in the possible receptions a text might elicit from the culture in
which (and by which) it was produced (*intentio operis*) than in determining authorial intentions (*intentio auctoris*). The goal was to understand what might come to
mind when someone in ancient Greek culture heard Hesiod's verses about Pandora and her "doggish mind" or Homer's heroes insulting one another with *dog
face;* what inferences did their cultural encyclopedia lead them to make? Retracing
this encyclopedia necessarily involved going into detailed ethnographic reconstruction: knowing what sorts of interactions, through what instruments (collars,
leashes), in what spheres (civil, military, domestic, public, sacred, hunting); what
possibilities of inclusion or exclusion; and what sorts of alignment with other
social categories the animal elicited and produced in that human community.

Although I was aware that, from the historical point of view, the very idea of an
assumed "Greek community" or "ancient Greek imagination" as a culture of meanings constituted an approximation (considering that the sources cover a vast tem-

poral span, belong to highly disparate genres, and hardly reflect the whole range of local cultures in Greece, at least not until the *koiné* of the Roman period), it still seemed like a necessary generalization. Only after I had identified the chief forms of relation with the animal and the salient traits of the dog's representation in common culture—in the most authoritative works of the poetic tradition and in common sense, as attested in proverbs, fables, and jokes[8]—was I able to try to understand how individual authors' depictions (whether literary or philosophical) either combined or contradicted these in order to adapt them to their specific communicative and ideological aims.

It is never easy for an outside observer to avoid unwarranted projections onto the object of their study, especially when the culture being observed is many centuries removed from the researcher's time. For a classicist, moreover, the "native" perspectives to be collected and described are predominantly intertwined in, or presupposed by, literarily sophisticated texts that, in their turn, conform to norms of genre and to particular and occasional interests and can intentionally make distorted or malicious use of common cultural models. And not only this: the information that the scholar uses to produce relevant readings comes from the very same texts that he or she then aims to interpret. How is one to proceed, then, in order to avoid a vicious circle?

To me it seemed good practice to treat the sources as raw material at first pass—taking them literally and abstracted from context—and organize them according to a criterion of repetition: I read the available passages, and each time a theme recurred more than twice, I included it in a relevant category. The large quantity of sources available on the dog ensured that repeated phenomena were statistically significant; the variety of sources made it less likely that repetitions reflected formulaic phenomena or genre conventions. For instance, the almost obsessive recurrence of the theme of food—whether it was the kind of food that dogs aspired to eat or the manner and place in which it was given to them—seemed like a good indicator of the cultural relevance of this trait for the Greeks in how they conceived their relation to the animal; so, too, the many references to canine madness—called by a name that more or less meant "wolf syndrome [*lyssa*]"—seemed to indicate that the dog's mental health was a central preoccupation in how the Greeks related to the animal. I proceeded in this way toward a description of what seemed like the dog's salient traits in Greek eyes. I tried as much as possible to adopt a "native" perspective in order to reconstruct what I've called "the entry *kyōn*" in the cultural encyclopedia of ancient Greece.[9]

This seemed to me to be the necessary first step to interpret not only how the term *kyon* was used as an insult but also all those texts (literary, mythographic, and in some cases even iconographic) in which the dog figures as protagonist, beginning with Hesiod's myth of Pandora. I could not see any other way to understand the wordplay and allusions, the irony and complex metaphorical texture of certain literary passages that, to make sense, surely relied on the collaboration of a listener who was competent and informed about current stereotypes regarding dogs. To recover this competence, avoiding as much as possible overlaying my own, was the task I set for myself (see chapter 2).

To this end, I mainly used literary sources, having recourse only at times to epigraphic and iconographic evidence. Visual art, as is known, employs codes all its own and thus deserves to be analyzed by experts in iconography. The same goes for the phenomena of ritual (purifications, lustrations, sacrifices) and of medicine and diet (the pharmacological or dietary use of parts of dogs), which I've mostly refrained from using, since I think they deserve to be studied with methods proper to disciplines such as history of religion and history of medicine. The chosen level of analysis has also not allowed me to take into consideration the differences of chronology, sociology (e.g., differences between dogs in "aristocratic" and "popular" spheres), or ethnicity and geography that might be detectable in the body of texts; I focused on representations of long duration and wide diffusion. My reconstructions, necessarily partial, thus anticipate being put to the test, and eventually refuted or corrected, by results achieved by other analytical methods, on other scales or with other evidence, including crucial data deriving from zooarchaeological sources (recovered remains of dogs in urban and extraurban spaces, sacred and profane, inhumations and cremations).

After identifying the salient aspects of the Greeks' way of seeing the dog and conceptualizing their relations with the animal (the dog's inclusion in the social hierarchy and the system of human alliances, its diet and the food pact, disturbances in the animal's cognitive capacity and techniques of control and concerns about canine agency), I was able to proceed with interpreting those Homeric passages alluding to acts of canine necrophagy that had led scholars to postulate a semiwild dog, showing how on the contrary, it was the image of a domestic dog, one sharing its owner's table, that gave the Homeric threats their power and pertinence (see chapter 3). I then focused on reconsidering why *kyon* is an insult and found a reason in the dog's special social position—privileged among animals but lowest of the low in the social hierarchy—and in the peculiar relationship that bound it to human partners, necessarily based on a measure of trust in the animal's capacity to recognize bonds and moral duties (chapter 4).

REPRESENTATIONS AND AFFORDANCES

Like any element of the world that the human mind decides to endow with the quality of a sign, so animals, taken as symbols, can be bent to any end, loaded with any value in the representations that human cultures produce. This assertion is theoretically true. There may be a thousand reasons to want to depict an elephant leaping and tumbling like a graceful dancer among the branches in a forest or spinning on the dance floor, and one can be sure that someone has imagined, or sooner or later will imagine, it thus. Yet the fact remains that an elephant, due to its size and weight, is not commonly taken as a symbol of nimbleness. Instead, in proverbial terms we speak of "an elephant in a china shop" (equivalent to the bull in the English version) or "an elephant step" (i.e., a heavy step) to describe a clumsy or heavy gait; "an elephant in the room" is used when someone stubbornly ignores an overwhelming presence that because of its size cannot be readily overlooked. In India and Thailand, the elephant is connected with "weighty" virtues such as wisdom, royalty, and the power to remove obstacles, certainly not with the agility of cunning, subterfuge, or expedience.

So if, in theory, one can say anything about animals—all the more so because they cannot refute us in public debates—in practice, representations of nonhuman species are almost never completely arbitrary. Their morphology, gait, and movements, odors and tactile effects, the sounds and noises they make, the places they appear or hide, their eating habits and abilities—not to mention the taste of their meat, the utility of their body parts (wool, hides) and their natural products (milk, whey, eggs, honey, wax)—all are traits of animals that offer the human imagination both possibilities and constraints.

To define how the aesthetic and ethological traits of an animal inspire and guide human symbol making in this way, Maurizio Bettini, in an important study on weasels in the ancient world,[10] borrowed from James J. Gibson's ecological psychology the term *affordance*: just as the environment affords a living being's body and perceptual system certain possibilities of action and prohibits others,[11] so an object in the world affords the human imagination concerned with it some opportunities for elaboration (rather than others). Just as the neuromotor system of a frog identifies the fly buzzing around it as possible nourishment and makes it flick its tongue, so a weasel slipping in and out of crevices and cracks offers the human symbolic mechanism certain possible symbolic projects (in preference to others).[12] In the case of the weasel, Greeks and Romans fostered the opportunity to shift the animal's slinky and sinuous agility toward the imaginary sphere of an easy birth; though other animals were available for representing slippery, slithering motion, (like the serpent, say) the weasel was preferred because of more affordances that oriented its representation toward the domestic and maternal spheres (a weasel lives in the house, where it guards against mice; it takes good care of its young, carrying them in its mouth).

Naturally, this does not mean that an animal will necessarily produce the same sort of elaborations the world over. Permutations are abundant and depend not only on the different practical and symbolic projects that a culture pursues but also on the total possibilities that an environment offers. A pig might be a source of nourishment for one human community and disgusting to others; so, too, some societies might spin out metaphors of birth exploiting possibilities afforded by the weasel, and others might use the serpent or the opossum in the same way; others might not even have symbolic projects on this topic, while still others might make use of plants or some other thing in the world besides an animal.

What is more, our cognitive system is not limited to working on sense data alone; it will spin new representations from other representations, giving rise to second-, third-, and fourth-degree representations in a virtually infinite chain of symbols. Obviously, in this process, representations of a higher order can deviate greatly from the initial cognitive project (that is, whatever was first given life by the affordance) and serve rather unpredictable aims or drift into completely arbitrary elaborations.[13] This is not to say, therefore, that every representation related to a certain animal has to do with an affordance: in many cases, we might find at a representation's origin other representations, which were, in their turn, products of intellectual activity (encyclopedic notions, definitions, and beliefs) instead of direct sense data. Unlike Bettini, I believe that any "representation of representation" should be kept distinct from *affordance,* to avoid the risk of stripping the Gibsonian concept of its inherent ecological quality.[14]

Although such symbolic drift is the norm, and more or less arbitrary and fantastic representations exhibiting surprising local variations may enrich the entry for an animal in the cultural encyclopedia (like anything that lies within our horizon of perception), the theory of affordances explains well the recurrence of some cultural elaborations on animals, especially some glaring cases of "convergence" in cultures far removed from each other.[15] With the weasel, as Bettini shows, Greco-Roman representations find surprising parallels in the Americas, among the Hopi of present-day Arizona: these people also attribute to species of the weasel family a special virtue in helping women avoid complications in childbirth.[16] In the case of the dog, as we have seen, the apparent "Greek" paradox whereby the animal most decisively involved in human activity and present in social spaces (including areas of rich symbolic content, such as eating and hunting) was taken as an abusive metaphor and gave rise to a whole host of negative judgments (which could be summed up in the charge of shamelessness) is no isolated phenomenon but one found in other cultural traditions. It makes one suspect that the dog possesses affordances liable to occasion these convergences.[17]

But which affordances, in particular? Anatomical and morphological traits help explain representations such as, for example, the dog's "eyes of fire," suggested by the *tapetum lucidum* in the canine eye. Other elaborations instead make sense in light of ethological characteristics: the taste for blood and raw meat and attacks of uncontrolled aggression were probably at the origin of figures of canine madness and discourses on dogs' kinship with wolves. Yet all these affordances spoke little to the problem that inspired my study: the charge of shamelessness (*anaideia*) and its disproportionate connection to female figures, to the point that doggishness was a typical trait of the "race of women." Traits listed by other scholars and adopted by some informers ancient and modern as causes of the phenomenon (tendencies toward coprophagy and necrophagy, toward incest and exhibitions of sexuality) seemed to me only to shift the problem: why, when other animals manifest the same behaviors, was it only the dog that earned the bad reputation of being an animal without restraint?

THE DOG AS PARTNER IN SOCIAL INTERACTIONS

An interesting article by Edward Reed concerning Gibson's concept of affordance helped me refocus the problem. Reed called attention to the fact that the identification of ecological information varies according to whether the object of focus is inanimate, animate, or socialized: while the affordances of inanimate objects offer possibilities for action, those of animate beings offer interactions (or "mutual affordances"), and only members of the same community, where shared norms of action prevail, offer possibilities of appropriate interaction. If I take a walk in the woods, the bed of leaves offers me the opportunity to walk on soft ground; if I walk in the woods and see a bear, the animal offers me more complex possibilities. I can choose from various moves, but all the options for action that the environment suggests to me depend not solely on me but also on how the bear will react to my presence, since I, in my turn, offer the bear certain affordances, which she may or may not choose to exploit for her own ends. Interaction becomes "appropriate," finally, with those subjects, typically members of my community who have had the same cultural training and with whom I know how to comport myself, who recognize certain gestures and behaviors as adequate or inadequate.[18] This holds for me just as for any other social animal—a baboon, within its baboon community, takes advantage of environmental affordances on the basis of social rules learned by and among its fellows during a period of acculturation.

Transferred from the plane of action to that of mental activity, agency, we may say, makes it such that the affordances the animal offers to human imagination include the conditions of relation, that is, how the respective behaviors of the subjects are modified in the shared environment.[19] Take the arena of hunting: animals such as deer that stake their chances for survival on flight will only with difficulty inspire elaborations on courage from their human predator; instead, the boar, stoutly defending itself against swarms of circling hunters, will foster representations of courageous self-defense. In every case, elaborations emerge from the mode of interaction between the subjects in a specific ecological context. But what particular kind of agency is involved in the diverse contexts of interaction between the dog and humans?

Plato says that dogs "are not to be classed among the animals that live in herds."[20] Some commentators find this observation curious, while to me it seems to capture a crucial fact about the canine condition in environments, such as ancient Greece, where dogs act as animal collaborators (guarding), cognitive prosthetics (hunting), and pets: in his daily experience, Plato evidently did not see packs of wild dogs but instead single dogs in the human community. This was the affordance the Athenian philosopher fixed on, leading him to exclude dogs from the class of herd animals (*agelaioi*).

Communities that decide to accommodate dogs are mixed societies, founded on relations and bonds that are interspecific. In these environments, the dog lives a life in promiscuous symbiosis with humans. It is placed in the society of *anthrōpoi*. If this happens, it is because the dog, by its morphoethological characteristics, enables (affords) this kind of interaction; in turn, we humans offer (afford) dogs the possibility of finding food in our houses instead of wandering in search of prey. Indeed, the species *Canis familiaris* arose just so, through a process of reciprocal molding that scholars now ever more often describe as having coevolutionary characteristics: some wolves decided to help humans in exchange for food, and the humans found it convenient to adopt some and keep them around.[21]

That the relationship with the dog was fundamentally based on this "pact" of reciprocal convenience seemed very clear to the Greeks, whose elaborations concerning the dog are rich in reflections not only on the importance of "nurturing" the animal so as to secure its services but also on dogs' interest in human food. The interaction with dogs, like any interaction with an animate subject, is thus a mutual affordance, involving harmony (or conflict) of interests in the shared environment.

In the dog's case, the relationship goes further. Dogs are not socialized by their conspecifics, except in early infancy, but by humans. The dog's agency, moreover, is not directed from the outside, as is the case with other collaborative animals (horses, mules, cows). Even when it performs tasks on a human being's behalf, the dog acts with autonomy: it's up to the dog to decide whether it will respect the command or not. For this reason, dogs are trained from the earliest age, and great importance is attached to this aspect of their relationship with humans.[22]

We can say, then, that the interaction between humans and dogs is one of competence—or better, that the dog, trained to live in a human community, is expected to behave appropriately. The animal's capacity to respond to the human educational process is the affordance that enables it to be thought of as acting consciously and responsibly.[23] The dog is required to not give in to uncontrolled impulses, to restrain its aggressions, to respect its owner, and to keep in its place: virtues that for the Greeks fell within the spectrum of *aidōs* (restraint).

Yet if the dog is represented in predominantly negative terms, often portrayed as lacking this virtue, this is because the dog, socialized and included, remains other than the humans among whom it lives. The animal's metonymic position, as a subject granted a degree of autonomous action, makes it slightly problematic and stirs anxieties about trespass (dogs intruding unwanted into social spaces or unleashing aggression in inappropriate directions) and betrayal of the bond that keeps it allied to the person who feeds it. The large number of ancient portrayals of dogs taking food not intended for them, being corrupted by their "brother" wolf and giving him a portion of livestock, accepting food from a thief in exchange for silence, and attacking their owner-hunter instead of the prey all seem attributable to the unease of having as an ally a being that cannot be fully assimilated.[24]

Confronted with representations of untrustworthy dogs, one sees a remarkable consonance in what Greek men said about women. Like Pandora, their mythic ancestor "with a dog's mind," women appear in men's eyes as other subjects—subject others—though ones inevitably established in the society of humans, capable of great solidarity and trustworthiness—indeed, indispensable cooperators for the survival of the race—yet vulnerable to adulterers' attempts to corrupt them and able to destroy the purity of the line, trained from the time they are small to serve the interests of males yet suspected of harboring deviant plans and hidden intentions of rebellion. For women too, restraint (*aidōs*) was the most demanded virtue and lack of restraint (*anaideia*) the defect most reproached.

Given the common destiny of dogs and women as subject others intimately rooted in the family of male humans, subordinated to those who demanded they share the interests of and show affection and loyalty to their masters, it does not seem so strange that *doggishness* was so often leveled as a reproach at feminine figures, nor is it surprising that, as popular stereotypes attested in proverbs would have it, the dog was treated as a feminine creature. Both were involved in a complexly interwoven rhetoric of mutual delegitimation (women are like dogs and dogs are like women, i.e., untrustworthy); by elaborating stereotypes about the lack of restraint in both women and dogs, Greek men were responding to their anxiety about the agency of subjects on whom they depended to protect the integrity of the house and secure its property; strict loyalty and devotion was demanded of them, and they were able to meet this claim, but also to delude even the most exacting investments of effort.[25] The ass, mule, or horse, acting mechanically and under strict control with saddles, reins, bits, and bridles, served the Greeks for representing practices of "taming" the virgin's wildness by man (her "horseman" and trainer);[26] dogs were used to represent the risks of feminine agency, the problematic loyalty of their wives and daughters and the no less problematic violence of uncontrolled maternal passions.

ANIMALS AS CATALYSTS FOR DISCOURSE ANALYSIS

The inclusion of individuals of the canine species in human society was so acute that it was bound to be problematic. This seemed to be the key to explaining not only the paradoxical and contradictory nature of the constellation of canine representations found in the sources but also the alignment of this problematic situation with the one involving the inclusion of the "race of women" (*genos gynaikōn*) in androcentric Greek society. The analysis that traced this alignment turned out to be valuable in disclosing an important aspect of ancient culture and shedding new light on certain texts in Greek literature. At the same time, it afforded a different angle—oblique and perhaps therefore more penetrating—on the ideology of gender and its discursive strategies. What Greeks said about their dogs reveals much about their relations with these animals, but it reveals even more about the humans, and especially the male humans (*andres*) who were the authorized narrators of those relations.

Here the question arises of the role that animals play in the processes by which humans model reality. This issue has long been debated in anthropology, especially since Lévi-Strauss proposed his interpretation of totemism as a rational method of organizing the social world: to impose order on the community, the schema of species differences—already there and available for use—is enlisted. The ordered variety of animal species is "good for thinking" about the social order. Thus for Lévi-Strauss, the animal world is not just a valuable reservoir of useful and edible products but also a mine for good representations with which to think about the human world.[27] Rodney Needham, who considered Lévi-Strauss's interpretive criteria "intellectualistic" and thus artificial and his conception of *l'esprit humain* overly rationalistic—"men do not often reason; they don't reason for long; and when they do reason, they don't do it very well"—countered that it would be more correct to say that animals are "good to imagine with": they are figures good to stimulate the imagination, especially the "evasive" sort that tends to construct worlds unbound by necessities (spatiotemporal, etc.) that reality normally imposes on thought.[28] Needham, that is, conceived of the imagination not as ordering but as disordering, one tending to work toward overcoming constraints and human limits.

However one wants to understand it, the importance of animals in human cultural production is undeniable and constitutes an anthropological universal. Human beings display an irrepressible need to narrate their relations with other species, to narrate their own lives through them, to "evade" life by imagining fantastic creatures, or to see their world reflected (whether on faithful or distorted lines, even fully upended) in the world of animals. Just think of how many cultural manifestations past and present take animality as a prototype for alterity: deviant, stranger, slave, woman, all have been marginalized in many cultures—and subcultures—by means of animalizing traits. But think too, on the contrary, how often a homology with animals is invoked to claim the perfect naturalness—and thus necessity—of a human behavior: whether it's aggression toward members of one's own species or male polygamy, the care for young as inscribed in feminine instinct, or competition for territory and dominance.[29] For this reason, studying representations of animals in human cultures does not impose a limit on the field of observation: instead, it plunges the scholar straight into basic processes of anthropopoiesis and social construction, including the politics of gender.

Tim Ingold notes that from classical times to the present day, animals have figured centrally in the Western construction of "man"[30]—and, we might add, of Western man's image of woman. In fact, the same thing seems to have happened (and still happens) in non-Western cultural traditions as well. In his famous reading of the Balinese cockfight, Clifford Geertz showed the way in which many complex questions (of social status, gender, and cultural sensibility) in an Asian culture could be "writ out in Aesopian terms" and be staged as a dramatic conflict between fighting roosters.[31] So too, a study begun with one literary text—Hesiod's account of the making of Pandora and the first woman's *kyneos noos*—can follow the tracks of doggishness into many important manifestations of ancient culture and touch on central themes in the Greek way of making the world.

An animal is an excellent term for analyzing extensive cultural complexes. Every species is incredibly diverse both in its cultural traits and in the texts and contexts in which it is put to use, so that reconstructing the ancient bestiary also means traversing many of the most important spaces of imagery in a community's cultural tradition. Bettini's study of the weasel is a clear example of how investigating the cultural representation of an animal can lead into the imagination and emotional life of a community, including births of heroes, knots and unknotting, midwives and witches, risky pregnancies and successful births, the magic of crossed knees and loose shoes. Similarly, studying the dog inevitably leads down many intersecting lines, some of them quite unexpected: the theme of identity as recognition and the problem of persistence beyond death, the question of asymmetrical solidarity (*philia*) and the definition of *philos*, the rupture in the ethical system between the set of masterly (male) virtues and the set of subordinate (feminine, servile, animal) virtues, and the strategic function of reputation and how it is used to create (or maintain) the social hierarchy, to mention just a few examples.

Observing how humans construct an animal can help us say much about how they construct themselves and their relations with the world around them. All the more so when an animal can guide and point us down trails otherwise little trodden and make us adopt an eccentric (and therefore privileged) perspective to observe wide-ranging and complicated cultural phenomena that often escape notice when looked at head on.[32] Working on the dog revealed, for example, how these animals played an important role in discursive practices that constructed and perpetuated gender inequality, opening new and unexpected avenues for further research.[33] But besides making possible thick ethnographic descriptions, thanks to which more competent readings of texts and deeper understanding of ideological processes arise—all the more difficult to identify when concealed beneath a veneer of trite banalities or staged in seemingly innocent "Aesopian terms"—research on animals is important in itself, since it focuses the attention of the observer, whether ethnographer, historian, or literary critic, on an aspect of life and history as important as it is neglected in humanities disciplines: human relationships with individuals of other species.

ANTHROZOOLOGY AND HUMAN-ANIMAL STUDIES

Anthropology, philosophy, sociology, and history have always regarded animals as important objects of human (economic and symbolic) activity. But only recently have they begun to consider the active role of other species in determining, conditioning, and promoting the activity and evolution of *Homo sapiens* in the common arena of life on planet Earth. The paradigm shift—from taking animals as means ("mirrors and windows"[34]) of analyzing prominent human facts to taking interspecies relations as ends of inquiry, from assuming animal "objects" and human cultural construction to considering animals as subjects and real partners of humans in a shared environment—is a stage of development for an emerging field of study that has not yet achieved the status of an academically recognized discipline but now has several notable institutions and scholarly publications devoted to it.[35] The field is variously labeled in different countries: *zooantropologia* in Italy, *anthropozoologie* in France, *anthrozoology* or *human-animal studies* (with the variant *critical animal studies,* radically concerned with animal rights) in English-speaking countries.

This broad project of reevaluating other species' roles in existence, in cultural and cognitive development, in short, in the current life and history of humanity, draws energy from many common concerns. Most of all is the ecological crisis, which has eroded the age-old trust in how the human species imposes its dominance on the rest of the planet. Already in the early 1970s, Lévi-Strauss denounced Western anthropology's culpability in this decline: the error of isolating cultural facts from their biological bases has alienated modern man and brought on ecological disaster from the so-called civilization that destroys the earth; humanity's will to isolate itself from other animal species, by construing itself as unique and ontologically distinct, reserving for itself the domain of "culture" and relegating all other species to "nature," has cut knowledge into programs of either "culturalistic" or "naturalistic" research—science and humanities—which do not dialogue with each other; this schism has led progressively to a dramatic impoverishment of research on humans.[36] Lévi-Strauss's call for a new holistic science, based on collaboration among disciplines and attention to the logic of relations and the dynamic complexity of reality (complex interactions, feedback loops, relational and processual dimensions, dynamic equilibria), dedicated not only to understanding action in the world but also to taking responsibility for action,[37] has inspired the interdisciplinary challenge of many research programs that are renegotiating the nature-culture (and science-humanities) opposition with the aim of reconstructing the human from a perspective no longer separatist and oppositional but continuous and inclusive (ecological).[38]

The rise of ethology and primatology, the discovery of animal languages and cultures, has further eroded the age-old human pretense to holding a monopoly on cultural production and transmission, as well as the capacity for socialization. Ways of life, forms of socializing, transmission of knowledge, languages and dialects, cognitive capacities, individual and historical variations in a species's behavior—information long exiled from zoological science, reduced to mere biological and taxonomical awareness of the animal kingdom—have become the very center of research on animals.[39] Meanwhile, traditional views of human culture, predominantly mentalist and representational, are being reconfigured: culture is not so much a system of symbols learned through the transmission of mental representations as a practice of training (mostly unreflective and involuntary) whereby human subjects learn through imitation and conformist adaptation. From this perspective, human culture is still distinct from that of other species, but not radically so.[40] All animal action is for the most part a tacit know-how (without explicit rules) embodied (the "mind" does not exist apart from the body and is only cognitive faculties within the body) and situated (calibrated to present circumstances and the local environment).[41] In this sense, we should be ready to recognize in other animals, too, a capacity for intentional action and thus personality (personhood).

Critical studies of varying inspiration, feminism prominent among them,[42] have favored extending the level of discussion from infraspecific relations (racial, colonial, gender, class) to interspecies relations between humans and subjects belonging to other animal species. As with any relation with others, those with nonhuman species should be studied in terms of subjugation and dominance, discrimination and reification; most human perspectives on the world are overrun with rhetoric that is not only ethnocentric and androcentric but also anthropocentric, and this species-ism has led not only to widespread phenomena of exclusion, segregation, and exploitation of nonhuman individuals, to the point of exterminating whole species, but also to a unilateral and partial reconstruction of human history.[43] Nonhuman animals are victims of the same strategies of domination that afflict and have afflicted other social groups: reduction to silence (cancelling their point of view), distancing and rejection (othering), or assimilation and negation of difference (saming).[44]

Even the postmodern question about identity and subject formation has had to reckon with the role of nonhuman animals.[45] Concepts such as "posthuman" and "more than human" are called to respond to the need to put forward a more inclusive conception of identity and subjects, more ecological and dynamic than classical ontology.[46]

The forecasted revolution clearly aims to interrogate many traditional disciplines, among them moral philosophy and law. By extending the promise of protection to all members of the human species, the Universal Declaration of Human

Rights has marked a new limit of exclusion that isolates human beings from other species and frames in novel terms the problem of the legitimacy of the latters' exclusion from the realm of rights. And this at the same time that the scientific community overwhelmingly accepts the Darwinian explanation, rendering ever more acute the need to acknowledge the common evolutionary history that binds *Homo sapiens* to many species, chiefly the anthropomorphic apes, and follow through on the consequences of this in regulating our relations with them. What is more, our acknowledgment of the role that domestication techniques have played in creating new species and in shaping infinite varieties for human use (cloning, extreme techniques of selective breeding) becomes ever clearer as biotechnology proliferates, placing questions of bioethics at the center of contemporary political agendas.[47]

Research programs that go under the name of anthrozoology or human-animal studies thus arise at the crossroads of critical reflections in philosophy of science, ethology, anthropology, sociology, psychology, biology, feminist and ecological thought, and bioethics, as revisions of the epistemological paradigm of classical anthropology and indictments of its anthropocentric character. Yet they are distinct from zoology, ethology, psychology, environmentalism, and animal activism in that they take into account matters of reflexivity, deal with interspecies relations, and aim to frame "the animal question" within a complex and problematic vision of cultural history.[48] They advocate a new and more generous evaluation of the animal presence in the history of the human species and in the reality of its cultures, which did not develop in a vacuum: humans interact with the environment, extracting, dumping waste products, but also exchanging and playing games (agonal, social, cognitive) with nonhuman species.[49] If contact with humans has shaped many animal species—this is radically true for domestic species, the dog in particular[50]—contact with other animals has shaped human groups as well. This is a matter not simply of differentiation and distancing (the human defined as non-animal) but also of situations of exchange, whether on the level of phylogeny (the human brain evolved in response to concerns involving other species; the dog developed its bark as an adaptive response to the need to communicate with humans), or, again, on the level of cultural history.[51] Humans exploit products of animal origin, but animals receive food, medicine, and shelters of human origin; humans and animals imitate one another's performances (swimming, flight, bipedalism, ritual gestures) and form genuine partnerships that structurally combine systems of diverse species to produce a superior cognitive or performative function.[52] Think of the pairings human-horse, hunter-dog, herdsman-dog, and plowman-ox and all those activities otherwise unthinkable that such pairings have enabled. But other cases exist where the extended possibility runs in the opposite direction: bees that exploit human signals to find honey, flocks and herds that shelter in buildings, pets that "exploit" their inclusion in human families.[53]

But what does it mean in practice to do anthropology or ethnography—or, as here, cultural history—from this new perspective? With the discipline still in an experimental stage, its approach is not yet stabilized, but it's generally safe to say that research from an anthrozoological perspective is concerned not only to draw attention to representations of animals in a culture (including fantastic animals and theriomorphic monsters) and seek reasons for their broad distribution but also to consider real animals in their ecological relations with human cultures (actions and reactions, feedback loops, complex interactions, hybridization and exchanges of knowledge and abilities);[54] to reconstruct the strategies of domination (tools, institutions, and rhetoric) that humans impose on other animals by investigating the ties between these and those designed to subordinate women, children, slaves, foreigners, the disabled, and other minorities; to take seriously indigenous ways of conceptualizing relations with individuals of other species in the form of social relations (notions of kinship, friendship, hospitality, and veneration, or else of hostility, rivalry, and competition); and to investigate the mutual morphoethological affordances that make such relations possible. This new perspective, in short, aims to take stock of societies in their hybrid nature as interspecific communities that include human beings and members of other species (dogs, horses, cows, and sheep, as well as insects and even bacteria and fungi).

This implies analysis that takes account of real animals—not just constructed or symbolic ones—and their real conditions of interaction. In my research, the theory of mutual affordances enabled me to intuit this perspective, by directing my inquiry toward those actual characteristics (cognitive and ethological) of humans and dogs that seemed to delimit their modes of interaction and the symbolic elaborations that accompany them in many cultures and by suggesting that in order to understand and describe specific expressions of Greek doggishness—not least their preferential connection with the feminine—it was necessary to determine what sorts of interactions the human-dog couple shared and how these were conceived in comparison to those with other species (such as wolves, foxes, and flies). At the time I was finishing the book, I still did not have much ethnographic literature at hand that took this perspective: works that have appeared more recently, such as Eduardo Kohn's study on human-dog relations in a Runa village of the upper Amazon,[55] would have been welcome help—and much comfort—as I developed my theoretical tools, despite the limited applicability of ethnographic methods to Greece of more than two millennia ago. To reconstruct interspecies relations, the classicist must rely on limited information mostly intermeshed in texts of a literary nature.

Nevertheless, it was evident to me that shifting attention from an animal object and animal representations to an animal subject and conceptualized relations was a move worth attempting. I felt I needed to take seriously the Greeks' belief that their dogs were able to understand, recognize, and respect certain social rules, as well as their anxiety in observing that this did not happen without exception.[56] The relationship had effects on the sociological level, establishing hierarchical positions, duties, and ethical norms; on the emotional level, it was a source of joy and sharing as well as illusions and anxiety. The relationship also put into play dynamics of identity and emotional investment—and we are speaking not just about pet dogs (though the observation holds for them, too) but of animals that humans entrusted with jobs such as guarding property, defending flocks from wolves, and pursuing and flushing out prey.

Without this kind of information, it is impossible to understand most of the elaborations on the dog. For example, one could not explain why the dog served as an effective term in the processes of identity formation (the dog's recognition and acknowledgment) or disintegration (cases of endogenous anthropophagy and failed recognition, such as those of Priam and Actaeon), nor why, among the women represented in canine terms, it is women of the home—wives, daughters, mothers, and female slaves born in the house—who are most prevalent. The attachment to the owner was undoubtedly a factor determining the relationship: the dog's specific agency could not be controlled with instruments but answered to rules that the animal had to internalize. The establishment of a bond between dog and owner is therefore an inescapable prerequisite. Certainly, the bond was asymmetrical: humans are unlikely to think of working for their dog, while we expect our dog to do this for us. Yet dogs were sometimes thought worthy of having tombs dedicated to them or would be saved portions of food when owners dined out.[57]

But this hierarchical distancing explained well both the use of the term *kyon* as an insult and its symbolic intersection with representations of the feminine. The authoritative subject of these elaborations was not an abstract "Greek man" but the adult male human (ἀνήρ) "master" (ἄναξ, δεσπότης), in the sense not only of "owner" but also of "ruler," in addition to the "raiser/nurturer" or "caretaker" (τροφεύς) who invests time and money to obtain the desired services from the one raised/nurtured.

The reconstruction was thus necessarily both an ethnographic description and a critique of the unilateral and ideological character of the sources that attest to the state of subjection that the same matrix of domination imposed on both dogs and women: creatures from whom the male expected respect, affection, and obedience and whose agency was felt to be problematic and a cause of disturbance and anxiety.

TOWARD A HISTORICAL ANTHROZOOLOGY OF THE ANCIENT WORLD

Tracing the history of barbed wire as an instrument for confining livestock that become a means of controlling a humiliated and reified humanity in concentration camps, Reviel Netz asserts that "human cultures do not grow in a vacuum but within a complex environmental system, rich with a multiform diversity of life presence. Our history is ecological and animals play a major role in it." To forget the relations with individuals of other species, as though they were irrelevant for reconstructing human history, is not just a moral error but an epistemological one as well: "When we set out to offer a history that mentions animals, we should understand that the history of animals is not merely an appendix, a note we should add because it is missing in our present traditional, human-focused history. Rather, the history of animals is part and parcel of history—that reality where all is inextricably tied together, humans, animals, and their shared material world."[58] Similarly, as Liliane Bodson stresses, even modern specialists in natural science cannot do without a historical perspective: even when focused on strictly biological processes, they cannot help but take account of the dynamics of historical interaction between human and nonhuman species. Cooperation among naturalists, historians, biologists, and archaeologists is often required in ecological preservation projects (reclamation or restoration) in habitats with declining or extinct populations of native or historically naturalized species.[59]

More and more cultural and literary history is being done in which animals are considered not simply as means to better observe human history from the margins but as genuine costars who deserve historiographical narratives in which they take center stage. Naturally, there are many ways to interpret the need to bring animals into the foreground. Many historical and ethnographic studies have taken animals as the main object of inquiry, as in monographs and collections dedicated to single species—the wolf (Ortalli 1997), the pig (Fabre-Vassas 1994; Walter 1999), the horse (Digard 2007), the bear (Pastoureau 2007)—or to single episodes or aspects of human history (Centini 1998; Darnton 1984; Ritvo 1987; Kete 1994); studies showing how focusing on animals can transform historical reconstruction (Ingold 1994a; Anthony 2007); studies on animals in the history of art, literature, film, and popular iconography (Baker 2001; De Cristofaro 2002; Spila 2002; Zambon 2007; Payne 2010; Spila 2012);[60] studies by trained historians and historiographies written by scholars trained in very different fields (ethnographers, naturalists, linguists).[61] Alongside more traditional approaches—which equate animals with either the biological history or the cultural representations of their species—titles such as *Les animaux ont une histoire* (Delort 1984), "How Domestic Animals Have Shaped the Development of Human Societies" (Clutton-Brock 2007), and *Creatures of Empire: How Domesticated Animals Transformed Early America* (Anderson 2004) give some idea of the change in perspective under way.[62] Of similar significance is the six-volume Berg editorial project *Cultural History of Animals* (including Kalof 2007).[63] The field is already so vast that any attempt to provide a meaningful synoptic view is futile; the works mentioned here serve only as indications of the strong interest in the animal question among historians, folklorists, and literary critics in recent decades.[64]

Even classical studies have in various ways responded to these concerns. The focus so far has mostly been on explicit forms of knowledge: zoology, zootechnics, and veterinary arts in Bodson's extensive corpus;[65] Aristotelian zoology in the works of David Mowbray Balme (1987; Balme and Gotthelf 2002); Jean-Louis Labarrière (2004), and Andrea Carbone (2011); zootechnics in Stella Georgoudi's research (1990). Much attention has been given to animals in the history of philosophical thought (Dierauer 1977; Sorabji 1993; Castignone and Lanata 1994; Cassin and Labarrière 1997; De Fontenay 1998; Labarrière 2005; Newmyer 2005; Newmyer 2011; Osborne 2011; Tutrone 2012), in religion (Gilhus 2006), and in medicine and pharmacological practices (Boehm and Luccioni 2008). General overviews on animals in ancient life and thought are abundant (from religion to art, from daily life to warfare).[66]

Given the prevalence of literary texts as sources of information on the ancient world, the interest in animals has also been evident in literary critical studies, with themes such as Homeric animal similes (Schnapp-Gourbeillon 1981; Lonsdale 1990), zoomorphic comic choruses (Rothwell 2006), and the animal world in ancient literature (Conti Bizzarro 2009; Camardese 2010; Payne 2010). Christophe Chandezon's work on breeding in ancient Greece (2003) is based instead on epigraphic sources. Timothy Howe has an interesting study on "pastoral politics" in Greece (2008; see also Whittaker 1988). Ever more common are classical conferences devoted to the animal question and interspecies relations (Bonnet, Jourdain-Annequin, and Pirenne-Delforge 1998; Gasti and Romano 2003; Santillo Frizell 2004; Alexandridis, Wild, and Winkler-Horaček 2008; Beta and Marzari 2010). There is also growing interest in fantastic zoology (Li Causi 2003), stories of metamorphosis (Forbes-Irving 1990; Frontisi-Ducroux 2003; R. Buxton 2009), the concept of the hybrid and hybridization (Li Causi 2008; Alexandridis 2009), hybrid creatures in the pantheon (Padgett 2003; Aston 2011), and the imagination of the monstrous (Atherton 2002).

New perspectives are opening that apply theoretical tools from ethnobiology and ethnolinguistics to the study of zoological classification (Lloyd 1998; Zucker 2005; Li Causi 2010) and of folk zoonyms (Zucker 2006; Guasparri 2007). Archaeology also has been reevaluating the role of animals in the story of civilization. There is a better understanding of the importance of faunal remains for reconstructing social conditions: zooarchaeology is considered an important subfield (Bodson 1998, 248–49; Reitz and Wing [1999] 2008²; Kotjabopoulou et al. 2003; MacKinnon 2004), and collections of finds being published constitute an important new body of evidence for anthrozoological research.

Also important are studies that have analyzed the role that animals played in anthropopoiesis: in ancient conceptions of the political (Detienne and Svenbro 1989), of crafty intelligence (Detienne and Vernant 1978), of dangerous seduction (Detienne 1979), and of language and human identity (Heath 2005), in articulating the relationship with violence (Andò and Cusumano 2010), and in thinking about the opposition between wild and civilized or domesticated (Charpentier 2004).

This list does not include the countless monographs and general collections on animals in Greece and Rome and ancient attitudes toward animals; an *Oxford Handbook of Animals in Classical Life and Thought* is currently in production. Thus, even in classical studies, it is impossible to provide an exhaustive picture of the works inspired by the animal question: one can get an idea of how this emerging subfield has flourished from the selective bibliography assembled by Thorsten Fögen (2006).

Against this voluminous activity—mainly oriented toward probing Greek and Roman ideas about animality, ancient modes of classification, and the role of animals in anthropopoiesis—not much has been done to reconstruct the conditions of relation that ancient peoples maintained with individual species. Anyone concerned with a particular animal and wanting to interpret its presence in a given text (literary, documentary, or iconographic) or context (ritual, economic, domestic) most often is forced to refer to entries in general works, which are often quite dated and, by their nature, can only with great care be used as adequate support to interpret specific texts and cultural formations.[67] Such texts all too rarely identify species accurately: ancient names, not corresponding to the Linnaean classification, are often ambiguous and require patient cross-disciplinary research to be connected with a specific animal (on this point see Franco 2006 and the reflections in Bodson 2009), along with all the problems that come with interpreting texts and rituals. With certain rare exceptions,[68] we lack extensive ethnographic descriptions of single species that would help reconstruct the morphoethological and relational affordances that oriented the representations—including the nonhuman actors' resistances to human pressures—and the sections of the ancient encyclopedia activated by an animal representation in a text, the rhetorical strategies into which the species had been co-opted.

Still, as I've tried to show, it is just this sort of work that is needed to understand what the presence of a species in a literary passage means, in myths and in other cultural elaborations. In a lucid synthesis, Bodson, in 1981, summarized the task of a historical "ethnozoology": "The questions that one formulates in the course of an ethnozoological inquiry are always very simple: what animal is mentioned? What role does it play? Is its presence obligatory? What is expected from it? How is it presented? treated? etc. But there are no answers that do not transcend the zoological, technical, or economic aspects and lead to deeper implications, where at last what gets called into question are the position and relations of every living being—including humans—that make up the animal kingdom."[69]

Identifying and reading these "deeper implications" requires preliminary labor to reconstruct not only the animal's entry in the ancient cultural encyclopedia but also the ecology in which relations with that species took place, interpretation that requires attention to detail and at the same time having an eye for broad phenomena of social intersections. What we want, to cite Donna Haraway, is a "natureculture" inquiry.[70] Without this, one risks either remaining confined to *Realien* or, on the contrary, taking animals only as constructions, reducing the real animal to a mere accident, devoid of interest.[71] For the Greek and Roman world, among other things, the sources are rather generous on this score: a marked encyclopedism in fact characterizes the whole ancient tradition of naturalistic treatises (Aristotle, Pliny, Aelian), whose value as anthrozoological sources therefore amply makes up for their "defect" in regard to scientific information;[72] these texts have preserved for us an extremely valuable quantity of information on ways of understanding the hearsay and prejudices that circulated about a certain animal, its relations, useful traits, and so forth. This information, carefully integrated with data from archaeology, zooarchaeology, iconography, and epigraphy, can provide reliable reconstructions of the ancient ways of living (and understanding) relations between species.

It would thus be valuable for classical studies—whether literary critical, cultural historical, historical religious, iconographic, or epigraphic documentary—to import from anthrozoology and human-animal studies certain perspectives and analytical tools to conduct research on humans and nonhumans in the ancient world. To offer just a few possible guidelines, such research would:

> Assume that any interpretation of possible meanings of an animal in a text or context (whether literary, documentary, or performative) must be preceded by a detailed and as complete as possible reconstruction of the assemblage of native notions and beliefs about the species, avoiding the application (at least at first pass) of any categories to the body of texts beyond those identifiable by their redundancy. To this end, reconstructing only "real" aspects (such as race, breeding, and utility), while important, is not sufficient; we need to understand how the culture elaborated these facts into notions and beliefs. With dogs, as I've tried to show, what the Greeks noted was their inclusion in the human community and at the same time their inability to behave according to human standards (rather than impurity or lust, as other studies have indicated).

> Pay attention to the interface between representation and the world, keeping in mind affordances—that is, morphoethological and cognitive characteristics—and the typology of interactions. For the "Greek" dog, these were identified as the animal's capacity for recognition and its ability to be bound by moral duties toward its caretaker. Recognizing mutual affordances also means restoring, to some degree, the animal's role as an active partner in the processes of cultural construction.[73]

> Pay attention to the animal's agency. In this way, it's possible to begin to plot a history of interspecies relations. As Jason Hribal emphasizes, "To simply study the history of cows does not mean then that the historical subjects . . . become actors" (2007, 101). A historical anthrozoology must take into

account ecological phenomena and the mutual interference in the life of those species but also important sociological factors such as the hierarchical relations within which interspecies relationships are realized—for example, how the relations with a certain animal intersect with relations of class and/or gender (Kohn 2007 is exemplary; see also Bird Rose 2011). Animal agency is not always easy to recover, yet in the case of the dog, I tried to do so, by restoring the spaces of freedom and resistances to social and educative pressures that the animal exerted and that were reflected in expressions of doubt and anxiety that the Greeks associated with the dog on a fairly regular basis. Like every attempt at social control, so, too, the clear-cut rules on which humans want their relations with individuals of other species to be based entail doubts and suspicions; the animal turns out to be capable of becoming a site of resistance to human attempts at normalization and of negotiating its own life conditions with the "weapons of the weak" (refusal to obey, simulated ignorance, work slowdowns, dragging its feet, etc.: J. C. Scott *apud* Hribal 2007, 103).

Pay attention to the conjunctive (rather than divisive) elements of interspecies relations. Classical ethnography concentrated mostly on dynamics of division rather than those of conjunction, relationship, contamination, and contact. The loci classici of reflection on animals have been sacrifice, hunting, and the animal as a site where alterity emerges (the monstrous, wild, "dark mirror" of the human soul; magic, witchcraft, divination). But ancient sources attest that this vision was not monolithically shared. Not only did movements such as Pythagoreanism and Orphism challenge these views, but a large number of anecdotes on love, recognition (between humans and pets but also work dogs, dolphins, horses, elephants, and even lions), adoption, teaching, and reciprocal inspiration between members of different species (one thinks of birdsong and poets, spider webs and weaving, the alphabet and the flight of cranes) attest to how common experience perceived humans not always as separate but also as included and integrated parts of the great family of animate beings. This doesn't mean embracing a "militant" animal rights perspective but rather simply correcting the distortions introduced by excessive attention devoted to bloody sacrifice as the founding moment in religion and ancient anthropology and by the rigidly separatist paradigm of the human as the space "between god and beast."[74]

Give attention to the undesired species that live with humans. In this case, too, we are dealing with correcting an imbalance in ethnographic attention toward fantastic and "exotic" animals on one hand and the animals used for meat and utilitarian uses on the other, to the disregard of all those species that, even when they have strict relations with humanity to the point of symbiosis (parasites, insects, rats), get pushed out of conscious awareness much more quickly and effectively than they are physically removed from human spaces. Though recently one has noted a growing interest in investigating this type of animal (Bodson 1991; Bodson 1994a; Bodson 2002; Conti Bizzarro 2009), exhaustive monographs conducted with up-to-date methods are lacking.

One final consideration: my teaching experience tells me that courses on historical anthrozoology of the ancient world attract students from various disciplines (classical studies, anthropology, philosophy, history, modern literature) and stimulate lively discussion of themes that feel meaningful at this particular historical moment.[75] That the histories of Greeks and Romans have much to tell us on these subjects is a good sign of how, if skillfully read, classical texts (like those of many other cultures) can pique the interest of a broad and diverse public. It is important for disciplinary boundaries in academia and curricular rigidity not to hamper these enterprises. The ethnoarchaeozoological installation *Zoomania: Animals, Hybrids and Monsters in Human Cultures,* conceived and built by an interdisciplinary team at the Archaeological Museum of Siena, was a great success with the public. The student workshop connected to the show conducted a successful experiment of anthrozoological education, aimed at promoting awareness of relational mechanisms and the human responsibility in interspecies relations.[76] The Center for Anthropology and the Ancient World at the University of Siena encourages doctoral students and its research fellows to take up these topics for their research and has now produced works on, besides the weasel and the dog, fish onomastics, the nightingale, the *striges,* and animal voices.[77] Although classics still do not appear in Margo DeMello's (2010) collection of syllabi inspired by human-animal studies, it is encouraging to know that the 2012 winner of the Animals and Society Course Award was Athena Kirk of the Classics Department at Washington and Lee University. I believe classical studies has much to gain from these new angles of regard on human and nonhuman relations, in terms of skilled interpretation of texts and reconstruction of classification systems and nomenclature in ancient cultures. But anthrozoology and human-animal studies will benefit no less from a historical perspective on the big topics of contemporary debate—vegetarianism and respect for animal life; co-optation of nonhuman animals into the politics of class and gender and into the rhetoric of naturalization; concepts of domestication; and deep reasons for the human propensity for pets, to name just a few—than from the diverse riches of cultural elaborations that the Greek and Roman world left to posterity in their texts, places, and artifacts that have survived the ravaging hands of humans and of time.

ABBREVIATIONS

COLLECTIONS

FGrH   *Die Fragmente der griechischen Historiker,* edited by F. Jacoby. Berlin and Leiden, 1923–58.

Orph. fragm.   *Orphicorum Fragmenta,* edited by O. Kern. Berlin, 1922.

Paroem. Gr.   *Corpus Paroemiographorum Graecorum,* edited by E. von Leutsch and F. G. Schneidewin. 2 vols. Hildesheim, 1965.

PCG   *Poetae Comici Graeci,* edited by R. Kassel and C. Austin. Berlin and New York, 1983–98.

PMG   *Poetae Melici Graeci,* edited by D. L. Page. Oxford, 1962.

SSR   G. Giannantoni, *Socratis et Socraticorum Reliquiae.* Naples, 1990.

TGrF   *Tragicorum graecorum fragmenta,* reviewed by A. Nauck. Leipzig, 1889[2].

VS   H. Diels and W. Kranz, *Die Fragmente der Vorsokratiker.* Berlin, 1966[12].

DICTIONARIES

LfgrE   *Lexikon des frühgriechischen Epos.* Göttingen, 1979–.

LSJ   H. G. Liddell, R. Scott, and H. S. Jones, *A Greek-English Lexicon.* Oxford, 1968.

INSCRIPTIONS

CIG   *Corpus Inscriptionum Graecarum.* Vols. 1–2, edited by A. Boeckhius. Berlin, 1828–43. Vol. 3, edited by J. Franzius. Berlin, 1853. Vol. 4, edited by E. Curtius and A. Kirchhoff. Berlin, 1877.

IG   *Inscriptiones Graecae.* Berlin, 1873–1927.

Kaibel	*Epigrammata graeca ex lapidibus conlecta,* edited by G. Kaibel. Berlin, 1878.
LSAM	F. Sokolowski, *Lois sacrées de l'Asie mineure.* Paris, 1955.
LSS	F. Sokolowski, *Lois sacrées des cités grecques,* supplement. Paris, 1962.
SEG	*Supplementum Epigraphicum Graecum.* Leiden, 1923–.
Syll[3]	G. Dittenberger, *Sylloge Inscriptionum graecarum.* Leipzig, 1920[3] [1901[2]].

NOTES

PREFACE

1. Carlo Ginzburg (1980) has called this epistemological mode the "conjectural paradigm."

2. On a deeper level, this tendency is perhaps related to a certain antidogmatic skepticism common to Continental traditions in the humanities: an attitude that, even without its holder taking a position of radical relativism, willingly acknowledges the component of rhetorical persuasion involved in any compelling argument. On the complex and fundamental link between rhetoric and historiography, see Ginzburg 1999.

PROLOGUE

1. Hesiod tells the myth of the origin of human misery in the *Theogony* (535–616) and in *Works and Days* (42–105). The reading offered here owes its coherence to the indispensable influence of Jean-Pierre Vernant's essay (1989, 21–86), which includes a detailed analysis of these two passages.

2. This story does not just narrate the fall of man from a primitive condition of happiness but also serves as a foundation myth for Greek sacrificial practice. The beast is sacrificed and then butchered: the ritual participants consume the meat and edible fat, while the bones and innards—destined for the gods—are placed on the altar and burned whole. In short, animal sacrifice constitutes in large part a ritualization of meat eating. With its norms and restrictions, it fixed the manners of men and stabilized their position on the vertical axis of the cosmic order: they are situated in the space of the cooked, intermediate between beasts (who eat raw foods) and gods (who receive completely burned food): see Vernant 1988a, 143–82; Detienne 1977, 37ff.; Camassa 1994, 90–99. On ancient sacrifice, see most recently Faraone and Naiden 2012.

3. Hesiod, *Theogony* 589.

4. Hesiod, *Works and Days* 58.

5. The Greek diction of *Works and Days* clearly marks this change: the term *anthrōpoi* (generic "human beings") designates humans in the first part of the myth, up to the theft of fire. In Zeus's reaction, which foreshadows the birth of woman, the text begins to speak instead of *andres* ("male human beings," 56). Thus, with the advent of woman, into the space of humanity another "race" creeps in, the *genos* of female people, a new and different breed but one specifically designed by Zeus to be insidiously similar to man, and necessary to his survival. In this terrible intrusion of woman into the midst of the happy assembly of primordial men, one can glimpse a reflex of the Greek fantasy of male autarchy, a utopian world with no need for women's presence: Loraux 1993b, 72–110; 2000, 23ff. Such a utopia was also expressed by myths of autochthony, in which heroes are born straight from the ground, without maternal mediation: Loraux 2000, 13ff.

6. Hesiod, *Works and Days* 81–82 points to the first etymology. Whatever it is taken to mean, the name of the first bride underlines the important role of the gift (*dōron*) in marriage practice: whether she is given, or whether she arrives full of all gifts, Pandora is the legitimate bride, "gifted" to her husband by her guardians as a precious good, well distinguished from both the concubine, whether kidnapped or bought, and the slave, captured as booty in war (Leduc 1990, 255–58). Another hypothesis holds instead that *Pandora* originally had an active meaning, "she who gives every gift": Hesiod would then have made this compound passive to elide its original positive value, inasmuch as Pandora in the most ancient myth would have been the Earth-woman "who gives everything," a characterization in obvious contrast with the idea of ruinous woman in the Hesiodic vision (Zeitlin 1995, 51). Much has been written on Pandora, especially after the rise of women's studies: a useful summary of the various interpretations of the myth up to 1993, with a good selection of bibliographical references, can be found in Lombardi 1994, 23–43. Vernant 1989 and Loraux 1993b are still fundamental for reading the Hesiodic passages.

7. For weaving as the domain of Athena and the primary education of a good Greek girl, see Brulé 1987, 99–105.

8. The grace (*charis*) that Aphrodite confers on Pandora is not an innocent elegance of movement and posture. According to the loaded valence of the Greek term, *charis* implies the enticement of availability: it is a sweetness containing the implicit promise of assent to another's desire (Brillante 1998, 7–34). On the psychology of *charis* in archaic poetry, see MacLachlan 1993, 35–72.

9. Hesiod, *Works and Days* 67.

10. Ibid., 704 (on the misfortune of getting a wife who "lies in ambush for dinners"), 374 ("whoever trusts a woman, trusts thieves"), but especially Hesiod, *Theogony* 594–602, which compares women to drones, parasitic members of the beehive, who take no part in productive labors. On this subject, see Zeitlin 1995, 49ff.; Arrighetti 1998, 457–67.

11. Hermes exhibited his extraordinary proclivity for theft while still in the cradle: a few hours after being born he managed to steal the cattle of his older brother, Apollo (*Homeric Hymn to Hermes* 4.17–19). On Hermes the thief and patron of thieves, see N. O. Brown 1947, 5–22.

12. I pass over for now the iambics of Semonides (fr. 7 Pellizer-Tedeschi), another milestone of Greek misogyny. They list a varied negative typology of women, each one linked to an animal exemplar: the dog-woman, the restless, curious, and talkative nuisance, is cer-

tainly not absent, but she is placed alongside the horse-woman, the weasel-woman, the pig-woman, the fox-woman, and so on. In this ancient anthology of abominable women, the dog does not feature as an exclusive paradigm of feminine bestiality, and the passage, therefore, cannot be counted among the sources that give preference to the woman-dog association. However, on the particular feminine characterization that may distinguish the figure of the dog-woman from the other animal-women in the Semonides poem, see especially Loraux 1993b, 96–98.

13. Homer, *Odyssey* 11.422–34.

14. Homer, *Iliad,* 3.180, 6.344, 6.356; *Odyssey* 4.145. See also Euripides, *Andromache* 630.

15. On the notion of a cultural encyclopedia, see Sperber 1975, 91ff.; Eco 1986, 68ff.; Sperber and Wilson 1986, 87–93; Bettini 2013, 143ff.

16. Loraux 1981, 102 n. 136. Her *chiennerie* is rendered as *bitchiness* in the English translation (1993b, 96 n. 136). On the symbolic density of the Hesiodic representation of Pandora's bitchiness see also King 1998, 24-25. Similarities to the Greek phenomenon might be found in the Roman world as well, unless Horace's Canidia—a disquieting and aggressive "bitch" of a figure—is an imitation of a Greek model (Oliensis 1991, 111ff.).

1. OFFENSIVE EPITHETS

1. For convenience, *kyōn* (the nominative form of *dog*) will be used when speaking about the animal, but since the abusive *dog* took the vocative form *kyon,* that will refer to the insult.

2. Scholz 1937, 7–10; Merlen 1971, 27; Lilja 1976, 21–25; Mainoldi 1984, 109, 119. Not much different, at bottom, is the explanation of Orth 1913, 2569, which instead identifies the insult's origin in the relevance of character flaws that may be attributed to the dog.

3. Merlen 1971, 27, compares the Greeks' supposed horror at dogs to that of Arabs and Israelites and concludes that without a doubt it was the presence of scavenging dogs that gave rise to the Greek insult "denoting shamelessness and audacity." Carla Mainoldi believes the insult can be attributed to a series of character traits already ascribed to the dog, but adds, "On the other hand, the aspect of the dog that seems most relevant to its metaphorical uses is without a doubt its scavenging trait, a sign of its latent savagery" (1984, 109).

4. FGrH 328f67 (Philochorus); Xenophon, *Cynegeticus* 5.25; Plutarch, *Roman Questions* 111 (290b); Strabo 10.5.5. The idea of the dog's impurity dominates Scholz 1937, 7–10, where the animal's "genuine" character, in Greece and the Near East, is that of a pariah endowed with dangerous "mana," while its positive image as a guardian, hunter, and valued helper in human affairs is an Indo-European tradition superimposed on the autochthonous substrate.

5. Gourevitch 1968, 267–75; Mainoldi 1984, 58, 69. There were also sacred dogs for the Sicilian god Adranus: Mainoldi 1984, 69; Cusumano 1992, 155–58; Cataldi 1992, 72–82. Some institutional presence of dogs in sanctuaries is attested: *IG* II², 3.1.4962 (Asclepeion of Piraeus); Aelian, *On the Nature of Animals* 7.13 (Asclepeion of Athens), 11.3 (temple of Hephaestus in Sicily), 11.5 (temple of Athena Ilias in Daunia).

6. Although the category of impure animals did not exist—the Greeks eventually spoke of animals as being more or less "valued" (Parker 1996², 357)—many studies nevertheless invoke the presumed impurity of the dog: see, e.g., Couroucli 2005; De Grossi Mazzorin 2008. The question of restricted access to sacred spaces must be addressed case by case: a

being—animal or person—was considered impure in certain places or specific circumstances and only rarely in absolute terms. Women, for example, were excluded from many ceremonies (see Cole 1992), but not from all, and some were of exclusive relevance to women. But the tendency to generalize the categories of pure and impure is rather common: for instance, the idea that women and animals, dogs included, were excluded from most sacred spaces for being subject to contaminating biological processes such as childbirth and abortion (Cole 1995, 188). It is not clear in what sense male domestic animals can be implicated in this sort of biological impurity.

7. Mainoldi 1984, 119–20.

8. Faust 1970, 23; Lilja 1976, 21–22.

9. Faust 1969, 54–125. This is the only study focused on animal insults in ancient languages and thus the work most often cited by modern commentators on the subject.

10. Metaphor sets in motion a rich semiotic activity, implying phenomena of condensation that play between the semantic properties of the vehicle and the tenor (Eco 1986, 87ff.), which neither simile nor literal statement is able to produce. However trite and conventional an insulting metaphor may be, to call someone a pig is not the same thing as calling them greedy or as greedy as a pig. See ch. 4, n. 2.

11. Faust 1969 provides a list of traits involved in each animal metaphor under discussion, but for the dog this is limited to the passing note that in German, *Hund!* is equivalent to "schmutzig, schlecht [dirty, bad]" (77).

12. *Scholia in Homeri Iliadem* 1.225, 8.423–24, 21.394 Erbse; *Scholia in Homeri Odysseam* 7.216, 11.423 Dindorf; *Scholia in Hesiodi Opera et Dies* 67, 67a Pertusi.

13. *Anaideia* may consist in a lack of respect toward a superior, a senior, or even the helpless. A warrior, for example, might be accused of *anaideia* for raging uncontrollably against the body of a conquered enemy (Vernant 1991, 52; Cairns 1993, 49). Essentially, then, *anaideia* can be any sort of excess, any behavior that exceeds the measure set by the sense of moral duty and honor.

14. Graver 1995, 45: "The *anaides* gloss is ultimately not very informative, and at some points risks reducing the text to tautology."

15. Homer, *Iliad* 1.149–71, 1.225–44, 18.396.

16. Homer, *Odyssey* 17.248 (*olophōia eidōs*). On the difficult term *olophōia*, see Russo 1987², 172.

17. Unlike the cow and the horse (e.g., Aristotle, *Historia Animalium* 572a–b, 575b31), the dog is never cited among the species whose females are known for their sexual excitation. The lasciviousness of the she-goat was proverbial: Plutarch, *Roman Questions* 111 (290a–b).

18. In Italian, *cane/cagna* and "son of a *cane/cagna*" are offensive epithets; in English, *dog* is an insult and even more so its feminine counterpart, *bitch;* in German, *dummer/ gemeiner Hund* is an expression of outrage. (Furthermore, the examples, as we will see, are not limited to European languages.) To these offensive usages can be added other negative expressions that play on the image of the dog: expressions such as the Italian *un male cane, un tempo da cani, porco cane!,* and *è andata da cani* can be compared with the English *sick as a dog, work like a dog, treat like a dog, it's gone to the dogs,* etc., and the French *un temps de chien, froid de chien, vie de chien,* and the variant of the last, *chienne de vie.* See Masson 1997, 41–42; for modern Greek, Couroucli 2005, 239–48.

19. Leach 1964, 23–63. For the anthropological and ethnographic literature inspired by this study, see Sperber 1996; Kilani 2000, 73–112, also contains echoes of the theory.

20. Halverson 1976, 505–16, offers detailed criticism.

21. Dierauer 1977, 5, advances a similar theory. The opposition of useful (despised) / useless (prized) identified by Jean-Pierre Digard to explain the different treatment that some domestic animals enjoy with respect to others might support the notion that subordination to man is an important discriminating factor in constructing hierarchies of estimation (1990, 234–35); cf. the objections of Rivera 2000, 67. On animal domestication as a model for all forms of subordination, see Digard 1990, 221; Fiorani 1999, 188–96.

22. Wijeyewardene 1968, 81.

23. Tambiah 1969, 424–57.

24. The Amazonian Achuar exhibit a similar attitude toward dogs (Descola 1993, 101). In the Thai culture that Stanley Tambiah describes (1969), the dog also features in matrimonial ritual: the newlyweds eat rice out of a conch shell like dogs, all the while being called dogs. According to Tambiah, in this case the dog represents incest and confusion among age classes. After behaving "like dogs" for the last time, the spouses abandon forever the sphere of sexual promiscuity and definitively enter the exogamous order of matrimonial life. In North American Indian traditions as well, the dog appears in stories of incest that precede the mythic foundations of exogamous marriage: Lévi-Strauss 1995, 153ff. The Mkako of Cameroon also associate the dog with incest (Copet-Rougier 1988, 113–14).

25. I use James Gibson's (1979) category of affordance in the sense that Bettini 2013, 125ff., suggests, to indicate a factual given of animal morphology or behavior that lends itself to use in the construction of symbolic representations. Understood in this sense, affordance allows one to regard cultural representations as inventions motivated by a perceived fact. On Gibson's psychological theory, see also the appendix; Reed 1988.

26. See Wijeyewardene 1968, 86; Harris 1985, 68–69. The theory that bases the low social status of both dogs and pigs on their coprophilia is common and seems to have— compared to theories that refer to anthropophagy or sexual incontinence—a wealth of supporting ethnographic evidence. This explanation is all the more interesting since some ethologists have proposed that dogs were domesticated spontaneously, attracted by human excrement: Haudricourt 1977, 125–26; Digard 1990, 94; Fiorani 1999, 199.

27. Balinese society, however, associates incest with pigs instead: Geertz 1973, 420 n. 8.

28. Plutarch, *Roman Questions* 111 (290a–c).

29. Freud 1961, 54 n. 1. In Nigeria, *dog* is used as an insult for a man who is sexually promiscuous. The animal's tendency toward coprophagy, on the other hand, does not seem in this context to be subject to taboo, since dogs are allowed to "wash" children after the latter defecate: Olowo Ojoade 1994, 215–21. On the ambiguous position of dogs in human cultural history, see Shepard 1996, 62–64, 248–49.

30. "The Individual as Species," in Lévi-Strauss 1966, 191–216.

31. Regarding pet names and identities in contemporary societies, see the numerous observations scattered throughout Marchesini 1999; see also Rivera 2000, 61–67; Marchesini 2000b, 119–20. Mentz 1933 contains an exhaustive list of dog names in ancient Greece.

32. On the vagueness to which analyses of animal symbolism seem doomed when based solely on a determination of the position an animal occupies in the cultural taxonomy, see Sperber 1996.

2. THE DOG IN GREECE

1. On Homeric animal similes, see Schnapp-Gourbeillon 1981; Lonsdale 1990; Minchin 2001. Redfield 1975, 193–99, also has important observations, especially with regard to dogs. Miller 2000, 73–81, provides a comparative view of the animals involved in the biographies of epic heroes. On the wild boar in particular, see Camerotto 2005; Franco 2006.

2. In both poems the collocation "dogs and men" occurs in thirteen of the thirty-three passages that mention the dog (excluding the group of *kyon* insults and the references to dogs in threats of outrage to corpses, which constitute, as we will see further on, two other typical cases of epic diction). This concept generates a verbal scheme that occurs with the following variants: κύνες θαλεροί τ᾽ αἰζηοί (Homer, *Iliad* 3.26 = 11.414; same position but in the accusative at 17.282); κύνες τ᾽ ἄνδρές τε νομῆες (ibid., 17.65); κυνῶν ἀλκτῆρα καὶ ἀνδρῶν (Homer, *Odyssey* 14.531 = 21.340); κύνες τε καὶ ἀνέρες ἀγροιῶται (*Iliad* 11.549 = 15.272); ἀνδρῶν τε κυνῶν τε (*Odyssey* 19.444); ἀνδρῶν ἠδὲ κυνῶν (*Iliad* 10.186 = 12.147); κύνας ἠδὲ καὶ ἄνδρας (ibid., 13.475); κύνες ἠδὲ καὶ αὐτοὶ (*Odyssey* 19.429, in the same metrical position as the preceding instance, of which it can be considered a modified form).

3. As the list in the previous note shows, in some of its variants the collocation appears to be a genuine formula (understood as a sequence of two or more words, in the same metrical position, occurring at least twice: Cantilena 1982, 58–81). This sharpens the impression that the whole spectrum of occurrences can be considered inflections of a single traditional semantic pattern, so in this sense we define the schema "dogs and men" as a formulaic nexus. See in this regard the definition Nagler 1967 proposes, according to which the "formula" is more of a conceptual image that the rhapsode would have time and again given voice to in similar but not necessarily identical verbal sequences united by a Wittgensteinian "family resemblance" (269–311). On the difficult problem of defining the formula and determining its degree of flexibility, see Hainsworth 1968; Cantilena 1982.

4. Homer, *Iliad* 11.414–20.

5. Ibid., 17.281–83.

6. To quote Redfield 1975, in these similes "dogs and men together form a functioning unit" (193).

7. Homer, *Iliad* 15.271–76.

8. Ibid., 22.188–92, 10.360–64, 15.579–81.

9. This occurs in the scene, already mentioned, where Ajax rushes to defend the body of Patroclus as a boar easily scatters "dogs and strong young men" simply by wheeling around and fighting head on (Homer, *Iliad* 8.338–40); likewise when Hector wheels around "in the midst of dogs and hunters" like a boar or lion exulting in its own strength, and whichever way it charges "there the ranks of men give way" (12.41–48). When Sarpedon scolds Hector's brothers and kinsmen for their lack of action, he describes them as dogs that shrink in fear around a lion (5.476), while in another passage the Trojans attack Ajax like dogs do a wounded boar, "but when the boar wheels on them, trusting in its strength, they shrink back, trembling in fear, on this side and that" (17.725–29).

10. Ibid., 17.61–67. Another passage compares the Teucrians to "dogs and men of the countryside" who drive a lion (Ajax) out of their corral (11.548–55).

11. Ibid., 15.579–88.

12. Mainoldi 1984, 113.

13. Homer, *Odyssey* 14.21–36.

14. Mainoldi 1984, 116.

15. Hainsworth 1961, 122–25. Cf., however, the judicious observations in Rose 1979, 218.

16. Homer, *Odyssey* 21.363–65.

17. Ibid., 16.4–6.

18. Plutarch, *On the Intelligence of Animals*, 15 (970e).

19. On the differing views that ancient philosophers and schools of thought expressed about animals, see Dierauer 1977; Ditadi 1994; Castignone and Lanata 1994; Lanata 2000; Labarrière 2000; Gilhus 2006; Kalof 2007; Newmyer 2011; Osborne 2011. For a synoptic view of the ancient debate between "utilitarians" and "animalists," see Franco 2001.

20. Aristotle, *Rhetoric* 2.3 (1380a): ὅτι δὲ πρὸς τοὺς ταπεινουμένους παύεται ἡ ὀργή, καὶ οἱ κύνες δηλοῦσιν οὐ δάκνοντες τοὺς καθίζοντας (That anger ceases toward those who humble themselves even dogs demonstrate, since they do not bite those who sit down). Aristotle does not explicitly mention the Homeric passage, and perhaps he refers to a common interpretation of canine behavior (see, e.g., Pliny, *Natural History* 8.146). A curious fact, showing both the empirical character and the variability of cultural elaborations about animals, is that the Japanese, in contrast to the Greeks, think dogs are sensitive to shows of strength and nonchalance, and they advise displaying confident indifference when dogs attack (Vetturini 1996, 163).

21. This Homeric episode has roused in modern commentators a strange interpretive persistence, with results even more bizarre than those already mentioned: one scholar has wanted to see in Odysseus's reaction to the dogs' threat the hero's particular "insight into the canine mind" (Lilja 1976, 29) instead of a strategy that was part of traditional practical knowledge, something any ancient wayfarer might know. The tendency to overinterpret the Homeric text, as though at each moment it were depicting heroic realities and priceless facets of mythic prehistory, can produce rather questionable results that strain credibility. Studies on oral culture have long since shown how traditional and "bourgeois" the contents of this genre of composition can be, a sort of mnemonic storehouse, dressed up in fantastic heroic trappings, that is meant to record and pass down practical notions and the culture's code of values: see Havelock 1978, 29–105.

22. Digard 1988, 34; Digard 1990, 79–81, 172–79; Fiorani 1999, 194. For critical revisions of the very notion of domestication, see Sigaut 1988; Digard 1990, 85–103; O'Connor 1997. When Carla Mainoldi appeals to a special "status" for the Homeric dog, she means a particular historical feature, some special position that the dog may have occupied in human society during the Homeric period, when it may not yet have been conceived of as a completely domesticated animal (1984, 119–20; see also, more recently, Kitchell 2004). Besides the fact that the passages we've analyzed so far do not seem to support the idea of a dog in a still-wild state in Homer, this assumption more simply risks the methodological error that Aristotle pointed out for those who classify animals according to the categories of domestic and wild: "Practically all the animals that are domesticated are also found in a wild state, for example, *human beings* [my italics], horses, cattle, dogs in India, pigs, goats, sheep" (*On the Parts of Animals,* 643b; see also Aristotle, *Problems* 895b25). An animal, even though domesticated, can never completely belong to the domain of culture, just as man can always slip back into being a "wild" animal.

23. Homer, *Odyssey* 17.61–62, 20.144–45 (ἅμα τῷ γε δύω κύνες ἀργοὶ ἕποντο).

24. E.g., Homer, *Iliad* 16.257 (οἳ δ' ἅμα Πατρόκλῳ μεγαλήτορι θωρηχθέντες ἔστιχον). In one passage in the *Iliad* (11.291–95), Hector incites his men against the Achaeans "like a hunter sets loose his white-toothed dogs against a wild boar or lion." It may be noted here that the regular term in Homer for a dog's master is *anax*, the Mycenaean "lord," head of the people and the army but also lord of the house, the master to whom the members of the *oikos*—women, slaves, nursemaids—owe obedience (see, e.g., Homer, *Odyssey* 1.397).

25. Homer, *Odyssey* 2.10–11.

26. Ibid., 6.84 (ἅμα τῇ γε καὶ ἀμφίπολοι κίον ἄλλαι).

27. An interpretation found already in Mahaffy 1874, 63 (cited in Lilja 1976, 27, 28 n. 53); see also Redfield 1975, 259 n. 66. According to Lilja, the Homeric expression οὐκ οἶος instead "only implies an allusion to the function of the dogs as guards" (28).

28. Homer, *Odyssey* 17. 309–10.

29. There is abundant iconographic evidence of dogs at their master's table: see Mainoldi 1984, 113, which reads the dog as a specific marker of the aristocratic feast; Schneider 2000, 18 n. 46.

30. Homer, *Iliad* 23.173–74. Two of these dogs would be slaughtered at their master's funeral pyre: see ch. 3.

31. Post-Homeric Greek had other terms for "parasite" as well, such as *entrapezitis, epitrapezidios,* and *trapezoleiktēs* (table-licker): Plutarch, *How to Distinguish Friend from Flatterer*, 3 (50c); Alciphron, *Epistles*, 3.9; Hesychius, s.v. ἐπιτραπεζίδιος; *Suda*, s.v. ἐντραπεζίτιδος. See also Ribbeck 1884, 99. On table dogs as idlers, see Oppian, *On the Hunt* 1.472–76.

32. Homer, *Odyssey* 18.105.

33. In Aesop, 342 Perry (216 Chambry³), wolves try to persuade herd dogs to hand over their flock, using as leverage the fact that men make dogs work but treat them poorly, giving them only leftovers to eat. This does not mean that the dog was considered a contemptible creature: in both the archaic and classical periods, to own dogs, just like horses, was a sign of distinction and affluence (Solon, fr. 23 West² [17 Gentili-Prato²]; Plato, *Lysis* 211e); simply being admitted to human tables already made the dog a privileged animal (Xenophon, *Memorabilia* 2.7.13).

34. See Aristophanes, *Knights* 413–16; Aristophanes, *Clouds* 489–91; Alciphron 3.8.2; Plutarch, *Life of Lycurgus* 12.9; *Suda*, s.v. ἀπομαγδαλία; Eustathius 1857.17, 1887.52. The term probably derives from the root ἀπομάσσω, perhaps through an adverb *ἀπομάγδην (Frisk 1954, 2:181). For the institutional function of "cleaner" that the dog plays in other cultures, see Milliet 1995, 83–87. In this sense dogs are like beggars, addressed as "garbage collectors" (δαιτῶν ἀπολυμαντῆρες) in Homer, *Odyssey* 17.220.

35. Homer, *Odyssey* 10.216–17. *Meiligmata thymou* refers to hunger satisfied by the food the master brings home (hence "soothing desire" in the sense of "restorative" morsels): *thymos* is the vital energy sustained by food as well as the desire that disturbs someone hungry (Caswell 1990, 16–17). But more generally, *thymos* is the emotive component that can manifest itself as boldness, courage, or desire, as well as anger, ferocity, or impetuosity. The latter set of propensities, as we will see (in the section "'Hungry like a Wolf' and Mental Disturbances"), man typically attributes to dogs and keeps in check by offering the animal food to render it gentle. This Homeric passage may therefore imply that the morsels the master brings home are meant to placate the dangerous ire of a famished dog, especially if we consider that the simile describes the behavior of the beasts bewitched by Circe (see Heubeck

1983, 235) and that the verb *meilissein* is typically used for "propitiating" enraged divinities. On magical means of soothing somebody's *thymos,* see Faraone 2004.

36. Aesop, 93 Hausrath[2] (91 Perry = 275 Chambry[3]). Besides the literary evidence describing the Maltese as the classic pet beloved of and pampered by its master—e.g., Aesop, 75 Hausrath[2] (73 Perry = 305 Chambry[3]), which attests to the common habit of bringing a Maltese or a monkey along for diversion on long sea crossings; Theophrastus, *Characters* 21.9, where the "snob" has a tomb built for his dead Maltese puppy; Plutarch, *On Peace of Mind* 13; Artemidorus, *The Interpretation of Dreams* 2.11—there are also images portraying children with their favorite pets, among which are dogs with characteristics (small size, long and flowing hair) that generally identify them as Maltese: Hamilton 1992, 84–111. See also Busuttil 1969. On animals as pets and play companions, see Musée de Marseille 1991, 64–71; Bodson 1994b, 63–74; Bodson 2000b; Fittà 1997, 65–72.

37. Besides the dog, only the pig is raised on human food, but it certainly does not share man's dining spaces.

38. Theophrastus, *Characters* 4.8.

39. These animals fall into the category of beasts "of burden" (*hypozygia*): Xenophon, *Oeconomicus* 18.4. Theophrastus's text may indicate simply a temporal concurrence between the meals of the bumpkin and his beasts of burden: he dines while his cows, donkeys, and horses eat, a situation recalling our saying, proverbially associated with country life, "Going to bed with the chickens." If instead it means that the bumpkin, during dinner, throws food to the farm animals, the image would be even more bizarre and comical: one would have to imagine a table surrounded not by dogs, as in the homes of the rich, but by farmyard herbivores; instead, with an even more marked reversal, one may suppose he goes out to eat in the barn. Arrian (*Cynegeticus* 9) also attests to the habit of sleeping with dogs.

40. Aesop, 283 Hausrath[2] (178 Chambry[3]).

41. Anaxandris, fr. 40.8–9 Kassel-Austin; Aristophanes, *Acharnians* 1156–60, *Knights* 1030–34, *Wasps* 835–972. When robbers wanted to distract guard dogs, they threw the animals bread and cakes, and it was thought that to attract a dog nothing worked better than the smell of well-roasted meat: Aelian, *On the Nature of Animals* 7.13, 14.27. On the prevalence of bread in the canine diet, see Arrian, *Cynegeticus* 8.2

42. Hesiod, *Works and Days* 604; compare ibid., 146–47, with the Homeric passages that define humans as those "who on earth eat *sitos*" (e.g., *Odyssey* 8.222, 9.89). *Works and Days* 606–7 calls food for cows and mules *chortos* (fodder) and *syrphetos* (gathered refuse). For cereal grains as plants subjected to the "cooking" of cultivation, see Detienne 1977, 12ff.

43. Aristotle, *History of Animals* 594a27–30, 612a6–7; Aelian, *On the Nature of Animals* 8.9. By contrast, straw and barley chaff—raw plant matter—are the typical diet of the other domestic, collaborative animals (donkeys, horses, cows): Aesop, 295 Hausrath[2] (264 Perry = 276 Chambry[3]).

44. Aristotle, *History of Animals,* 502a7. By contrast, the pig, which likes human food but is not one of the *karcharodonta,* also eats raw vegetables, especially roots (ibid., 595a16–19). Dogs tend to drink the blood of wounded prey: Arrian, *Cynegeticus* 25.9.

45. Aesop, 342 Perry (216 Chambry[3]).

46. Plato, *Laws* 906d.

47. Aesop, 276 Hausrath[2] (267 Perry = 314 Chambry[3]).

48. Dion of Prusa, *Oration* 7.17.

49. Aristotle, *History of Animals* 607a1–8; see also Aelian, *On the Nature of Animals* 4.19, 8.1; Xenophon, *Cynegeticus* 3.1; Pollux 5.38. There is no lack of other analogies between dogs and lions. Aristotle (*History of Animals* 497b) emphasizes the similar structure of the dog and the lion: the difference is that dogs have cervical vertebrae, while lions have a single bone in their neck; as to digestive organs, Aristotle classifies man, dog, and lion among the animals with a small belly, as opposed to the pig and the bear, which have larger stomachs (495b, 507b). The pseudo-Aristotelian treatise on physiognomy also associates the lion with large-breed dogs, in their *megalopsychia* (high-mindedness, arrogance; 811a20), and again, lions and "barking dogs" are examples of how a deep voice is a sign of courage (807a20); lions and dogs demonstrate that those with slim waists are particularly well suited for hunting (810b5). The dog's relationship with the fox is well attested, and perhaps their nearness explains the reluctance to use dogs to hunt this animal: according to Xenophon, when dogs chase foxes they get corrupted and can't be found when they're needed (*Cynegeticus* 6.3). If dogs easily acquire the bad habits of the fox, it is probably because they are "genetically" very similar (see Babrius 95).

50. Xenophon, *Cynegeticus* 4.4, 6.15. Aelian explains that hunting dogs consider captured prey a prize due to them only if the master consents: the dog hunts out of desire for honor (*philotimia*), not for the meat (*On the Nature of Animals* 8.2). See also Arrian, *Cynegeticus* 18.

51. Xenophon, *Cynegeticus* 7.9 (see also Arrian *Cynegeticus* 25.9). The Aesop fable (139 Hausrath[2] [136 Perry = 182 Chambry[3]]) that illustrates doubtful wavering (*amphibolos*) is perhaps based on the behavior of a hunting dog that immobilizes its prey but doesn't kill it, bites but doesn't eat it: see ch. 5, n. 41.

52. Aesop, 222 Hausrath[2] (206 Perry = 312 Chambry[3]): a herdsman throws stillborn lambs and the corpses of sheep to his dog; 134 Hausrath[2] (254 Perry = 183 Chambry[3]): a dog steals entrails from the kitchen. The habit of tossing the prey's entrails to the hounds was still common in aristocratic hunts in eighteenth-century Europe; nonaristocratic hunters instead would roast and eat the innards themselves on the spot: Padiglione 1994, 187.

53. Lincoln 1975 discusses at length the meaning of *lyssa*, with comparative Indo-European material. Note that the current objection to this etymology—raised already by Ernout 1948 and revived by Mainoldi 1984, 186 n. 108—claims that if lyssa were indeed connected with the wolf, we should find more evidence of wolves inflicted with the disease. But lyssa is not "a malady typical of the wolf" (Chantraine 1968, s.v. λύσσα) but rather a typical illness of dogs that consists, as Lincoln has well shown, in "turning wolf," in becoming "like a wolf," and how can this happen to a wolf, which is already such by nature? On the contrary, if anything, it is the passage in Theocritus (4.11) that speaks of wolves with lyssa that calls for explanation: see Gow 1952[2], 79. On the close proximity of dogs and wolves, see Plato, *Sophist* 231a6.

54. *Lyssa* is used of canine rabies properly speaking in Aristotle, *History of Animals* 7.22.604a4–10, but already in Homer it appears associated with dogs. Mainoldi 1984, 175, is somewhat hesitant to assert that lyssa was the disease of rabies from the time of Homer: in the epics it referred instead to an entirely human condition of martial frenzy and only later took on the specialized meaning of the canine pathology (this is the position of *LSJ*, which glosses λύσσα in Homer only as "martial rage": see Chantraine 1968, s.v. λύσσα). But the passage where Hector is a "rabid dog" (*Iliad* 8.299) is sufficient evidence that at least from Homer on, the dog was considered subject to lyssa, whether or not this is understood "clin-

ically" as the disease of rabies. The connection between dogs and lyssa then occurs regularly, beginning at least with Aristophanes (*Lysistrata* 298), and the krater by the Lycaon painter (see below, n. 58) provides clear evidence for the middle of the fifth century. Thus, it is not Xenophon who first references canine lyssa (as Chantraine maintains) but Homer, followed by Aristophanes.

55. *FGrH* 26f1.19 (Conon); Pausanias 1.43.7–8; Callimachus frr. 26–31 Pfeiffer; Athenaeus 3.29e; Statius, *Thebaid* 1.571–672 (where dogs that have been inflicted with *dira rabies* dismember Linos). See also Russell 1955. Another myth speaks of a priest's son being torn apart by a dog in the sanctuary on Delos (Callimachus, fr. 664 Pfeiffer); this was the *aetion* for the exclusion of dogs from the island. See Acosta-Hughes 2002, 188.

56. Plato, *Republic* 416a1–7.

57. Demosthenes 25.40.8 (*Against Aristogeiton* 1).

58. Apollodorus gives both motivations in his version, *Bibliotheca* 3.4.4. The version in which lyssa motivates Actaeon's dogs must be ancient: on a krater by the Lycaon painter (Boston, Museum of Fine Arts, inv. 00.346; ARV² 1045, mid-fifth century B.C.E.), next to Actaeon being attacked by his own dogs is a female figure in hunting attire, from whose head a small dog's head is coming out, accompanied by the inscription ΛΥΣΑ. We see here canine lyssa personified, in the act of setting dogs against Actaeon, who shows signs of his metamorphosis into a stag (antlers and ears). In both motivations given in the mythic variants—Actaeon's metamorphosis into a stag and the dogs' attack by madness—the mechanism concerns the dogs' inability to recognize their master, a distortion of their perception of reality: Frontisi-Ducroux 1997.

59. The wolf is the *makellarios* (butcher) par excellence, with which one cannot expect collaboration since its nature leads it to see in other animals only meat and food (Aesop, 97, 187, 209, 267, 366 Perry [107, 281, 313, 314, 315 Chambry³]).

60. Plato, *Republic* 416a1–7, mentioned above, says that herd dogs can turn wolf through intemperance, hunger, or any bad habit to which their imprudent master has accustomed them. If a dog happens to taste the meat of a dead sheep, it is no longer a trustworthy guardian: it will tend to attack the flock (*Geoponica* 18.2.13).

61. Homer, *Iliad* 8.299.

62. For instances of lyssa as an altered mental state in humans, see Ciani 1974, 72ff.; Mainoldi 1984, 175; Grmek and Gourevitch 1998, 117–18. That lyssa appears as a type of human madness predominantly in the poets suggests that its origin may lie in canine "madness," of which human "rabies" was a metaphorical extension. In the *Corpus Hippocraticum* we find only one mention of lyssa (*On Ancient Medicine* 19), describing the state of painful irritation caused by an excess of bile.

63. Homer, *Iliad* 9.238–39 (see also 9.305). At ibid., 13.53, Hector is "raving mad like fire [λυσσώδης φλογὶ εἴκελος]." As Lincoln 1975, 104, emphasizes, lyssa makes the hero invincible and his attack irresistible: it's no accident that in Homer, it is only attributed to Achilles and Hector, the extreme models of martial virtue. Moreover, in war, the hero has to display blind and savage violence, as shown by the many similes comparing the brave warrior to a wild, carnivorous beast: see Vermeule 1979, 83–116; Clarke 1995. That "raving" Hector regards neither men nor gods clearly shows the ambiguity of this heroic virtue: this kind of madness may be valued in war, where violence is required, but should not, for this very reason, be considered an unconditional good.

64. Homer, *Iliad* 21.542–43. On this point, see also Vernant 1991, 51ff.

65. All in the *Odyssey*: 16.4–6, where Eumaeus's dogs greet Telemachus as he arrives, recognizing him as a friend of their master; 17.301–2, where the only creature on Ithaca to recognize Odysseus after his twenty-year absence is his dog Argus, who raises his ears and wags his tail on seeing his master approach; 16.162, where Athena appears and only Odysseus and the dogs see her. A fragment of Heraclitus (*VS* 22b97) says, "Dogs bark at those they don't know." On the canine nous (as the faculty of recognition) in Homer, see Heath 2005, 49–50.

66. See Homer, *Odyssey* 8.575–76, which contrasts wild men with "hospitable" (*philoxeinoi*) peoples.

67. Theophrastus, *Characters* 4.10.

68. Plato, *Republic* 375e–376b. On animal figures in Plato, see Pinotti 1994, 103–22.

69. How sophistic and provocative this wholly positive Platonic model of the dog's capacity of recognition is may be inferred by comparing it to other evidence that presumably adheres to the traditional image of the dog's inability to distinguish between benevolent and malevolent as a clear sign of its limited rationality. Still, it should be noted that the traditional model does not deny canine intelligence but only criticizes its gray areas. The dog's intelligence was a productive theme among philosophers. Hunting dogs, for example, were cited as a paradigm of syllogistic reason, for their ability to pick out from several options the right track for quarry, as Plutarch relates (*On the Intelligence of Animals*, 13 [969b]; see also Aelian, *On the Nature of Animals* 6.59; Sextus Empiricus, *PH* 1.62–72; Decleva Caizzi 1993; Floridi 1997). With his characteristic good sense, Plutarch stresses the speciousness of such arguments: the dog finds the trail by means of its subtle senses alone; its intelligence is to be seen not in situations involving recognition with its senses (scent or vision) but when it exercises discernment and judgment, as, for example, when it obeys a command.

70. Theophrastus, *Characters* 14.5–6.

71. Homer, *Odyssey* 20.14–16. Many translators into modern languages have understood the expression ἄνδρ' ἀγνοιήσασ' ὑλάει to mean that the she-dog barks at a man she doesn't know: in English, for example, Fagles 1996 has "growls, facing a stranger," Fitzgerald 1961 "howl and bristle at a stranger," and Lattimore 1965 "facing an unknown man." But in such a situation, a she-dog with puppies would not behave any differently than any other dog whatsoever. Instead, in my view, the line should be understood as "she barks at the man she does not recognize," that is, her master (for *agno[i]ein* of recognizing a known person, see *Odyssey* 23.95, 24.218; *LfgrE*, s.v. ἀγνο[ι]έω; in Aeschylus, *Suppliants* 499, Danaus warns, "Beware, lest boldness give birth to fear, for through ignorance [ὑπ' ἀγνοίας] men have slain those they love"), since the specificity of a mother dog protecting her pups is that she does not allow anyone near, not even those she would at other times treat as friends: Semonides's infamous iambic about the races of women shows this clearly (fr. 7.33–36 West²). See also Oppian, *Halieutica* 1.719–23: the new mother barks at the shepherd "even if he was a friend before [εἰ καὶ πάρος ἦεν ἑταῖρος]." In *History of Animals* 571b29–31, Aristotle notes that animal aggression increases for males during the mating season, for females after giving birth, and he gives the examples of the she-bear and the she-dog. In *Problems* 894b13, Aristotle cites the sow in addition to the she-dog for this same postpartum behavior.

72. Epithets commonly used for the dog are *irascible/excitable* (ὀργίλος: Aesop, 107 Hausrath² [105 Perry = 139 Chambry³]; δυσόργητος: Pseudo-Aristotle, *Physiognomonica*

811a32) and *impulsive/impetuous* (θυμικός: Aristotle, *History of Animals* 488b22; see also θυμοειδής in Plato, *Republic* 375a–e).

73. Aelian, *On the Nature of Animals* 15.11.

74. The *karcharias* shark was the "sharp-toothed" (*karcharos*) fish par excellence: Thompson 1947, 106, 136. Isidore of Seville confirms the etymology (*Etymologiae* 12.6.5): "Canes in mari a terrenis canibus nuncupati, quod mordeant" (Dogs in the sea are named after land dogs, because they bite); see also Pliny, *Natural History* 9.34. It has recently been argued that in later times the basilisk was called κινάδης for a similar reason: Barbara 2005. On the mechanisms of transposing names from the terrestrial to the aquatic realm, see Guasparri 1998, 408–14.

75. The anecdote is alluded to in three epigrams in the *Palatine Anthology* (9.17, 9.18, 9.371), the first two attributed to Germanicus (the brother of the emperor Claudius), the third anonymous (Page 1981², 557–58). An interesting epigram by Antipater of Thessalonica (*Pal. Anth.* 9.268) may figure a dogfish as an animal instrument of an avenging Keres that devours the evildoer: see Gow and Page 1968, 106 (the reading Κηρῶν is the result of emendation and thus uncertain). Regarding the "dog" fish, Aelian (*On the Nature of Animals* 13.4) cites an interesting fragment of the comic poet Anaxippus (fr. 2 Kassel-Austin), in which an irate character threatens an adversary with these words: "If you keep provoking me and making my bile boil like a *callionymus* [a type of fish], you'll find out I'm no different from a sword-dog [ξιφίου κυνός]!" This is perhaps a play on words between a dogfish, or "sea dog" (*kyōn thalattios*), and a swordfish (*xiphias*), based on the threatening aggression of the sea "dog": if you don't stop, we are going to come to blows, and then you'll find, the character says, continuing the fish imagery begun with the mention of the callionymus, that I'm a complete "dogfish with a sword." Here, it's worth recalling that the terrible, human-eating sea monster in the *Odyssey* is called Scylla, a name that Homer intentionally plays off the similar *skylax* (puppy). A voracious and aggressive fish seems to have been imagined fairly regularly as a dog of the sea.

76. Aristotle, *History of Animals* 502a20. Aristotle classifies the baboon, or *kynokephalos*, as among the species of monkeys held to be intermediate between man and quadrupeds in some complex way (502a16); thus, for him, even baboons are in some sense anthropomorphic. Modern taxonomy instead distinguishes between anthropomorphic primates (humans, chimpanzees, orangutans, gorillas) and cynomorphic primates (baboons, mandrills, and various other species). Among "Greek" monkeys, the *kynokephaloi* in particular provided fodder for popular fantasies of marvelous fabled societies of half-human beings with dog heads, which ancient geography located in distant lands at the world's edges: Herodotus mentions them in his description of Libyan fauna (4.191) alongside other marvelous creatures, such as those "without heads," which have eyes in their chests, and the "wild men." See Romm 1992, 77–81; 1996, 133–35. Colorful descriptions of these "dogheaded" monkey-men are found in Aelian, where it's notably impossible to tell whether the accounts are about identifiable animals such as baboons or about the half-human beings of mythic geography (*On the Nature of Animals* 4.46, 6.1, 7.19, 10.30). See also Fischer and Wecker 1924, 24–26; White 1991, 47–70.

77. Aelian, *On the Nature of Animals* 14.24, 14.27. The two stories about pankynion and kynosbatos display an obvious parallelism: one repeats the same formula in the sea as on the land. We'll encounter these "canine" plants again later on.

78. Plutarch, *Greek Questions* 15.294e–f; see also Aristotle, fr. 572 Gigon. Athenaeus (2.70c) also mentions the myth.

79. A lost drama of Sophocles mentioned a *kynaros akantha,* which the grammarian Didymus (*apud* Athenaeus 2.70c; see also Hesychius, s.v. κύναρος) conjectured referred to the kynosbatos, with its rough and harmful spines. But it could be the artichoke, which was called *kinara* but had a graphic variant, *kynara,* that eventually prevailed—and determined the modern taxonomic name of the plant group (Cynara). Chantraine 1968 (s.v. κίναρα) suggests that this variant arose under the influence of *kyōn:* it's difficult to judge, but if indeed *kyōn* played a role, the artichoke's prickliness and spines may well have been the relevant factors.

80. Xenophon, *Cynegeticus* 5.15. See also Arrian, *Cynegeticus* 7.3, 25.5. Elsewhere, Xenophon recommends gentle means to calm excited dogs in the presence of the prey: one should use a soft and reassuring tone and not assail them (*Cynegeticus* 6.10). Such methods were not always employed. In Homer, when Eumaeus's dogs surround Odysseus, the swineherd drives them away with rocks (*Odyssey* 14.35–36), and in Aesop, we find reference to the fact that dogs were often beaten (342 Perry [216 Chambry³]).

81. Similarly, the proverbial aggression of a bitch protecting her puppies was represented as a form of genuine madness (Semonides, fr. 7.33 West²: μαίνεται), since it involved the animal losing its normal cognitive faculties. That lyssa served as evidence that dogs, as a rule, possessed rationality and self-control was already argued in antiquity. Just as a sick man can lose the reason he is endowed with, so, too, a rabid dog is out of its usual senses because it has lost one of its natural faculties: Plutarch, *On the Intelligence of Animals* 5 (963c–f).

82. Because of their extraordinary strength, Indian dogs were well suited for boar hunting (Xenophon, *Cynegeticus* 10.1) and were used in warfare by the Persians (Herodotus 1.192.15–20, 7.187.4–5). Alexander the Great saw a famous spectacle when the Indians wanted to show the incredible daring and ferocity of their dogs, which scorned all lesser adversaries and would take on only a lion as their equal: the Indian dog did not let go of its prey even when its owners started cutting its tail and legs; it gave up only when they cut off its head (Aelian, *On the Nature of Animals* 8.1; Plutarch, *On the Intelligence of Animals* 15 [970f–971a]; Diodorus Siculus 17.92; Pollux 5.42–44). On their origin in cross-breeding with a tiger, see Aristotle, *History of Animals* 607a; Aristotle, *Generation of Animals* 746a; Aelian, *On the Nature of Animals* 8.1. See also Pomelli 2003.

83. Pollux 5.38.

84. Homer, *Odyssey* 17.291–94. The episode is quite famous and its reception widespread: Most 1991, 144ff. It has mainly been interpreted as an example of dogs' fidelity, but its function within the Homeric text is rather to stress the dog and master's common status of outcasts from the palace and to stage a unique scene of mutual recognition (Köhnken 2003, 391–96).

85. A theory that has found some favor is that *Argus*—usually interpreted as a proper name and connected by ancient commentators with the adjective *argos,* "swift" (or perhaps "white, shining")—was originally a common noun that meant "dog." If this is true, the Homeric line would have originally meant simply "the dog of long-suffering Odysseus": Carpenter 1950 (endorsed by West 1978, 160, 368–69).

86. Ballarini 1999, 319–24.

87. On hypozygia, see Xenophon, *Oeconomicus* 18.4. According to Aelian (*On the Nature of Animals* 6.8), the names for the upbringing of dogs and birds were respectively

σκυλακοτροφική and ὀρνιθοτροφία—from *troph,* "rearing,"—whereas that of horses was πωλοδαμνική, from *dama-/damn-/dmā-,* "taming."

88. On the lexicon of taming, see Benveniste 1973, 242–51. For the metaphor of the yoke: Dumortier 1935, 12ff.; Onians 1951, 407. The bridle and the charioteer as metaphors of control and mastery are found, for example, in the famous Platonic image of the chariot of the soul (Plato, *Phaedrus* 246b) and in Aeschylus on the madness of Orestes, which feels like a charioteer no longer in control of his horses (*Choephori* 1022); on this topic, see Myrick 1994. The metaphorical uses of reins and bit (*chalinos*) are quite numerous, as a look at their entries in modern dictionaries will indicate. On the importance that the bit played in the economy of relations between man and horse in Greece, duly reflected in myth, see the seminal Detienne and Vernant 1978, 183–213.

89. Hesiod, *Works and Days* 795–97.

90. Xenophon, *Cynegeticus* 6.11–14; Aelian, *On the Nature of Animals* 8.2. The herd dog is the guide of the flock: Aesop, 153 Perry (158 Hausrath[2] = 217 Chambry[3]).

91. Terms such as *deraion, kloios* (collar), *kynouchos* (leash or perhaps muzzle: Reinach 1928), and *himas* and *kyneira* (leash) were not generally used as metaphors of domination. This does not mean that, especially in Aesop, the dog was not also portrayed as man's slave, in opposition to wild animals, and that the sign of this subordination was not, besides poor food and occasional beatings, the collar that led it (Aesop, 342 Perry [216 Chambry[3]], 294 Hausrath[2] [226 Chambry[3]], 329 Perry [179 Chambry[3]], 346 Perry).

92. Aelian, *On the Nature of Animals* 9.54. See also *Geoponica* 18.2.16–17.

93. Aelian, *On the Nature of Animals* 9.54–55. On the magic of knots and their interpretation by James Frazer, see Bettini 2013, 74–77, 80–82.

94. Aristotle, *Rhetoric* 1406b26–29. Aggressive dogs used as guards were kept tied up during the day and let loose at night: Xenophon, *Anabasis* 5.8.24. A dangerous dog should be restrained with a three-cubit-long rope: Plutarch, *Life of Solon* 20.4.

95. Xenophon, *Cynegeticus* 7.11–12.

96. Xenophon explicitly advises treating dogs with kindness rather than force: they should be coaxed, encouraged, called by name (ibid., 6.10, 17.22, 17.25). Violent means were most often used to punish dogs for insubordination (Anaxandrides fr. 40 Kassel-Austin) or to drive out those that were rabid (Demosthenes 25.40.8 [*Against Aristogeiton* 1]), but there do not seem to be examples of dogs induced to perform their work through coercive means: although violence was sometimes used, it did not become a characteristic element in the cultural representation of the collaborative man-dog relationship.

97. Morris 1987, 1; Masson 1997, 133; Johns 2008, 9. The use of this type of "immaterial bond" (*attachement immatériel*) is a widespread technique of domestication: Digard 2006, 159–62.

98. Lorenz (1954) 2002, 7–9. The theory that dogs descend from jackals is no longer accepted, and the prevailing view today is that all dog breeds share a single descent from the wolf: Morris 1987, 13; Vigne 2004, 32–33.

99. Hesiod, *Works and Days* 604–5.

100. Lapucci 1995, 74.

101. Isocrates, 1.29 (Κακοὺς εὖ ποιῶν ὅμοια πείσει τοῖς τὰς ἀλλοτρίας κύνας σιτίζουσιν· ἐκεῖναί τε γὰρ τοὺς διδόντας ὥσπερ τοὺς τυχόντας ὑλακτοῦσιν οἵ τε κακοὶ τοὺς ὠφελοῦντας ὥσπερ τοὺς βλάπτοντας ἀδικοῦσιν).

102. The two episodes are in Aelian, *On the Nature of Animals* 7.13, 12.33.

103. Plato, *Republic* 416a. This chapter's earlier section "'Hungry like a Wolf' and Mental Disturbances" also discusses this passage.

104. The verses come from the so-called Homeric epigrams transmitted in the biography of Homer falsely attributed to Herodotus: *Homeri Opera,* vol. 5, 206 Allen. Markwald 1986, 190ff., interprets the advice as referring only to the time to feed the dogs and not to the place where they should be stationed, but this reading doesn't explain why feeding them before setting the table would make them—as the text says—perceive a danger before it arrives at the hall. In any event, the relationship between the place where a dog is fed and its tendency to stay there is shown in Xenophon, *Cynegeticus* 7.11-12 (also cited in n. 95, above).

105. *Paroem. Gr.* I, append. 3.53 Leutsch-Schneidewin. For the expression's Latin and modern variants, see Tosi 1991, 456. On the question of the preferred place for guard dogs, see Aesop, 268 Hausrath² (252 Perry = 180 Chambry³), where a dog, in the service of his friend a rooster, lies down at night "at the door" (in this case the base of the tree in which the rooster sleeps).

106. Aeschylus, *Prometheus Bound* 462-66.

107. *Scholia in Lycophronis Alexandram* 359, 520 Scheer; Pausanias 2.4.1. For Athena's role as the goddess of techniques of control, see Detienne and Vernant 1978, 177ff.

108. Xenophon, *Cynegeticus* 1.1.

109. Homer, *Odyssey* 7.91-94. These dogs were apotropaic talismans, a kind of product in which Hephaestus specialized. In antiquity, and especially in eastern Mediterranean cultures (Assyrians, Sumerians, Hittites, Egyptians, Persians), metal and terra-cotta dogs—but also sphinxes, lions, and other theriomorphic figures—were placed before gates to protect houses and on the thresholds of tombs to guard against evil spirits; the dogs of Alcinous's palace served this protective purpose and are thus described as "immortal" and alive since they were magically active and effective *phylaktēria* (Faraone 1992, 21-29). Even today, stone and terra-cotta dogs are often placed on the side pillars and in the entryways of many country houses, a legacy perhaps from their ancient function as magical guardians of the threshold.

110. Antoninus Liberalis, *Metamorphoses* 36.1-2; *Scholia in Homeri Odysseam* 20.66 Dindorf. Roscher 1896, 5-8, relates the story of Pandareus's theft of this dog. According to Pollux 5.39, which refers to a version in Nicander, another work of Hephaestus was the bronze dog that Zeus gave to Europa, which eventually passed to Procris and Cephalus and was used to hunt the fierce, uncatchable Teumessian fox; see also *Scholia in Homeri Odysseam* 19.518 Dindorf.

111. On Hephaestus's automatons, see Faraone 1992, 18-29; Pugliara 2002. These were, just like other implements forged by the god of metallurgy, divine and thus perfect instruments of service.

112. Homer, *Odyssey* 17.306-17. For the table dog as a model of the parasite, see this chapter's section "The Table Companion" and above, n. 31.

113. Aesop, 94 Hausrath² (92 Perry = 175 Chambry³). The hunting dog's work was the most valued and was thought to be the most difficult perhaps because it directly procured the master's food.

114. Aesop, 294 Hausrath² (226 Chambry³). The fact that the dog expects to be fed rather than getting its own food places it in an inferior moral position relative to wild animals and to humans. As noted in relation to its dining habits, the dog plays the role of a beggar at the

human table, and stories express this bottommost social position in various ways: one is the contempt that wild animals feel for the subordination to man that the dog accepts. Aelian, *On the Nature of Animals* 3.1, relates that in Mauretania, when a hungry lion approaches a house in search of food and there are no men there to drive it away, the women resort to a technique of persuasion and address it thus: "Aren't you ashamed, you who are a lion, king of the beasts, to come to my hut looking for food, seeking help from a woman, and, like some invalid man staring at the hands of women, to get through pity and moaning what you need? You should be in the mountains, pouncing on deer and antelope and whatever else is worthy food for a lion; instead you'd rather be fed and cared for [παρατραφῆναι] like a pitiful little puppy [κυνιδίου δὲ ἀθλίου]!" At these words the lion would go away, filled with shame.

115. Aesop, 329 Perry (179 Chambry³).

116. Aelian, *On the Nature of Animals* 14.1. I am aware of the fact that Aelian is not an unproblematic source for Greek cultural representations. Whenever possible, I support his statements with evidence from genuine Greek authors; by the same token, I avoid drawing dogmatic conclusions when *On the Nature of Animals* is the only evidence available. I believe that the reward is worth the risk: since the majority of Greek authors from whom Aelian derived his information are irremediably lost, if we repudiate him as a source for the Greeks we forego all chance of retrieving at least a small part of this data.

117. This passage can be contrasted with the story about the astounding domestic wolves of Conopeon: these were faithful companions of fishermen, and "to look at them, you'd say they were no different from house dogs"; "when they receive a part of the catch they establish a peace treaty between themselves and the fishermen; when they do not, they rend and destroy the fishermen's nets and make them pay the penalty for the wolves' lost share" (Aelian, *On the Nature of Animals* 6.65). Despite being domesticated, the wolves are still true to their aggressive nature and are represented as dangerous racketeers.

118. *Tropheia* and *threptēria* are the normal words used to speak about the debt of nourishment, one of the most strongly felt moral bonds in ancient Greece, to the extent that one of the distinguishing signs of wickedness among the men of the Iron Age—an unjust and wretched race in whom every moral value was corrupted—was that children no longer paid back their aged parents for their rearing (Hesiod, *Works and Days* 187–88). On the debt of nourishment's fundamental ethical-normative importance in Greece, where it was manifest in juridical norms as well, see Broadbent 1968, 139; Harrison 1968, 77–78; Maffi 1983, 14; Pomeroy 1997, 141. For a discussion of how this Greek norm developed in the Roman declamation schools, see Beltrami 1997, 79–97.

119. Much more of interest could be said about the priority of the feeding bond over that of blood relations—seen here in the mackerel's feeling bound more to their feeders than to their conspecifics—but it would go beyond the scope of this study, since it would concern only animals that hunt members of their own species to help men (and thus would not apply to the dog). The theme is also found in Aesop (238 Perry [282 Chambry³], 265 Perry [285 Chambry³]).

120. The model of eating companion also applies to the cohunting dolphins that Pliny describes (*Natural History* 9.9): fishermen awarded them not only a portion of the fish caught but also wine-soaked bread (*intrita panis e vino*). The use of dolphins as helpers in fishing still occurs on the coast of Mauritania (Digard 1990, 124).

121. Aelian, *On the Nature of Animals* 6.25. This episode recalls one that Xenophon narrates about the death of Cyrus (*Anabasis* 1.8.26), when only his intimate dining companions remained by him. Once again we find notions of commensality and raising/feeding interwoven.

122. Aelian, *On the Nature of Animals* 7.10; ibid., 7.29, has an almost identical incipit, which tells another story of canine fidelity. A large number of the stories in Aelian are also in Plutarch, *On the Intelligence of Animals* 13 (969c–970b).

123. Plutarch, *On the Intelligence of Animals* 13 (969d).

124. Ibid., 969e.

125. Aelian, *On the Nature of Animals* 10.41. On this story and a possible funeral stele for Eupolis and his dog, see Grassl 2009. It's notable that even in this case Aelian chooses the verb *hypagein* to indicate the master's gradual enticement of the dog.

126. Plutarch, *Themistocles* 10.9–10; Plutarch, *Cato the Elder* 5.4; Aelian, *On the Nature of Animals* 12.35.

127. Aelian, *On the Nature of Animals* 6.62. Herodotus 2.65.2 uses the term *syntrophos*, literally "sharing in nourishment" or "raised together," to indicate domestic as opposed to wild animals. The Aelian passage, by contrast, uses the term for the human cohabitating with the animal; such reciprocity, with a human described as *philos* and *syntrophos* of an animal, is not common: normally the dog is called *philos* of its master and not the reverse.

128. See especially Aristotle, *Nicomachean Ethics* 8.6 (1157b). On Greek *philotes* see Blundell 1989, 39–59.

129. As far as I know this occurs only in Bion, *Lament for Adonis* 18; Aelian, *On the Nature of Animals* 7.10; Oppian, *On the Hunt* 4.52. See also *Palatine Anthology* 6.176.4 (dog as *hetairos*). The only examples of a master being his dog's philos seems to be in Aelian, *On the Nature of Animals* 6.62, and, albeit indirectly, *IG* 12.2.459 (from Lesbos), where the person who erected the gravestone to the dear dog Parthenope advises the passerby to get himself a "good friend [χρηστὸν φίλον]" that will be loving to him in life and take care of his burial after death (in Herrlinger 1930, 42). The scarcity of evidence does not mean that the Greeks were incapable of feeling affection for their pets: see Bodson 1994b, 63–74.

130. Aristotle, *Nicomachean Ethics* 8.13 (1161b1–8).

131. Ibid., 8.7–8 (1158b11–29). See Campese 1983, 34–39; Pakaluk 1998, 91–107. On the vocabulary of philia, see Benveniste 1973, 273–88; Konstan 1997, whose denial of the status of philoi for relatives (53–72) is not convincing, especially since his argument does not take into account Aeschylus's use of the adjective *philos* in the *Oresteia* (Belfiore 2000, 19–20, raises a similar objection). On the fact that a husband in classical Athens would not have admitted to loving his wife, see Flacelière 1962, 125.

132. According to Aristotle, just as between man and cow or horse, so also between master and slave qua slave there can be neither philia nor a standard of justice (*dikaion*), but between master and slave qua human these can exist, since philia and dikaion are possible wherever both parties are able to participate in a convention, whether a law or a contract (*Nicomachean Ethics* 8.11.6–7). Isn't a dog an animal capable of recognizing the bond of a pact with its master? To push this problem a bit, we might take advantage of the ambiguity of the Aristotelian distinction (Pakaluk 1998, 125–26) and argue that although we may not

allow that a dog qua animal can maintain relations of a conventional or contractual sort, when perceived qua human it might very well give and take in philia. Labarrière 1997, 31–32, even proposes using Aristotle's classification to define the status of companion animals, with whom we form bonds of (Aristotelian) philia based on pleasure. For dogs (and horses) as philoi of their masters, see Belfiore 2000, 168. On the dog's attachment to its master, see Arrian, *Cynegeticus* 5.1–6.

133. Aristophanes, *Wasps* 766–972. On the dog as a member of the family, see Aristophanes, *Wealth* 1103–6; *Palatine Anthology* 10.86.2; Alciphron, *Epistles* 2.15.

134. E.g., Theophrastus, *Characters* 21.9; *Palatine Anthology* 7.211. See also Herrlinger 1930; Bodson 1994b, 72; Chamoux 2001. Epigrams for dead dogs became a literary genre, well attested in the *Greek Anthology*. See also the two epitaphs for the hound Tauron found in a papyrus of the Zenon archive (*P. Cair. Zen.* 4.59532 = *SH* 977): Buzón and Cavallero 1993; Purola 1994; Pepper 2010.

135. Aesop, 342 Perry (216 Chambry³).

136. Even in the above-mentioned passage in Aelian about Darius's dog (*On the Nature of Animals* 6.25), the animal remains by the body "so as not to betray [μὴ προδούς]" its master.

137. Aesop, 209, 267, 366 Perry (313, 314, 315 Chambry³).

138. Aeschylus, *Agamemnon* 716–26.

139. See Eduard Fraenkel's comment on the passage: "So paying his τροφεῖα" (1950, 340).

140. Aesop, 267 Perry (276 Hausrath² = 314 Chambry³).

141. Parallel to the lion cub in Aeschylus that dines on the herds of those who raised it, in the Aesop fable the wolf slaughters the herdsman's sheep as though making a sacrifice (θύων) and consumes the victim in a feast (ἐθοινεῖτο): on wolves as an alternative society that practices *isonomia* and sacrificial cuisine see Detienne and Svenbro 1989, 148ff. In Aesop many carnivorous animals eat their food in the form of sacrificial meals. All these animals are thought of as composing alternative societies ("metaphorical," as Lévi-Strauss would say: see "A Metonymic Subject," the last section of ch. 1) like that of the wolves. But no dog ever organizes a meal. Even more interesting is the fact that in some cases a dog joins the meal of another animal as an invited guest: in this Aesop fable the dog participates in the wolf's sacrificial meal, while in another (129 Hausrath² [171 Chambry³]) a crow that is offering a sacrifice to Athena invites a dog to dinner. Even these details seem highly indicative of the dog's strange, liminal position, forever poised between perfect symbiosis with man and a tendency to take advantage of other forms of conviviality (whether antagonistic to or simply different from those of humans).

142. Aesop, 215 Chambry³ (see also 343 Perry, which includes Babrius's verse rendition). The dog prefers to be with the man who raises it instead of its congeners, with which it feels no solidarity. Dogs, says Aelian (*On the Nature of Animals* 7.19), are not willing to share food and will often maul one another in fighting over a bone. Plato (*Politicus* 266a3) says that the dog is not among the animals that live in groups (τὸ γὰρ τῶν κυνῶν οὐκ ἐπάξιον καταριθμεῖν γένος ὡς ἐν ἀγελαίοις θρέμμασιν). Even when they work in packs, as when hunting, it's only because the hunter compels them to, and as soon as they are able they tend to go back to minding their own business (Xenophon, *Cynegeticus* 7.10).

143. Philemon, fr. 93 Kassel-Austin.

3. FOOD FOR DOGS

Epigraph: Giovanni Jervis, *Presenza e identità: Lezioni di psicologia* (Milan: Garzanti, 1984), 150.

1. On the "Homeric dog" question and for bibliography see Lilja 1976, 13–21. Scholars have been keen to know "Homer's attitude to dogs" (13), an ambiguous phrase that conflates questions of value judgment about dogs in archaic Greek culture with the epic poet's personal attitude toward the animal. So, for instance, the frequent mention of corpse-eating dogs in the *Iliad* is not evaluated, as would be sensible, in terms of symbolic implications and reasons of expression that underlie any semantic choice but is considered instead as a sign of Homer's "negative attitude" toward dogs. For some, Homer was an absolute dog lover, for others a complete despiser of dogs. See also Beck 1991, 167, which concludes with the statement "The poet liked dogs." On the treatment of dogs as a basis for judgment in the thorny "Homeric question," see again Lilja 1976, 13.

2. For the idea of Disneyfication, see Baker 2001, 174–75; Bettini 2013, 138–9.

3. Eco 1986, 83ff.; Sperber and Wilson 1986, 88–93; Bettini 2013, 143ff.

4. Lloyd 1990, 14ff., has a useful reminder of the difficulties connected with analyzing cultural objects, particularly the false problems that can arise when observers unconsciously overlay their categories on the cultural context that they're studying.

5. It seems that even the so-called pariah dogs—the Asian feral dogs that rummage food from refuse and eat carrion—were not a genuine semidomestic breed but differed from house dogs only through not having been raised in a house (Milliet 1995, 86). Edmondo De Amicis in his 1878 book *Constantinopoli* had already spoken of Asian feral dogs as having a different "social condition" than house dogs, but the naturalist Michele Lessona challenged this view and instead—more in line with contemporaneous stereotypes of evolutionistic anthropology—answered the question with an appeal to "savagery," comparing the difference between pariah dogs and European dogs to those between a "savage cannibal of Fiji" and a refined Parisian (1996², 1–10).

6. For the various scholarly views and relevant bibliography see Lilja 1976, 14–21. A conspicuous instance of how the need for such a distinction derives from our cultural mode of conceptualizing the dog's image—one rooted in the desire to find a repugnant "nondog dog" for the origin of an insult—can be seen in a comment by Bryan Hainsworth on a passage of the *Iliad*: "Greek draws no linguistic distinction between the hound, a noble creature ... to which heroes in their pride might be compared, and the scavenging mongrel cur implied by the use of κύων as a term of abuse or insult" (1993, 191).

7. See the statement that Plutarch puts in the mouth of Gryllus—one of Odysseus's comrades changed into a beast by Circe—who in an amusing dialogue asserts the superiority of the animal condition over the human: "Surely from hunger sometimes even a dog, driven by need, has eaten human flesh, or a bird partaken of it" (*That Brute Beasts Make Use of Reason* 7 [991a]).

8. Thucydides 2.50.

9. The Greeks also observed dogs' attraction to human vomit: Aristotle, *History of Animals* 594b3; Aelian, *On the Nature of Animals* 7.22; Pliny, *Natural History* 8.44 (106). On the fact that categories such as domestic and wild are too generic and ill defined to be useful in cultural analysis, see the important remarks of O'Connor 1997, 150–52.

10. The corpse-eating *kynes* in Homer could just as easily be jackals or hyenas, given that the Greeks undoubtedly considered, for example, the Egyptian god Anubis—whom many modern scholars describe as having a jackal's head—to be dogheaded (cynocephalous). But such modern distinctions are not relevant for my purposes here. If the poet calls them *kynes,* it is because he classifies them in the same category as house dogs, hunting dogs, herd dogs, and guard dogs. Thus even the corpse-eating *kynes*—of whatever type they were—are simply dogs and deserve to factor into the complex of ideas that constitute the entry *kyōn* in the Greek cultural encyclopedia.

11. Vernant 1989, 39–41; 1991, 62ff.

12. Dogs, vultures and other birds, worms, flies, eels, and fish all appear in Homer (the beasts at *Odyssey* 5.473 are mentioned as possible attackers of Odysseus in his sleep, so this passage is not included in the instances of necrophagy). In tragedy, corpses are most often abandoned to vaguely specified *thēres,* while crows are the most frequently mentioned corpse-eating animals in comedy. For the corpse-eating tendency of swine—exceedingly omnivorous animals to which are also attributed cannibalism and the habit of eating their young—see Aelian, On *the Nature of Animals* 10.16.

13. Homer, *Iliad* 21.203–4. Other cases more like descriptions than expressions of threat or fear include: in the *Iliad*'s famous proem, Achilles's wrath is responsible for the deaths of many heroes, whose bodies "make feasts for dogs and all the birds" (1.4); at *Iliad* 17.153, Glaucus reproaches Hector for not being able to save Sarpedon from the dogs; at *Iliad* 23.184–85, dogs do not throng to Hector's corpse, as Achilles would like, because Aphrodite keeps them at bay; *Odyssey* 3.270–71 says that Aegisthus condemned to death the bard whom Agamemnon left at Argos to supervise Clytemnestra by marooning him on a desert island "to become prey and spoil for birds."

14. Mainoldi 1984, 122, has a complete list of the passages. For the use of abusive slang in exhortations of comrades to battle, see Slatkin 1988, 119–32; Martin 1989, 72–73. For the role played by the motif of the mutilation of corpses at the end of the *Iliad,* see Segal 1971. The threat and fear of ending up as food for dogs or swine were commonplace in Mesopotamia as well: Finet 1993, 137–38.

15. Some statistics: There are a total of thirty-nine instances of necrophagy in both poems, thirty-one involving dogs; of these, eleven speak of "dogs and birds," while the other twenty (roughly two-thirds) mention only dogs. The motif of a corpse devoured by beasts in general is much more frequent in the *Iliad* (thirty-three cases versus six in the *Odyssey*), especially in the sections devoted to the death of Patroclus and the recovery of his body (book 17 alone contains six instances of the motif) and those about Hector's death and the attempt to recover his body (ten instances in books 22–24).

16. Vernant 1991, 70ff.

17. Homer, *Iliad* 22.345–37. For the insult *Dog!* hurled at a defeated enemy, see ch. 4.

18. *Aidōs* is the complex of cultural restraints that govern social relations and in particular respect, whether that owed by an inferior to a superior or that of a superior toward a subordinate, against whom the social norm demands that the superior not vent violent rage: Vernant 1991, 52; Cairns 1993, 49.

19. As we have seen, this is the effect of the warrior's *lyssa,* which causes the hero to have no respect for man or god (see ch. 2). On the paradoxical extremism on which the Homeric warrior's valor is based and his "inhumanity," which often spills over into

bestial ferocity, see Vernant 1991; Clarke 1995. Hecuba's address to Hector (Homer, *Iliad* 24.207–8) also emphasizes Achilles's lack of pity and *aidōs*, significantly calling the hero killer "raw-eating" (*ōmēstēs*), like a beast. Similarly, Apollo describes Achilles as a lion that "with only savage thoughts" ranges through the ranks of men "hunting for prey" (ibid., 24.40–45). Achilles's *anaideia* is thus figured rather emphatically as anthropophagy: Faust 1970, 24.

20. Homer, *Iliad* 22.348–54.

21. The aim of depersonalizing the individual by reducing him to edible flesh is also evident in expressions such as "You will glut dogs and birds with fat and flesh" (or "with white fat"): see Homer, *Iliad* 8.380, 13.832; Heath 2005, 136–38.

22. In Vernant's interpretation, it is a matter of falling on the slain enemy like a beast on its prey: "One assails the corpse and, failing to eat it raw oneself—as the phrase desires—one dismembers and devours the flesh through dogs and birds as proxies" (1991, 67); see also Rahn 1953, 471; Faust 1970, 24; Vermeule 1979, 107. Another example of a cannibalistic connotation deeply rooted in the figuring of the treatment of enemy corpses is the simile at *Iliad* 18.161–64, which compares Hector, trying to drag off Patroclus's body, to a famished lion that herdsmen are unable to drive from the carcass it has plundered.

23. Homer, *Iliad* 17.150–53.

24. Homer, *Odyssey* 3.271 uses the same phrase, of the bard condemned to death by Aegisthus (see n. 13 above); *Odyssey* 5.473 is similar; *Odyssey* 24.292 uses *helōr* on its own; *Iliad* 1.4, *helōria*; *Iliad* 17.272, *kyrma* alone.

25. Homer, *Iliad* 13.831, 17.241.

26. Ibid., 17.127, 17.255, 17.272, 18.179. On the use of the feminine, see ch. 5.

27. Homer, *Iliad* 22.339, 24.409.

28. As Redfield 1975, 200, notes, "The warrior *allows* his enemy to be eaten by birds; he *causes* him to be eaten by dogs."

29. Specifically spatial language often emphasizes the importance of the place where the corpse will lie and become prey to corpse-eating beasts: at *Iliad* 16.836, for example, Hector tells Patroclus, "But here [ἐνθάδε] the vultures will eat you," that is, on Trojan land. Obviously for the Greeks, to remain a corpse at Troy is a figure of nonreturn, the sad fate of those who will neither see relatives again nor receive funeral honors and rites of mourning from them. When it's a Trojan who dies on the field before the city, the theme of nonreturn is figured by the transfer of the corpse to the Greek ships, a sort of strange, distant place where it will be isolated "far away," "separated" from parents, shut off from the mourning of loved ones: see Homer, *Iliad* 22.88–89, 22.508, 24.211–12.

30. Following Geertz 1973, we will attempt to trace a "thick description" of the formulaic threat that invokes outraging a corpse; such "thickness" naturally correlates with the importance of the imagery of the deceased body in the ancient world.

31. Aeschylus, *Prometheus Bound* 1021–25.

32. Recall, for example, that in Circe's halls wandered beasts that wagged their tails like puppies (Homer, *Odyssey* 10.216–19). On Circe as "mistress of animals" and dangerous divine *parthenos*, see Franco 2010, 129–44. Again in Aeschylus's *Prometheus*, the fabled griffins are Zeus's "dogs" (803). The gods sometimes have other natural elements as "dogs": e.g., fiery flames are the "dogs of Hephaestus" (Alexis, fr. 153 [16 Kassel-Austin]; see also Eubolus, fr. 75 [7 Kassel-Austin]). But minor divinities can themselves be "dogs," that is, attendants

and servants: Iris is like a faithful "she-dog" to Hera (Callimachus, *Hymns* 4.228), while Pan is the "dog" of Arcadia's great goddess (Pindar, fr. 96 Snell-Maehler).

33. Lilja 1976, 54; Mainoldi 1984, 155.

34. It's worth noting that the epithet *aklētos* was reserved from the earliest period for the parasite: Ribbeck 1884, 77; Guastella 1988, 84 n. 13.

35. Aeschylus, *Agamemnon* 730–31.

36. Homer, *Iliad* 8.380, 13.832.

37. Homer, *Odyssey* 21.362–65.

38. Ibid., 14.22, states that Eumaeus raised his own dogs.

39. Segal 1971, 14. By contrast, Mainoldi 1984, 106, seems to believe that the suitors have recourse to this image because they know the particular ferocity of Eumaeus's dogs, so savage that they would devour their trainer. But it seems far more reasonable to connect the violent image to the suitors' savage ferocity and believe that Homer wanted to emphasize this, not the ferocity of Eumaeus's dogs.

40. Stein 1936, 71–72: "I am I because my little dog knows me . . . but perhaps he did not and if he did I would not be I. Oh no oh no."

41. Homer, *Iliad* 22.66–76.

42. Vernant 1991, 64ff.

43. Note how at *Iliad* 22.71 Priam stresses that wounds do "not disfigure [πάντ' ἐπέοικεν]"—more literally, are "entirely fitting" to—a young hero's body: the glory acquired in battle guarantees this harmonious seemliness to the warrior's body.

44. The text expresses the agitated state in which Priam's dogs, having drunk their master's blood, are imagined going back to lie down at the palace gate ("alyssontes peri thymōi") with the verb *alyssō*, a derivative with strengthening -*k*- from the root *alyō*, indicating a state of emotional distress, almost a constant dysphoria (desperation or melancholy), but according to Chantraine 1968, s.v. ἀλύω, it's fair to speculate that its similarity with *lyssa* encouraged the formation of *alyssō*. If this is so, Priam's dogs would be in a state of nearly rabid frenzy that consists, as we saw in ch. 2, in turning wolf. On the Homeric passage see also Schnapp-Gourbeillon 1981, 167–68. Interestingly, Tryphiodorus recycles the motif, in *The Taking of Ilium* 607–12.

45. On canine images as a structural pattern in the second half of the *Odyssey*, see Rose 1979; the Argus episode in particular may be "something of a paradigm in the series of recognition scenes in the second half of the poem" (223). This function for Argus might also help explain the presence of the dog in the common iconographic theme of the hero's departure; the dog beside the warrior heading off to battle would stand as a sign of good omen prefiguring its master's return: Schneider 2000, 22–23.

46. The man-eating tendency is part of the dog's constitutional "blindness," on par with its inability to acknowledge hospitality (see ch. 2). But note nevertheless that conversely, the dog was considered highly respectful of the taboo against cannibalism ("Canis caninam non est," "Dog does not eat dog," to use Varro's words: *On the Latin Language* 7.31), which was common among wolves, swine, and other animals: Aelian, *On the Nature of Animals* 4.40.

47. The mentioned variants trace the dogs' failure to recognize their master to a perceptual disorder (lyssa inflicted on them by Artemis) or to the alteration of the identifying traits of the hunter (whom Artemis transforms into or disguises as a deer), but whatever the

explanation given for the event, what remains constant is the dogs' inability to see in Actaeon their master. See Frontisi-Ducroux 1997.

48. Euripides, *Bacchae* 338–39.

49. Callimachus, *Hymns* 5.114–15.

50. Aristophanes, *Wasps* 967–72.

51. The beggar, constantly distressed by the trouble to find food, suffers perpetual hunger, even when faced with a full plate: he lays into the food with the voraciousness of one uncertain about his next chance to eat. Given the similarity in their position as retainers, there are many convergences between the dog and the parasite. To give just a few examples: parasites, not unlike dogs, were considered to be at the bottom of the social scale; like table dogs, parasites at a table were also a sign of the house's wealth; the parasite practiced flattery, and the dog, as we will see, was also accused of being a flattering animal. On the parasites' typology see Ribbeck 1884; Longo 1985, 14–22; Avezzù 1989, 235–40. On the animal (the dog among them) metaphors in the representation of parasites, see Ribbeck 1884, 93–100; Guastella 1988, 87–105.

52. Aristophanes, *Wasps* 904; *Knights* 1033–34. As it happens, Chytroleiktēs (Potlicker) is also the name of one of the parasites in Alciphron (*Epistles* 3.18); see also Guastella 1988, 93–94.

53. Aristophanes, *Peace* 481–83 (see also 641); Plato, *Republic* 539b.

54. According to Pisani 1984², 89, the adage "It's hard for a dog to taste the *chorion*" (Theocritus 10.11; see also Apostolius 18.11, in *Paroem. Gr.* 2.719 Leutsch-Schneidewin) also played on the meagerness of the dog's diet, as a reminder to the poor to stay away from luxuries. This reading takes the term *chorion* (literally "membrane" and specifically "placenta") to mean "sausage," as is common in comedy: these were sausages stuffed with milk and honey (Gow 1952², 188; Chantraine 1968, s.v. χόριον; Arnott 1996, 531). The meaning of the proverb is nevertheless much debated: G. Williams 1959 makes the argument that *chorion* means all the skin, bones, cartilage, etc., of a carcass, and he interprets this as a warning not to taste anything that will then become an irresistible temptation—like an animal carcass is to a dog—or not to try an experience that could become a source of wicked vices, like a dog that has tasted a carcass and can no longer be trusted as a herd dog. Most recently, however, Luzzatto 2001 convincingly suggests that the phrase is instead to be connected to an Aesopic fable preserved by Phaedrus (1.20), in which some dogs ogle a piece of leather (*corium*) at the bottom of a river and think the easiest way to get it is to drink up all the water: they end up bursting. Thus interpreted, the sentence better fits the Theocritean context and can be taken as evidence of dogs' love of leather.

55. Pherecrates, fr. 28 Kassel-Austin.

56. The fragment, of doubtful origin, is found in both comic (*PCG, adesp.* 142 Kassel-Austin) and tragic (*TGrF, adesp.* 118 Nauck²) collections.

57. Alciphron, *Epistles* 3.15.3 (see also 3.8.2, where the unsuccessful parasite must be content with apomagdaliai like the dogs).

58. Aristophanes, *Clouds* 489–91. See also *Wasps* 916, where with Aristophanes's typical comic wit, a "Cydathenaean dog," who stands for the demagogue Cleon, laments the fact that another dog, Labes, accused of theft, has not been willing to "throw before" (*proballein*) him even the tiniest scrap. Plutarch, *On the Intelligence of Animals* 13 (969f) also uses *proballein* of offering food to dogs.

59. When the sausage maker in Aristophanes's *Knights* brags about being raised on apomagdaliai (414), he does so only because beating his adversary depends on proving that he is cruder, nastier, and more beggarly.

60. Perpillou 1998, 325–39. A *skybalon* may also originally have been a kind of apomagdalia. For offal, varied organic refuse, and excrement in the dog's diet, see Aesop, 222 Hausrath[2] (206 Perry = 312 Chambry[3]), 134 Hausrath[2] (254 Perry = 183 Chambry[3]); Aristophanes, *Peace* 24–25; Pseudo-Aristotle, *On Reported Marvels* 841b6–8.

61. The passages, mentioned earlier, are Homer, *Iliad* 22.339, 24.409. In the first, Hector entreats Achilles not to let the Achaeans' dogs tear him apart beside the ships; in the second, Priam asks Hermes whether his son's body is still beside the ships (i.e., intact) or whether it has been "cut to pieces, and Achilles has already served him up to his dogs." Priam uses the verb *protithēmi*, often used of "setting out" a meal, placing it on the table: Achilles's action is thus configured as ritually codified aeikia.

62. See, e.g., Sophocles, *Electra* 1113; Plato, *Phaedo* 86c.

63. Euripides, fr. 469 Nauck[2] (which accepts Siegfried Mekler's supplement δείπνου). This is a line that Athenaeus cites (3. 97a) in reference to Cynics, who wasted no opportunity to behave "like dogs" even at dinners, making ostentatious displays of how much they enjoyed the bones.

64. Heraclitus, *VS* 22b96: νέκυες γὰρ κοπρίων ἐκβλητότεροι. Plutarch cites this line in discussing the diet of Homeric heroes, specifically their use of salt as a preservative: meat, Plutarch says, is dead flesh and part of a corpse and thus should be thrown out like refuse— as Heraclitus says—if salt did not intervene to revive it, giving it, as it were, a new *psychē* (*Convivial Questions* 4.4.3).

65. Interesting in this respect is the scene on a red-figure Attic skyphos by the Brygos painter (ca. 490 B.C.E., Kunsthistorisches Museum, Vienna) where Achilles is eating, knife in hand, with Hector's wounded corpse lying underneath the *kline*, a space usually occupied by table dogs.

66. Sophocles, *Ajax* 830.

67. See, e.g., Aristophanes, *Clouds* 489; Aristophanes, *Wasps* 916; Herodotus 9.112.

68. Homer, *Odyssey* 22.475–77.

69. The view that it is his corpse rests on a single detail, that the rope used to tie him up beforehand is described as *oloos* (fatal) (Cantarella 1991, 30). Ritual mutilation of the corpse also occurred in the historic period in Greece: what was known as *maschalismos* was one means by which murderers sought to protect themselves from the dead man's vengeance, by cutting off his hands and feet (Rohde 1925, 582–86; Johnston 1999, 156–59).

70. However, the treatment of entrails is debated. The prevailing view is that the Greeks considered nearly all parts of animals edible, except bones and cartilage: "Not only the muscle but almost every other part of the major domestic animals was tried as food in classical Greece" (Dalby 1996, 61). The *splanchna*—heart, liver, and kidneys—were deemed edible but reserved for sacrifices to the gods (Vernant 1989, 226 n. 17), while the gallbladder was saved for the gods but was, like bones, considered inedible (*PCG, adesp.* 142 Kassel-Austin = *TGrF, adesp.* 118 Nauck[2]). Other parts, such as the pancreas and the genitals, were perhaps not normally eaten and were discarded during the butchering stage: dogs may well have taken advantage of these. Dogs' love of entrails is possibly attested in a proverb (*Paroem. Gr.* 1.264 Leutsch-Schneidewin) that says to set "a dog [to guard] entrails [κύων

παρ' ἐντέροις]" was the height of stupidity: G. Williams 1959, 98-99; Mcdonough 1999, 467-68. The *Suda*, s.v. κύων παρ' ἐντέροις, has a diametrically opposite interpretation, which understands ἔντερα as "guts" that dogs don't eat: "a dog by the guts" thus describes someone who cannot enjoy what they have.

71. Homer, *Odyssey* 18.85-87.

72. Homer, *Iliad* 21.453-55.

73. Herodotus 9.112.

74. I'm proposing here an explanation that follows from the dog's positive implications in funerary symbolism, which Carla Mainoldi treats instead as a contradictory element, one simply juxtaposed to the negative and monstrous side of the "dog scavenger": the first represents the animal's domestic and civilized aspect, the second its savage aspect (Mainoldi 1984, 39, 51). Taking the opposite tack, I've tried to show that it is the whole set of the dog's domesticated properties that made it a good subject for representing the outrage of corpses, but a fortiori the dog also served well to represent the opposite, namely the permanence of the deceased's identity. Such a double function for the animal is well attested in Indo-European funerary symbolism, where one sometimes finds the image of two infernal hounds, a white one able to restore life and a black one that instead brings death: Schlerath 1954; Lincoln 1979, 275-80.

75. Homer, *Iliad* 23.19-23.

76. Ibid., 23.179-83.

77. For the image of funereal "jaws of flame," see Aeschylus, *Choephori* 324. On the parallelism between the devouring effects of the grave, of fire, and of corpse-eating beasts: Vermeule 1979, 108-9. The difference is that dogs devour the entire corpse, while cremation—as Homer describes it—preserves the hero's bones, purified through calcination and completely white (Poplin 1995, 257). In fact, once the fire is out, Patroclus's comrades gather his bones from the ashes and arrange them in a golden urn to be placed in his grave (Homer, *Iliad* 23.236-42).

78. Homer, *Iliad* 23.171-76.

79. Similar human and animal sacrifices to dead people of high status are attested, for instance, in ancient Mesopotamia (Limet 2000), Scythia (Herodotus 4.71-72), and Gaul (Caesar, *De Bello Gallico* 6.19.4). Dog skeletons have also been found in Mycenaean graves: Day 1984; Hamilakis 1996, 161-66.

80. Schnapp-Gourbeillon 1982, 82-83, instead sees in the funeral rites for Patroclus an expression of Achilles's excessive and emotionally explosive nature: the "execution" of dogs and horses here is intentionally "monstrous" because of their status as "companions of heroes."

81. For the iconographic evidence, see Mainoldi 1984, 38-39; Woysch-Méautis 1982, 53-60, 124-30; Zlotogorska 1997; Schneider 2000. See also Ridgway 1971; Papaoikonomou 1981; Canós i Villena and Németh 1996; T. Visser 2001; Le Bohec-Bouhet 2011, 496-515.

82. Aristotle, *Rhetoric* 1401a20; Theocritus 21.15; Longus, *Daphnis and Chloe* 1.16.2. In Aelian, *On the Nature of Animals* 6.10, a poor person unable to afford a servant uses a dog for the same purpose. See also Schneider 2000, 28-29.

83. Solon, fr. 17 Gentili-Prato² (23 West²). See also Theognis 1253-56.

84. This iconographic model, common in vase painting as well, was most likely the typical way to visually present the animal's bond with its master. For dogs on funerary monuments see Toynbee (1973) 1996², 110-22.

85. References in Mainoldi 1984, 39.

86. Aelian is especially full of these sorts of stories, some of which surely go back to the classical period: *On the Nature of Animals* 1.8, 6.25, 7.10, 7.28, 10.41, 11.13, 12.35. He even tells about dogs that throw themselves onto the funeral pyres or into the graves of their masters: 7.40.

87. Ibid., 7.10. The dog restores the master's honor even against an adulterer who has seduced his wife: 7.25.

88. Pollux 5.46–47.

89. The entire epigram, attributed to Pisander of Rhodes, is at *Palatine Anthology* 7.304. See also Page 1981², 80ff.

90. With the expression "together with you [ἅμα σοὶ]," Achilles tells Patroclus he will not go to the pyre alone (Homer, *Iliad* 23.182); see also ch. 2 on "together with him [ἅμα τῷ]." The earliest dog skeleton found so far in a human burial dates to twelve thousand years ago (Snyder 1998, 70). On animal burials in antiquity see Day 1984; Bodson 2000a.

4. SAD FATES, LOW MORALS, AND HEINOUS BEHAVIORS

1. Homer, *Iliad* 22.345.

2. Searle 1976, 10ff. On speech-act theory in general, see Austin (1962) 1975², 91ff.; Sbisà 1995².

3. E.g., Homer, *Iliad* 21.393. Martin 1989 analyzes the language of the Iliadic hero from a performative perspective (16–18, 65–77, on insults specifically; 34, on threatening someone that he would be "food for the beasts" as another form of "authoritative speech"). See also Parks 1990, 96–126. On the meaning of *mythos* in the archaic period, see Martin 1989, 18–42; Lincoln 1997.

4. Even more specialized metaphors such as *ass* and *pig* derive their offensive force from the general principle of degrading the interlocutor to the animal level: they are outrageous because *ass* and *pig* first and foremost indicate inferiority; if this were not so, it would be hard to see why the terms that the tropes substitute for, such as the adjectives *stubborn* or *filthy*, should not be just as effective. In these cases it is a specific, conventionally determined stereotype—the ass's stubbornness, the pig's filthiness—that defines the expression's semantic content, something that hardly ever happens with the dog, whose name can function as an insult even without the metaphor referring to a specific trait of observed animal behavior. This is why, in my view, the interpretation of metaphors of insult proposed in Manfred Faust's classic study (1969) misses the mark, especially with insults like *Dog!*, and his theory has little explanatory value. The scheme Faust proposed is inadequate for two reasons. First, by not taking into account the pragmatic aspect of the utterance, it precludes the possibility of identifying the trait most pertinent to the outrageous metaphor—its denigrating effect—and impedes understanding why, for some animals, negative features are selected primarily or exclusively, while for others the features selected have a positive value; simply saying that these selections occur merely states the obvious rather than adding anything significant. Second, Faust's understanding of metaphor does not explain why natural languages choose to express insults in metaphorical terms: essentially, it fails to explain the deeper relation that links insult to metaphor. The law of economy that governs communicative phenomena dictates that the speaker is led to choose one expression over another when it is deemed able

to convey more information, not the opposite (see Grice 1975, 41–58; Sperber and Wilson 1986, 48–50, 233–37). When we use *Ass!* to insult a stubborn person, we do it not to make communication more opaque but rather because the term is rich and dense, because it can convey in one word, besides the information "stubborn," other, supplementary information: it evokes a host of connotations that, if listed out, would entail a long series of propositions of the sort "animal" + "beast of burden" + "that is beaten" + "is unworthy of respect" + "x^n"—that is, all the characteristic traits that the encyclopedic entry *ass* might evoke. In short, the entire complex of "assness." To put it another way, even when it is strongly codified, an animal metaphor activates a much richer frame than the term for which it substitutes. The metaphor's fluid margin, its implicit and always virtually "open" (Eco 1986, 118ff.) quality of communication, constitutes its richness, its surplus value compared to explicit, literal messages. I agree with Gottesman 2008, 5ff., that in expressions of abuse "the crucial element [is] not meaning but force," but I suspect that the semantic richness of the metaphor has something to do with the insult's strength. On the importance of metaphors and similes as ways of describing but also of conceiving what is difficult to imagine analytically, see Lloyd 1966, 172ff.; Lakoff and Johnson 1980; Lakoff 1987.

5. Homer, *Iliad* 11.362–66 = 20.449–53.

6. Graver 1995, 49.

7. Adkins 1969, 14ff., shows how important it is to consider the pragmatic aspects of language in interpreting Homeric diction. In a society so preoccupied with what people say, the field of verbal exchange becomes a kind of chessboard on which subjects make moves with words, and each subject tends to evaluate every verbal move of an adversary for the effects it will have on the balance of power and considers an interlocutor's discourse as potentially able to diminish or augment (or leave intact) his own "good name [κλέος]." Clearly insulting plays an essential role in this game: indeed, it is a typical move, an aggression stereotyped by linguistic convention. On the theme of praise and blame in ancient epic see Nagy 1979; Martin 1989; Parks 1990; Scodel 2008. Létoublon 1983, 31–48, discusses the importance of verbal challenges and insults in the strategy of combat in the *Iliad*. On invective in Homer, see Koster 1980, 42ff.; Gottesman 2008. On challenges and the verbal strategies of characters in the *Iliad*, see Martin 1989. More on verbal taunting in Homer and in Indo-European epic traditions is Miller 2000, 232–36.

8. Homer, *Iliad* 8.526. The sense of the phrase is found in the following line (οὓς κῆρες φορέουσι, etc.), which is almost unanimously considered an explanatory gloss of the hapax κηρεσσιφορήτους, "devoted to death," not, as Graver 1995, 49, understands it, "bearers of death": see Chantraine 1968, s.v. κῆρ; Kirk 1990, 338. A person borne by a Ker or an evil Moira (Fate) is destined to meet a bad end: see, e.g., Homer, *Iliad* 2.302, 2.834, 5.613–14.

9. Aristophanes, *Wasps* 898; Hesychius, s.v. κύνειον θάνατον; *Paroem. Gr.* 2.182 Leutsch-Schneidewin. One may also recall here how in the *Odyssey* Polyphemus kills two of Odysseus's companions by beating them on the ground "like puppies" (9.289).

10. On food for dogs, see ch. 3. Erinyes of dogs: *Paroem. Gr.* (appendix) 2.20 Leutsch-Schneidewin, comparable with the "Erinyes of beggars" at Homer, *Odyssey* 17.475.

11. Aristophanes, *Knights* 289. In a fragment (40.8–9 Kassel-Austin) of the comic poet Anaxandris, a Greek contrasts his people's customary treatment of dogs with the Egyptians': "You venerate the dog, I beat it when I catch it eating my food." The Egyptians' veneration of the dogheaded god Anubis made a great impression on the Greeks. Plato's Socrates com-

monly uses the exclamation "by the dog" as a substitute for the common "by the gods," which in one instance appears as "by the dog god of the Egyptians" (*Gorgias* 282b5). The exclamatory "by the dog" was a form of euphemistic swearing by what is right and just called the oath of Rhadamanthus (other forms were "by the goose" and "by the ram"). Used as a cliché filler phrase, and thus semantically empty and noncommittal, the oath avoided troubling the gods and substituted for them the more harmless domestic animals (Dillon 1995, 146–47; Geus 2000). Thus when Socrates invokes the "dog god of the Egyptians" he plays on the expression's euphemistic force: for a Greek the dog replaces a god and desacralizes the oath, but for an Egyptian to swear by the dog is indeed a sacred act.

12. Hesychius, s.v. κύων; *Scholia in Platonis Lysidem* 206e; Pollux 9.100; Eustathius, *Ad Iliadem* 23.87–91 (289.63–64); Eustathius, *Ad Odysseam* 1.108–10 (1397.40–41). It is possible that this is not originally a Greek expression but rather a translation by Suetonius (in his lost treatise *Peri paidion*) of the corresponding Latin *canis*: see Faust 1969, 113–14; Fittà 1997, 114. The dog's function in such phrases does not seem to differ much from its use in Italian expressions like "è andata da cani" (it's going badly) and "stare da cani" (to be bad or miserable).

13. On the Cynics' *talaipōria* see Goulet-Cazé 1996, 62.

14. The dog was not, as Parker 1996², 230, claims, "the most despised of animals," but rather the most despised of human beings.

15. A few scholars have spoken in favor of the view that the animal's cultural representation needs to be evaluated in relation to the dog's peculiar position in the human community (e.g., Schlerath 1954, 38; Redfield 1975, 193–99), but they have remained for the most part unheeded, as we've seen, by the majority of scholars working on the dog in Greece. Metaphors such as *lion,* by contrast, tend to have a laudatory character, most likely because the lion—like the boar, the tiger, the wolf, etc.—is an independent animal, free and untamable, a worthy human antagonist: in short, an alternative model ("metaphoric" in Lévi-Strauss's sense—see ch. 1) to humanity and therefore able to be figured as superhuman, as opposed to the dog, the ass, and the pig, metonymic subordinates thus presented on a subhuman level.

16. Homer, *Iliad* 8.477–84. Line 483 expresses Hera's rage with the verb σκύζεσθαι, "growl (with rage)," which, according to Lamberterie 1994, works with the insult οὐ κύντερον ἄλλο that follows to create an offensive allusion to the growls of a bitch in heat. Later the technical term for she-dogs being in heat was σκυζᾶν, probably derived from the Homeric σκύζεσθαι.

17. Homer, *Odyssey* 17.248–50.

18. A dog is chained or confined when it is bad, to keep it from causing harm (Aeschylus, *Choephori* 446: "I was shut out of the inner chambers as if I were some rabid dog"), or when one is expecting a guest, to keep it from performing its usual guard duty (*Palatine Anthology* 5.30.3–4; see also ch. 2 on dogs and strangers).

19. A proverbial Greek expression of the "nursing a serpent at the breast" sort warns against the threat of ingratitude from children and others whom one rears: "Raising wolf cubs is to raise dogs that will eat you!" (Theocritus 5.38; for the strange anticlimax see Gow 1952², 101–2). Another parable of ingratitude concerned a dog in a well: the master jumps down a well to save his dog, which has fallen in, and instead of giving thanks the frightened creature attacks him (Aesop 122 Hausrath² [120 Perry = 155 Chambry³]).

20. In this regard it is quite instructive to read the widespread practical manuals of animal behavior aimed at dog owners, which offer advice on how to train one's pet not to have "undesired behaviors." Behaviors typical of the species are treated here by humans as aberrant and "corrected" through more or less punitive interventions. A striking example of this attitude by dog lovers is the manual by Ferdinand Brunner, which, despite its good-natured title (*Der unverstandene Hund,* "The misunderstood dog"), devotes a considerable portion of its treatment of dog psychology to the problem of how to change unruly behaviors and unwanted tendencies in one's dog.

21. It is surely no accident that the Cynics chose the dog as the symbol for their subversive project of vaunting the revolutionary superiority of natural law over cultural conventions. Poverty of means and lack of restraint, which in traditional culture are signs of the dog's inferiority, became for the Cynics the virtues of the new sage. See *SSR* 4:491–97; Long 1996, 28–46; Goulet-Cazé 1996, 62.

22. Lack of restraint (*anaideia*) is invariably the mark of "doggishness" in ancient commentators: see *Scholia in Homeri Iliadem* 1.225 (associated with untrustworthiness, *apistia*), 8.423–24, 13.623c, 21.394 Erbse; *Scholia in Homeri Odysseam* 7.216, 11.423 Dindorf; *Scholia in Hesiodi Opera* 67 Pertusi.

23. Note that the expression "I don't care one bit [*ouk alegizō*]," with which Zeus scornfully dismisses Hera as a dog in the Homeric passage cited above, also appears in diametrically opposite situations: it is used of an inferior ("dog") "having no regard" for a superior (Homer, *Odyssey* 19.154) and is thus an accusation of shameless irreverence (*anaideia*). Just as the principle of aidōs has a double sense, so too *doggishness* lends itself to distinct functions relative to the power relations implied by the context: for one claiming superiority, the inferior is a dog and unworthy of aidōs; in turn, an inferior not showing the respect due a superior is a dog for not recognizing the norm regulating hierarchical distance and is lacking in aidōs. The dog cannot but exercise the virtue of respect, since all are its superiors—and it cannot expect to receive respect from anyone. In this it marks the lower limit of the human condition.

24. Recall the sausage maker in Aristophanes who boasts of being raised on dog food to outdo his opponent in being the more ignoble (see ch. 3, n. 59). The pimp was nicknamed "dog fox [*kynalōpēx*]," ignoble, hustling swindler that he was (Aristophanes, *Knights* 1067–79; *Lysistrata* 957). Parasites complain of being treated like dogs (Alciphron, *Epistles* 3.8, 3.15) and often indeed not only must be satisfied with leftovers but are also beaten and driven out with blows: in short, they are not considered worthy of respect.

25. Although aidōs is moral restraint in two directions—both reverence toward a superior and clemency toward the helpless and powerless—naturally enough, the dog is mostly conceived of in the direction of low toward high: stationed at the lowest societal rank, the dog must see every human as a source of subjugation. The same is true for human subordinates: finding themselves in positions of inferiority and possessing little prestige, children, women, and slaves must mainly exercise aidōs of the reverential sort: see Cairns 1993, 121–2; Carson 1990, 142.

26. According to Plutarch, the dog's intelligence is clearly manifest in its various actions and reactions but also in the "obligations [*kathēkonta*]" that it is able to fulfill: *On the Intelligence of Animals* 13 (969b–c).

27. Homer, *Iliad* 8.421–24.

28. In the complex of ethical restraints that combine to form good conduct—that of a person who is "wise," "prudent," "of sound mind" (*sōphrōn*)—deos is of fundamental importance. Given the strict correlation between the system of expected behavior and the social rank of the subjects involved, the root of "fear" is also found in the adjective *deinos*, used of someone who is "fearsome" and thus "respected," "powerful": Cairns 1993, 88; see also 372, on the strict relation between *deos* and aidōs.

29. Domestic conflict: Homer, *Iliad* 3.180, 6.344, 6.356, 8.423, 8.483, 18.396, 21.394, 21.421, 21.481; *Odyssey* 4.145, 8.319, 11.424–27, 18.338, 19.91, 19.154, 19.372. Internal rivalry: *Iliad* 1.159, 1.225, 9.372–73.

30. Homer, *Iliad* 21.481–88.

31. Homer, *Odyssey* 22.35–40.

32. Aristotle, *Rhetoric* 1380a23–24.

33. See Cairns 1993, 213–14, 235–36, on the importance of *phobos* and *deos* as ethical restraints, in relation to aidōs and the concept of good sense, the sense of proper limits (*sōphrosynē*).

34. Plutarch, *On the Intelligence of Animals* 15 (970f); Aelian, *On the Nature of Animals* 8.1; Pollux 5.43. Indian dogs are recommended for hunting boars (Xenophon, *Cynegeticus* 10.1), a sport in which the hunter must be willing to see many of his dogs killed (ibid., 10.21), and in the East they were even used in warfare (Herodotus 1.192, 7.187). It is worth recalling that the job of herd dogs in ancient Greece was not herding or leading livestock but guarding them against predators and thieves (Chandezon 2003, 53 n. 49).

35. The two forms are equivalent: only the Attic dialect developed a tendency to distinguish between tharsos, "good courage," and thrasos, "bad courage": see West 1978, 237; Chantraine 1968, s.v. θάρσος.

36. See, e.g., Pindar, *Isthmians* 1.13; Aeschylus, *Suppliants* 758; Aristophanes, *Wasps* 1402; Theocritus 15.53.

37. On this polarity (*andreia/anaideia*), which disambiguates the concept of tharsos, see the interesting passage in Pseudo-Aristotle, *Physiognomonica* 805b, which claims that the courageous (*andreios*) and the impudent (*anaidēs*) have the same bodily traits, although very different temperaments.

38. See, for example, Plutarch, *On the Intelligence of Animals* 4 (987f–988b); Xenophon, *Oeconomicus* 7.25. On the virtues of subordinates, see Aristotle, *Politics* 1260a, where he admits a female andreia but defines it as being of a "subordinate" nature to distinguish it from the "dominant" andreia of the male. Women, children, and slaves have "their" virtues, but they can never attain the perfection that the adult male must measure up to: they can also practice courage, temperance, and justice, but in a different and, at any rate, deficient way. A passage in Hesiod (*Works and Days* 319) asserts that "aidōs is for the poor, tharsos is for the rich," which may be an interesting version of the idea that subordinates, people of inferior rank, cannot venture any courage that does not end up in anaideia: Cairns 1993, 148–49 (for other interpretations of the passage see West 1978, 237).

39. In these instances the dog displays the manly virtue of andreia: Aristotle, *History of Animals* 608a31. The dog that bites people is, on the contrary, a symbol of malice: Aesop 64 (332 Perry = 177, 186 Chambry[3]).

40. Homer, *Iliad* 1.158–60.

41. Agamemnon says, "You will know well how much more powerful I am than you, and no one else will be willing to speak to me as equal and measure himself against me" (Homer, *Iliad* 1.185–87); Achilles responds, "You'd rather steal the gifts from someone who speaks to you face to face" (1.229–30).

42. Ibid., 1.225.

43. Cairns 1993, 158.

44. The dog's gaze as a symbol of effrontery also appears in a compound verb that the Atticist Phrynichus mentions (*Praeparatio sophistica* 84 De Borries): Κυνοφθαλμίζεται: ἀναιδῶς καὶ ἰταμῶς ὁρᾷ, τρόπον ματρύλλου (To cast dog glances: i.e., to look shamelessly and brazenly, like a pimp). In an opposite direction from the dog's gaze as looking straight in the eyes—but no less important for the connection between shamelessness and the gaze—is the scholiastic note on the Homeric insult *kynamyia,* "dog-fly" (*Scholia in Homeri Iliadem* 21.394b Erbse), to which we will return later on. It states that in his commentary on Homer, Neoptolemus of Parion wrote *kinamyia* and understood the compound (taking it as derived from *kinein,* "move," and *mysis,* "closing" the eyelids) as "blinking the eyes," with reference to the brazen behavior of someone who doesn't look straight in the eyes but instead casts leering and sidelong glances. Here the fixed and settled gaze is thus characteristic of the wise and temperate, while the wandering, sidelong gaze is typical of the shameless; compare this with Seneca, *Epistles* 52.12 ("impudicum et incessus ostendit . . . et flexus oculorum," "the impudent man is given away by his gait . . . and his shifty eyes"). Thus, gazes too fixed and too wandering can both be interpreted as signs of shamelessness: Rizzini 1998, 74–75.

45. Homer, *Iliad* 9.344–45, 371, 375–76. The accusations of "doggishness" that Achilles levels at Agamemnon do not rule out a reference to a betrayal of the *philotēs* that binds the Achaean chiefs in a pact of alliance: the traitor is another of the dog masks, as we will see.

46. Ibid., 9.372–73.

47. Aeschylus, *Suppliants* 758; see also Theocritus 15.53.

48. The fly, like the dog, can be described as "living with [*syntrophos*]" and "dining with [*homodiaitos, homotrapezos*]" humans: Lucian, *Muscae encomium* 4. For this insect's characteristic thrasos, see Aelian, *On the Nature of Animals* 7.19, 2.29, 15.1; Lucian, *Muscae encomium* 5 (where the distinction between thrasos as impudence and tharsos as valued courage is obviously specious); *Scholia in Homeri Iliadem* 21.394 Erbse. For the fly's parasitism and intrusiveness into human spaces, see *Iliad* 2.469–71, 19.25; Lucian, *Muscae encomium* 8. "To swat the flies off someone" was a proverbial expression for concerned and protective behavior: Aristophanes, *Wasps* 597 (see also Homer, *Iliad* 4.130–31). The fly has the courage to bother not just humans but other fierce, large animals as well: an unequal contest does not frighten it (Lucian, *Muscae encomium* 6). See also Davies and Kathirithamby 1986, 150–64; Beavis 1988, 219–25. Parasitic dietary practice is at any rate already connected with impudence (e.g., see Theophrastus, *Characters* 9): whoever must ask others for food cannot afford the luxury of shame. The Homeric beggar, once welcomed to the table of the rich, had to politely put aside his shame, since aidōs could only get in the way of asking for and getting what he needs. See Cairns 1993, 106.

49. Aelian, *On the Nature of Animals* 11.8, 5.17. An entry ban to the temple of Cronus associates flies and dogs: *FGrH* 81 F 33. The smell of blood on the sacrificial altars would obviously attract both animals, who would not hesitate to fall on offered victims (Mcdonough

1999, 467–77) and perhaps for this reason were unwanted in such sacred spaces. A dog "thief" of sacrificial meat appears in the foundation myth of the cult of Heracles at Kynosarges: *Suda*, s.v. Κυνόσαργες.

50. Pausanias 5.14.1. On this point see the note in Maddoli and Saladino 1995, 259–60.

51. Lucian, *Muscae encomium* 10. Myia in this myth can be compared with the dog-woman in the infamous Semonides fragment on the types of women (Semonides fr. 7 West² [Pellizer-Tedeschi], 12–20), whose chief trait is a nosy peevishness that leads her to wander around shamelessly butting into everything and meddling in everyone else's business.

52. See ch. 3. Similar anxieties about dogs trespassing through their ambition to climb the ladder of human honors may also lurk within the stories of dogs that fall in love with girls and boys or become adulterers by seducing their master's wife (e.g., Aelian, *On the Nature of Animals* 1.6, 7.19). In connection with this, recall also the previously mentioned (in ch. 1, n. 24) stories of incest in Native American mythology in which a dog plays the role of a blood relation who sleeps with a woman (Lévi-Strauss 1995, 153).

53. Homer, *Iliad* 21.394–95.

54. Ibid., 21.421–30.

55. *Scholia in Homeri Iliadem* 21.394 Erbse; Eustathius, 1243.25. Relative to this see Davies and Kathirithamby 1986, 155–57; Mcdonough 1999, 475–76.

56. Aelian, *On the Nature of Animals* 4.51, 6.37. For the variant *kynomyia* (with analogical *-o-*) see Chantraine 1968, s.v. κύων. Aelian asserts a parallel with the horsefly, but this relates only to size, not the tendency to bite. Lucian (*Muscae encomium* 12) says that certain large flies were called *kynes* or "soldier flies [*stratiōtides*]." Yet it is possible that *kynomyia* and the Homeric *kynamyia* are not variants but rather two distinct terms in either formation or meaning: according to Dubielzig 1995, the first is a sarcastic insult, like *kynalōpēx* (dog-fox) or *grypalōpēx* (griffin-fox), lacking a real-world referent and comparable to the German insult *Schweinehund* (pig-dog); the second means "the fly of dogs" and indicates a horsefly or a tick, as well as the plant otherwise known as Pulicaria, or fleabane. Beavis 1988, 238, considers both *kynamyia* and *kynomyia* to be purely linguistic inventions, neither indicating a specific, real-world insect. According to Lamberterie 1994, 37–38, on the other hand, the original offensive coinage *kynamyia* was slightly modified to *kynomyia* for use in the Septuagint to translate the name of the insect that God sent against the Egyptians (which in Hebrew sounds like "hybrid, mixture"; thus the compound *dog-fly* would render in Greek the idea of monstrous intermingling); from this origin it would then have passed into technical language, becoming a genuine, specific zoonym.

57. Beavis 1988, 222–23.

58. Homer, *Iliad* 17.570–72.

59. Aelian, *On the Nature of Animals* 9.15, 11.8.

60. Lucian, *Muscae encomium* 3 (see also Aelian, *On the Nature of Animals* 6.11).

61. Theocritus, *Idylls* 25.78–83. The passage is likely an imitation of the arrival of Odysseus at Eumaeus's hut in Homer; for a detailed discussion of Homeric references in the Theocritus passage see Chryssafis 1981, 94–111.

62. Certain conspicuous lacks in the dog's capacity for discernment only limits, not destroys, the admiration for its cognitive virtues in this passage; if the animal's intelligence did not exhibit a few faults it would be perfect, making it a true double of humans. Chryssafis 1981, 109, believes instead that the comparison between the dog and other animals at

line 82 is not very apt and thus proposes to change the text for a different interpretation: "Not even [human] guardians could compete with them in honor [οὐδ᾽ ἄν οἱ θηρῶντες ἐδήρισεν περὶ τιμῆς]." The emendation does not seem justified. The intelligence of dogs was a common topic of discussion among philosophers (Sorabji 1993, 25–26, 89), who loved to emphasize aspects surprisingly close to human rationality, in stark contrast with the tendencies in popular culture, which were more attentive to deviant and deficient aspects, consistent with the concerns of those who relied on dogs from day to day.

63. The way a dog barks when it hears a knock at the door, before it knows whether the knocker is friend or stranger, is for Aristotle an illustration of impulsiveness (*Nic. Eth.* 1149a25–32); this can be compared with how the old cowherd of Augeas calls the dogs "impulsive," "unreflective" (*epiméthes*) in the Theocritus passage. Impulsiveness is one form of intemperance (*akrasia*).

64. Aidōs is also the respect owed to strangers, whether guest, beggar, or suppliant: Cairns 1993, 105–13.

65. Apollonius Rhodius, *Argonautica* 3.192–93. Noteworthy here is the way that Babrius (74 Luzzatto–La Penna) recounts the Aesopic fable about the ages of man: to repay a man who has given them hospitality during the winter, a horse, a cow, and a dog each give him some years of their life. The horse gives years of youth, when cocksure boldness prevails; the cow gives the mature years, responsible and industrious; finally, the dog gives the years of old age, when one becomes angry and grumpy; "For this reason," Babrius says, "all old people fawn only on those who feed them, but always bark at the rest and do not care for strangers/guests." The bumpkin in Theophrastus's *Characters* 4.9 reveals his lack of tact in proudly boasting of his guard dog's impressive efficacy to a guest who has just arrived.

66. Theocritus, *Idylls* 25.76–77: χαίρων ἐν φρεσὶν ἧσιν, ὀθούνεκεν αὖλιν ἔρυντο / αὐτοῦ γ᾽ οὐ παρεόντος. Chryssafis 1981, 102–4, prefers the reading ὀθούνεκεν αἰὲν ἔρυντο / αὐτοῦ που παρεόντος, understood as "rejoicing that they [the dogs] are always restrained when he is nearby."

67. In Xenophon, bad hunting dogs are *apsychoi* and good ones *eupsychoi*. The two adjectives refer primarily to a physical characteristic, the dog's breath (according to the concrete meaning of *psyché*): those with short breath can't stand the heat and will give up the chase, while those with good lung capacity will not give up even when they get very heated (*Cynegeticus* 3.3, 4.6). However, *eupsychos* and *apsychos* also commonly mean "courageous" and "cowardly," respectively. A timid dog that, out of fear, does not obey its master is despicable, like a soldier who avoids the fray because of cowardice: Homer, *Iliad* 5.476.

68. See Hesiod's description of Cerberus: *Theogony* 310–12, 764–73. In Etruria, Hades was depicted with a dog's head: Mainoldi 1984, 43. For the iconography of Orthros, see ibid., 42–43. In Pindar, a pack of dogs that are also "full of thrasos" instead protect Geryon's flocks (*Isthmians* 1.13). A lack of pity can be a form of anaideia, specifically the lack of aidōs toward those who are in a position of inferiority (Cairns 1993, 49, 92–93).

69. Aelian, *On the Nature of Animals* 10.41., 7.13, 11.19; Plutarch, *On the Intelligence of Animals* 969e–f. For similar stories in a Roman context, see Aelian, *On the Nature of Animals* 7.10.

70. Pindar, fr. 96 Maehler; Callimachus, *Hymn to Delos* 228–32. On the positive valence of the metaphor "dog of X" to indicate a faithful servant, see Lehnus 1979, 158–59. For the

list of bloodthirsty beasts denoted with this formula, such as the eagle of Zeus that feasts on Prometheus and the Hydra of Lerna, see Mainoldi 1984, 154-55.

71. Here the entire plot of Aristophanes's *Wasps* is exemplary (see Taillardat 1962, 405–6), but the metaphor also appears in Aristophanes, *Knights* 46–60, 1017–19 (see Worthington 1990; Desfray 1999); Aristophanes, *Peace* 313, 754–56; Demosthenes 25.40 (*Against Aristogeiton* 1); Theophrastus, *Characters* 29.5. The Cynics were derided along the same lines (Athenaeus 13.611b–d; *Palatine Anthology* 11.153, 154, 158), but they embraced the name *Dogs* with an altogether different understanding: they assumed doggishness as a conscious marker of provocation and so anticipated the derision they endured.

72. Homer already describes the Erinyes in ownership terms akin to those of the dog-master relationship, calling them "Erinyes of X," someone's faithful agents of defense and vengeance (Homer, *Iliad* 21.412; *Odyssey* 2.135, 9.280, 17.475). See also *Iliad* 15.204, which says the Erinyes "follow [*hepesthai*, the usual verb for a dog following its master]" the more elderly, in the sense of being at their service. But the Erinyes become genuine bitches only with Aeschylus (*Choephori* 924, 1054; *Eumenides* 130–32, 230). For the bacchantes, see Euripides, *Bacchae* 731, 977, 1189–90. The Harpies are "she-dogs of Zeus" in Apollonius of Rhodes, *Argonautica* 2.289.

73. Sperber 1996.

74. Aeschylus, *Choephori* 1054: μητρὸς ἔγκοτοι κύνες (see also 924: φύλαξαι μητρὸς ἐγκότους κύνας). I agree with Heath 2005, 239–42, that the *Oresteia* does not represent the Erinyes exclusively as dogs: they show traits of different species (dogs, serpents, wild beasts), reflecting a monstrous and indistinct prepolitical chaos, and are conceived as "a disgusting conflation, a combination of elements that makes them part beast, part human, certainly divine but excluded from the ranks of all three categories" (239). I think nevertheless that the dog element in the hybrid is worth being analyzed separately and in the context of the entire depiction; after all, Euripides will dub the same Erinyes *kynōpides* (*Orestes* 260). The dog and doggishness are among the most productive motifs in the *Oresteia*: Dumortier 1935, 152–54; Lebeck 1971, 66–67; Harriott 1982; Mainoldi 1984, 165–69; Saayman 1993. See also ch. 5.

75. The Erinyes unleash against their human prey a violence blind to any call for pity or moderation: see the list of terrible mutilations that according to Apollo constitute the means by which they attain their justice at Aeschylus, *Eumenides* 185–90. Theognis 347–51 already uses the dog metaphor to represent vampirism (i.e., the drinking of human blood) and the desire for vendetta: see Napolitano 1996.

76. Aeschylus, *Agamemnon* 1188–89. On giving blood to dogs, see Pollux 5.51; Hull 1964, 47. At Aeschylus, *Eumenides* 244–53, the Erinyes track the trail of blood that Orestes has left and, once they've found their prey, say, "The odor of human blood greets me with a smile" (253): they are man-eating, vampiric she-dogs (see also Aeschylus, *Choephori* 183–84; *Eumenides* 264–66, 305). In Euripides as well, the Erinyes that pursue Orestes are hellish executioners with dog and Gorgon gazes at once: *Orestes* 260–61 (see also *Eumenides* 48). On the other hand, John Heath, who denies that Aeschylus's Erinyes have a specifically "canine" vocation (1999, 34–35), instead takes their vampiric features as "designed to accentuate the distance of the goddesses from both human and animal" (2005, 241).

77. The Erinyes cannot be placated (Aeschylus, *Eumenides* 384; see also Sophocles, *Electra* 1388: ἄφυκτοι κύνες). They preside over all those powers activated by effective speech, those sorts of utterances that are capable of shaping reality to conform with their content: a

typical case is a curse, which causes what it evokes to take place (see Faraone 1991, 3ff.; Giordano 1999, 13ff.). This is why the Erinyes, who attend to curses and oaths, are not revocable. They also pursue those who violate hospitality (*Eumenides* 270), but this is simply another aspect of their "canine" cooperation, inasmuch as their justice is completely aligned with the injured party who sets them loose, who may be a violated guest.

78. Euripides, *Electra* 1252 (see also 1342, which alludes to Orestes's punishing furies simply as κύνας). See also Apollonius Rhodius, *Argonautica* 4.1666 (with a Ker as a "swift bitch of Hades"). Recall too that in Aeschylus the other gods despise the Erinyes as the epitome of horror, of blind pursuit and anthropophagy (e.g., *Eumenides* 179–90): they are bitches to everyone except Clytemnestra, their mistress, who rebukes them for the opposite reason, for not attacking Orestes with blind vehemence (*Eumenides* 94–99).

79. It would take a long list to catalog the many sources, beginning with Homer, that represent the Erinyes as guardians not just of the honor of murdered dead but also of moral principles such as respect for the elderly, for beggars, and for oaths: see the comprehensive list in Wüst 1956 and the study in Visser 1980. Pseudo-Heraclitus, *Epistles* 9.20 Bernays, expressly describes the Erinyes as "guardians" against transgressions of Justice (πολλαὶ Δίκης Ἐρινύες, ἁμαρτημάτων φύλακες).

80. See the fragment of Heraclitus (*VS* 22b94) where the philosopher states that if the sun trespasses its limits, the Erinyes, helpers of Dikē, will find it out.

81. Faraone 1992, 26, 45–48.

82. For the Erinyes as guardians of the tomb, see, e.g., *IG* 12, fasc. 9, 1179 (*SEG* 28 [1978]: 721); Strubbe 1991, 45–47. For the Erinyes as plague demons, see Faraone 1992, 45. On their responsibility for the death of children and women in labor, see, e.g., *IG* 3, pt. 2, 1354 (Kaibel 162); *SEG* 18 (1962): 456; *CIG* 2415 (Kaibel 218).

83. Hippocrates, *On the Sacred Disease* 1.38.

84. Plutarch, *Roman Questions* 51 (276f–277a), restating in his own way Ovid's explanation (*Fasti* 5.133–42): "Causa tamen positi fuerat cognominis illis / quod praestant oculis omnia tuta suis: / stant quoque pro nobis et praesunt moenibus urbis, / et sunt praesentes auxiliumque ferunt. / At canis ante pedes saxo fabricatus eodem / stabat: quae standi cum Lare causa fuit? / Servat uterque domum, domino quoque fidus uterque: / compita grata deo, compita grata cani. / Exagitant et Lar et turba Diania fures: / pervigilantque Lares, pervigilantque canes." On probable dog sacrifices for defensive walls and gates, see Robert 1993.

85. See ch. 2.

86. Useful here are the observations that Jean-Pierre Digard has collected on guard dogs in various traditional societies: they are trained to be as aggressive as possible, but this creates the problem of ensuring that their aggression is always directed toward outsiders, which obviously cannot be guaranteed without exception (1990, 164). See also *Geoponica* 18.1.1: a good dog must not attack at random and without motive.

87. Homer, *Iliad* 19.87 (the Erinyes among the deities responsible for the *atē* of Agamemnon); *Odyssey* 15.234 (a single Erinys as the agent of the *atē* of the seer Melampus).

88. Aeschylus, *Eumenides* 500.

89. Euripides, *Bacchae* 977. The same occurs with the maenads in a lost tragedy of Aeschylus (*Xanthriae* fr. 169). The Euripides text treats *kynes* as feminine, and most Italian translations render this as "swift bitches of Lyssa." For reasons I will explain shortly, I adhere

once again to the more generic *dogs*. On the homology of dogs of Lyssa and the Erinyes, see Dodds's comment on this passage of the *Bacchae* (1960², 199).

90. Euripides, *Bacchae* 1189–91.

91. Euripides's tragedy twice models the rabid canine madness of the Bacchic women on the myth of Actaeon (ibid., 337–40, 1291). Once possessed by Artemis, the dogs of Actaeon switch masters, changing their allegiance. Executing the goddess's will, they recognize her and not their former master, whom they now see only as prey. On the parallels between Pentheus and Actaeon and the theme of recognition, see Frontisi-Ducroux 1997, 437–38. On the myth of Actaeon as a representation of the slaying of a *philos*, see Belfiore 2000, 168.

92. Homer, *Iliad* 8.299. Diogenes, the "dog" philosopher, parodied this Homeric line to describe the madness of the trials that Fortune (Tychē) set against him, given his impassivity to her blows, which he welcomed as chances to exercise the superior morality of the sage (Goulet-Cazé 1996, 56). With a provocative reversal of perspective typical of the Cynics (see, e.g., their praise of cannibalism: Daraki 1982), Diogenes boasts that he is a "rabid dog" that Fortune is unable to beat: *SSR*, Diogenes (V B) fr. 148.

93. Homer, *Iliad* 9.238–39; see also 9.305. Rabid dogs were killed: Demosthenes, 25.40.8 (*Against Aristogeiton* 1).

94. The poet of the *Iliad* never calls Achilles a dog, despite his raging like a bloodthirsty cannibal; even when he is a raging predator, in the grip of martial lyssa, he is always a lion (Nagy 1979, 227 n. 6). Only his enemies would call him a dog, since only in the eyes of those who suffer an aggression is that aggression hateful, execrable, and not a virtue (Schubert 2000, 59–80). On the paraenetic use of insults in the *Iliad*, see Slatkin 1988, which shows how comrades-in-arms often upbraid one another as a goad to action. Nevertheless, no hero ever calls a comrade a dog, which is an insult reserved for enemies.

95. People with whom one has a relationship of *philia* are *aidoioi* (to be treated with aidōs, proper respect), particularly those who have raised and nurtured one: Cairns 1993, 91. Thus, the transgression of the dog-traitor is once again a form of anaideia.

96. Homer, *Odyssey* 18.338, 19.91, 19.154, 19.372.

97. Ibid., 18.338–39.

98. See ch. 5. At Homer, *Odyssey* 19.372–73, the nurse calls the maidservants *bitches* for the mockery and insults they have heaped on the disguised beggar Odysseus.

99. Homer, *Odyssey* 18.322–25.

100. The maidservants do not escape punishment by Odysseus, who inflicts on them an "unclean death" (ibid., 22.462), as traitors deserve.

101. Ibid., 19.91–95.

102. Ibid., 19.154.

103. Ibid., 8.317–20. In the compound *kynōpis* it is not *kyn-* but rather the second element that carries the marker of feminine gender: thus, in this case as well, I translate it as *dog* rather than *bitch*, which would add a layer of ambiguity in identifying the animal referent (see the end of this section, "Sixth Mask: The Traitor").

104. *Sōphrosynē*, the opposite of immoderation, is the ability to restrain impulses and desires through rational control. See the scholiastic comment on this passage, *Scholia in Homeri Odysseam* 8.320 Dindorf: οὐκ ἐχέθυμος] οὐκ ἔχουσα θυμὸν ὃν δεῖ, ἢ οὐ κρατοῦσα τὴν ἐπιθυμίαν, οἷον ἄκρατος καὶ ἀκόλαστος.... οὐ σώφρων ἤτοι οὐ κρατοῦσα τῆς ἐπιθυμίας, οὐ λογισμὸν ἔχουσα.

105. There is one case where a son attributes doggishness to his mother (*Iliad* 18.396): poor Hephaestus, in recalling how his mother, Hera, threw him down from Olympus because he was lame, calls her "dog-faced." This case of doggishness also possibly includes failed recognition of a philia: i.e., the affection for a child expected of a mother. See, however, the section "Seventh Mask: The Furious Mother."

106. Recall that one term used to refer to the process of inducing a dog's solidarity is *hypagein*, "to subdue" but also "to lure, attract" (see ch. 2); another is *kolakeuein*, "to flatter."

107. In reality, this payment for a wife was the Homeric practice of giving *hedna*, which some scholars claim an opposite practice replaced in a later period, whereby the bride's father had to pay a dowry to the son-in-law (Vernant [1980] 1988; Redfield 1982, 186–88; Sealey 1990, 114–27). According to others, hedna and dowries were instead elements of a single transaction: hedna were perhaps a "counter-dowry" that the bridegroom gave in exchange for the bride with the dowry (Vérilhac and Vial 1998, 125–35) or else a display of wealth and rank that a successful suitor proffered in agreement to the future father-in-law, who then gave his daughter and a dowry (Leduc 1990, 255–65). The parallel between the matrimonial transaction and the transfer of a dog does not rest, however, on the idea of paying a price: a dog, like a wife-to-be, may be transferred for free, given as a gift, and so forth.

108. On this point, see Xenophon, *Oeconomicus* 7.10–15, where the husband is concerned to induce his wife's feelings of attachment and solidarity to gain her fullest participation in caring for the household; see also Plutarch, *Precepts on Marriage* 12, which recommends persuasion rather than force to ensure the new bride's docile submission.

109. By *seduction,* I mean the work of a dog's new master or a woman's new guardian to reorient the direction of their solidarity. Given the dangers inherent in a woman's seducibility, Greek husbands preferred to think about this work in terms of domestication: see the image of the virgin as a "filly" to be tamed (Calame 1997, 185ff.) and the idea of marriage, of which "cow-eyed" Hera was the patron, as a "yoke" (e.g., Euripides, *Iphigeneia at Aulis* 698; *Phoenician Women* 1366; *Bacchae* 468). Even more reassuring must have been the metaphors of one's bride as a field to be plowed or earth to be sowed (DuBois 1988, 65ff.; Sissa 1990; Loraux 2000, 95ff.). According to Plutarch (*Precepts on Marriage*), the husband needs to teach his bride to be affectionate to him. Still, Greek husbands could not avoid noticing that winning a woman's affections was a sort of seduction: Lysias, *Against Eratosthenes* 33, says that adulterers corrupt others' wives by inducing them to become affectionate friend-companions of the seducer rather than, as they should be, their husbands. The metaphor of woman as dog represents precisely this worrisome aspect of marital relations. On the anxieties of Greek husbands about female seducibility, see Cohen 1991, 136–46.

110. Homer, *Iliad* 3.161–80.

111. Ibid., 3.162, 3.172. *Aidoios* means "worthy of aidōs." On the etymological connection between *deinos* and *deos,* the proper "fear" that an inferior must display toward a superior, see above, n. 28.

112. Homer, *Iliad* 3.180 (δαὴρ αὖτ' ἐμὸς ἔσκε κυνώπιδος).

113. Ibid., 6.344 (δᾶερ ἐμεῖο κυνὸς κακομηχάνου ὀκρυοέσσης), 6.356 (εἵνεκ' ἐμεῖο κυνὸς καὶ Ἀλεξάνδρου ἕνεκ' ἄτης).

114. Homer, *Odyssey* 4.145–46 (ἐμεῖο κυνώπιδος εἵνεκ' Ἀχαιοὶ / ἦλθεθ' ὑπὸ Τροίην, πόλεμον θρασὺν ὁρμαίνοντες).

115. See especially the two monographs Clader 1976 and N. Austin 1994; also Graver 1995, dedicated to the problem of "dog" Helen in Homer; Worman 2001's analysis; most recently, Blondell 2010 and 2013.

116. For another perspective, see Clader 1976, 46ff., which sees in the doggishness of Helen and other Argive figures in Homer—Clytemnestra and Agamemnon—a subtle link to the frequent connection between the dog and the adjective *argos* in epic diction and further postulates that *kynōpis* might be a cult epithet for Helen, comparable to *boōpis* for Hera and *glaukōpis* for Athena. Graver 1995, 53, suggests instead that Helen's calling herself a dog evokes a negative version of her myth already common in other poetic traditions (though first evidenced only in Stesichorus), which the epic rhapsodes countered with their positive vision.

117. Cantarella 1986, 40-43; Cohen 1991, 99-132; Todd 1993, 279. Ancient Greek did not even have a word designating the woman in an adulterous affair, but it called the seducing man *moichos*. In Athenian law, the cheated-on husband had to divorce his wife, who was then excluded from public religious festivals, but she was not put on trial and could even remarry. As Cohen 1991, 123 n. 74, says, in punishing only the adulterer, Athenian law was concerned with the public consequences of illicit sex, not its moral and private aspects.

118. The adultery laws that provide the data for this reconstruction belong to a much later period than Homer, of course, and thus do not amount to secure evidence for the world described in epic poetry, but this does not mean that such legislation did not reflect models and concerns already active in traditional culture for many generations, so they may, therefore, be of use in understanding certain dynamics of imagination attested in earlier periods. For example, female characters in Homer do not seem to have a social or juridical position very different from those of the majority of Greek women in later periods: see Cantarella 1986, 24ff., for the relevant bibliography and discussion.

119. Homer, *Iliad* 13.623 (to be precise, Menelaus calls the Trojans *bitches*, but see the later detailed discussion of the gendering in this passage); Euripides, *Trojan Women* 864-66.

120. Responding to this need to safeguard the divine figure of Helen, Stesichorus gives a well-known radical answer in his *Palinode*: it wasn't Helen who went to Troy, only a phantom. On the ambiguous figure of Helen, ever oscillating between marvelous divine object of male desire and an active, perilous, malign spirit of feminine seduction, see Loraux 1995, 194-210. According to Worman 2001, 28-29, on the other hand, this peculiar form of self-abuse is part of Helen's seductive rhetorical skill: by accusing and disparaging herself, she disarms her interlocutors, removing their opportunity and willingness to insult her.

121. Homer, *Iliad* 3.404 (ἐθέλει στυγερὴν ἐμὲ οἴκαδ' ἄγεσθαι). Perhaps a hint at the probability that the lawful husband, having taken his wife back, would punish her privately within the home.

122. Blondell 2010 articulates this dichotomy in a way that I find persuasive: Helen's self-blame "constitutes self-disempowering, gender-appropriate, and evidently endearing behavior" but at the same time "empowers Helen in a different way, by providing her with a space in which she can assert her own subjectivity and reclaim the agency that is denied to her by men" (14). In reclaiming her subjectivity, Helen implicitly reclaims "the subjectivity of the Greek wife" (18) and the problem of assessing her complicity in her abduction "thus mirrors the problem of identifying women's subjectivity in the Greek wedding,

and more generally their finely-calibrated position between coercion and consent in marriage" (19).

123. In the common ideal model, the house a woman belongs to—whether as daughter or wife—constitutes the space within which she can legitimately move at will; any movement of a woman into or toward the outside is preferably controlled by a male will and not conducted according to the woman's volition: Vernant (1980) 1988, 73ff.; Vernant 1983, 127–75; Cantarella 1986, 46ff. On the problem of controlling female movement, see especially Visser 1986; also Woodbury 1978, 297; Carson 1990; Cohen 1991, 136–70, notes the need of distinguishing ideal models from actual social practices. Recall here Plutarch's comments (in *Roman Questions* 29) on the Roman practice of a marriage party carrying a new bride across the threshold of her husband's house rather than having her walk in. Perhaps, he says, this is because the Romans want to symbolize that the wife is not to enter or exit the house at her pleasure but can only be forced to enter or exit; a similar symbol occurs in Boeotian marriage rites, in which "they burn the axle of the marriage chariot in front of the door, to show that the wife must remain within, since her means of transport has been destroyed."

124. Aeschylus, *Agamemnon* 716–25. Metaphorically, Helen behaved as though she were a cute puppy when she first came to Troy, but then, with the outbreak of the war caused by her adultery, she proves to be a dangerous beast.

125. Euripides, *Andromache* 630 (προδότιν αἰκάλλων κύνα).

126. Aelian, *On the Nature of Animals* 8.2, 11.3, 11.20; Phrynichus, *Praeparatio Sophistica* 36 De Borries.

127. McClure 1999, 190, by a different tack, concludes that Euripides's Menelaus is "feminized" and placed on the same level as his wife in being unable to control his desires and resist sexual seduction, a reading that harmonizes with mine. The episode is a proverbial example of male susceptibility to erotic temptation: see, e.g., Aristophanes's *Lysistrata* 155–56, where Lampito cites Menelaus as evidence that the women's sexual extortion of their husbands will be successful: "Didn't Menelaus drop his sword when he caught sight of Helen's naked 'apples'?"

128. For the Homeric passages about "dog" Clytemnestra, see ch. 5. For the motif of her doggishness in Aeschylus's trilogy, see *Agamemnon* 606–8, 914, 1228. In the *Choephori*, these canine traits are transferred to Clytemnestra's avengers, the Erinyes.

129. Aeschylus, *Agamemnon* 1231, comparable with Lycophron, *Alexandra* 612, which describes the adulterous wife of Diomedes—who, like Clytemnestra, tries to kill her husband on his return—as θρασεῖα θουρὰς κύων (bold, impetuous bitch).

130. Aeschylus, *Choephori* 613–22. Also, Scylla, the sea monster in Homer, is etymologically connected to *skylax*, "little dog," "puppy," probably because it is a devouring creature like the sea dog (*kyōn thalattios*; see ch. 2, n. 75).

131. Apollodorus, *Bibliotheca* 3.15.8. The same oscillation between greed for riches and erotic weakness is attested for Helen's adultery: Plutarch, *Precepts on Marriage* 21 (φιλόπλουτος ἡ Ἑλένη).

132. Rather, lasciviousness was attributed to the dog in general: Plutarch, *Precepts on Marriage* 7; Aelian, *On the Nature of Animals* 7.19 (explicitly about male dogs).

133. There are many examples, some already cited in the discussion of the dog's relationship to human food (see chs. 2 and 3). Here we may recall just the brilliant comic bit in Aristophanes's *Wasps* where the Cydathenaean dog—who stands in for the demagogue

Cleon, the "dog of the people"—delivers a prosecution speech against the dog Labes (Snatcher) centering on the fact that Labes has not shared a stolen cheese with him: a dispute, in other words, between two greedy, thieving dogs. The Cydathenaean dog calls Labes "of all dogs, the man most greedy [κυνῶν ἁπάντων ἄνδρα μονοφαγίστατον]" (923); this striking turn of phrase uses *dog* on three levels, referring to the character in the play, to the traditional insult, and, by allusion, to the general Laches, who lay behind the mask of Labes.

134. As we've seen, the seducibility of Helen, Clytemnestra, and Scylla can be portrayed as the result of erotic lust but also of lust for riches and power.

135. Hunter 1994, 111–16; McClure 1999, 60–61, 162–63, 179.

136. As already mentioned (in n. 103), in the compound *kynopis*, the second element (*-ōpis*), not the first (*kyn-*), carries the marker of feminine gender.

137. Semonides fr. 7 West² (Pellizer-Tedeschi), 32–36.

138. Homer, *Odyssey* 20.17–18: στῆθος δὲ πλήξας κραδίην ἠνίπαπε μύθῳ· / τέτλαθι δή, κραδίη· καὶ κύντερον ἄλλο ποτ᾽ ἔτλης. See ch. 2. Note that *kradiē* is feminine, which adds to the coherence of the simile.

139. Odysseus rebukes his heart by literally beating it (πλήξας). Plato uses this Homeric passage to illustrate the theory of the rational principle charged with keeping at bay the irrational part of the soul, as a master does his dog: *Republic* 441b–c.

140. Euripides, *Hecuba* 1265 (κύων . . . πύρσ᾽ ἔχουσα δέργματα), 1273 (κυνὸς ταλαίνης σῆμα).

141. Burnett 1994.

142. Aristotle, *History of Animals* 542a, 545b; Aesop 223 Perry (251 Hausrath² = 342 Chambry³), which tells about a contest between a she-dog and a sow over their fecundity. On she-dogs and deities of childbirth, see Bettini 2013, 99. The Xenophon passage (*Cynegeticus* 7.4), with what Burnett 1994 cites as an example of the she-dog as a positive maternal model, in fact recounts in rather cold terms the normal process of weaning, during which the mother keeps the puppies warm with her breath and within her "embrace." There is one case of the she-dog held up as a model mother, by Antipater of Sidon (*Palatine Anthology* 7.425; see also the note on this epigram in Gow and Page 1965, 59).

143. The fact that puppies are born blind was imputed to the she-dog's haste in giving birth, before they had completely formed. In Italian, the cat plays this proverbial role. The expression is quite ancient and appears in Sumerian and Akkadian contexts (West 1997, 500). For the Greek proverb, see Archilochus, fr. 196a.39–41. West²; Aesop 223 Perry (251 Hausrath² = 342 Chambry³), where a she-dog boasts of her fecundity, while a sow retorts that her puppies are born blind; Aristotle, *History of Animals* 574a; Aristotle, *Generation of Animals* 770a–b, 774b. For the variant of the proverb in Aristophanes, which surprisingly replaces the she-dog with a goldfinch, see Bettini 2013, 249 n. 39. On the doggishness of Hephaestus's mother, see Homer, *Iliad* 18.396–97 (μητρὸς ἐμῆς ἰότητι κυνώπιδος, ἥ μ᾽ ἐθέλησε / κρύψαι χωλὸν ἐόντα).

144. This fury, justified or not, is the characteristic trait of the she-dog with puppies in both Homer and Semonides. Oppian (*Halieutica* 1.722–23) explicitly describes the indiscriminate aggression of a she-dog protecting her pups as a temporary loss of aidōs. The *Palatine Anthology,* alongside the sole ancient Greek example of a she-dog as a positive model of maternal care (7.425), contains at least two instances of cruel and rabid bitch-mothers (7.433, 7.531).

145. Some scholars have already noted the importance of the traditional model of the she-dog with puppies for Hecuba's metamorphosis (references in Mossman 1995, 195 n. 68, 196 n. 71). For other interpretations and bibliography, see ibid., 194–201; Gregory 1999, xxxiii–xxxvi. The Erinyes are divine apparitions of the avenging mother's aggressive rage in the myths of Orestes, Alcmeon, Meleager (Homer, *Iliad* 9.471), and Oedipus (Homer, *Iliad* 11.280). Even Telemachus expresses fear of the Erinyes of Penelope, his mother (*Odyssey* 2.135), and Ares is urged to fear those of his mother, Hera (*Iliad* 21.412).

146. On the dreadfulness that the Greeks attributed to a mother's grief, see Loraux 1998, 9ff., 35ff.

147. Semonides, fr. 7 Pellizer-Tedeschi (West²), 12–15.

148. Lloyd-Jones 1976, 68, interprets *autométora* as "her mother's own child"; Loraux 1993b, 96–97, as "true daughter of her mother."

149. Phocylides, fr. 2.6 Gentili-Prato (χαλεπή τε καὶ ἄγριος). For the priority of Semonides over Phocylides, see Pellizer and Tedeschi 1990, xxxv–xxxvi. It's worth noting that Semonides expresses the dog-woman's implacability with οὐδ' ἂν μειλίχως μυθεόμενος (she never utters a gentle word) and implies her difficult stubbornness with ἄπρηκτον (impossible, unmanageable).

150. Homer, *Iliad* 24.212–14. Burnett does not cite this passage and claims that Euripides's Hecuba is "the first appearance of the Queen of Troy as an avenger" (1994, 161). What the Homeric Hecuba longs for is a "canine" vengeance for her son's demise, which she would accomplish by mauling Achilles to death.

151. Pausanias 8.25.4 (see also Antimachus, fr. 35 Wyss). Elsewhere in Arcadia, wrathful Demeter was called Black (Μέλαινα): Pausanias 8.42.1.

152. *Homeric Hymn to Demeter* 83 (ἄπλητον . . . χόλον), 90 (ἄχος αἰνότερον καὶ κύντερον).

153. Ibid., 305–6. This model may have played some role in the case of "bitch" Clytemnestra in Aeschylus. She claims, after all, to have killed Agamemnon as payback for the sacrifice of Iphigeneia: *Agamemnon* 1525–29.

154. *PMG*, 965 Page.

155. On Hecate and childbirth, see Bettini 2013, 99. Explicit evidence of this connection is rare and specifically concerns a tripartite Hecate-Artemis-Eileithyia: Johnston 1999, 211–15; Von Rudloff 1999, 107–11; Ricciardelli 2000, 234, 238–39. For the strict tie between Hecate and dogs, see especially Theocritus 2.11–13; also *Anecdota Graeca* 327.13, 336.31 Bekker; Hesychius, s.v. Ἑκάτης ἄγαλμα; Apollonius Rhodius, *Argonautica* 3.1040, 1212–17; Lycophron, *Alexandra* 77; Nonnus, *Dionysiaca* 3.74; *Orphic Hymns* 2.5. Hecate is one of the few deities who seems to have received dog sacrifices: Aristophanes, fr. 209 Kassel-Austin; Sophron, fr. 8 Olivieri. According to a little-known but rather significant myth, she was originally an ill-tempered woman who did not give hospitality to Artemis, who turned her into a bitch (Callimachus, fr. 461 Pfeiffer): the Hecate-dog nexus is once again situated in the negative trait of aggression against strangers rather than the image of a fecund she-dog.

156. Euripides, fr. 968 Nauck²: Ἑκάτης ἄγαλμα φωσφόρου κύων ἔσῃ.

157. The association is more explicit in Lycophron, *Alexandra* 1174–89, where Hecuba becomes a dog in the goddess's retinue.

158. Homer, *Iliad* 22.25–32. The comparison, focalized through Priam's eyes, is prophetic: Achilles will soon bring fire and destruction to the Trojan kingdom. On the danger of the Dog Star, see Hesiod, *Works and Days* 587.

159. Hyginus, *Astronomia* 2.36. On the rich mythic tradition surrounding the Dog Star, see Gundel 1927; Ceragioli 1992; Condos 1997, 65–70.

160. On the warrior as a burning flame, see Homer, *Iliad* 13.53. For madness and lyssa as a burning fire, see Aristophanes, *Thesmophoriazusae* 680.

161. See Athenaeus 3.99e, which attests to how wild aggression, canine lyssa, and the dog days could function in a system of reciprocal relations. According to a tradition cited in *Scholia in Apollonium Rhodium* 2.526, the inhabitants of Ceos greeted Sirius with a yearly ritual, expectantly waiting under arms for the Dog Star to rise (μεθ' ὅπλων ἐπιτηρεῖν τὴν ἐπιτολὴν τοῦ Κυνός): see Bettini 1991, 244–45. Perhaps the ritual served to symbolically oppose the rabid onslaught of Sirius with an army ready to unleash an equally effective martial lyssa. Similarly, the sacrifice of a dog at the Porta Catularia in Rome was probably a ritual expulsion of the devastating effects of the Dog Star: Faraone 1992, 42. The association between the dog and the hot summer dog days was still alive in medieval European folklore: Schmitt 1983, 149ff.

162. Callimachus, fr. 75.34–35 Pfeiffer; Nonnus, *Dionysiaca* 5.221, 47.219–55; Hyginus, *Myths* 130; Hyginus, *Astronomia* 2.4; Pollux 5.42; *Scholia in Ap. Rhod. Argon.* 2.498–527. This tradition, dating back perhaps to Eratosthenes (Rosokoki 1995, 47–59), had a rich reception in Latin culture, which referred to the Dog Star as *canicula*.

163. Lycophron, *Alexandra* 334. In this version of the Trojan myth, the Greeks are angered by Hecuba's curses and stone her to death (*Suda*, s.v. Κυνὸς σῆμα).

164. *Homeric Hymn to Hermes* 194; Theocritus 20.25. For "yellow, amber" as a possible meaning of *charopoi*, see Pseudo-Aristotle, *Physiognomonica* 812b, which uses the word to describe the eyes of eagles and lions; the anonymous Latin translation of this treatise uses the adjective *subnigri* (light brown). Arrian (*Cynegeticus* 4.5), on the other hand, distinguishes the "fiery [*pyropa*]" eyes of lions, leopards, and lynxes from *charopa* eyes. *Geoponica* 19.2.1 advises choosing charopoi dogs and those with a lionlike appearance (*leontoeidēs*). Oppian says the swiftest dogs are those with *kyanoi* eyes, while dogs used for hunting big game should have *pyroentes* and charopoi eyes (*On the Hunt* 1.403–21). See also the useful discussion in Gow 1952², 227–28.

165. An old tradition, which Empedocles took up, maintains that bright eyes see well at night because they are made of fire (Aristotle, *Generation of Animals* 779b). This was of obvious importance for guard dogs, while hunting dogs need to see well by day, so dogs with darker eyes were preferred for this (Xenophon, *Cynegeticus* 3.3, 4.1). More generally, the ancient Greek theory of optics supposed that eyesight depended on interaction between the fire inside the eye and the external fire of sunlight: Plato, *Timaeus* 45b–46c. The connection between emanations of light and fiery heat—i.e., what make one see—and the visual faculty of the source of light—i.e., what sees—is implicit in the mythic figure of Helios, the sun god, "who sees all [πανόπτης]," in, e.g., Aeschylus, *Prometheus Bound* 91. The fiery trait of the gaze seems to stem and be developed from the dog's luminous eyes, which, just like the cat's, possess what's called a *tapetum lucidum*, a layer at the back that enables them to see even in very low light and explains why they glow in the dark (Morris 1987, 69ff.).

166. See ch. 2. Lions and eagles are charopoi in Pseudo-Aristotle, *Physiognomonica* 812b. For *pyrōdeis* dragons, see Theocritus 24.18. On the fieriness of wolves, see Detienne and Svenbro 1989. The gaze of fire (πυρώδης) is, among other things, a sign of anaideia in Pseudo-Aristotle, *Physiognomonica* 812b9, which cites dogs as evidence. Another important

passage in the same text (812a22) maintains that people with a fiery red complexion are "mad [μανικοί]," because the parts of the body "excessively heated are the color of flame, and those who are overheated are mad." In Hippocrates (*On Diet* 1.35.9–11), the beings in which fire prevails over water are "half-mad [ὑπομαινόμενοι]," and it takes only the least amount of inflammation for their excessive fieriness to drive them mad.

167. Euripides, *Hecuba* 1173.

168. Ibid., 1100–1105.

169. A similar episode of blinding occurs in the story of Orion, who recovers thanks to direct intervention from the Sun: Apollodorus, *Bibliotheca* 1.4.3.

170. Polymestor's speech recounting the dreadful scene of infanticide carried out by Hecuba and her accomplices has a complex hunting image, in which the Trojan women are a savage pack of human predators that Polymestor, a beast blinded by the she-dogs, tries to hunt down (Euripides, *Hecuba* 1132–75). On mother goddess figures—mothers turned avengers by rabid fury, then pacified and incorporated into the polis as "guardians of justice" (e.g., Mother of the Gods [Meter Theon], the Erinyes-Eumenides, Demeter Thesmophoros)—see Loraux 1998, 67ff.

171. *Orphicorum fragmenta* 42 Kern; Proclus, *Hymns* 6.2 Vogt; Aristophanes, *Wasps* 804; Aristophanes, *Frogs* 366; Aristophanes, *Lysistrata* 64. See also Kraus 1960, 63, 69–70, 107; Faraone 1992, 6–9; Johnston 1999, 207–8.

172. Johnston 1999, 241–87. The Erinyes are nearly always depicted as hunters, in short tunics and high leggings, and often brandishing torches: Wüst 1956, 138–66. Theocritus (2.14) calls Hecate δασπλῆτις, "dreadful," a Homeric epithet for the Erinyes (Homer, *Odyssey* 15.234; see also Hesiod fr. 280.9 Merkelbach-West). Moreover, it is well known that Hecate—called, inter alia, "driver of dogs [σκυλαγέτις]" (*Papyri Graecae Magicae* 4.2722) and "protector of dogs [σκυλακῖτις]" (*Orphic Hymns* 1.5 Ricciardelli)—was subject to a fairly early overlay with Artemis, the divine hunter par excellence and, later on, the goddess of moonlight. On Hecate brandishing a torch, see *Homeric Hymn to Demeter* 52. For the association of Hecate with a torch and dogs, see Mainoldi 1984, 47; Johnston 1999, 211–12; Von Rudloff 1999, 102, 120; Ricciardelli 2000, 236. For Hecate's connection with madness in the mysteries at Aegina, see Johnston 1999, 137, 144–45.

173. Homer, *Odyssey* 7.91–94.

174. Hermesianax fr. 6.10–11 Powell (describing Orpheus's encounter with Cerberus): ἠδὲ καὶ αἰνοτάτου βλέμμ' ὑπέμεινε κυνός, / ἐν πυρὶ μὲν φωνὴν τεθοωμένου, ἐν πυρὶ δ' ὄμμα (and he also endured the gaze of the dreadful dog, whose voice in fire, whose eye in fire was sharpened). The participle τεθοωμένου, indicating the sharpness of Cerberus's voice and gaze, recalls the brand that Odysseus sharpened and hardened in fire to blind Polyphemus (Homer, *Odyssey* 9.327–28). Similarly, in Hesiod, Cerberus has a metallic voice "of bronze" (*Theogony* 311).

175. Pausanias 9.34.5 (ἀνωτέρω δέ ἐστιν Ἡρακλῆς Χάροψ ἐπίκλησιν· ἐνταῦθα δὲ οἱ Βοιωτοὶ λέγουσιν ἀναβῆναι τὸν Ἡρακλέα ἄγοντα τοῦ Ἅιδου τὸν κύνα). Heracles was also venerated as, inter alia, a "Guardian" spirit: Faraone 1992, 58.

176. Euripides, *Heracles* 822–24.

177. Euripides, *Hecuba* 1271–73.

178. On the use of the signal fire (*tekmar*), see Aeschylus, *Agamemnon* 281–315. For the dangerous jutting headland of Kynossēma, see Thucydides 8.104.5. Concerning Kynossēma,

Faraone 1992, 45, 52 n. 72, revives W. H. Roscher's view (1896) that Euripides's treatment of Hecuba reflects a local myth about Hecate (interpreting the heroine's name, Hekabe in Greek, as nothing but a variant of the goddess's name). The myth would have told about a plague sent by Hecate to the realm of King Polymestor; the dog with the fiery gaze would have been the malign, demonic form in which she revealed herself to the kingdom's inhabitants.

179. Aristotle, fr. 398 Rose. It may be that the promontory had this name for another reason, as an allusion to the myth of Hecuba being stoned to death (see above, n. 163): in fact, in these stories there seems to be an active morphological similarity between the rocky promontory and a rudimentary grave (like those given to dogs?) made of a simple pile of rocks (see Euripides, *Hecuba* 1272: μορφῆς ἐπωιδὸν, ἢ τί, τῆς ἐμῆς ἐρεῖς;). The allusion could also recall the situation of a dog being pelted with stones. The theme of the bitch's gaze of fire connected to Kynossēma, on the other hand, seems explicable only as an allusion to a lighthouse. For the medieval motif of the grave of the poor dog, one that died for its master or was killed for its master's mistake, see Schmitt 1983.

180. On the important signaling function of hunting dogs, see Xenophon, *Cynegeticus* 6.23.

181. Dogs sense and give warning of divine presences: Homer, *Odyssey* 16.162. Hermes passes unnoticed by dogs: *Homeric Hymn to Hermes* 145. For Hermes Kynanchās, see Hipponax fr. 3a.1 West² (fr. 3 Masson); Antoninus Liberalis, *Metamorphoses* 23.2.

182. For the sources on the *kyneē*, see Mainoldi 1984, 43. Cassandra is represented as "a she-dog that sniffs out the tracks" and reveals with her prophetic vision what others cannot see: Aeschylus, *Agamemnon* 1093–94. But note the ambiguity of the image: Cassandra is both priestess of Apollo and mad visionary, both grief-stricken victim who contemplates her imminent death and rabid bitch who declares vengeance against her malefactors. For nighttime barking and strange behavior of dogs as *omina*, see Pausanias 1.19.3, 4.13.1, 4.21.1. Dog entrails used in divination: ibid., 6.2.5. Dogs barking at night signaled the arrival of Hecate: Theocritus 2.35–36. On dogs' ability to interpret signs, see Xenophon, *Cynegeticus* 6.22. Note that in Roman culture as well, the dog was eminently *sagax*, "keen-sensed," and soothsaying witches were called *sagae*.

183. See, e.g., *SEG* 18 (1962), 561, a funeral inscription that invokes for the tomb's protection, and to punish those who desecrate it, Helios, "who sees all," Olympian Zeus, Pluto, Demeter-Kore, the Erinyes, "dogs of Artemis-Hecate," chthonic Hermes, and all the gods that "have care and thought for good souls"; *CIG* 916 (*IG* 3, pt. 2, 1423); *IG* 12, fasc. 9, 1179.21–22 (*Syll*³, 1240, *omisso epigrammate*). See also Faraone 1992, 22.

184. Aelian, *On the Nature of Animals* 14.24, 14.27.

185. As Laura Gibbs kindly pointed out to me, Josephus tells a similar story about a plant called *baaras* (*Jewish War* 7.6.3).

186. Recall also that the story of Orion—the master of Sirius, transformed into a constellation with him—was one of blindness healed: having been blinded, he was guided by a young boy toward the east, where a ray of sunlight struck him and restored his sight (Apollodorus, *Bibliotheke* 1.4.3; Lucian, *De Domo*, 29; Hyginus, *Astronomia* 2.34).

187. The rule that Faust 1969, 69, sets down, that an animal category functions as a metaphorical insult only when it refers to a person, needs revision.

188. Homer, *Iliad* 10.503.

189. Homer, *Odyssey* 7.216.

190. See, for example, the passage in the pseudo-Herodotean *Life of Homer* that is framed by the epigram cited in ch. 2 about the importance of feeding dogs before setting the table, so they don't harass the diners with their noisy clamoring for food: *Homeri Opera,* vol. 5, 206 Allen.

191. See ch. 5.

192. In addition to remarks on the parasite dog in chs. 2 and 3, see *Palatine Anthology* 16.9: "Oh belly, dog-fly, for which flattering parasites sell their share of freedom for a bowl of soup! [Ὦ γαστὴρ κυνάμυια, δι' ἣν κόλακες παράσιτοι ζωμοῦ πωλοῦσιν θεσμὸν ἐλευθερίης.]"

193. Homer, *Odyssey* 20.18–20.

194. *Homeric Hymn to Demeter* 90, 305–6.

195. See also two passages in Apollonius Rhodius, *Argonautica,* one describing the suicide of Clite as *kynteron* (1.1064), the other calling *kynteron* the daily inhuman miseries of someone who must labor to expiate a crime against the gods (2.474). See also Burnett 1994, 153.

196. Chantraine 1958, 259.

197. Homer, *Iliad* 22.93; Homer, *Odyssey* 10.212; Sophocles, *Philoctetes* 391; Euripides, *Bacchae* 1141.

198. Homer, *Iliad* 9.69, 9.160, 9.392, 10.239; *Odyssey* 15.533.

199. Benveniste 1971, 239ff. On Benveniste's theory of delocutive derivatives, see Turpin 1980, 362–63, which also mentions a more complex version of the theory (proposed by Benoît de Cornulier [1976]) that distinguishes three phases of derivation, which would, for our case, expect the following development: *kyōn,* "dog" (sense A: animal of the species dog) - *Kyon!,* "Dog!" (sense B: derived delocution that constitutes the insult) - *kynteros* "more dog," and *kyntatos,* "most dog" (nominal adjectives derived from the delocution *Kyon!*).

200. This process may be compared with that which gave rise to the Latin *oculissime,* a superlative derived from the noun *oculus* through delocution from *mi ocule,* in the sense of "my dearest," "my treasure" (see, e.g., Plautus, *Curculio* 122, 203). Given that such nominal comparatives and superlatives often formed on roots indicating a level in a hierarchy— including *kyōn, basileus,* and *doulos* (slave)—or from nouns indicating worth (as with *oculissime*), one might suppose that they were often employed as vocatives, to express deference (*Basileu!,* "My king!") or to humiliate (*Kyon!,* "Dog!"; *Doule!,* "Slave!"), and on this account gave rise to the delocutions in question.

5. RETURN TO PANDORA

1. Plutarch, *On the Intelligence of Animals* 13 (969c).

2. Notable here again is Aristotle's classification of virtues in *Politics* 1260a, where he distinguishes between so-called masterly (*archikē*) virtue, the complete virtue of the adult male, and the "servile [*hypēretikē*]" virtue of women and subordinates.

3. Arrian meant his *Cynegeticus* to be an addition to Xenophon's and presents himself as the namesake of Xenophon (Arrian, *Cynegeticus* 1.1–4; see Stadter 1980, 190).

4. Arrian, *On Hunting* 5.1–6.

5. On the similar expectations that aristocrats had of slaves, horses, dogs, and women (at least in the world of Xenophon's *Oeconomicus*), see Vilatte 1986.

6. Plutarch, *On the Intelligence of Animals* 13 (969d–e); Aelian, *On the Nature of Animals* 6.25, 7.29.

7. Aristotle, fr. 398 Rose; Aelian, *On the Nature of Animals* 6.25, 7.10, 7.28, 7.29, 7.40, 10.41 (the grave of Eupolis on Aegina, nicknamed Κυνὸς Θρῆνος because his dog laid down there and died of grief), 11.13, 12.35; Plutarch, *On the Intelligence of Animals* 13 (969c–970b), 14 (970c). Examples of dogs mourning their owner's death: Bion, *Lament for Adonis* 18; Cassius Dio 58.1.3; Nonnus, *Dionysiaca* 5.381; Quintus Smyrnaeus 2.578–79 (see Seneca, *Phaedra* 1108: "maestaeque domini membra vestigant canes").

8. See ch. 3. Dogs can function as mirrors of identity or as "funeral monuments" in various ways. Among the Nzema of southwestern Ghana, they are given names that recall the death of a relative (Death, They Left Me Alone) or descriptive names expressing different states of mind of their owner (for example, They Said Something is the name given to the dog of someone who wanted to ridicule their neighbors' malice, while Remember the Past is the dog of someone who has not received due gratitude from a friend): Wade-Brown 1974, 163–68. On the dog as a mirror of its master's identity, see also Vilatte 1986, 280–84.

9. Euripides, *Alcestis* 83–85, 150–51, 235–36, 442, 623–24. Another exemplary wife, who does not long outlive her husband, is Laodamia, the subject of a lost play of Euripides, *Protesilaos*, whose plot is not known with certainty. According to the mythographer Hyginus (*Myths* 103, 104), there were at least two accounts of Laodamia's death. In one version, she is able to gain her husband's return to life for a few hours, but when Protesilaos has to go back to Hades, she cannot control her grief and dies in his arms; in the other version, Laodamia has a statue made in her husband's likeness and consoles herself by caressing and kissing his image, but her father, to stop his daughter tormenting herself, has it thrown in the fire. Laodamia then throws herself on the flames and perishes with the image of her husband (see Guidorizzi 2000, 360–61). For the second version in particular and the motif of the lover's image, see Bettini 1999, 9ff.

10. Aelian, *On the Nature of Animals* 6.25. On Evadne's suicide, see Euripides, *Suppliant Women* 980–1071; Pseudo-Apollodorus, *Bibliotheke* 3.7.1; Hyginus, *Myths* 243; see also Guidorizzi 2000, 498. Hyginus names Evadnes, Alcestis, and Laodamia among the women "quae castissimae fuerunt" (*Myths* 256).

11. Aelian, *On the Nature of Animals* 7.28. This encyclopedia of animals is of great interest less for its zoological and ethological contents than for being the first work to focus attention on the relations between animals and humans and on the cultural models produced through this relation: as such, Aelian might be called the first "anthrozoologist" of antiquity (Gibbs 1999).

12. The existence of a collection of anecdotes about the life of Aesop is attested already in Aristophanes: see Adrados 1999², 647–65; Ferrari 1997, 5–7; Jedrkiewicz 1989, 41–68.

13. *Life of Aesop* 45.

14. See ch. 2.

15. Aeschylus, *Agamemnon* 606–8.

16. Ibid., 914.

17. Besides the Aeschylus passage cited, other examples of wives as guardians of their husband's house and goods are Xenophon, *Oeconomicus* 7.25, 7.42 (see Demosthenes,

Against Neaera 122: τῶν ἔνδον φύλακα πιστήν). The verb *oikourein* typically refers to the secluded, inactive life, the woman's "staying at home," contrasted with the male's free movement and activity, to the point that Euripides can use the substantive *oikourēma* (what stays at home) as an antonomastic reference to woman (*Orestes* 928), and to call a man *oikouros* is to insult him by applying a "female" trait (Aeschylus, *Agamemnon* 1626). For the *oikouros* dog, see Aristophanes, *Wasps* 970; Aesop, 92 Perry (94 Haurath[2] = 175 Chambry[3]); Aelian, *On the Nature of Animals* 6.65. In Aelian (ibid., 6.22), one finds the interesting claim that what dogs fear most is being driven out of doors (ἐκ τῶν τεγῶν): a bit like women, dogs outside the home are in danger. The metaphor of the dog that preserves and keeps watch recurs in a later speech of Clytemnestra's (*Agamemnon* 896), referring to Agamemnon: in her first speech to her husband, she hails him as "dog of the sheepfold." But the fact that the positive metaphor of guard dog might be used for a husband does not seem to diminish the force of my argument.

18. For the opposition between feminine immobility and masculine mobility represented by the divine couple Hestia and Hermes, see Vernant 1983, 127–75. If the house dog provided good imaginative fodder for thinking about women, what about the hunting dog? With its outdoor and typically masculine activity of hunter, one might expect it to have formed a systematic opposition to the house dog and thus gone on to become one pole of a symbolic paradigm within the masculine-feminine dialectic. But this dichotomy (house dog/woman–hunting dog/man) does not occur. Even the hunting dog is seen primarily as a subaltern element, "at the service" of man, and thus does not offer a foothold for symbolic elaborations on manliness. Whether keeping guard at home or going out to hunt with the master, the dog remains first and foremost a *kyōn:* a subordinate bound to obey, quite similar to women and slaves inasmuch as it can never resemble the master of the house. An interesting interpretation occurs in Artemidorus 2.11: dreaming of a guard dog refers to wives, children, and stored-up goods; dreaming of hunting dogs refers simply to gains deriving from outside.

19. Thucydides 2.45.2. On silence as the ideal condition of a woman's life, see Cantarella 1985; Loraux 1993a, 126–27; McClure 1999, 19–24; Blok 2001, 97. On birth as the only feminine *ponos* worthy of public notice, see Loraux 1995, 32ff. To speak of cultural representations of "Greek women" is in reality to use a convenient approximation, since the great majority of sources on which reconstructions are based are Athenian and date to the classical period; the cultural image of women discussed here aligns for the most part with married Athenian women in the fifth and fourth centuries B.C.E. and does not take account of possible differences over time, nor of the diverse images that must have characterized foreigners, slaves, and courtesans or respectable women from other cities. It's well known, for example, that Spartan women were markedly different from women in Athens, even as far as freedom of speech was concerned. On different typologies of women and their relative differences of position, see Pomeroy 1995[2]; McClure 1999, 261–62. On Spartan women, see Redfield 1977–78; Paradiso 1993; McClure 1999, 164–68; Cartledge 2001, 106–26. The Greek tradition of misogyny, with its literary topos of *psogos gynaikōn*, is nonetheless attested in the most diverse cultural areas and over the whole span of Greek history, and this justifies the use, in a study focused on this tradition, of a category like "the Greek woman."

20. Regarding silence in the work of slaves, see again Loraux 1995, 47.

21. Cohen 1991, 54–69; Hunter 1994, 96–119.

22. Also, just as the dialectical pairing of mental health and madness can be inscribed in the frame of ideological strategies of a culture, so canine *lyssa* may be counted among the beliefs that made the dog into a social agent. In Greek thought, madness and transgression were quite contiguous categories, such that a criminal act could be conceived in terms of both moral error and blind madness. Besides the madness of sacrilegious impurity—Orestes and Alcmeon being two well-known mythic examples of this—one need only consider the complex web of terms needed to translate the idea of *atē* (Dodds 1951, 2–8; Doyle 1984, 146–47). After all, the concept of mental pathology only coalesced in the history of medicine, and very slowly, out of a complex concept of "disease of the soul," indicating various altered states of cognition, perception, control, and transgressions understood as disturbed behaviors: see Pigeaud 1981, 529. The typical antonym for various terms for madness was *sōphrosynē*, literally "sanity, integrity of *phrenes*," a comprehensive category for the complex of moral and physiological notions of "state of mental health," "capacity of control," "respect for moral limits," "wisdom" (Adkins 1960, 339; Simon 1978, 92, 149; Padel 1992, 23; Padel 1995, 128). From the perspective of ideological strategies, the concept of *sōphrosynē* was of fundamental importance: social subordinates, such as women and dogs, were thought of as particularly needing *sōphrosynē* (or rather, tending to lack this virtue and thus being transgressive and excessive by nature), understood as the norm—moral and hygienic—that defines the duty to obey (for women, see Carson 1990, 142–43). Thus, it is not farfetched for the particular predisposition to altered mental states attributed to the dog to be interpreted as a strategic assertion of a "hygienic" and moral norm imposed on the animal as an element from whom *sōphrosynē* was expected.

23. With regard to women on this point, see Campese 1983, 25–28; Carson 1990, 142.

24. For women, see again Carson 1990, 153–64; on woman as leaky container, flux, and continual loss, see Sissa 1990, 127ff.

25. Homer, *Odyssey* 11.423–34.

26. Ibid., 11.441–43, 54–56.

27. It's also possible that within this framework lay a profound psychological dynamic concerning how the male and master constructed his identity. In the "recognizing" eyes of his dog and in the gaze of his wife, the man loves to see reflected back his identity as undisputed head of family, loved and adored: when such a reflection fails, when the dog or the woman refuses to be a faithful "mirror" reflecting back this image, the illusion of perfect symmetry falls to pieces and dogs and women go from tools that confirm identity to masks of hostile alterity and threats of dissolution. On the ideal woman as a mirror of her husband, see Plutarch, *Precepts on Marriage* 14 (139f). There are also signs that the dog could be thought of as faithful reflection of the master. A comic fragment attributed to Apollodorus (fr. 15 Kassel-Austin) says that you can know the mood of a house's master as soon as you cross the threshold by observing the dog's mood, and "Like *kyōn*, like master" was a proverbial phrase: see Plato, *Republic* 8.14 (563c). Zeitlin 1978 discusses the cultural dynamic whereby a rebellious woman who refuses to recognize male superiority necessarily becomes, in the imagination, a murderous monster, a woman who wants to eliminate the male and found an exclusively feminine society.

28. Hesiod, *Works and Days* 67, 78.

29. On the explanatory and amplifying nature of the description of Pandora's construction in accord with Zeus's orders, see Arrighetti 1998, 410–11.

30. Homer, *Odyssey* 17.248.

31. Proteus: ibid., 4.460, and compare to 4.410, "I will tell you all the old man's tricks [ὀλοφώια]." Circe: ibid., 10.289. On Proteus's *olophōia* as hidden, harmful actions, see Zatta 1997, 83–84; Scuderi 2012. On Circe's dangerous tricks, see Franco 2010, 31–144, 227–51.

32. On the cunning of animals, see Detienne and Vernant 1978, 27–54. For the proverbial guile of wolves and foxes, animal tricksters par excellence, see Aesop, 37, 107, 124, 153, 157, 154, 234 Perry; 54, 119, 165, 199, 217, 218, 220, 225, 229 Chambry[3].

33. Hesiod, *Theogony* 771; Aesop, 91 Perry (93 Hausrath[2] = 275 Chambry[3]).

34. A passage in Aeschylus (*Agamemnon* 797–98) clearly attests that the Greeks also saw in the dog's fawning an expression of affection, of friendliness (*philotēs*). The common interpretations of animal expressiveness and ethological theory are incompatible, but see the provocative work of J. M. Masson (1997), who maintains that the traditional vision has the greater scientific credibility. For canine sainein as a sign of recognition of a friend/familiar, see Homer, *Odyssey* 16.4–6; as a sign of joy and display of friendship (metaphorically compared to human behavior), see Pindar, *Pythians* 1.50–52; *Olympians* 4.5.

35. See, e.g., Xenophon, *Cynegeticus* 6.22–23.

36. Xenophon, ibid. 3.4–10: "cheat" (ἐξαπατῶσιν, ἐξαπατᾶν πειρῶνται); "try to make the false appear true" (ἀληθῆ τὰ ψευδῆ ποιούμεναι); "deceptively" (πεπλασμένως). Xenophon (6.3) also advises against training dogs to hunt foxes, because this, he says, completely corrupts them (διαφθορὰ γὰρ μεγίστη)—perhaps because they would learn to follow the example of the clever animal par excellence?

37. This connotation seems conspicuous in, for example, Pindar, *Pythians* 1.49–51: Hiero, a new Philoctetes, will enter the fray and force "even the haughty" to sainein before his martial virtue. On sainein as part of the lexicon for flatterers and *kakoi, see* Ribbeck 1884, 93–97; Harriott 1982, 14; the note of Cingano to Pindar, *Pythians* 2.82 (in Gentili et al. 1995, 399).

38. Aesop, 91 Perry (93 Hausrath[2] = 275 Chambry[3]).

39. For this general interpretation of the ode's conclusion, see Brillante 2000.

40. Pindar, *Pythians* 2.81–83.

41. Note that Aristotle (*History of Animals* 488b) attributes the ability to flatter specifically to dogs while not citing the same ability for foxes; in Aesop, too, the fox is a great trickster, but it does not seem to employ the language of flattery. In one fable (Aesop, 206 Perry [222 Hausrath[2] = 312 Chambry[3]]), a dog that jumps fawningly around the flock but in reality hopes for a sheep to die so he can eat it is an emblem of the flatterer. In another (136 Perry [139 Hausrath[2] = 182 Chambry[3]]), a dog is an emblem of ambiguity: a hunting dog catches a rabbit and holds it between its paws, biting it a little and licking its nose a little; the poor creature, confused by the dog's behavior, says, "Either stop biting me or stop kissing me, so I'll know if you're friend or foe." The affordance for elaborating a figure of ambiguity seems to be supplied here by the hunting dog's behavior in catching prey: it must not eat it but restrain it as much as possible until the hunter arrives. In Artemidorus (*Interpretation of Dreams* 2.11), dreaming of a dog fawning on its master is a good sign, while dreaming of a dog fawning on someone else is a premonition of tricks and traps from wicked men or women.

42. Pindar, *Pythians* 2.83–85.

43. Theognis 363–64; Pindar, *Isthmians* 4.48; a late echo in Plutarch, *How to Take Advantage of Enemies* 9 (91c). See again Brillante 2000; see also M. Napolitano 1996, 74–79.

44. E.g., Aristophanes, *Lysistrata* 629, where the chorus of Athenian elders claims that one can't trust the Spartans any more than one can a hungry wolf (οἶσι πιστὸν οὐδὲν εἰ μή περ λύκῳ κεχηνότι).

45. Konstan 1997, 42–52.

46. Solon, fr. 36 West² (30 Gentili-Prato²), 26–27.

47. According to Blaise 1995, 34–35, Solon's wolf metaphor may also indicate his standing "outside"—like the wolf, a marginal, asocial animal—that is, he is above factions: with neither the people nor the nobles (the dogs circling him), Solon presents himself as *super partes*, and only thus, from outside, can he impose laws in the interest of all. Like a wolf, Solon did use his cunning *mētis* in his activity (on this "dark side" of his personality, see Vox 1983; Vox 1984, 127–40; Giammarco Razzano 2001, 79–81), but never to harm his fellows. On Solon's fragment, see now Noussia Fantuzzi 2010, 455–85, which does not seem aware of my reading of the passage.

48. Plutarch, *How to Tell a Flatterer from a Friend* 19 (61c), and see *Dinner of the Seven Wise Men* 2 (147b); Plato, *Republic* 565e–566a (see *Phaedo* 82a). On the wolf as a figure for the tyrant, see Mainoldi 1984, 193–94; Visintin 1992, 115–19. In a passage from Artemidorus (*Interpretation of Dreams* 2.12), the fox replaces the dog in the same opposition: ἀλώπηξ τὰ μὲν αὐτὰ τῷ λύκῳ σημαίνει, διαφέρει δὲ ἐν τῷ τοὺς ἐχθροὺς οὐκ ἐκ τοῦ φανεροῦ ἐπιθησομένους σημαίνειν ἀλλὰ λάθρα ἐπιβουλεύσοντας. Ὡς δὲ ἐπὶ τὸ πλεῖστον γυναῖκας σημαίνει τὰς ἐπιτιθεμένας. Here too, the wolf stands for the male, its counterpart (the fox) for the female.

49. See Chantraine 1968; Frisk 1960–70, s.v. λαίθαργος. The connection with λήθαργος is uncertain and does not shed much light on the meaning, unless we suppose a sly dog trick of feigning lethargic dozing in order to bite in treachery. Λήθαργος is the proper name of a dog in *Palatine Anthology* 7.304 (see ch. 3).

50. Hesychius, s.v. <λήθαργος· κύων ὁ προσαίνων μέν, λάθρα δὲ δάκνων (Soph. fr. 800); <λαίθαργοι· κύνες κρύφα δάκνοντες; <λάθαργοι· κύνες κρυφίως δάκνοντες (and see λαιθάργῳ ποδί· λαθραίῳ). The adverb λάθρα in context means the dog does not display any intention to bite, thus doing it "secretly" in the sense of "treacherously," "without one expecting it." See Phrynichus, *Sophistic Preparations* 87.9 De Borries: a λαίθαργος dog is one that comes up and bites without barking (λαίθαργος κύων: ὁ λάθρα προσαλλόμενος καὶ χωρὶς ὑλακῆς δάκνων. τοῦτο δὲ οἱ πολλοὶ παραφθείραντες λαθροδήκτην καλοῦσιν; see 84.5: κέρκῳ σαίνειν· ἐπὶ τῶν κυνῶν τῶν προσσαινόντων μὲν τῇ οὐρᾷ, κακὸν δέ τι διανοουμένων λάθρα δρᾶσαι). In Aristophanes (*Knights* 1033–34), to behave "doggishly" (κυνηδόν) is to act undetected in the dark of night (λήσει σε κυνηδὸν νύκτωρ). In an Aesop fable (186 Chambry³ [the verse version of Babrius: 332 Perry]), an owner whose dog has a habit of biting treacherously (λάθρα) puts a rattle on its neck, to alert people to its presence.

51. Hipponax, 74 West² (66 Masson): ὕστερον τρώγει (on the proverbial σκυτοτραγεῖν, see G. Williams 1959, 99; below, n. 91); Aristophanes, *Knights* 1068 (see *scholia ad loc.*: λαίθαργοι κύνες λέγονται αἱ λάθρα προσιοῦσαι καὶ δάκνουσαι); Sophocles, fr. 885 Radt: σαίνεις δάκνουσα καὶ κύων λαίθαργος εἶ. The adverb ὕστερον in the Hipponax fragment may mean not "then" but "behind" (as in, e.g., Xenophon, *Cynegeticus* 5.3.42), in which case the laithargos dog of Hipponax would attack "from behind," over the shoulder (but cf. Degani 1984, 260). On the "foxlike" dog, see Xenophon, *Cynegeticus* 3.1. Recall again (see

above, n. 36) how Xenophon (6.3) advises against having dogs hunt foxes, lest they adopt their bad habits.

52. Aristophanes, *Knights* 1031.

53. In Homer (*Odyssey* 10.215), the beasts around Circe's house are like big dogs fawning on their master. Similarly, the Phrygian Great Mother is able to tame savage beasts (Apollonius Rhodius, *Argonautica* 1.1145), as are Artemis (ibid., 3.883) and Aphrodite (*Homeric Hymns* 5.70, where wolves, lions, bears, and panthers fawn on the goddess as she passes). Docile, tail-wagging lions are also found at the temple of Anaitis (a Babylonian goddess) in Aelian, *On the Nature of Animals* 12.23. On the fascination with wild and ferocious animals made tame and docile and displayed in shows and parades, see Franco 2008a, 61–64.

54. Aeschylus, *Choephori* 420–22.

55. Many interpretations have been proposed for this obscure passage: see Garvie 1986, 156. Modern scholars most often interpret the neologism *asantos* in a passive sense: "what cannot be flattered/charmed" (see Odysseus's *akeletos noos* in Homer, *Odyssey* 10.329). According to Hesychius (s.v. ἄσαντος: οὐ σαίνων), it means instead "that does not fawn." Maybe the Hesychian gloss deserves consideration, since one characteristic of the wolf is precisely that it does not *sainein*. Moreover, Aeschylus otherwise always uses the verb *sainein* to describe the behavior of someone who attempts to avoid their harsh fate out of cowardice (*Seven against Thebes* 383, 704). Electra's heart could thus be *asantos* in the sense that it does not "fawn back" to Clytemnestra's luring flattery. This reading is supported by, among other things, a passage in Sophocles's *Electra*. There, Electra rejects the advice of her sister Chrysothemis, who urges resigned acceptance of their fate as orphans, overpowered as they are by Aegisthus and Clytemnestra. Electra expresses her outrage at her sister's passivity once again with a canine metaphor: Electra refuses outright the "fawning" (*thōpeuein*) of a dog (on this other verb typical of a dog's fawning, see below). Chrysothemis can, if she wants, fawn like a dog (σὺ ταῦτα θώπευε) in their situation, but fawning before suffering and those that cause it is not for Electra (397). Sophocles's heroine wishes to adopt the ideal of *andreia*—manly courage (rather a wolfish trait)—to which her sister responds with the dogma of female (doggish) exclusion according to the logic of the fight between equals: "You were born a woman, not a man" (997). Yet in the other interpretation, that Electra's "wolf heart" will not be fawned upon, the dog-wolf opposition on the level of *sainein* still remains valid, only in this case, fawning does not suit the wolf, inasmuch as it is an animal that does not give in to such deceptive flattery (Brillante 2000).

56. In this sense also, Electra's *thymos* "comes from" her mother.

57. On the metaphorical uses of *sainein* in Aeschylus, see now Caramico 2009.

58. It is worth recalling Arrian's passage on the dog Hormē quoted above: the dog would fawn on the person who she thought was angry at her, in an attempt to appease his rage.

59. Aeschylus, *Choephori* 194.

60. Vernant 1989, 78–86.

61. Hesiod, *Theogony* 767–73.

62. Hades is πάνδοκος (Aeschylus, *Seven against Thebes* 860), πολυδέγμων (*Homeric Hymn to Demeter* 17).

63. Aristotle, *History of Animals* 488b.

64. The verb θωπεύειν is connected with the roots of θάμβος and τέθηπα and thus probably referred to a reaction of shocked surprise, of enthusiasm: Chantraine 1968, s.v.

θώψ; Burton 1993, 3–7. According to Otto Ribbeck (1884, 95), however, the original sense of the verb more likely referred to the kind of gratifying caresses one uses with horses. For αἰκάλλειν as a verb for canine fawning see, e.g., Aelian, *History of Animals* 8.2, 11.3 (σαίνουσι καὶ αἰκάλλουσι). Hesychius notes the metaphorical use (s.v. αἴκαλος· κόλαξ).

65. See especially Plato, *Theaetetus* 173a, *Laws* 634a, *Republic* 590c; Sophocles, *Oedipus at Colonus* 1003, 1336; Aristophanes, *Knights* 46–48.

66. Aristophanes, *Lysistrata* 1037: ὡς ἐστὲ θωπικαὶ φύσει. See also Aeschylus, *Prometheus* 937 (θώπτω), and the above-mentioned passage in Sophocles's *Electra* (397), as well as Euripides, *Suppliant Women* 1103 (θωπεύματα), all instances of feminine *thōpeuein*.

67. Aristophanes, *Wasps* 605–12.

68. The verb is *hypothōpeuein*. For *aspazesthai* used for canine behavior, see, e.g., Plato, *Republic* 376a6. The Aristophanes passage can be compared with Arrian's description of his affectionate dog (*Cynegeticus* 5.2–6), quoted above.

69. On the possible relationships—even etymological—among Helen, poison, and seductive deception, see Tasinato 1982, 32–38. The word of an erotically attractive woman was always regarded with suspicion, precisely because the sweetness of her words and the loveliness of her voice were part of her weapons of seduction: McClure 1999, 62–68. On the deceptive words of women and their exclusion from authoritative discourse, see Lincoln 1997, 352–67.

70. Besides the passage in Aeschylus's *Choephori* (194) discussed above, see Aristophanes, *Thesmophoriazusae* 869.

71. Plato, *Laws* 781a. For the oppositions between male-courage-open action and female-weakness-trickery, see also Pseudo-Aristotle, *Physiognomonica* 808b–809a.

72. Aeschylus, *Agamemnon* 1636: τὸ γὰρ δολῶσαι πρὸς γυναικὸς ἦν σαφῶς.

73. The passage in Sophocles's *Electra* discussed above (n. 55) is worth recalling: Chrysothemis urges resigned acceptance, but Electra rejects her sister's doggish passivity; Chrysothemis can, if she wants, fawn like a dog (σὺ ταῦτα θώπευε), but fawning before suffering and those who cause it is not for Electra (397). To Chrysothemis, who behaves like a doggish woman, Electra responds with a manly (wolfish) attitude.

74. See, for instance, the way that the old men in *Lysistrata* call the women's insurrection *thrasos* in an attempt to suppress it, while the women extol their thrasos to assert it as a synonym for *andreia*, the masculine virtue of good courage, from which men exclude them by definition (318, 379, 545–49, 1109). The women of "virile" initiative in another of Aristophanes's comedies also assert their andreia: see *Assembly Women* 519. Another woman who boasts of her andreia is, significantly, Sophocles's Electra, the daughter "entirely of her father," with an unwavering thirst for vengeance (*Electra* 983). For a detailed list of the male virtues, from which females of every animal species are excluded by nature, see Aristotle, *History of Animals* 608b (only female bears and leopards are not inferior to the males in courage).

75. For Clytemnestra's deeds as causing *stasis*, see Aeschylus, *Agamemnon* 1117.

76. Aeschylus, *Agamemnon* 1228–30. The passage is gravely corrupted, and the translation offered follows the text in the Loeb edition: Tyrwhitt's emendation of λέξασα (saying) to λείξασα (licking) looks innocent, but I have found no evidence that licking was a relevant part of the dog's fawning for the Greeks. See West 1990, 212–14, on these difficult lines. On the polysemy and constant code-switching that characterizes Clytemnestra's deceptive art of rhetoric, see McClure 1999, 70–92.

77. Aeschylus, *Agamemnon* 1093–94, 1184–85.

78. Aeschylus, *Persians* 111–13: φιλόφρων γὰρ ποτισαίνουσα τὸ πρῶτον παράγει βροτὸν εἰς ἄρκυας Ἄτα. In this image, Atē is probably being figured as a hunting dog that wags her tail to lead the huntsmen to the nets, only to have them fall in.

79. Aeschylus, *Agamemnon* 606–8.

80. Plutarch, *Precepts on Marriage* 19 (140c): Ἰδίους οὐ δεῖ φίλους κτᾶσθαι τὴν γυναῖκα, κοινοῖς δὲ χρῆσθαι τοῖς τοῦ ἀνδρός.

81. Given its derogatory connotations, the term *bitch* is avoided nowadays, at least among pet owners, but it is still used in specific contexts (among hunters, dog handlers, and other people who work with dogs) to refer to an unspayed female.

82. Aristophanes, *Clouds* 660. This is why Socrates teases Strepsiades, telling him that he can't even distinguish male from female and suggesting a distinction between the rooster (*alektryōn*) and the "roosteress," a nonexistent *alektryaina*. For discussion of this passage, which is not always correctly understood, see Guidorizzi 1996, 274–75. Dionysius Thrax's grammar (12.8) gives *kyōn* and *hippos* (horse) as examples of nouns of common gender; see also Lallot 1998², 48, 130. On Greek nouns of *genus commune,* see Schwyzer 1959², 31.

83. Homer, *Iliad* 13.623.

84. Ibid., 17.127, 17.255, 17.272, 18.179, 24.409.

85. The insult *Woman!* was itself traditional: Menelaus in the *Iliad* (7.96) provides an example when, exhorting his comrades to accept Hector's challenge, he calls them "Achaean women, not Achaean men [Ἀχαιΐδες οὐκέτ᾽ Ἀχαιοί]." Thersites uses the same form of abuse at 2.235.

86. Euripides, *Bacchae* 338–39. Euripides's sinister image of Actaeon torn to pieces by his own rabid bitches, moreover, echoes the drama's main action, in which the Bacchae, at once "dogs" and "women," a savage, raving pack of the mad hunter Dionysus, are set loose to blindly hunt a man of their own family. Aristophanes is perhaps satirizing the dreadful symbolism of these man-eating bitches when he makes "bitches" of Artemis a characteristic trait of Euripides's poetry (*Frogs* 1360).

87. Callimachus, *Hymns* 5.114–15.

88. Xenophon, *Cynegeticus*; *Oeconomicus* 5.6.

89. In Italian, this would mean to call the animal *la cane* and treat the noun in a similar fashion to *la tigre,* a feminine noun that denotes an instance, whether male or female, of the species *Panthera tigris,* but with this significant difference: Italian *tigre* is, properly speaking, what is called an epicene noun, unlike *kyōn,* which has common gender. Epicene nouns (of the type |*giraffa*| and |*tigre*|) have a definite grammatical gender (in these cases, feminine) but can be used to refer to either sex: for example, "a [*una*] male-giraffe" or "a [*una*] male-tiger" (Doleschal 1999, 118–19). Greek *kyōn,* on the other hand, does not have a definite, predetermined gender, so in a generic usage it can be made—as we have seen—to agree with either masculine or feminine modifiers.

90. Isocrates 1.29 (Κακοὺς εὖ ποιῶν ὅμοια πείσει τοῖς τὰς ἀλλοτρίας κύνας σιτίζουσιν· ἐκεῖναι τε γὰρ κτλ).

91. Alciphron, *Epistles* 3.11.4: οὐδὲ γὰρ κύων σκυτοτραγεῖν μαθοῦσα τῆς τέχνης ἐπιλήσεται; Lucian, *Adversus indoctum* 25.23: οὐδὲ γὰρ κύων ἅπαξ παύσαιτ᾽ ἂν σκυτοτραγεῖν μαθοῦσα. See also G. Williams 1959, 99. This proverb may be related to the shoemaker in Herodas (7.62–63) who, as he advertises his wares, guarantees that anyone who comes into his shop will understand "why women and dogs 'gnaw on' leather [σκύτεα γυναῖκες καὶ

κύνες τί βρώζουσιν]." This is probably a sexual joke based on the use of the *olisbos:* just like a dog that has learned to chew on leather, so a woman who has learned to use a leather phallus never loses the habit, and thus she will not leave the shoemaker's shop without buying one (Cunningham 1971, 183).

92. Theocritus 21.44–45 (καὶ γὰρ ἐν ὕπνοις πᾶσα κύων ἄρτον μαντεύεται); Diphilus comicus, fr. 91 Kassel-Austin (παρ' ἧς τὸν ἄρτον ἡ κύων οὐ λαμβάνει). Another theory that should be noted is in Lilja 1976, 50, which proposes that the feminization of *kyōn* might be explained by the fact that Greeks historically tended to call dogs, even as adults, *skylax,* a term that originally meant "puppy," and *skylax* was predominantly used in the feminine. But this theory is unsatisfying, in my view, for several reasons. First and foremost, Lilja cites no textual evidence showing an ancient tendency to call the dog *skylax;* it's true that in modern Greek, the dog is *to skylì,* but this proves nothing for ancient Greek, and besides, the modern word is neuter, not feminine (on modern Greek usage, see now Couroucli 2005). Second, this explanation merely begs the question: if indeed *skylax* tended to be considered feminine, what was the reason for that?

93. Some examples in Doric: Theocritus 2.35, 6.29–30, 15.43, 21.45 (but *kyōn* in the masculine is not absent: see 5.106, 8.27, 25.68, 29.38); Epicharmus, fr. 168 Olivieri; Sophron, fr. 4.7 Olivieri; *Palatine Anthology* 9.604. Even non-Doric writers treat Laconian *kynes* as feminine: Plato, *Parmenides* 128c; Pindar, frr. 106–7 Maehler; Sophocles, *Ajax* 7–8; Theophrastus, *Characters* 5.8; Aristotle, *History of Animals* 574a16 (but masculine at 607a3). Note that these are all authors who otherwise treat *kyōn* as masculine. It is not the case, as is often maintained, that the feminine is used generally for all hunting dogs: while Arrian, following Xenophon, treats *kynes* as feminine, Oppian in his *Cynegeticus* treats *kyōn* as masculine. On this entire question, see now F. Williams 1999.

94. Aristotle, *History of Animals* 608b25–29. See also Arrian, *Cynegeticus* 32. It should be noted that Greek does tend to treat some other animal names as feminine when using the plural, especially with groups (flocks, herds), a fact that may be due to flocks and herds being composed mainly of females (sheep, cows, sows, mares), with a few males kept for breeding: see Georgoudi 1990, 233–34. According to Eustathius (692.18–19), on the other hand, treating animal names in the plural—such as *boes, hippoi,* and *kynes*—as feminine was typical in the Ionian dialect. However, in the case of dogs, there are many instances of feminine generic, even in the singular.

95. Apollodorus, fr. 15 Kassel-Austin; Anaxandrides, fr. 40 Kassel-Austin; Pherecrates, fr. 179 Kassel-Austin. The expression "flay a flayed [f.] *kyōn*" (Aristophanes, *Lysistrata* 158) is an obscene reference to masturbation—male according to Taillardat 1962, 71 (*kyōn* was in fact used as a phallic metaphor: see Taillardat 1967, 126; Henderson 1991², 127), but female according to Henderson 1991², 133; according to the scholia on the passage, it refers instead to the erotic use of a leather phallus (*olisbos*).

96. Plato, *Republic* 5.469d–e. See Wissman 2012 for a thorough discussion of this proverbial metaphor.

97. Aristophanes, *Lysistrata* 298 (κύων λυττῶσα), 1215 (εὐλαβεῖσθαι τὴν κύνα).

98. Ibid., 363 (κοὺ μή ποτ' ἄλλη σου κύων τῶν ὄρχεων λάβηται): meaning, my jaws can bite as well as speak. On this passage, see Sommerstein 1990, 171; Henderson 1987, 114.

99. Semonides, fr. 7.16–17 Pellizer-Tedeschi. Barking dogs were often imagined as aggressive, annoying, overtalktative, and untalented speakers whose harsh and unpleasant

rhetoric is doomed to fail: Franco 2007a. On the *canina facundia* in the Roman world, see La Penna 1973; Bonsangue 2005; Masselli 2011.

100. The dog bite was a common metaphor for blame: Steiner 2001; Nagy 1979, 226.

101. On gender characterization effected through different uses of obscene language in comedy, see McClure 1999, 205–18, which notes that female characters (with the exception of elderly women) typically tend to avoid explicit obscenities, especially in the presence of men, and use euphemism and innuendo instead. When a female character uses strong, direct language with a man, it is a sign of a world upside down: the adoption by females of a masculine code indicates a subversion of normal civic hierarchies and a resulting inversion of roles, whereby women command men and exercise power in political affairs.

102. Aristophanes, *Acharnians* 1159–60.

103. Aristophanes, *Wealth* 1103–6.

104. Dogs and pigs are both animals *syanthrōpeuomena* (that live with man): Aristotle, *History of Animals* 572a6.

105. Lazzeroni 1993.

106. Grammatical gender is one of the most mysterious and often discussed phenomena in linguistics. Significant difficulties still persist about both the origin and the nature of this kind of classifying function, as well as how it develops (Corbett 1991, 1; Lazzeroni 1993, 3; Weber 1999, 495–509). For a synopsis of recent discussions, see Unterbeck et al. 1999. In general, these range from claims that the distribution of nouns into different grammatical genders is absolutely arbitrary (Eco 1976, 92, which holds, nonetheless, that the noun's grammatical marker lends its semantic content an aura of gendered connotation) to admissions, more or less detailed, of motivating rationale, especially regarding the names of animal beings, for the most part distributed into classes of grammatical gender corresponding to the referent's sex in each language (e.g., |marito [husband]| masc. vs. |moglie [wife]| fem.; |cane| masc. vs. |cagna| fem.). Yet there do seem to be cases where it's hard to rule out the possibility that a noun (even the name of an inanimate object) has been assigned a grammatical gender for reasons of structural order, based on classes of masculine or feminine entries in the cultural encyclopedia: in some Afro-Asiatic languages, for example, masculine nouns tend to denote objects that are large, robust, and long, while small, fragile, and rounded objects have feminine names (a "semantically loaded gender marking system": Hurskainen 1999, 680–87). In my view, the concept of polarization helps explain the case of Greek *kyōn* all the more, since the noun's feminization is not the result of morphological change but is instead a semantic shift: the noun, while formally keeping its indefinite gender, changes its agreement, which is the factor that, in the case of a generic referent, signals that it belongs in a "covert category" of semantic gender.

107. All this may seem strangely similar to the theory of "metaphorical gender" endorsed by eighteenth- and nineteenth-century linguistics, whereby |earth|, for example, is feminine since it is fertile and welcoming and |luck| would also be feminine, inasmuch as women are also fickle and unpredictable (Baron 1986, 101–5), but the similarity is only superficial. Polarization theory applies not as a general organizing principle for grammatical gender but only to a specific case; it concerns not the gender of every noun but rather a given binary pairing in a given culture; and it does not concern the "masculinity" or "femininity" of referents per se but outlines the possibility that their opposition, in terms of cultural polarity, has been represented on the grammatical level by a gender opposition.

108. Pseudo-Aristotle, *On Reported Marvels* 116 (841b6). For the dating of this work, see Giannini 1964, 133–34.

109. Consistent with my argument, Alessandro Giannini (1966, 283) offered the following Latin translation of the Pseudo-Aristotle passage: "Nec porcum nec canem ullum audere stercora hominum attingere." For *hys* (f.), see especially Aelian, *On the Nature of Animals* 8.19, 10.16. For feminine *kyōn*, see ibid., 7.40, 13.14, 13.24, 16.24. The two pieces of evidence from the Aristotelian treatise and from Aelian cast doubts on a statement in the scholia on Euripides that says the use of the feminine for common nouns was an especially poetic usage (*Scholia in Euripidis Phoenissas* 3).

110. On this cultural polarity in the swine family, see now Franco 2006.

111. Female wild boars can be extremely dangerous, as the myth of the murderous Crommyonian sow killed by Theseus shows.

112. According to Jeffrey Henderson (1987, 161), the joke—understood as a metaphor for "I will vent my anger freely"—draws its significance from the fact that swine terms were often used to indicate female sexuality.

113. Aristophanes, *Lysistrata* 682–84. The boar's fury was recognized in the species generally, whether it was male or female, and thus the joke might very well be understood as simply a metaphor for anger, with no play on words: "I am going to set loose the boar inside me!" (Taillardat 1962, 207–8, 191). The relevance of my reading obviously depends on the correctness of the assumption that in classical Athenian Greek, the feminine of *hys* was used to designate the domesticated pig. According to Sommerstein 1990, 192, "Here the gender of the animal simply follows that of the speaker." It's true that the feminine is required in order to agree grammatically with the metaphor's referent, but this does not mean that it occurred "simply." Instead, the agreement may have an insulting charge, all the more biting for being ironically cast as a slip by the characters speaking.

114. Dog stands in relation to wolf as tamest to wildest (κυνὶ λύκος, ἀγριώτατον ἡμερωτάτῳ: Plato, *Sophist* 231a6). It is worth noticing that in the passage from Plato's *Republic* mentioned above (n. 96), the dogs [f.] that "get angry at the stones" instead of attacking those who have hurled them are compared to a man with a "womanish and petty mind" (5.469d–e) who despoils the dead body of the enemy instead of bravely confronting his antagonist alive. The importance of gender categories for classifying the natural world is confirmed by how often they were used in botanical classification. Greek names for plants were almost all feminine, but that was no hindrance to almost every type of plant being categorized as masculine or feminine depending on whether or not it was fruit bearing or whether its wood was soft (a feminine plant) or hard and difficult to work (a masculine plant). A significant exception to the rule that all plant names were feminine is that the domesticated fig was called *sykea* (a feminine noun), while the wild fig was called *erineos* or *olynthos* (masculine nouns): Foxhall 1998.

115. See Solon, fr. 36 West² (30 Gentili-Prato²); see also this chapter's earlier section "A Dog's Mischief." The cultural polarity wolf/dog had in essence reoriented the grammatical gender of |*kyōn*|, switching it from a generic masculine to a generic feminine: thus the phenomenon may be considered a result of what Umberto Eco (1976) calls the "semantic reverberation" of the gender marker (see n. 106 above).

116. In Semonides (fr. 7 Pellizer-Tedeschi), annoying idle chatter is typical of the dog-woman, but the entire race of women is given by nature to faultfinding and insults

(μεμψιμοιρότερον καὶ φιλολοίδορον): Aristotle, *History of Animals* 608b10. For the dog's aggressive chattering, see, e.g., Aeschylus, *Agamemnon* 1631 (νήπια ὑλάγματα), 1672 (μάταια ὑλάγματα), but examples of canine garrulity as a symbol of empty aggression—merely verbal and thus ineffective—and of *loidoria* are quite abundant: see Franco 2007a. On women's annoying, senseless prattling, see McClure 1999, 56–62, 170–71.

117. On curiosity and intrusiveness, see again the dog-woman in Semonides (fr. 7 Pellizer-Tedeschi). The dog as thief of human food needs no further support; as for woman, however, recall Hesiod's description of the wife as always "lying in wait for dinner" (δειπνολόχος: *Works and Days* 704). The topos of feminine voraciousness, a consequence of her parasitic condition, appears again in Xenophon, who says that one of the most important things to consider in choosing a bride is that her stomach has been well trained (*Oeconomicus* 7.6). On the dog's impulsive and fiery nature, characteristics that almost always place it in the domain of thrasos, or unwarranted and reckless courage, see ch. 4. As an example of feminine fieriness, one can recall Hesiod's woman who "burns" and parches man (Vernant 1989, 66); an assertion of woman's combustible nature occurs in Aristophanes, *Lysistrata* 1014–15.

118. In Aristophanes's *Wasps* (1401–5), a bakeress comes to Philocleon to demand compensation for damages. In response, the wily old man tells her an obliquely insulting anecdote from the life of Aesop: one day the fabulist scolded a *kyōn* [f.] that, "bold and drunk," had dared to bark at him, urging it to σωφροσύνη, saying, "*Kyon, kyon!* If you'd sell your wicked tongue for a bit of grain, I'd think you'd be acting with some sense!" The expression reappears in Callimachus (*Aitia* fr. 75.4 Pfeiffer) as a call to silence: "*Kyon, kyon!*" the poet says to himself at a moment when he wants to refrain from saying something he shouldn't. Thus, the phrase has been interpreted as a typical idiom for situations when one must hold one's tongue: Pontes 1995. In other words, when you needed to silence someone or yourself, you told the tongue, "Sit! Down!" by calling it *Dog!* See also Sappho, fr. 158 Voigt (γλῶσσαν μαψυλάκαν).

119. See this chapter's earlier section "Intimate Enemies." Of course, abstract nouns were generally feminine in Greek, so terms such as *hope, ruin,* and *poverty* were usually feminine by sheer morphological accident; obviously, then, when such concepts were personified, they would be represented as women. Nevertheless, the fact that such words were grammatically feminine could retrospectively motivate their interpretation in mythopoetic terms: a being such as Atē or Elpis might be attributed "womanly" cultural traits or occasion reflections on the fact that these beings were, "like women," enigmatic and inscrutable (see Martin 2001, 73).

120. Plato, *Republic* 607b (*Lyr. Adesp.* 987 Page): λακέρυζα πρὸς δεσπόταν κύων; *Laws* 967c–d.

121. Epicharmus, fr. 168 Olivieri (οἵαπερ ἁ δέσποινα, τοία χὰ κύων); Plato, *Republic* 563c6 (ἀτεχνῶς γὰρ αἵ τε κύνες κατὰ τὴν παροιμίαν οἷαίπερ αἱ δέσποιναι).

122. *FGrH* 81f33 (Philarchus). On dogs and flies as thieves of meat sacrificed on altars, see ch. 4.

123. *LSS* 91; *LSAM* 51. See Cole 1995. We could also add the dog-corpse association to this list, but in that case the symbolic contact between the two cultural representations doesn't seem to play out on the same level of images of *aeikeia*: the prohibition seems instead to establish a link between the sphere of birth and the cultural status of corpses, both of which probably involved ritual pollution (on this point specifically, I agree with the interpretation of Cole 1995, 183).

124. Pausanias 7.27.10.

125. This recalls again the wolf/male–dog/female opposition. When a wolf brutally attacks, it is truly being a wolf, coherently manifesting its proper, competitive nature, but when a dog attacks with savage determination, it has "turned wolf" (*lyssētēr*), become denatured, crazed, and detestable, needing care or to be put down as soon as possible. The dog's position is that of a subordinate excluded from the ethic of competition and fully invested with the ethics of feminine *sōphrosynē*: restraint of impulses, every excess forbidden. That over time the Greek language opted to designate the dog with the word for puppy (Modern Greek, το σκυλί) does not fundamentally conflict with this interpretation. The association between dog and child, both of them in debt for their upbringing, has been discussed above (chs. 2 and 4), so the dog-infant intersection was available since antiquity, but one may add that the ancient imagination likened women to a sort of eternal child, incapable of autonomy and always in need of a guardian (Campese 1983, 19–28; Cantarella 1986, 41–42).

126. Aristotle, *History of Animals* 607a4–9.

127. Aelian, *On the Nature of Animals* 8.1.

128. I cannot here go into the vast topic of Greek conceptions of generation and the role that the female body played in this, a subject that has been well studied: see Sissa 1983; Loraux 2000, 95ff.; M.L. Napolitano 1985, 40–50; DuBois 1988, 85ff. For my purposes, it suffices to show how in this fantastical account of genesis, the dog acts as the feminine element in opposition to the tiger (a wild animal and thus masculine) and as the force that degenerates the father's wild virility, bending its savage and fiercely independent nature over three generations until the offspring assume the desired gentleness and docility of the mother: the litter (completely like their father) of an untamable creature is transformed into a litter of animals docile to man (like their mother), whose genes preserve the memory of their wild ancestry. On the importance of the principle of polarity in Greek thought, see Lloyd 1966, 15–71.

129. On the "Pandora complex," i.e., women seen as the weakest link in the chain of the Greek family (*oikos*), see A.S. Brown 1997, 42–46.

130. Aristophanes, *Lysistrata* 283–84. On the contradictory, two-sided reputation of Euripides, who according to another interpretation brought novel, "feminist" requests to the Athenian stage, see Nancy 1984.

131. Satyrus, *Life of Euripides*, fr. 39.21 Arrighetti; Hermesianax, fr. 7.67–68 Powell; Sotades fr. 15.15 Powell; *Palatine Anthology* 7.44, 7.51 (commentary in Page 1981², 158; Gow and Page 1968, 5–6). On this traditional variant of the legend, also mentioned in the *Genos Euripidou* and the *Suda*, see the discussion in Arrighetti 1964, 145ff. The mother of the Molossian dogs that tore Euripides apart was apparently King Archelaos's she-dog: Le Bohec-Bouhet 2011, 493.

APPENDIX

In order that the reader may more easily trace the chronological development of the ideas discussed below, relevant dates of first publication are given in brackets.

1. For Scholz, the Greek dog combines the idea of an "impure" animal, endowed with dangerous "mana" and deriving from a pre-Indo-European cultural contempt for pariah dogs, with a positive vision of the Aryan invaders, who had a dog-loving culture (1937,

7–10). For Merlen (1971, 27), the insulting force of the term *kyon* would have derived from the observation of corpse-eating habits of pariah dogs; Lilja (1976, 17–35) reviews the scholarly history of the question and concludes that "the complicated Homeric concept of dogs as bloodthirsty beasts and unclean scavengers is an unsolved puzzle to me" (35). Mainoldi (1984, 107–20) also seems unable to provide a convincing explanation and oscillates between the idea that the insult was born of contempt for the "scavenging" dog and that the dog was a good metaphor for a host of moral transgressions "parce que le chien est *lui-même* traître, dévergondé, insubordonnéé" (109; emphasis mine).

2. Lévi-Strauss 1966, 191–216 [1962].

3. Trinquier 2004.

4. E.g., olpe of Berlin, Staatliche Mus. 1915 (the sacrifice of a tuna; under the *trapeza* are two dogs with mouths open, perhaps waiting for their share); olpe of Heidelberg, Universität 253; *Corpus vasorum antiquorum*, Deut. 10, plate 39 (two figures preparing sacrificial meat on spits; two dogs are shown, one eating a piece of meat and the other waiting with open mouth).

5. As Tambiah 1969 says, animals are good not only—in Levi-Strauss's words (1963, 89) [1962]—to "think with" but also to "prohibit with." See also Brandes 1984; for physiognomy, Gleason 1995, 55–81. On the pragmatic and normative function of important metaphors, see Lakoff and Johnson's observations in their chapter "Metaphors, Truth, and Action" (1980, 156–58).

6. On the necessity of good comparison and the utility of categories that are "neither too local nor too generic" as points of entry for comparative experiment, see Detienne 2002 (quotes on 74); 2009.

7. Eco 1979; 1990.

8. On "common sense" as a cultural system capable of producing order through a heterogeneous and contradictory set of beliefs and bits of popular "wisdom," see Geertz 1983, 73–93.

9. Following Bettini 2013, 123ff. [1998, 229ff.]. Further reflections on this point in Franco 2003.

10. Bettini 2013, 125ff. [1998, 202ff.].

11. On Gibson's affordances, see Gibson 1979.

12. I prefer to call such projects symbolic (whereas Bettini defines them as "metaphoric"), inasmuch as they include not only metaphors (figures, proverbs, and so forth) but also ritual acts and beliefs, which have a psychological status distinct from that of rhetorical figures: on this point see Sperber 1975, 103ff. [1974, 100ff.].

13. Giorgio Raimondo Cardona has observed ([1985] 1995³, 53), for instance, that dietary prohibitions "do vary according to the traits included in the animal's definition: but instead of being sensitive to those concerning the referent's morphological features (that is, immediately transparent and, once identified, invariantly present) they rather seem to respond to those of a symbolic sort, capable of being read and understood in accord with subjective and variable schemata"; as such, for instance, the pig is taboo to nomadic peoples, as it symbolizes sedentary peoples, and likewise, sedentary peoples place restrictions on cattle and sheep because they are animals of "the enemy." Such symbolic elaborations obviously have nothing to do with the affordances offered by swine, cattle, and sheep species.

14. To be effective, I think the notion of affordance should be reserved for traits that objects of the world offer to a certain psychomotor (and by extension, cognitive) system to

be acted on in some practical (and by extension, intellectual) form. An affordance, in other words, concerns relationships between the environment and a subject immersed in it and determines the spectrum of (necessarily limited) possibilities for action that the subject has in the world. An affordance does not necessarily produce representations. Nor does a representation always respond to affordances, because it might arise from other representations and so may not have anything to do with the system of possibilities and environmental constraints in which the subject is enmeshed. Unless, that is, we also take a subject's culture as part of the environment, in which case we abandon the possibility of distinguishing between the world and constructions of it (radical constructivism) and give up the project of investigating the relations between symbolic systems and the reality in which they arise (see Reed 1988, 101). If it is true that symbolic knowledge takes mental representations of the world, not the world itself, as its object (Sperber 1975, 109–10 [1974, 105–6]), it is no less the case that such knowledge often assumes mental representations formed in the world (as with, for example, some encyclopedic propositions). The encyclopedic notion "the weasel gives birth from its mouth," which arose from the affordance that the weasel carries its babies in its mouth, was taken up as a symbolic device to elaborate an action that fostered easy birth. Obviously, these considerations all presuppose a representational conception of culture that is much contested, not least by anthropologists (such as Tim Ingold) who appeal to Gibson's ecological psychology. For them, the differences between cultures reside not in diverse ways of elaborating representations but in different trained habits of perceiving and noticing the things in the world (see, e.g., Ingold 2000, 285–97).

15. Therefore, the claim that "animals quite obviously cannot and do not . . . represent themselves to human viewers" (Mullan and Marvin 1987, 3) should be qualified. Animals may not be able to represent themselves, and certainly do not use human language to do so, but they surely do "present" themselves to humans (see on this issue the important remarks in Kohn 2007, 5), and humans usually do not conceive of species in totally arbitrary ways (although trivialization and fantastic imagination are always possible).

16. Bettini 2013, 128 [1998, 206].

17. Only recently, many years after completing my study of the Greek dog, did I happen on Kohn's article (2007) on the relationships that the Runa have with their dogs, a study offering surprising analogies with my reconstruction for ancient Greece.

18. Reed 1988, 112–23.

19. If it's the case that mental and semantic categories are always conditioned by the interactional model that the categorizing human being entertains with the world (Violi 2001, 139ff. [1997, 159ff.]), then clearly, from the perspective of epistemology as well, to exclude the interactional aspect from the object's fundamental attributes would greatly impoverish our knowledge of how we know that object. If "dog" and "cat" are categories of the same basic sort as "fish" and "bird," while the latter also occupy a distinct, more generic place in the lexicon, this fact most likely depends on the different interactions that bind humans to dogs and cats.

20. Plato, *Politicus* 266a.

21. On the coevolution of humans and dogs see, e.g., the interesting article Schleidt and Shalter 2003.

22. In the Greek world, treatises on hunting with dogs attest this attention, but there is little doubt that guard and herd dogs, as well as pets, were subject to some form of disci-

plined training and socialization. The Runa of the Amazon educate their dogs with a level of care comparable to that in their education of children: the dog's probability of survival, on the other hand, depends on its ability to behave "like humans" (Kohn 2007, 9–10). On the social character of the relationship with dogs among the Nuaulu of Indonesia and the expectations that this entails, see Ellen 1999, 63–64.

23. On this point, see Hare et al. 2002.

24. Another important study that I had not yet found at the time of first publication is J. Buxton 1968, which shows how among the Mandari of northern Sudan as well, the dog's metonymic position entails anxieties absent from relationships with other domestic animals (39–46).

25. For ideology as a structured symbolic response to structured social tensions, see Geertz 1973, 204ff. ("Ideology as a Cultural System").

26. Franco 2008b; 2008c.

27. Lévi-Strauss 1963 [1962].

28. Needham 1978, 51ff.

29. A strategy already well tried in the ancient world: see Franco, forthcoming.

30. Ingold 1994b, 14.

31. Geertz 1973, 412–53 (quote on 419).

32. Roy Willis claims that the way humans relate to animals, "when subjected to the detailed examination of a structuralist analysis, [can] be used as a key to 'read off' certain otherwise inaccessible information about the way human beings conceived of themselves" (1974, 7, quoted in Baker 2001, xxxv). See also Shanklin 1985, 377: "Like the study of women, which has provided corrective and sometimes alternative views of how societies operate at many levels, the study of human-animal interaction now offers a stimulating and specific view of how humans operate at many levels."

33. Inquiry into how Greeks and Romans articulated grammatical gender, semantic gender, and discourses on animal species has since become a principal research focus of mine; the first fruits of this topic are found in Franco 2006; 2008b; 2008c. Juliana Schiesari has undertaken a similar project (2010) in Renaissance studies.

34. Mullin 1999.

35. Courses and programs are now found in universities around the world, which the Animals and Society Institute (ASI) tracks (at www.animalsandsociety.org/courses). The best introductions to the already vast bibliography are Marchesini 2000a; Marchesini and Tonutti 2007; DeMello 2012; Hurn 2012. Marchesini 1999 and Rivera 2000 are two collected volumes important for Italian zooanthropology. Notable among the proliferating research centers and programs, besides the ASI, are the International Society for Anthrozoology (ISAZ), Minding Animals International (MAI), the Culture and Animals Foundation (CAF), and the subgroup H-Animal in Humanities and Social Sciences Online (H-Net). A mere sampling of specialist journals, also expanding rapidly, includes *Society and Animals, Anthrozoös, Antennae, Journal of Critical Animal Studies, Human-Animal Interaction Bulletin,* and *Anthropozoologica* (in French). In November 2008, the journal of the European Union Research Commission (*Research*Eu)* devoted a special volume to the theme humanity/animality. Linda Kalof, Seven Mattes, and Amy Fitzgerald in the Animal Studies Program at Michigan State University maintain an annotated bibliography (www.animalstudies.msu.edu/bibliography.php), which is limited to publications in English and thus

overlooks important works such as, for example, those of Philippe Descola (1994 [1986]; 2011; 2013 [2005]) and Jean-Pierre Digard (1990; 1999) in France and Roberto Marchesini and Sabrina Tonutti in Italy.

36. Lévi-Strauss 1971. As a population's genetics shows, Lévi-Strauss says, it is simply not true that cultures are systems independent of biological bases: cultural choices condition the selection of some genes over others, not only among domesticated animals (this is the basic principal of domestication) but also in human populations. Between biological evolution and cultural developments exist complex relations of action and reaction that cannot be investigated without the joint effort of different disciplines.

37. Ingold 1990, 225.

38. Lutri, Acerbi, and Tonutti 2009. What we commonly call culture and retain as an exclusive human prerogative is by no means a well-defined object; it has hundreds of different definitions (Ingold [1988] 1994², 84–97).

39. In some measure, this serves to reconcile the new science with the ancient encyclopedic tradition of *historia animalium,* as Bodson 1998 rightly points out.

40. The overestimation of the rational-representational element in human activity (as though people actually on average acted rationally and were guided by symbols) has always been one of the capstones widening the gap between humans and nonhumans: Ingold [1988] 1994², 85–97. For an account of recent changes of perspective in anthropology, see Hurn 2012.

41. Ingold 1997, 109ff.; Grasseni and Ronzon 2004.

42. See Adams and Donovan 1995; now also the reflections in Battaglia 2008; Castignone 2009, 121–40; Gruen and Weil 2010.

43. Even an ethnographer committed to combating racist tendencies will quickly come to realize that problems such as ethnocentrism "reflect on a human scale a much vaster problem, whose solution is still more urgent: the relations between man and other living species . . . , because the respect we'd like to see man have for his congeners is only a particular case of the respect he should feel for all forms of life. By isolating man from the rest of creation, by defining too rigidly the limits that separate them from one another, Western humanism, inherited from antiquity and the Renaissance, has deprived him of a defensive bulwark and, as experience in the last century and our own proves, has exposed him without sufficient defense to assaults that have grown up inside the very citadel" (Lévi-Strauss 1971). Perhaps no ethnographer in the field today could do what Edward Evans-Pritchard did with the "oracular chickens" of the Azande: after he had poisoned a certain number of them, he decided that making decisions on the basis of that crude ordeal was not all that bad (1937).

44. According to the theory of intersectionality, these forms of oppression are in fact correlated and form a system of power based on the intersection of multiple forms of discrimination.

45. Haraway 2003; Derrida 2008 [2006]; Braidotti 2006.

46. Marchesini 2002; Wolfe 2010.

47. The bibliography on animal rights is by now enormous; see De Mori 2007 for a recent synoptic treatment.

48. Mannucci 2008, 19–28. Italian anthropology is undergoing a revival of interest in the animal question, seen in the special edition of the journal *Lares* (74, no. 1, including

Padiglione 2008) devoted to this topic. The provocative views of Sergio Dalla Bernardina (2006) are important for the reflexive dimension: he sees in the contemporary obsession with the animal question a new collective ritual of self-absolution and catharsis.

49. According to Marchesini, human culture is formed not through distancing from the animal (as the humanistic paradigm proposes) but, on the contrary, through a progressive absorption of the theriomorphic: humans receive from the animal world challenges and checkmates as well as examples and collaborations that have stimulated adaptive and evolutionary responses (think of animals as a source of recognition of our deficiencies—physical, perceptual, etc.—that has triggered technological development). The animal has thus had a mentoring role and also constitutes a "vocabulary of models for the imagination to draw on for new forms of existence" (Marchesini and Andersen 2003, 16). The very human capacity to contaminate ourselves with the animal has permitted our species to become a "hybrid," transcending the possibilities that genetic endowments and innate behaviors alone offer. In this paradigm, therefore, culture arises along with and thanks to animals, though paradoxically, this ends up being the trait that substantially differentiates *Homo sapiens* from other species. The animal is above all "present and alive in our culture but not in the form of an object so much as a partner able to convey humans beyond their genetic destiny toward that immense repertoire of anthropopoietic possibilities that we call culture" (20).

50. In their coevolution with humans, they have lost many abilities of their wild ancestors while acquiring new ones. For instance, dogs have learned to use humans to solve problems instead of looking for solutions on their own: DeMello 2012, 89.

51. The idea of humanity's debt to other species is a wide field for reflection, pioneered by Paul Shepard (1978; 1996).

52. In a radical theory proposed by Marchesini, humans were able to gather the greatest fruits from interacting with other species on account of being animals in continual formation. The human characteristic of having a very long phase of formation and a "learning window" virtually always open rendered individuals of our species both more curious and more prone to being shaped in contact and encounter with other animals (Marchesini and Andersen 2003, 49–55).

53. Serpell 1986, 73–86. On the mutual benefits of domestication generally, see Budiansky 1997.

54. E.g., the program of multispecies ethnography, which is dedicated to analyzing "how a multitude of organisms' livelihoods shape and are shaped by political, economic, and cultural forces" (Kirksey and Helmreich 2010, 545).

55. Kohn 2007. Other, older works that escaped me at the time include Ellen 1999; Ariel de Vidas 2002.

56. The view of animals as biological machines that run purely on automatic instincts is a counterintuitive theory (developed by scientists and philosophers) that would seem truly bizarre to most peoples, who have, generally speaking, very good reasons to think their relations with other animals are a form of social interaction and to attribute to individuals of other species intentions, emotions, and desires. The obsessive avoidance of anthropomorphism can lead to epistemological errors worse than those fallen into with a naïve vision of interspecific relations.

57. We can add that while there is some evidence of dog sacrifices, and the eating of dog meat is attested (though scarcely) in the Greek world (see Dalby 1996, 60), someone who

sacrificed or ate their own dog would probably have aroused horror. I do not know of any case of this, whether real or mythical. The sacrifice of dogs and horses of the dead on the latters' tombs is obviously a very different situation.

58. Netz 2004, xiii–xiv. Many scholars have criticized the way in which traditional approaches have glossed over, if not kept silent on, the crucial role animals have played in human social history, as partners, competitors, or symbionts of *Homo sapiens* in the various complex ecological systems in which cultures, human and nonhuman, are embedded: see Marchesini and Tonutti 2007; Montgomery and Kalof 2010. On the importance of a historical perspective in anthrozoology, see Marchesini 2000a, 341; Ritvo 2002.

59. See Bodson 1998, which rightly emphasizes that "l'histoire des animaux, qui se situe au carrefour des sciences naturelles et humaines, ne peut plus se concevoir en dehors de la pratique interdisciplinaire" (250). An interesting recent example is the reintroduction of the purple swamphen (*Porphyrio porphyrio*) to Sicily, spurred by studies on the animal's presence there in the Roman period and involving collaboration between a classicist and a naturalist: see Andreoni and Andreotti 2010.

60. On animals and film, see also Porter 2010. On animals and literature, see also Rohman 2010; DeMello 2012, 325–41.

61. François Poplin organizes a yearly seminar, "Anthropozoologie: Histoire naturelle et culturelle des animaux vrais," where naturalists, anthropologists, archaeologists, and historians participate in a multidisciplinary project ("L'Homme et l'Animal") hosted by the National Museum of Natural History in Paris, which publishes the semiannual journal *Anthropozoologica* (now also online: www.bioone.org/loi/anth).

62. Still, there were some pioneers of this perspective: see, for instance, *Animals, Men, and Myths: A History of the Influence of Animals on Civilization and Culture* by Richard Lewinsohn (1954 [1952]) or *L'Animal civilisateur de l'homme* by Michel Rousseau (1962). On this topic, see the crucial article by Bodson (1998).

63. On the history of "history of animals" from Aristotle to Buffon, see again Bodson 1998.

64. On animals and history, see also Ritvo 2002; Montgomery and Kalof 2010.

65. Bodson's works on the history of zoology and the animal question in the ancient world more generally are too numerous to list, and their importance is hard to overstate. Bodson has worked since the 1970s (see, e.g., Bodson 1975) as both a researcher and a promoter of anthrozoological studies; her long bibliography can be found online (http://promethee.philo.ulg.ac.be/Zoologica/lbodson/bibl/#1). She organizes the "Colloques d'histoire des connaissances zoologiques," whose proceedings the University of Liège publishes.

66. To cite just a few: Prieur 1988; Dumont 2001; Amat 2002; Goguey 2003; Kalof 2007; Kitchell 2013. For a recent collection of essays on ancient serpents, see Barbara and Trinquier 2012.

67. E.g., entries such as those on specific animals in the Pauly-Wissowa *Realencyclopädie* (see Orth 1913; Fischer and Wecker 1924; Gundel 1927; Wüst 1956) and texts such as Thompson (1895) 1936²; Keller 1909–13; Jennison 1937; Thompson 1947. More useful, up-to-date tools include Toynbee (1973) 1996²; Davies and Kathirithamby 1986; Beavis 1988; Arnott 2007.

68. Outstanding among them are Bettini 2013 [1998]), on the weasel, and McInerney 2010, on cows in Greece. Scullard 1974 focuses much attention on the uses of elephants in

warfare; Levêque 1999, on the frog, focuses on comparative religious facts. See also Hyland 1990, on the horse in Rome, and Engels 1999, on cats in the ancient world. Mainoldi's monograph on the dog and the wolf in Greece (1984) has the conspicuous merit of gathering and discussing a great number of sources, but the conceptual tools with which these are organized now seem dated.

69. Bodson 1981, 240.

70. Haraway 2003.

71. The eradication of real animals (and of real naturecultural relations) from symbolic analysis is the reason, in my view, that so many interpretations produced to date end up proposing poor "explanations," which take the animal as "chthonic" or "infernal" or connected with "fertility" or "royalty." The dog, owl, cock, serpent, butterfly, horse, and many other animals are said to have had a chthonic value, being associated with the lower world, connected with the sphere of the dead and with impurity, but these labels point to very generic symbolic values rather than explain the meaning(s) of individual species in a specific text or context.

72. Cardona maintains that the model for the ethnoscientist is not the modern scientist but rather the ancient naturalist, for whom the rupture between current knowledge and scientific knowledge was not very deep and who was a *curiosus* who aimed to make critical observations and synthesize varied specialized forms of knowledge (from experts in hunting, fishing, pharmacopoeia, etc.), as Aristotle did: a "curious outside" observer "who compares, analyzes, cuts off bits of knowledge in time by comparing a before and after" ([1985] 1995³, 35–36).

73. On the cultural debt that the human community owes animals, see Marchesini and Andersen 2003, 16–21.

74. I'm referring to the influential reconstructions of Walter Burkert (1983 [1972]) and Jean-Paul Vernant (1989 [1979]). The collection of studies edited by Christopher Faraone and F. S. Naiden (2012) has again taken up the entire question of ancient sacrifice, submitting the grand theories of the past to critique and carefully situating them in their original historical contexts.

75. I offered courses on the anthrozoology of the ancient world while holding a teaching position in classical philology at the University of Siena in 2004–8. Some of my students chose topics relating to human-animal studies for their theses (such as animals as teachers of technical skills in ancient folklore, human relations with monkeys, and interspecies parental care in Greek and Roman texts).

76. See Franco 2007b.

77. We've said plenty about the dog and the weasel. On animal voices, see Bettini 2008; fish nomenclature, Guasparri 2005; nightingales, Zambon 2007; *striges*, Cherubini 2010.

Acosta-Hughes, B. 2002. *Polyeideia: The Iambi of Callimachus and the Archaic Iambic Tradition*. Berkeley: University of California Press.

Adams, C. J., and J. Donovan, eds. 1995. *Animals and Women*. Durham and London: Durham University Press.

Adkins, A. W. H. 1960. *Merit and Responsibility: A Study in Greek Values*. Oxford: Oxford University Press. Translated by Riccardo Ambrosini as *La morale dei Greci da Omero ad Aristotele*. Rome and Bari: Laterza, 1987.

———. 1969. "Threatening, Abusing and Feeling Angry in the Homeric Poems." *Journal of Hellenic Studies* 89: 7–21.

Adrados, F. R. 1999². *History of the Greco-Latin Fable*. Vol. 1. Leiden, Netherlands: Brill.

Alexandridis, A. 2009. "Shifting Species: Animal and Human Bodies in Attic Vase Painting of the 6th and 5th Centuries B.C." In *Bodies and Boundaries in Graeco-Roman Antiquity*, edited by Thorsten Fögen and Mireille Lee, 267–86. Berlin and New York: de Gruyter.

Alexandridis, A., M. Wild, and L. Winkler-Horaček, eds. 2008. *Mensch und Tier in der Antike: Grenzziehung und Grenzüberschreitung*. Wiesbaden: Reichert.

Amat, J. 2002. *Les animaux familiers dans la Rome antique*. Paris: Les Belles Lettres.

Anderson, V. D. 2004. *Creatures of Empire: How Domestic Animals Transformed Early America*. Oxford and New York: Oxford University Press.

Andò, V., and N. Cusumano. 2010. *Come bestie? Forme e paradossi della violenza tra mondo antico e disagio contemporaneo*. Caltanissetta and Rome: Salvatore Sciascia.

Andreoni, M., and A. Andreotti. 2010. "In difesa del pollo sultano." *Archeologia viva* 29, no. 143: 66–69.

Anthony, D. W. 2007. *The Horse, the Wheel, and Language: How Bronze-Age Riders from the Eurasian Steppes Shaped the Modern World*. Princeton: Princeton University Press.

Ariel de Vidas, A. 2002. "A Dog's Life among the Teenek Indians (Mexico): Animals' Participation in the Classification of Self and Other." *Journal of the Royal Anthropological Institute* 8, no. 3: 531–50.

Arnott, W. G. 1996. *Alexis: The Fragments: A Commentary*. Cambridge: Cambridge University Press.

———. 2007. *Birds in the Ancient World from A to Z*. London and New York: Routledge.

Arrighetti, G., ed. 1964. *Satiro: Vita di Euripide*. Pisa: Libreria Goliardica.

———. 1998. *Esiodo: Opere*. Turin: Einaudi-Gallimard.

Aston, E. 2011. "Mixanthrôpoi: Animal-Human Hybrid Deities in Greek Religion," supplement, *Kernos* 25. Liège: Centre International d'Étude de la Religion Grecque Antique.

Atherton, C., ed. 2002. *Monsters and Monstrosity in Greek and Roman Culture*. Nottingham Classical Literature Studies 6. Bari: Levante.

Austin, J. L. (1962) 1975². *How to Do Things with Words*. Cambridge, MA: Harvard University Press.

Austin, N. 1994. *Helen of Troy and Her Shameless Phantom*. Ithaca, NY, and London: Cornell University Press.

Avezzù, E. 1989. "Il ventre del parassita: Identità, spazio e tempo discontinuo." In *Homo Edens: Regimi, miti e pratiche dell'alimentazione nella civiltà del Mediterraneo*, edited by O. Longo and P. Scarpi, 235–40. Verona: Diapress/Documenti.

Baker, S. 2001. *Picturing the Beast: Animals, Identity, and Representation*. Urbana and Chicago: University of Illinois Press.

Ballarini, G. 1999. "La domesticazione animale come conquista culturale zooantropologica." In *Zooantropologia*, edited by R. Marchesini, 312–69. Como: Red.

Balme, D. M. 1987. "The Place of Biology in Aristotle's Philosophy." In *Philosophical Issues in Aristotle's Biology*, edited by A. Gotthelf and J. G. Lennox, 9–20. Cambridge: Cambridge University Press.

Balme, D. M. and A. Gotthelf, eds. 2002. *Aristotle: Historia Animalium*. Vol. 1, *Books I–X: Text*. Cambridge: Cambridge University Press.

Barbara, S. 2005. "Exégèse d'un zoonyme oublié: Le basilic κινάδης." *Revue de philologie de littérature et d'histoire anciennes* 79, no. 1: 17–34.

Barbara, S., and J. Trinquier, eds. 2012. "Ophiaca: Diffusion et réception des savoirs antiques sur les Ophidiens / Ophiaca: Diffusion and Reception of Ophidian Lore in Antiquity." Special issue, *Anthropozoologica* 47, no. 1.

Baron, D. 1986. *Grammar and Gender*. New Haven and London: Yale University Press.

Battaglia, L. 2008. "Femminismo e animalismo: Una nuova alleanza?" In *Lares*, special issue, 74, no. 1: 31–46.

Beavis, I. C. 1988. *Insects and Other Invertebrates in Classical Antiquity*. Exeter: University of Exeter Press.

Beck, W. 1991. "Dogs, Dwellings, and Masters: Ensemble and Symbol in the Odyssey." *Hermes* 119: 158–67.

Belfiore, E. S. 2000. *Murder among Friends: Violation of Philia in Greek Tragedy*. New York and Oxford: Oxford University Press.

Beltrami, L. 1997. "I doveri alimentari erga parentes." In *Pietas e allattamento filiale, Atti del colloquio di Urbino, 2–3 maggio 1996*, edited by R. Raffaelli, R. M. Danese, and S. Lanciotti, 73–101. Urbino: Quattro Venti.

Benveniste, E. 1971. *Problems in General Linguistics.* Translated by Mary Elizabeth Meek. Coral Gables, FL: University of Miami Press. Originally published as *Problèmes de linguistique générale.* Paris: Gallimard, 1966.

———. 1973. *Indo-European Language and Society.* Translated by Elizabeth Palmer. Coral Gables, FL: University of Miami Press. Originally published as *Le vocabulaire des institutions indo-européennes.* Paris: Les Éditions de Minuit, 1969.

Beta, S., and F. Marzari, eds. 2010. *Animali, ibridi e mostri nella cultura antica.* Florence: Cadmo.

Bettini, M. 1991. *Anthropology and Roman Culture.* Translated by John Van Sickle. Baltimore: Johns Hopkins University Press. Originally published as *Antropologia e cultura romana.* Rome: La Nuova Italia Scientifica, 1986.

———. 1999. *The Portrait of the Lover.* Translated by Laura Gibbs. Berkeley: University of California Press. Originally published as *Il ritratto dell'amante.* Turin: Einaudi, 1992.

———. 2008. *Voci: Antropologia sonora del mondo antico.* Turin: Einaudi.

———. 2013. *Women and Weasels.* Translated by Emlyn Eisenach. Chicago: University of Chicago Press. Originally published as *Nascere: Storie di donne, donnole, madri ed eroi.* Turin: Einaudi, 1998.

Bird Rose, D. 2011. *Wild Dog Dreaming: Love and Extinction.* Charlottesville: University of Virginia Press.

Blaise, F. 1995. "Solon, Fragment 36 W: Pratique et fondation des normes politiques." *Revue des Études Grecques* 108: 24–37.

Blok, J. H. 2001. "Virtual Voices: Towards a Choreography of Women's Speech in Classical Athens." In *Making Silence Speak: Women's Voices in Greek Literature and Society,* edited by A. Lardinois and L. McClure, 95–116. Princeton and Oxford: Princeton University Press.

Blondell, R. 2010. "'Bitch That I Am': Self-Blame and Self-Assertion in the *Iliad*." *Transactions of the American Philological Association* 140, no. 1: 1–32.

———. 2013. *Helen of Troy: Beauty, Myth, Devastation.* Oxford: Oxford University Press.

Blundell, M. W. 1989. *Helping Friends and Harming Enemies: A Study in Sophocles and Greek Ethics.* Cambridge: Cambridge University Press.

Bodson, L. 1975. *Hiera Zōia: Contribution à l'étude de la place de l'animal dans la religion grecque ancienne.* Brussels: Académie Royale de Belgique.

———. 1981. "L'apport de l'éthnozoologie à l'éxplication des auteurs grecs et latins." *Les études classiques* 49: 239–49.

———. 1991. "Les invasions d'insectes dévastateurs dans l'antiquité gréco-romaine." In *Contributions à l'histoire des connaissances zoologiques: Journée d'étude, Université de Liège, 17 Mars 1990,* edited by Bodson and R. Libois, 54–69. Liège: Université de Liège.

———. 1994a. "Ancient Views on Pests and Parasites of Livestock." *Argos* 10: 303–10.

———. 1994b. "L'animale nella morale collettiva e individuale dell'antichità greco-romana." In *Filosofi e animali nel mondo antico,* edited by S. Castignone and G. Lanata, 53–85. Pisa: ETS.

———. 1998. "L'histoire des animaux." In *Si les lions pouvaient parler: Essais sur la condition animale,* edited by B. Cyrulnik, 231–55. Paris: Quarto Gallimard.

———, ed. 2000a. *Ces animaux que l'homme choisit d'inhumer: Contributions à l'étude de la place et du rôle de l'animal dans les rites funéraires.* Liège: Université de Liège.

256   REFERENCES

———. 2000b. "Motivations for Pet-Keeping in Ancient Greece and Rome: A Preliminary Survey." In *Companion Animals and Us: Exploring the Relationships between People and Pets,* edited by A. L. Podberscek, E. S. Paul, and J. A. Serpell, 27–41. Cambridge: Cambridge University Press.

———. 2001. *La sépulture des animaux: Concepts, usages et pratiques à travers le temps et l'espace.* Liège: Université de Liège.

———. 2002. "Amphibians and Reptiles: Evidence from Wall Paintings, Mosaics, Sculpture, Skeletal Remains, and Ancient Authors." In *The Natural History of Pompeii,* edited by W. Feemster Jashemski and F. G. Meyer, 327–56. Cambridge: Cambridge University Press.

———. 2009. *L'interprétation des noms grecs et latins d'animaux illustrée par le cas du zoonyme sēps-seps.* Brussels: Académie Royale de Belgique, Classe des Lettres.

Boehm, I., and P. Luccioni, eds. 2008. *Le médecin initié par l'animal: Animaux et médecine dans l'Antiquité grecque et latine.* Lyon: Maison de l'Orient de la Méditerranée–Jean Pouilloux.

Bonnet, C., C. Jourdain-Annequin, and V. Pirenne-Delforge, eds. 1998. "Le Bestiaire d'Héraclés," supplement, *Kernos 7.* Liège: Centre internationale d'étude de la religion grecque antique.

Bonsangue, V. 2005. "'Canina eloquentia': Cicerone, Quintiliano e il causidico strillone." *Pan* 23: 131–40.

Braidotti, R. 2006. *Transposition: On Nomadic Ethics.* Cambridge, U.K., and Malden, MA: Polity.

Brandes, S. 1984. "Animal Metaphors and Social Control in Tzintzuntzan." *Ethnology* 23: 207–15.

Brillante, C. 1998. "Charis, bia e il tema della reciprocità amorosa." *Quaderni Urbinati di Cultura Classica,* n.s., 59: 7–34.

———. 2000. "Il messaggio del poeta nel finale della Pitica seconda di Pindaro." In *Poesia e religione in Grecia: Studi in onore di G. A. Privitera,* edited by M. Cannati Fera and S. Grandolini, 101–18. Naples: Edizioni Scientifiche Italiane.

Broadbent, M. 1968. *Studies in Greek Genealogy.* Leiden, Netherlands: Brill.

Brown, A. S. 1997. "Aphrodite and the Pandora Complex." *Classical Quarterly* 47, no. 1: 26–47.

Brown, N. O. 1947. *Hermes the Thief.* Madison: University of Wisconsin Press. Reprint, Great Barrington, MA: Lindisfarne, 1990².

Brulé, P. 1987. *La fille d'Athènes.* Paris: Les Belles Lettres.

Brunner, F. 1974. *Der unverstandene Hund.* Melsungen, Germany: Neudamm. Translated by Tiziana Prina as *Come capire il cane e farsi capire da lui.* Milan: TEA, 1998.

Budiansky, S. 1997. *The Covenant of the Wild.* London: Phoenix.

Burkert, W. 1983. *Homo necans.* Translated by Peter Bing. Berkeley: University of California Press. Originally published in German under the same title. Berlin and New York: Walter de Gruyter, 1972.

Burnett, A. P. 1994. "Hekabe the Dog." *Arethusa* 27: 151–64.

Burton, C. R. 1993. "Greek τέθηπα, Etc." *Glotta* 71: 1–9.

Busuttil, J. 1969. "The Maltese Dog." *Greece and Rome* 16: 205–8.

Buxton, J. 1968. "Animal Identity and Human Peril: Some Mandari Images." *Man* 31: 35–49.

Buxton, R. 2009. *Forms of Astonishment: Greek Myths of Metamorphosis.* Oxford: Oxford University Press.

Buzón, R. P., and P. A. Cavallero. 1993. "Dos epigramas funerarios al perro de Zenón (*P. Cairo Zen.* 59532): Edición y estudio." In *VII reunião anual da SBEC: Araraquara, 30 de agosto a 05 de setembro de 1992*, edited by S. M. S. de Carvalho et al., 75–86. Araraquara: Sociedade brasileira de estudos clássicos.

Cairns, D. L. 1993. *Aidōs: The Psychology and Ethics of Honour and Shame in Ancient Greek Literature*. Oxford: Clarendon.

Calame, C. 1997. *Choruses of Young Women in Ancient Greece*. Translated by Derek Collins and Jane Orion. Lanham, MD: Rowman and Littlefield. Originally published as *Les choeurs de jeunes filles en Grèce archaïque*. Rome: Edizioni dell'Ateneo, 1977.

Camardese, D. 2010. *Il mondo animale nella poesia lucreziana tra "topos" e osservazione realistica*. Bologna: Patron.

Camassa, G. 1994. "Frammenti del bestiario pitagorico nella riflessione di Porfirio." In *Filosofi e animali nel mondo antico*, edited by S. Castignone and G. Lanata, 89–100. Pisa: ETS.

Camerotto, A. 2005. "Cinghiali eroici." In *Animali tra zoologia, mito e letteratura nella cultura classica e orientale*, edited by E. Cingano, A. Ghersetti, and L. Milano, vol. 1, 107–28. Padua: Sargon.

Campese, S. 1983. "Madre materia: Donna, casa, città nell'antropologia di Aristotele." In *Madre materia: Sociologia e biologia della donna greca*, edited by Campese, P. Manuli, and G. Sissa, 15–79. Turin: Boringhieri.

Canós i Villena, I., and G. Németh. 1996. "Theophilos, Philomousos, Ioukounda: A Greek family in the Roman Imperial Period." *Acta Classica Universitatis Scientiarum Debreceniensis* 32: 51–57.

Cantarella, E. 1985. *Tacita muta*. Rome: Riuniti.

———. 1986. *Pandora's Daughters: The Role and Status of Women in Greek and Roman Antiquity*. Translated by Maureen Brown Fant. Baltimore: Johns Hopkins University Press. Originally published as *L'ambiguo malanno*. Rome: Riuniti, 1985².

———. 1991. *I supplizi capitali in Grecia e a Roma*. Milan: Rizzoli.

Cantilena, M. 1982. *Ricerche sulla dizione epica 1: Per una studio della formularità negli Inni omerici*. Rome: Edizioni dell'Ateneo.

Caramico, A. 2009. "Un caso di dilatazione semantica: L'uso eschileo del verbo σαίνω." *Lexis* 27: 447–56.

Carbone, A., ed. 2002. *Aristotele: Le parti degli animali*. Milan: Rizzoli.

———. 2011. *Aristote illustré: Représentations du corps et schématisation dans la biologie aristotélicienne*. Paris: Classiques Garnier.

Cardona, G. R. (1985) 1995³. *La foresta di piume*. Rome and Bari: Laterza.

Carpenter, R. 1950. "Argeiphontes: A Suggestion." *American Journal of Archaeology* 54: 177–83.

Carson, A. 1990. "Putting Her in Her Place: Woman, Dirt, and Desire." In *Before Sexuality*, edited by D. M. Halperin, J. J. Winkler, and F. I. Zeitlin, 135–69. Princeton: Princeton University Press.

Cartledge, P. 2001. *Spartan Reflections*. London: Duckworth.

Cassin, B., and J.-L. Labarrière, eds. 1997. *L'animal dans l'antiquité*. Paris: Vrin.

Castignone, S. 2009. "Il Verde Paradiso Perduto: Appunti su Ecofemminismo e Animalismo." In *Animali ed ecologia in una rilettura del mondo al femminile*, edited by V. Baricalla, 121–42. Bologna: Alberto Perdisa.

Castignone, S., and G. Lanata, eds. 1994. *Filosofi e animali nel mondo antico*. Pisa: ETS.

Caswell, C. P. 1990. *A Study of Thumos in Early Greek Epic*. Leiden, Netherlands: Brill.

Cataldi, S. 1992. "Popoli e città del lupo e del cane in Italia meridionale e in Sicilia tra realtà e immagine." In *Autocoscienza e rappresentazione dei popoli nell'antichità,* edited by M. Sordi, 55–82. Milan: Vita e pensiero.

Centini, M. 1998. *Le bestie del diavolo: Gli animali e la stregoneria tra fonti storiche e folklore*. Milan: Rusconi.

Ceragioli, R. C. 1992. *Fervidus ille canis: The Lore and Poetry of the Dog Star in Antiquity*. Diss., Harvard University.

Cerulli, E., ed. 1991. *Tra uomo e animale*. Bari: Dedalo.

Chamoux, F. 2001. "Chiens cyrénéens." *Comptes Rendus de l'Academie des Inscriptions et Belles-Lettres* 3: 1307–13.

Chandezon, C. 2003. *L'élevage en Grèce (fin Vᵉ–fin Iᵉʳ s. a.C.): L'apport des sources épigraphiques*. Bordeaux: Ausonius.

Chantraine, P. 1958. *Grammaire homérique 1: Phonetique et morphologie*. Paris: Klincksieck.

———. 1968. *Dictionnaire étymologique de la langue grecque*. Paris: Klincksieck.

Charpentier, M.-C., ed. 2004. *Les espaces du sauvage dans le monde antique: Approches et définitions*. Colloque Besançon, 4–5 May 2000. Besançon: Presses universitaires de Franche-Comté.

Cherubini, L. 2010. *Strix: La strega nella cultura romana*. Turin: UTET.

Chryssafis, G. 1981. *A Textual and Stylistic Commentary on Theocritus' Idyll XXV*. Amsterdam: Gieben.

Ciani, M. G. 1974. "Lessico e funzione della follia nella tragedia greca." *Bollettino dell'Istituto di Filologia greca dell'Università di Padova* 1: 70–110.

Clader, L. L. 1976. *Helen: The Evolution from Divine to Heroic in Greek Epic Tradition*. Leiden, Netherlands: Brill.

Clarke, M. 1995. "Between Lions and Men: Images of the Hero in the *Iliad*." *Greek Roman and Byzantine Studies* 36: 137–59.

Clutton-Brock, J. 2007. "How Domestic Animals Have Shaped the Development of Human Societies." In *A Cultural History of Animals in Antiquity,* edited by L. Kalof, 71–96. Oxford and New York: Berg.

Cohen, D. 1991. *Law, Sexuality, and Society: The Enforcement of Morals in Classical Athens*. Cambridge: Cambridge University Press.

Cole, S. G., 1992. "*Gunaiki ou Themis*: Gender Difference in the Greek *Leges Sacrae*." *Helios* 19: 104–22.

———. 1995. "Women, Dogs, and Flies." *Ancient World* 26: 182–91.

Condos, T. 1997. *Star Myths of the Greeks and Romans: A Sourcebook*. Grand Rapids, MI: Phanes.

Conti Bizzarro, F. 2009. *Comici entomologi*. Alessandria: Edizioni dell'Orso.

Copet-Rougier, E. 1988. "Le Jeu de l'entre-deux: Le chien chez les Mkako (Est-Cameroun)." *L'Homme* 108: 108–21.

Corbett, G. 1991. *Gender*. Cambridge: Cambridge University Press.

Cornulier, B. de. 1976. "La notion de dérivation délocutive." *Revue de linguistique romane* 40: 116–43.

Couroucli, M. 2005. "Du cynégétique à l'abominable: À propos du chien comme terme d'injure et d'exclusion en grec moderne." *L'Homme* 174: 227–52.

Cunningham, I. C., ed. 1971. *Herodas: Mimiambi*. Oxford: Clarendon.

Cusumano, N. 1992. "I culti di Adrano e di Efesto: Religione, politica e acculturazione in Sicilia tra V e IV secolo." *Kokalos* 38: 151–89.

Dalby, A. 1996. *Siren Feasts: A History of Food and Gastronomy in Greece*. London and New York: Routledge.

Dalla Bernardina, S. 2006. *L'éloquence des bêtes: Quand l'homme parle des animaux*. Paris: Métailié.

Daraki, M. 1982. "Les fils de la mort: La nécrophagie cynique et stoïcienne." In *La mort, les morts dans les sociétés anciennes*, edited by G. Gnoli and J.-P. Vernant, 155–76. Cambridge and Paris: Cambridge University Press.

Darnton, R. 1984. *The Great Cat Massacre and Other Episodes in French Cultural History*. New York: Vintage Books.

Davies, M., and J. Kathirithamby. 1986. *Greek Insects*. London: Duckworth.

Day, L. P. 1984. "Dog Burials in the Greek World." *American Journal of Archaeology* 88: 21–32.

De Amicis, E. 1878. *Constantinopoli*. Milan: Treves.

Decleva Caizzi, F. 1993. "L'elogio del Cane: Sesto Empirico, Schizzi pirroniani I 62–78." *Elenchos* 14: 305–30.

De Cristofaro, F. 2002. *Zoo di romanzi: Balzac, Manzoni, Dickens e altri bestiari*. Naples: Liguori.

De Fontenay, E. 1998. *Le silence des bêtes: La philosophie à l'épreuve de l'animalité*. Paris: Fayard.

Degani, E. 1984. *Studi su Ipponatte*. Bari: Adriatica.

De Grossi Mazzorin, J. 2008. "L'uso dei cani nel mondo antico nei riti di fondazione, purificazione e passaggio." In *Uomini, piante e animali nella dimensione del sacro*, edited by F. D'Andria, De Grossi Mazzorin, and G. Fiorentino, 71–81. Bari: Edipuglia.

Delort, J. 1984. *Les animaux ont une histoire*. Paris: Seuil.

DeMello, M., ed. 2010. *Teaching the Animal: Human-Animal Studies across the Disciplines*. New York: Lantern Books.

———. 2012. *Animals and Society: An Introduction to Human-Animal Studies*. New York: Columbia University Press.

De Mori, B. 2007. *Che cos'è la bioetica animale?* Rome: Carocci.

Derrida, J. 2008. *The Animal That Therefore I Am*. Translated by David Wills. New York: Fordham University Press. Originally published as *L'animal que donc je suis*. Paris: Galilée, 2006.

Descola, P. 1993. *Les lances du crépuscule: Relations Jivaros, Haute-Amazonie*. Paris: Plon.

———. 1994. *In the Society of Nature*. Translated by Nora Scott. Cambridge: Cambridge University Press. Originally published as *La nature domestique*. Paris: Éditions de la MSH, 1986.

———. 2011. *L'écologie des autres: L'anthropologie et la question de la nature*. Paris: Quae.

———. 2013. *Beyond Nature and Culture*. Translated by Janet Lloyd. Chicago: University of Chicago Press. Originally published as *Par-delà nature et culture*. Paris: Gallimard, Bibliothèque des sciences humaines, 2005.

Desfray, S. 1999. "Oracles et animaux dans les 'Cavaliers' d'Aristophanes." *L'Antiquité Classique* 68: 35–56.

Detienne, M. 1977. *The Gardens of Adonis*. Translated by Janet Lloyd. Hassocks, U.K.: Harvester. Originally published as *Les Jardins d'Adonis*. Paris, Gallimard, 1972.

———. 1979. *Dionysos Slain*. Translated by Leonard Muellner and Mireille Muellner. Baltimore and London: Johns Hopkins University Press. Originally published as *Dionysos mis à mort*. Paris: Gallimard, 1977.

———. 2002. "L'art de construire des comparables." *Critique internationale* 14: 68–78.

———. 2009. "Historical Anthropology? Comparative Anthropology?" *Arion* 17, no. 1: 61–83.

Detienne, M., and J. Svenbro. 1989. "The Feast of the Wolves, or the Impossible City." In *The Cuisine of Sacrifice among the Greeks,* edited by Detienne and J.-P. Vernant, 148–63. Translated by Paula Wissing. Chicago: University of Chicago Press. Originally published as "Les loups au festin ou la cité impossible." In *La cuisine du sacrifice en pays grec,* edited by Detienne and Vernant, 218–21. Paris: Gallimard, 1979.

Detienne, M., and J.-P. Vernant. 1978. *Cunning Intelligence in Greek Culture and Society*. Translated by Janet Lloyd. Atlantic Highlands, NJ: Humanities. Originally published as *Les ruses de l'intelligence*. Paris: Flammarion, 1974.

———, eds. 1989. *The Cuisine of Sacrifice among the Greeks*. Translated by Paula Wissing. Chicago: University of Chicago Press. Originally published as *La cuisine du sacrifice en pays grec*. Paris: Gallimard, 1979.

Dierauer, U. 1977. *Tier und Mensch im Denken der Antike*. Amsterdam: B. R. Grüner.

Digard, J.-P. 1988. "Jalons pour una anthropologie de la domestication animale." *L'Homme* 108: 27–58.

———. 1990. *L'homme et les animaux domestiques: Anthropologie d'une passion*. Paris: Fayard.

———. 1999. *Les Français et leur animaux*. Paris: Fayard.

———. 2006. "Domestication animale et attachement: De la corde au sentiment." In *De l'éthnographie à l'histoire: Le monde de Carmen Bernand,* edited by J.-P. Castelain, S. Gruzinski, and C. Salazar-Soler, 155–71. Paris: L'Harmattan.

———. 2007. *Une histoire du cheval: Art, techniques, société*. Arles: Actes Sud.

Dillon, M. 1995. "By Gods, Tongues, and Dogs: The Use of Oaths in Aristophanic Comedy." *Greece and Rome* 42: 135–51.

Ditadi, G. 1994. *I filosofi e gli animali*. Este: Isonomia.

Dodds, E. R. 1951. *The Greeks and the Irrational*. Berkeley: University of Berkeley Press.

———, ed. 1960². *Euripides: Bacchae*. Oxford: Clarendon.

Doleschal, U. 1999. "Gender Assignment Revisited." In *Gender in Grammar and Cognition,* edited by B. Unterbeck, M. Rissanen, T. Nevalainen, and M. Saari, 117–65. Berlin and New York: Mouton de Gruyter.

Doyle, R. E. 1984. *ΆTH: Its Use and Meaning: A Study in the Greek Poetic Tradition from Homer to Euripides*. New York: Fordham University Press.

Dubielzig, U. von, 1995. "Κυνάμυια/κυνόμυια: Varianten eines Wortes oder zwei Wörter?" *Glotta* 72: 44–57.

DuBois, P. 1988. *Sowing the Body: Psychoanalysis and Ancient Representations of Women*. Chicago: University of Chicago Press.

Dumont, J. 2001. *Les animaux dans l'Antiquité grecque*. Paris: L'Harmattan.

Dumortier, J. 1935. *Les images dans la poésie d'Eschyle*. Paris: Les Belles Lettres.

Eco, U. 1976. *A Theory of Semiotics*. Bloomington: Indiana University Press.

———. 1979. *Lector in fabula*. Milan: Bompiani.

———. 1986. *Semiotics and the Philosophy of Language*. Bloomington: Indiana University Press. Originally published as *Semiotica e filosofia del linguaggio*. Turin: Einaudi, 1984.

———. 1990. *The Limits of Interpretation*. Bloomington: Indiana University Press. Originally published as *I limiti dell'interpretazione*. Milan: Bompiani, 1990.

Ellen, R. 1999. "Categories of Animality and Canine Abuse: Exploring Contradictions in Nuaulu Social Relationships with Dogs." *Anthropos* 94: 57–68.

Engels, D. 1999. *Classical Cats: The Rise and Fall of the Sacred Cat*. London: Routledge.

Ernout, A. 1948. "Lyssa." *Revue de philologie de littérature et d'histoire anciennes* 22: 154–56.

Evans-Pritchard, E. E. 1937. *Witchcraft, Oracles and Magic among the Azande*. Oxford: Clarendon.

Fabre-Vassas, C. 1994. *La bête singulière*. Paris: Gallimard.

Fagles, R. 1996. *The Odyssey*. New York: Viking.

Faraone, C. A. 1991. "The Agonistic Context of Early Greek Binding Spells." In *Magika Hiera: Ancient Greek Magic and Religion*, edited by Faraone and D. Obbink, 3–32. Oxford: Oxford University Press.

———. 1992. *Talismans and Trojan Horses: Guardian Statues in Ancient Greek Myth and Ritual*. New York and Oxford: Oxford University Press.

———. 2004. "Thumos as Masculine Ideal and Social Pathology in Ancient Greek Magical Spells." In *Ancient Anger: Perspectives from Homer to Galen*, edited by S. Braund and G. W. Most, 144–62. Yale Classical Studies 32. Cambridge: Cambridge University Press.

Faraone, C. A., and F. S. Naiden, eds. 2012. *Greek and Roman Animal Sacrifice: Ancient Victims, Modern Observers*. Cambridge and New York: Cambridge University Press.

Faust, M. 1969. "Metaphorische Schimpfwörter." *Indogermanische Forschungen* 74: 54–125.

———. 1970. "Die künstlerische Verwendung von kyôn (Hund) in den homerischen Epen." *Glotta* 48: 8–31.

Ferrari, F., ed. 1997. *Romanzo di Esopo*. Milan: Rizzoli.

Finet, A. 1993. "Le comportement du chien, facteur de son ambivalence en Mésopotamie." In *L'histoire de la connaissance du comportement animal*, edited by L. Bodson, 133–42. Liège: Université de Liège.

Fiorani, E. 1999. "Domestico/Selvaggio." In *Zooantropologia*, edited by R. Marchesini, 188–214. Como: Red.

Fischer, C. T., and O. Wecker. 1924. "Kynokephaloi." In *Realencyclopädie der classischen Altertumwissenschaft*, edited by A. F. Pauly and G. Wissowa, vol. 121, coll. 24–26. Stuttgart: Druckenmüller.

Fittà, M. 1997. *Giochi e giocattoli nell'Antichità*. Milan: Leonardo Arte.

Fitzgerald, R. 1961. *The Odyssey*. Garden City, NY: Doubleday.

Flacelière, R. 1962. *Love in Ancient Greece*. Translated by James Cleugh. New York: Crown. Originally published as *L'amour en Grèce*. Paris: Hachette, 1960.

Floridi, L. 1997. "Scepticism and Animal Rationality: The Fortune of Chrysippus' Dog in the History of Western Thought." *Archiv für Geschichte der Philosophie* 79, no. 1: 27–57.

Fögen, T. 2006. "Animals in Greco-Roman Antiquity and Beyond: A Select Bibliography." www.telemachos.hu-berlin.de/esterni/Tierbibliographie_Foegen.pdf.

Forbes-Irving, P. 1990. *Metamorphosis in Greek Myths*. Oxford: Clarendon.

Foxhall, L. 1998. "Natural Sex: The Attribution of Sex and Gender to Plants in Ancient Greece." In *Thinking Men: Masculinity and Its Self-Representation in the Classical Tradition*, edited by Foxhall and J. Salmon, 57–70. London and New York: Routledge.

Fraenkel, E. 1950. *Aeschylus: Agamemnon*. Vol. 2. Oxford: Clarendon.

Franco, C. 2001. "L'ingiustizia dei macellai: Vegetarianismo e rispetto della vita animale nell'antichità classica." *I viaggi di Erodoto* 43–44: 208–23.

———. 2003. "Animali e analisi cuturale." In *"Buoni per pensare": Gli animali nel pensiero e nella letteratura dell'antichità*, edited by F. Gasti and E. Romano, 63–81. Atti della II Giornata ghisleriana di Filologia classica, Pavia, 18–19 April 2002. Pavia and Como: Ibis.

———. 2006. "Il verro e il cinghiale: Immagini di caccia e virilità nel mondo greco." *Studi Italiani di Filologia Classica* 4, no. 1: 5–31.

———. 2007a. "Callimaco e la voce del cane." *Annali Online di Ferrara—Lettere* 1: 45–68.

———, ed. 2007b. *Zoomania: Animali ibridi e mostri nelle culture umane*. Siena: Protagon.

———. 2008a. "Circe e le belve spettacolari: Nota a Virgilio, *Eneide* VII 8–24." *Annali Online di Ferrara—Lettere* 3, no. 2: 54–73.

———. 2008b. "Questioni di genere e metafore animali nella letteratura greca." *Annali Online di Ferrara—Lettere* 3, no. 1: 73–94.

———. 2008c. "Riflessioni preliminari per uno studio su animali e costruzione di genere nel mondo antico." In *Mensch und Tier in der Antike: Grenzziehung und Grenzüberschreitung*, edited by A. Alexandridis, M. Wild, and L. Winkler-Horaček, 265–84. Wiesbaden: Reichert.

———. 2010. "Il mito di Circe." In *Il mito di Circe*, by M. Bettini and Franco, 25–381. Turin: Einaudi.

———. Forthcoming. "L'utopia dell'animale naturale in Grecia e a Roma." In *De Utopías y Animales: VIII Jornadas sobre pensamiento utópico, 24–25 de noviembre de 2011*. Madrid: Universidad Carlos III de Madrid, Instituto de Estudios Clásicos Lucio Anneo Séneca.

Freud, S. 1961. *Civilization and Its Discontents*. Translated and edited by James Strachey. New York: W. W. Norton. Originally published as *Das Unbehagen in der Kultur*. Vienna: Internationaler Psychoanalytischer Verlag, 1930.

Frisk, H. 1960–70. *Griechisches Etymologisches Wörterbuch*. Heidelberg: Winter.

Frontisi-Ducroux, F. 1997. "Actéon, ses chiens et leur maître." In *L'animal dans l'antiquité*, edited by B. Cassin and J.-L. Labarrière, 435–49. Paris: Vrin.

———. 2003. *L'homme-cerf et la femme-araignée*. Paris: Gallimard.

Garvie, A. F., ed. 1986. *Aeschylus: Choephori*. Oxford: Clarendon, 1986.

Gasti, F., and E. Romano, eds. 2003. *"Buoni per pensare": Gli animali nel pensiero e nella letteratura dell'antichità*. Atti della II Giornata ghisleriana di Filologia classica, Pavia, 18–19 April 2002. Pavia and Como: Ibis.

Geertz, C. 1973. *The Interpretation of Cultures*. New York: Basic Books.

———. 1983. *Local Knowledge*. New York: Basic Books.

Gentili, B., P. A. Bernardini, E. Cingano, and P. Giannini, eds. 1995. *Pindaro: Le Pitiche*. Milan: Valla.

Georgoudi, S. 1990. *Des chevaux et des boeufs dans le monde grec*. Paris and Athens: Daedalus.

Geus, K. 2000. "'. . . Beim Hund': Historische Anmerkungen zum Eid des Sokrates." *Gymnasium* 107, no. 2: 97–107.

Giammarco Razzano, M. C. 2001. *La vecchiaia di Solone*. Rome: Carocci.

Giannini, A. 1964. "Studi sulla paradossografia greca: Da Callimaco all'età imperiale." *Acme* 17: 99–140.

———. 1966. *Paradoxographorum graecorum reliquiae*. Milan: Istituto Editoriale Italiano.

Gibbs, L. 1999. "Aelian's Ancient Encyclopedia of Animals." Paper presented at the American Folklore Society Annual Meeting, Memphis, October.

Gibson, J. 1979. *The Ecological Approach to Visual Perception*. Boston: Houghton Mifflin.

Gilhus, I. 2006. *Animals, Gods, and Humans: Changing Attitudes to Animals in Greek, Roman, and Early Christian Ideas*. London and New York: Routledge.

Ginzburg, C. 1980. "Morelli, Freud, and Sherlock Holmes: Clues and Scientific Method." Translated by Anna Davin. *History Workshop* 9: 5–36. Originally published as "Spie: Radici di un paradigma indiziario." In *Crisi della ragione*, edited by A. Gargani, 59–106. Turin: Einaudi, 1979.

———. 1999. *History, Rhetoric, and Proof*. Hanover and London: University Press of New England.

Giordano, M. 1999. *La parola efficace: Maledizioni, giuramenti e benedizioni nella Grecia arcaica*. Pisa and Rome: Istituti Editoriali e Poligrafici Internazionali.

Gleason, M. W. 1995. *Making Men: Sophists and Self-Presentation in Ancient Rome*. Princeton: Princeton University Press.

Goguey, D. 2003. *Les animaux dans la mentalité romaine*. Brussels: Latomus.

Gottesman, A. 2008. "The Pragmatic of Homeric Kertomia." *Classical Quarterly* 58, no. 1: 1–12.

Goulet-Cazé, M.-O. 1996. "Religion and the Early Cynics." In *The Cynics: The Cynic Movement in Antiquity and Its Legacy*, edited by R. Bracht Branham and Goulet-Cazé, 47–80. Berkeley: University of California Press.

Gourevitch, D. 1968. "Le chien, de la thérapeutique populaire aux cultes sanitaires." *Mélanges d'Archéologie et d'Histoire de l'École Française de Rome* 80: 247–81.

Gow, A. S. F. 1952². *Theocritus*. Vol. 2. Cambridge: Cambridge University Press.

Gow, A. S. F. and D. L. Page. 1965. *The Greek Anthology: Hellenistic Epigrams*. Vol. 2. Cambridge: Cambridge University Press.

———. 1968. *The Greek Anthology: The Garland of Philip*. Vol. 2. Cambridge: Cambridge University Press.

Grasseni, C., and F. Ronzon. 2004. *Pratiche e cognizione: Note di ecologia della cultura*. Rome: Meltemi.

Grassl, H. 2009. "Ein Dichter, ein Sklave und ein Hund: Äginetische Gedankenspiele." In *Aiakeion: Beiträge zur klassischen Altertumswissenschaft zu Ehren von Florens Felten*, edited by C. Reinholdt, P. Scherrer, and W. Wohlmayr, 21–23. Vienna: Phoibos.

Graver, M. 1995. "Dog-Helen and Homeric Insult." *Classical Antiquity* 14: 41–61.

Gregory, J. 1999. *Euripides: Hecuba: Introduction, Text, and Commentary*. Atlanta: Scholars Press.

Grice, H. P. 1975. "Logic and Conversation." In *Syntax and Semantics: Speech Acts*, edited by P. Cole and J. L. Morgan, 41–58. New York and London: Academic Press.

Grmek, M., and D. Gourevitch. 1998. *Les maladies dans l'art antique*. Paris: Fayard.

Gruen, L., and Weil, K. 2010. "Teaching Difference: Sex, Gender, Species." In *Teaching the Animal: Human-Animal Studies across the Disciplines*, edited by M. DeMello, 127–42. New York: Lantern Books.

Guasparri, A. 1998. "Varrone linguista: Impositio nominum e creatività linguistica in una tassonomia esemplare." *Bollettino di studi latini* 28, no. 2: 408–14.

———. 2005. "Aquatilium vocabula ad similitudinem: Lessico antropologico-linguistico degli animali acquatici nel mondo latino." Doctoral thesis, Università di Siena.

———. 2007. "Etnobiologia e mondo antico: Una prospettiva di ricerca." In "Animali, animali fantastici, ibridi, mostri," edited by A. M. Andrisano. Special issue, *Annali Ferrara Online*: 69–90.

Guastella, G. 1988. *La contaminazione e il parassita*. Pisa: Giardini.

Guidorizzi, G., ed. 1996. *Aristofane: Le nuvole*. Milan: Valla Mondadori.

———. 2000. *Igino: Miti*. Milan: Adelphi.

Gundel, H. 1927. "Sirius." In *Realencyclopädie der classischen Altertumwissenschaft*, edited by A. F. Pauly and G. Wissowa, vol. 3, A.1, coll. 314–51. Stuttgart: Druckenmüller.

Hainsworth, J. B. 1961. "Odysseus and the Dogs." *Greece and Rome* 8: 122–25.

———. 1968. *The Flexibility of the Homeric Formula*. Oxford: Clarendon.

———. 1993. *The Iliad: A Commentary*. General editor G. S. Kirk. Vol. 3. Cambridge: Cambridge University Press.

Halverson, J. 1976. "Animal Categories and Terms of Abuse." *Man*, n.s., 11, no. 4: 505–16.

Hamilakis, Y. 1996. "A Footnote on the Archaeology of Power: Animal Bones from a Mycenaean Chamber Tomb at Galatas, NE Peloponnese." *Annual of the British School at Athens* 91: 153–66.

Hamilton, R. 1992. *Choes and Anthesteria: Athenian Iconography and Ritual*. Ann Arbor: University of Michigan Press.

Haraway, D. 2003. *The Companion Species Manifesto: Dogs, People, and Significant Otherness*. Chicago: Prickly Paradigm.

Hare, B., M. Brown, C. Williamson, and M. Tomasello. 2002. "The Domestication of Social Cognition in Dogs." *Science* 298, no. 5598: 1634–36.

Harriott, R. M. 1982. "The Argive Elders, the Discerning Shepherd and the Fawning Dog: Misleading Communication in the *Agamemnon*." *Classical Quarterly* 32: 9–17.

Harris, M. 1985. *Good to Eat: Riddles of Food and Culture*. New York: Simon and Schuster.

Harrison, A. R. W. 1968. *The Law of Athens*. Vol. 1. Oxford: Clarendon.

Haudricourt, A. G. 1977. "Note d'ethnozoologie: Le rôle des excrétats dans la domestication." *L'Homme* 17: 125–26.

Havelock, E. A. 1978. *The Greek Concept of Justice from Its Shadow in Homer to Its Substance in Plato*. Cambridge, MA: Harvard University Press.

Heath, J. 1999. "Disentangling the Beast: Humans and Other Animals in Aeschylus' *Oresteia*." *Journal of Hellenic Studies* 119: 17–47.

———. 2005. *The Talking Greeks: Speech, Animals, and the Other in Homer, Aeschylus, and Plato*. Cambridge: Cambridge University Press.

Henderson, J., ed. 1987. *Aristophanes' Lysistrata*. Oxford: Clarendon.

———. 1991². *The Maculate Muse: Obscene Language in Attic Comedy*. Oxford: Oxford University Press.

Herrlinger, G. 1930. *Totenklage um Tiere in der antiken Dichtung*. Stuttgart: W. Kohlhammer Verlag.

Heubeck, A., ed. 1983. *Omero: Odissea*. Vol. 3. Milan: Valla Mondadori.

Heubeck, A., and S. West, ed. 1987². *Omero: Odissea*. Vol. 1. Milan: Valla Mondadori.

Howe, T. 2008. *Pastoral Politics: Animals, Agriculture and Society in Ancient Greece.* Claremont, CA: Regina Books.

Hribal, J. C. 2007. "Animals, Agency, and Class: Writing the History of Animals from Below." *Human Ecology Review* 14, no. 1: 101–12.

Hull, D. B. 1964. *Hounds and Hunting in Ancient Greece.* Chicago: University of Chicago Press.

Hunter, V. J. 1994. *Policing Athens: Social Control in the Attic Lawsuits, 420–320 B.C.* Princeton: Princeton University Press.

Hurn, S. 2012. *Humans and Other Animals.* London: Pluto.

Hurskainen, A. 1999. "Noun Classification in African Languages." In *Gender in Grammar and Cognition,* edited by B. Unterbeck, M. Rissanen, T. Nevalainen, and M. Saari, 665–87. Berlin and New York: Mouton de Gruyter.

Hyland, A. R. 1990. *Equus: The Horse in the Roman World.* London: Batsford.

Ingold, T., ed. (1988) 1994^2. *What Is an Animal?* London and New York: Routledge.

———. 1990. "An Anthropologist Looks at Biology." *Man,* n.s., 25, no. 2: 208–29.

———. 1994a. "From Trust to Domination: An Alternative History of Human-Animal Relations." In *Animals and Human Society,* edited by A. Manning and J. Serpell, 1–22. New York: Routledge.

———. 1994b. "Humanity and Animality." In *A Companion Encyclopedia of Anthropology,* edited by Ingold, 14–32. London and New York, Routledge.

———. 1997. "Eight Themes in the Anthropology of Technology." In "Technology as Skilled Practice," edited by P. Harvey. Special issue, *Social Analysis* 41, no. 1: 106–38.

———. 2000. "Evolving Skills." In *Alas Poor Darwin: Arguments against Evolutionary Psychology,* edited by H. Rose and S. Rose, 273–97. London: Jonathan Cape.

———. 2001. *Ecologia della cultura.* Rome: Meltemi.

Jedrkiewicz, S. 1989. *Sapere e paradosso nell'Antichità: Esopo e la favola.* Rome: Edizioni dell'Ateneo.

Jennison, G. 1937. *Animals for Show and Pleasure in Ancient Rome.* Manchester: University of Manchester Press. Reprint, Philadelphia: University of Pennsylvania Press, 2005.

Jervis, G. 1984. *Presenza e identità: Lezioni di psicologia.* Milan: Garzanti.

Johns, C. 2008. *Dogs: History, Myth, Art.* Cambridge, MA: Harvard University Press.

Johnston, S. I. 1999. *Restless Dead: Encounters between the Living and the Dead in Ancient Greece.* Berkeley: University of California Press.

Kalof, L., ed. 2007. *A Cultural History of Animals in Antiquity.* Oxford and New York: Berg.

Keller, O. 1909–13. *Die antike Tierwelt.* 2 vols. Leipzig: W. Engelmann.

Kete, K. 1994. *The Beast in the Boudoir: Petkeeping in Nineteenth-Century Paris.* Berkeley: University of California Press.

Kilani, M. 2000. "La 'mucca pazza', ovvero il declino della ragione sacrificale." In *Homo sapiens e mucca pazza: Antropologia del rapporto con il mondo animale,* edited by A. Rivera, 73–112. Bari: Dedalo.

King, H. 1998. *Hippocrates' Woman.* London and New York: Routledge.

Kirk, G. S. 1990. *The Iliad: A Commentary.* General editor G. S. Kirk. Vol. 2. Cambridge: Cambridge University Press.

Kirksey, S. E., and S. Helmreich. 2010. "The Emergence of Multispecies Ethnography." *Cultural Anthropology* 25, no. 4: 545–76.

Kitchell, K. F. 2004. "Man's Best Friend? The Changing Role of the Dog in Greek Society." In *Pecus: Man and Animal in Antiquity—Proceedings of the Conference at the Swedish Institute in Rome, September 9–12, 2002,* edited by B. Santillo Frizell, 177–82. Rome: Swedish Institute in Rome.

———. 2013. *Animals in the Ancient World, from A to Z.* London and New York: Routledge.

Kohn, E. 2007. "How Dogs Dream: Amazonian Natures and the Politics of Transspecies Engagement." *American Ethnologist* 34, no. 1: 3–24.

Köhnken, A. 2003. "Perspektivisches Erzählen im homerischen Epos: Die Wiedererkennung Odysseus: Argos." *Hermes* 131, no. 4: 385–96.

Konstan, D. 1997. *Friendship in the Classical World.* Cambridge: Cambridge University Press.

Koster, S. 1980. *Die Invektive in der grieschischen und römischen Literatur.* Meisenheim am Glan: Hain.

Kotjabopoulou, E., Y. Hamilakis, P. Halstead, C. Gamble, and P. Elefanti, eds. 2003. *Zooarchaeology in Greece: Recent Advances.* London: British School at Athens.

Kraus, T. 1960. *Hekate: Studien zu Wesen und Bild der Göttin in Kleinasien und Griechenland.* Heidelberg: C. Winter.

Labarrière, J.-L. 1997. "Animal de compagnie, animal domestique et animal sauvage: Une tentative de définition." In *L'animal de compagnie: Ses rôles et leurs motivations au regard de l'histoire,* edited by L. Bodson, 15–33. Liège: Université de Liège.

———. 2000. "Raison humaine et intelligence animale dans la philosophie grecque." *Terrain* 34: 107–22.

———. 2004. *Langage, vie politique et mouvement des animaux: Études aristotéliciennes.* Paris: Vrin.

———. 2005. *La condition animale: Études sur Aristote et les Stoïciens.* Louvain-la-Neuve, Belgium: Peeters.

Lakoff, G. 1987. *Women, Fire, and Dangerous Things.* Chicago: University of Chicago Press.

Lakoff, G., and M. Johnson. 1980. *Metaphors We Live By.* Chicago: University of Chicago Press.

Lallot, J. 1989². *La grammaire de Denys le Thrace.* Paris: Éditions du Centre National de la Recherche Scientifique.

Lamberterie, C. de. 1994. "Grec ΣΚΥΖΑΝ, ΣΚΥΖΕΣΘΑΙ et les grognements d'Héra." *Revue des Études Grecques* 107: 15–46.

Lanata, G. 2000. "Credenze e saperi sugli animali." *I Quaderni del ramo d'oro* 3: 7–38.

La Penna, A. 1973. "Una polemica di Sallustio contro l'oratoria contemporanea?" *Rivista di Filologia e Istruzione Classica* 101: 88–91.

Lapucci, C. 1995. *L'arca di Noè.* Milan: Vallardi.

Lattimore, R. 1965. *The Odyssey.* New York: Harper and Row.

Lazzeroni, R. 1993. "Il genere indeuropeo: Una categoria naturale?" In *Maschile/Femminile: Genere e ruoli nelle culture antiche,* edited by M. Bettini, 3–16. Rome and Bari: Laterza.

Leach, E. 1964. "Anthropological Aspects of Language: Animal Categories and Verbal Abuse." In *New Directions in the Study of Language,* edited by E. H. Lenneberg, 23–63. Cambridge, MA: MIT Press.

Lebeck, A. 1971. *The Oresteia: A Study in Language and Structure.* Washington DC: Center of Hellenic Studies.

Le Bohec-Bouhet, S. 2011. "Les chiens en Macédoine dans l'Antiquité." In *"Philologos Dionysios": Mélanges offerts au professeur Denis Knoepfler*, edited by N. Badoud, 491–515. Neuchâtel, Switzerland: Université de Neuchâtel, Faculté des lettres et sciences humaines.

Leduc, C. 1990. "Come darla in matrimonio? La sposa nel mondo greco, secoli IX–IV a.C." In *L'Antichità*, edited by P. Schmitt Pantel, 246–314. Vol. 1 of *Storia della donne in Occidente*, edited by G. Duby and M. Perrot. Rome and Bari: Laterza.

Lehnus, L. 1979. *L'Inno a Pan di Pindaro*. Milano: Cisalpino-Goliardica.

Lessona, M. 1996². *La storia naturale dei cani*. Padua: Muzzio. Originally published as *I cani*. Florence: Barbera, 1886.

Létoublon, F. 1983. "Défi et combat dans l'*Iliade*." *Revue des Études Grecques* 96: 27–48.

Levêque, P. 1999. *Les grenouilles dans l'antiquité*. Paris: De Fallois.

Lévi-Strauss, C. 1963. *Totemism*. Translated by Rodney Needham. Boston: Beacon. Originally published as *Le totémisme aujourd'hui*. Paris: PUF, 1962.

———. 1966. *The Savage Mind*. Chicago: University of Chicago Press. Originally published as *La pensée sauvage*. Paris: Plon, 1962.

———. 1971. "Race et culture." *Revue internationale des Sciences sociales* 23, no. 4: 647–66.

———. 1995. *The Story of Lynx*. Translated by Catherine Tihanyi. Chicago: University of Chicago Press. Originally published as *Histoire de Lynx*. Paris: Plon, 1991.

Lewinsohn, R. 1954. *Animals, Men, and Myths: A History of the Influence of Animals on Civilization and Culture*. Translated by Edward Ballard Garside. New York: Harper and Row. Originally published as *Eine Geschichte der Tiere, ihr Einfluss auf Zivilisation und Kultur*. Berlin: Rowohlt, 1952.

Li Causi, P. 2003. *Sulle tracce del manticora: La zoologia dei confini del mondo in Grecia e a Roma*. Palermo: Palumbo.

———. 2008. *Generare in comune: Teorie e rappresentazioni dell'ibrido nel sapere zoologico dei Greci e dei Romani*. Palermo: Palumbo.

———. 2010. "I generi dei generi (e le specie): Le marche di classificazione di secondo livello dei Romani e la zoologia di Plinio il Vecchio." *Annali Online di Ferrara—Lettere* 2: 107–42.

Lilja, S. 1976. *Dogs in Ancient Greek Poetry*. Helsinki: Societas Scientiarum Fennica.

Limet, H. 2000. "Le contenu archéozoologique des tombes «royales» d'Ur: Réflections sur son interprétation." In *Ces animaux que l'homme choisit d'inhumer*, edited by L. Bodson, 41–61. Liège: Université de Liège.

Lincoln, B. 1975. "Homeric λύσσα: 'Wolfish Rage.'" *Indogermanische Forschungen* 80: 98–105.

———. 1979. "The Hellhound." *Journal of Indo-European Studies* 7: 273–86.

———. 1997. "Competing Discourses: Rethinking the Prehistory of Mythos and Logos." *Arethusa* 30: 341–67. Reprinted in *Theorizing Myth: Narrative, Ideology, and Scholarship*, 3–18. Chicago: University of Chicago Press, 1999.

Lloyd, G. E. R. 1966. *Polarity and Analogy*. Cambridge: Cambridge University Press.

———. 1990. *Demystifying Mentalities*. Cambridge: Cambridge University Press.

———. 1998. "Humains et animaux: Problèmes de taxonomie en Grèce et en Chine anciennes." *Etudes de Lettres* 3–4: 73–91. Reprinted in *La fabrication de l'humain dans les cultures et en anthropologie*, edited by C. Calame and M. Kilani, 73–91. Lausanne: Payot, 1999.

Lloyd-Jones, H. 1976. *Females of the Species: Semonides on Women.* London: Duckworth.

Lombardi, T. 1994. "Alcune considerazioni sul mito di Pandora." *Quaderni Urbinati di Cultura Classica,* n.s., 46: 23–34.

Long, A. A. 1996. "The Socratic Tradition: Diogenes, Crates, and Hellenistic Ethics." In *The Cynics: The Cynic Movement in Antiquity and Its Legacy,* edited by R. Bracht Branham and M.-O. Goulet-Cazé, 28–46. Berkeley: University of California Press.

Longo, O. 1985. *Alcifrone: Lo spazio del piacere.* In *Alcifrone: Lettere di parassiti e di cortigiane,* edited by E. Avezzù and O. Longo, 14–41. Venice: Marsilio.

Lonsdale, S. H. 1990. *Creatures of Speech: Lion, Herding and Hunting Similes in the Iliad.* Stuttgart: Teubner.

Loraux, N. 1993a. "Aspasia, la straniera, l'intellettuale." In *Grecia al femminile,* edited by Loraux, 125–54. Rome and Bari: Laterza.

———. 1993b. "On the Race of Women and Some of Its Tribes: Hesiod and Semonides." In *The Children of Athena,* 72–110. Translated by Caroline Levine. Princeton: Princeton University Press. Originally published as "Sur la race des femmes et quelques unes des ses tribus." *Arethusa* 11, nos. 1–2 (1978): 43–87. Collected in *Les enfants d'Athéna,* 75–117. Paris: Maspero, 1981.

———. 1995. *The Experiences of Tiresias.* Translated by Paula Wissing. Princeton: Princeton University Press. Originally published as *Les expériences de Tirésias: Le féminin et l'homme grec.* Paris: Seuil, 1989.

———. 1998. *Mothers in Mourning.* Translated by Corinne Pache. Ithaca, NY: Cornell University Press. Originally published as *Les mères en deuil.* Paris: Seuil, 1990.

———. 2000. *Born of the Earth: Myth and Politics in Athens.* Translated by Selina Stewart. Ithaca, NY: Cornell University Press. Originally published as *Né de la Terre.* Paris: Seuil, 1996.

Lorenz, K. (1954) 2002. *Man Meets Dog.* Translated by Marjorie Kerr Wilson. London and New York: Routledge. Originally published as *So kam der Mensch auf den Hund.* Vienna: Borotha-Schoeler, 1950.

Lutri, A., A. Acerbi, and S. Tonutti., eds. 2009. *"Umano, troppo umano": Riflessioni sull'opposizione natura/cultura in antropologia.* Florence: SEID.

Luzzatto, M. J. 2001. "Teocrito ed Esopo (*Id.* X 11 e il cane impazzito)." *Maia* 53, no. 2: 355–58.

MacKinnon, M. 2004. *Production and Consumption of Animals in Roman Italy: Integrating the Zooarchaeological and Textual Evidence.* Portsmouth, RI: Journal of Roman Archaeology.

MacLachlan, B. 1993. *The Age of Grace: Charis in Early Greek Poetry.* Princeton: Princeton University Press.

Maddoli, G., and V. Saladino, eds. 1995. *Pausania: Guida della Grecia, Libro V (L'Elide e Olimpia).* Milan: Valla Mondadori.

Maffi, A. 1983. "Padri e figli fra diritto positivo e diritto immaginario nella Grecia classica." In *La paura dei padri nella società antica e medievale,* edited by E. Pellizer and N. Zorzetti, 5–27. Rome and Bari: Laterza.

Mahaffy, J. P. 1874. *Social Life in Greece from Homer to Menander.* London: Macmillan.

Mainoldi, C. 1984. *L'image du loup et du chien dans la Grèce ancienne d'Homère à Platon.* Paris: Ophrys.

Mannucci, A. 2008. "Introduzione." In *Lares,* special issue, 74, no. 1: 19–28.

Marchesini, R., ed. 1999. *Zooantropologia*. Como: Red.

———. 2000a. *Lineamenti di zooantropologia*. Bologna: Calderini.

———. 2000b. "La fabbricazione dei viventi: Dall'animale-partner all'animale-macchina." In *Homo sapiens e mucca pazza: Antropologia del rapporto con il mondo animale*, edited by A. Rivera, 113–47. Bari: Dedalo.

———. 2002. *Post-human: Verso nuovi modelli di esistenza*. Turin: Bollati Boringhieri.

Marchesini, R., and K. Andersen. 2003. *Animal Appeal*. Bologna: Hybris.

Marchesini, R., and S. Tonutti. 2007. *Manuale di zooantropologia*. Rome: Meltemi.

Markwald, G. 1986. *Die Homerischen Epigramme: Sprachliche und inhaltliche Untersuchungen*. Meisenheim am Glan: Hain.

Martin, R. P. 1989. *The Language of Heroes: Speech and Performance in the Iliad*. Ithaca, NY: Cornell University Press.

———. 2001. "Just like a Woman: Enigmas of the Lyric Voice." In *Making Silence Speak: Women's Voices in Greek Literature and Society*, edited by A. Lardinois and L. McClure, 55–74. Princeton and Oxford: Princeton University Press.

Masselli, G. M. 2011. "Caninam facundiam exercere: Forme dell'invettiva nella cultura pagana." *Auctores nostri* 9: 105–29.

Masson, J. M. 1997. *Dogs Never Lie about Love*. New York: Crown.

McClure, L. 1999. *Spoken like a Woman: Speech and Gender in Athenian Drama*. Princeton: Princeton University Press.

Mcdonough, C. M. 1999. "Forbidden to Enter the Ara Maxima: Dogs and Flies, or Dog-flies?" *Mnemosyne* 52, no. 4: 464–77.

McInerney, J. 2010. *The Cattle of the Sun: Cows and Culture in the World of the Ancient Greeks*. Princeton: Princeton University Press.

Mentz, F. 1933. "Die klassischen Hundenamen." *Philologus* 88: 104–29, 181–202, 415–42.

Merlen, R. H. A. 1971. *De canibus: Dog and Hound in Antiquity*. London: Allen.

Miller, D. A. 2000. *The Epic Hero*. Baltimore and London: Johns Hopkins University Press.

Milliet, J. 1995. "Manger du chien? C'est bon pour les sauvages!" *L'Homme* 136: 75–94.

Minchin, E. 2001. "Similes in Homer: Image, Mind's Eye, and Memory." In "Speaking Volumes: Orality and Literacy in the Greek and Roman World," edited by J. Watson, 5–52. Supplement, *Mnemosyne* 218. Leiden, Netherlands: Brill.

Montgomery, G. M., and L. Kalof. 2010. "History from Below: Animals as Historical Subjects." In *Teaching the Animal: Human-Animal Studies across the Disciplines*, edited by M. DeMello, 35–47. New York: Lantern Books.

Morris, D. 1987. *Dogwatching*. New York: Crown.

Mossman, J. 1995. *Wild Justice: A Study of Euripides' Hecuba*. Oxford: Clarendon.

Most, G. W. 1991. "Ansichten über einen Hund: Zu einigen Strukturen der Homerrezeption zwischen Antike und Neuzeit." *Antike und Abendland* 37: 144–68.

Mullan, B., and G. Marvin. 1987. *Zoo Culture*. London: Weidenfeld and Nicolson.

Mullin, M. 1999. "Mirrors and Windows: Sociocultural Studies of Human-Animal Relationships." *Annual Review of Anthropology* 28: 201–24.

———. 2002. "Animals in Anthropology." *Society and Animals* 10, no. 4: 387–93.

Musée de Marseille. 1991. *Jouer dans l'antiquité: Musée d'Archéologie Mediterranéenne, Centre de la Vieille Charité, 22 novembre 1991–16 février 1992*. Paris: Réunion des Musées Nationaux; Marseilles: Musée de Marseille.

Myrick, L. D. 1994. "The Way Up and Down: Racehorse and Turning Imagery in the Orestes Plays." *Classical Journal* 89, no. 2: 131–48.

Nagler, M. N. 1967. "Towards a Generative View of the Oral Formula." *Transactions and Proceedings of the American Philological Association* 98: 269–311.

Nagy, G. 1979. *The Best of the Achaeans.* Baltimore and London: Johns Hopkins University Press.

Nancy, C. 1984. "Euripide et le partie des femmes." *Quaderni Urbinati di Cultura Classica,* n.s., 17: 111–36.

Napolitano, M. 1996. "Del bere sangue e di Teognide-cane (a proposito di Theogn. 341–50)." *Eikasmos* 7: 65–79.

Napolitano, M. L. 1985. "Donne spartane e ΤΕΚΝΟΠΟΙΙΑ." *Annali dell'Istituto Orientale di Napoli: Sezione archeologia e storia antica* 7: 19–50.

Needham, R. 1978. *Primordial Characters.* Charlottesville: University of Virginia Press.

Netz, R. 2004. *Barbed Wire.* Middletown, CT: Wesleyan University Press.

Newmyer, S. T. 2005. *Animals, Rights and Reason in Plutarch and Modern Ethics.* London and New York: Routledge.

———. 2011. *Animals in Greek and Roman Thought: A Sourcebook.* London and New York: Routledge.

Noussia Fantuzzi, M. 2010. *Solon the Athenian: The Poetic Fragments.* Leiden, Netherlands, and Boston: Brill.

O'Connor, T. P. 1997. "Working at Relationships: Another Look at Animal Domestication." *Antiquity* 71: 149–56.

Oliensis, E. 1991. "Canidia, Canicula, and the Decorum of Horace's Epodes." *Arethusa* 24: 107–38.

Olowo Ojoade, J. 1994. "Nigerian Cultural Attitudes to the Dog." In *Signifying Animals: Human Meaning in the Natural World,* edited by R. G. Willis, 215–21. Reprint, London: Routledge.

Onians, R. B. 1951. *The Origins of the European Thought about the Body, the Mind, the Soul, the World, Time, and Fate.* Cambridge: Cambridge University Press.

Ortalli, G. 1997. *Lupi genti culture.* Turin: Einaudi.

Orth, F. 1913. "Hund." In *Realencyclopädie der classischen Altertumwissenschaft,* edited by A. F. Pauly and G. Wissowa, vol. 8, 2540–82. Stuttgart: Druckenmüller.

Osborne, C. 2011. *Dumb Beasts and Dead Philosophers: Humanity and the Humane in Ancient Philosophy and Literature.* Oxford: Clarendon.

Padel, R. 1992. *In and Out of the Mind: Greek Images of the Tragic Self.* Princeton: Princeton University Press.

———. 1995. *Whom Gods Destroy: Elements of Greek and Tragic Madness.* Princeton: Princeton University Press.

Padgett, J. M. 2003. *The Centaur's Smile: The Human Animal in Early Greek Art.* New Haven: Yale University Press.

Padiglione, V. 1994. *Il cinghiale cacciatore: Antropologia simbolica della caccia in Sardegna.* Rome: Armando.

———. 2008. "Animalscape: La diaspora animale nel nostro quotidiano." In *Lares,* special issue, 74, no. 1: 211–33.

Page, D. L., ed. 1981^2. *Further Greek Epigrams.* Revised edition by R. D. Dawe and J. Diggle. Cambridge: Cambridge University Press.

Pakaluk, M. 1998. *Aristotle: Nicomachean Ethics, Books VIII and IX*. Oxford: Clarendon.

Papaoikonomou, Y. 1981. "L'enfant aux astragales: À propos d'une stèle funéraire crétoise." *Bulletin de correspondance Hellénique* 105: 255–63.

Paradiso, A. 1993. "Gorgo, la Spartana." In *Grecia al femminile*, edited by N. Loraux, 109–22. Rome and Bari: Laterza.

Parker, R. 1996². *Miasma: Pollution and Purification in Early Greek Religion*. Oxford: Clarendon.

Parks, W. 1990. *Verbal Dueling in Heroic Narrative*. Princeton: Princeton University Press.

Pastoureau, M. 2007. *L'ours: Histoire d'un roi déchu*. Paris: Seuil.

Payne, M. 2010. *The Animal Part: Human and Other Animals in the Poetic Imagination*. Chicago and London: University of Chicago Press.

Pellizer, E., and G. Tedeschi, eds. 1990. *Semonides: Testimonia et fragmenta*. Rome: Edizioni dell'Ateneo.

Pepper, T. W. 2010. "A Patron and a Companion: Two Animal Epitaphs for Zenon of Caunos (*P.Cair.Zen.* IV 59532 = SH 977)." In *Proceedings of the Twenty-Fifth International Congress of Papyrology: Ann Arbor, July 29–August 4, 2007*, edited by T. Gagos, 605–22. Ann Arbor: Scholarly Publishing Office, University of Michigan Library.

Perpillou, J.-L. 1998. "Du manger de chien." *Revue des Étude Anciennes* 100: 325–39.

Pigeaud, J. 1981. *La maladie de l'âme*. Paris: Les Belles Lettres.

Pinotti, P. 1994. "Gli animali in Platone: Metafore e tassonomie." In *Filosofi e animali nel mondo antico*, edited by S. Castignone and G. Lanata, 103–22. Pisa: ETS.

Pisani, V., ed. 1984². *Teocrito: Idilli*. Rome: Nuovo Istituto Editoriale Italiano.

Pomelli, R. 2003. "Il cane indiano: Sondaggi da una rappresentazione culturale." In *"Buoni per pensare": Gli animali nel pensiero e nella letteratura dell'antichità*, edited by F. Gasti and E. Romano, 147–81. Atti della II Giornata ghisleriana di Filologia classica, Pavia, 18–19 April 2002. Pavia and Como: Ibis.

Pomeroy, S. B. 1995². *Goddesses, Whores, Wives, and Slaves: Women in Classical Antiquity*. New York: Schocken Books.

———. 1997. *Families in Classical and Hellenistic Greece: Representations and Reality*. Oxford: Clarendon.

Pontes, H. 1995. "The Double Dog in Callimachus and Aristophanes." *Philologus* 139: 251–55.

Poplin, F. 1995. "L'homme et l'animal dans le bûcher de Patrocle (*Iliade*, XXIII)." *Anthropozoologica* 21: 253–65.

Porter, P. 2010. "Teaching Animal Movies." In *Teaching the Animal: Human-Animal Studies across the Disciplines*, edited by M. DeMello, 18–34. New York: Lantern Books.

Prieur, J. 1988. *Les animaux sacrés dans l'antiquité*. Rennes: Ouest-France.

Pugliara, M. 2002. *La meraviglia e l'artificio*. Rome: L'Erma di Bretschneider.

Purola, T. 1994. "*P.Cair.Zen.* 4.59532: Two Epitaphs for a Hunting Dog called Tauron." *Arctos* 28: 55–62.

Rahn, H. 1953. "Tier und Mensch in der Homerischen Auffassung der Wirklichkeit." *Paideuma* 5: 274–97, 431–80.

Redfield, J. 1975. *Nature and Culture in the Iliad*. Chicago and London: University of Chicago Press.

———. 1977–78. "The Women of Sparta." *Classical Journal* 73: 146–61.

———. 1982. "Notes on the Greek Wedding." *Arethusa* 15: 181–201.

Reed, E. S. 1988. "The Affordances of the Animate Environment: Social Science from the Ecological Point of View." In *What Is an Animal?*, edited by T. Ingold, 110–26. London and New York: Routledge.

Reinach, T. 1928. "Κυνοῦχος." *Revue de philologie, de littérature et d'histoire anciennes* 54: 97–100.

Reitz, E. J., and E. S. Wing. (1999) 2008². *Zooarchaeology.* Cambridge: Cambridge University Press.

Ribbeck, O. 1884. "Kolax: Eine ethologische Studie." *Abhandlungen der philol.-hist. Classe der Königl. Sächsischen Gesell. der Wissenschaft* 21: 1–113.

Ricciardelli, G., ed. 2000. *Inni orfici.* Milan: Valla Mondadori.

Ridgway, B. S. 1971. "The Man-and-Dog Stelai." *Jahrbuch der Deutschen Archaeologischen Instituts* 86: 60–79.

Ritvo, H. 1987. *The Animal Estate: The English and Other Creatures in the Victorian Age.* Cambridge, MA: Harvard University Press.

———. 2002. "History and Animal Studies." *Society and Animals* 10, no. 4: 403–6.

Rivera, A., ed. 2000. *Homo sapiens e mucca pazza: Antropologia del rapporto con il mondo animale.* Bari: Dedalo.

Rizzini, I. 1998. *L'occhio parlante: Per una semiotica dello sguardo nel mondo antico.* Venice: Istituto veneto di scienze, lettere ed arti.

Robert, R. 1993. "Rites de protection et de défense: À propos des ossements d'un chien découverts au pied du rempart de Paestum." *Annali dell'Istituto Orientale di Napoli: Sezione archeologia e storia antica* 15: 119–42.

Rohde, E. 1925. *The Cult of Souls and Belief in Immortality among the Greeks.* Translated by W. B. Hillis. London: K. Paul, Trench, Trubner. Originally published as *Psyche: Seelencult und Unsterblichkeitsglaube der Griechen.* Freiburg in Brisgau and Leipzig: Mohr, 1890–94.

Rohman, C. 2010. "Animal Writes: Literature and the Discourse of Species." In *Teaching the Animal: Human-Animal Studies across the Disciplines,* edited by M. DeMello, 48–59. New York: Lantern Books.

Romm, J. S. 1992. *The Egdes of the Earth in Ancient Thought.* Princeton: Princeton University Press.

———. 1996. "Dog Heads and Noble Savages: Cynicism before the Cynics?" In *The Cynics: The Cynic Movement in Antiquity and Its Legacy,* edited by R. Bracht Branham and M.-O. Goulet-Cazé, 121–35. Berkeley: University of California Press.

Roscher, W. H. 1896. *Das von der "Kynanthropie" handelnde Fragment des Marcellus von Side.* Leipzig: S. Hirzel.

Rose, G. P. 1979. "Odysseus' Barking Heart." *Transactions and Proceedings of the American Philological Association* 109: 215–30.

Rosokoki, A. 1995. *Die Erigone des Eratosthenes: Eine kommentierte Ausgabe der Fragmente.* Heidelberg: Winter.

Rothwell, K. S., Jr. 2006. *Nature, Culture, and the Origins of Greek Comedy: A Study of Animal Choruses.* Cambridge: Cambridge University Press.

Rousseau, M. 1962. *L'Animal civilisateur de l'homme.* Paris: Masson.

Russell, H. L. 1955. "Dog-Slaying at the Argive Sheep Festival." *Classical Bulletin* 31: 61–62.

Russo, J., ed. 1987². *Omero: Odissea.* Vol. 5. Milan: Valla Mondadori.

Saayman, F. 1993. "Dogs and Lions in the *Oresteia.*" *Akroterion* 38: 11–18.

Santillo Frizell, B., ed. 2004. *Pecus: Man and Animal in Antiquity: Proceedings of the Conference at the Swedish Institute in Rome, September 9–12, 2002*. Projects and Seminars 1. Rome: Swedish Institute.

Sbisà, M., ed. 1995². *Gli atti linguistici: Aspetti e problemi della filosofia del linguaggio*. Milan: Feltrinelli.

Scarpi, P., ed. 1996. *Apollodoro: I miti greci*. Milan: Valla Mondadori.

Schiesari, J. 2010. *Beasts and Beauties: Animals, Gender, and Domestication in the Italian Renaissance*. Toronto; Buffalo, NY; and London: University of Toronto Press.

Schleidt, W. M., and M. D. Shalter. 2003. "Co-evolution of Humans and Canids." *Evolution and Cognition* 9, no. 1: 57–72.

Schlerath, B. 1954. "Der Hund bei den Indogermanen." *Paideuma* 6, no. 1: 25–40.

Schmitt, J.-C. 1983. *The Holy Greyhound: Guinefort, Healer of Children since the Thirteenth Century*. Translated by Martin Thom. Cambridge: Cambridge University Press. Originally published as *Le Saint Levrier: Guinefort, guérisseur d'enfants depuis le 13. siècle*. Paris: Flammarion, 1979.

Schnapp-Gourbeillon, A. 1981. *Lions, héros, masques: Les répresentations de l'animal chez Homère*. Paris: Maspero.

———. 1982. "Les funérailles de Patrocle." In *La mort, les morts dans les sociétés anciennes*, edited by G. Gnoli and J.-P. Vernant, 77–88. Cambridge and Paris: Cambridge University Press.

Schneider, C. 2000. "Herr und Hund auf archaischen Grabstelen." *Jahrbuch des Deutschen Archäologischen Instituts* 115: 1–36.

Scholz, H. 1937. *Der Hund in der griechisch-römischen Magie und Religion*. Dissertation, Friedrich Wilhelms University of Berlin (now Humboldt University of Berlin). Berlin: Triltsch and Huther.

Schubert, P. 2000. *Noms d'agent et invective: Entre phénomène linguistique et interprétation du récit dans les poèmes homériques*. Hypomnemata 133. Göttingen: Vandenhoeck and Ruprecht.

Schwyzer, E. 1959². *Griechische Grammatik*. Vol. 2. Munich: Beck'sche Verlagsbuchhandl.

Scodel, R. 2008. *Epic Facework: Self-Presentation and Social Interaction in Homer*. Swansea: Classical Press of Wales.

Scuderi, A. 2012. *Il paradosso di Proteo: Storia di una rappresentazione culturale da Omero al postumano*. Rome: Carocci.

Scullard, H. H. 1974. *The Elephant in the Greek and Roman World*. Ithaca, N.Y.: Cornell University Press.

Sealey, R. 1990. *Women and Law in Classical Greece*. Chapel Hill and London: University of North Carolina Press.

Searle, J. R. 1976. "A Classification of Illocutionary Acts." *Language in Society* 5: 1–23.

Segal, C. 1971. *The Theme of the Mutilation of Corpse in the Iliad*. Leiden, Netherlands: Brill.

Serpell, J. A. 1986. *In the Company of Animals: A History of Human-Animal Relationships*. Oxford and New York: Blackwell.

Shanklin, E. 1985. "Sustenance and Symbol: Anthropological Studies of Domesticated Animals." *Annual Review of Anthropology* 14: 375–403.

Shepard, P. 1978. *Thinking Animals: Animals and the Development of Human Intelligence*. New York: Viking.

———. 1996. *The Others: How Animals Made Us Human.* Washington DC: Island.

Sigaut, F. 1988. "Critique de la notion de domestication." *L'Homme* 108: 59–71.

Simon, B. 1978. *Mind and Madness in Ancient Greece: The Classical Roots of Modern Psychiatry.* Ithaca, NY, and London: Cornell University Press.

Sissa, G. 1983. "Il corpo della donna: Lineamenti di una ginecologia filosofica." In *Madre materia: Sociologia e biologia della donna greca,* edited by S. Campese, P. Manuli, and G. Sissa, 83–145. Turin: Boringhieri.

———. 1990. *Greek Virginity.* Translated by Arthur Goldhammer. Cambridge, MA: Harvard University Press. Originally published as *Le corps virginal.* Paris: Vrin, 1987.

Slatkin, L. 1988. "Les amis mortels: À propos des insultes dans les combats de l'*Iliade.*" *L'Ecrit du Temps* 19: 119–32.

Snyder, L. M. 1998. "Our Best, and Oldest, Friends." *Archaeology* 51: 70–78.

Sommerstein, A. H., ed. 1990. *Aristophanes: Lysistrata.* Warminster, U.K.: Aris and Phillips.

Sorabji, R. 1993. *Animal Minds and Human Morals: The Origins of Western Debate.* London: Duckworth.

Sperber, D. 1975. *Rethinking Symbolism.* Translated by Alice L. Morton. Cambridge: Cambridge University Press. Originally published as *Le symbolisme en général.* Paris: Hermann, 1974.

———. 1996. "Why Are Perfect Animals, Hybrids, and Monsters Food for Symbolic Thought?" *Method and Theory in the Study of Religion* 8, no. 2: 143–69. Originally published as "Pourquoi les animaux parfaits, les hybrides et les monstres sont-ils bons à penser symboliquement?" *L'Homme* 15, no. 2 (1975): 5-24.

Sperber, D., and D. Wilson. 1986. *Relevance: Communication and Cognition.* Oxford: Basil Blackwell.

Spila, C., ed. 2002. *Cani di pietra: L'epicedio canino nella poesia del Rinascimento.* Rome: Quiritta.

———. 2012. *Animalia tantum: Animali nella letteratura dall'Antichità al Rinascimento.* Naples: Liguori.

Stadter, P. A. 1980. *Arrian of Nicomedia.* Chapel Hill: University of North Carolina Press.

Stein, G. 1936. *The Geographical History of America, or The Relation of Human Nature to the Human Mind.* New York: Random House.

Steiner, D. 2001. "Slander's Bite: Nemean 7.102–05 and the Language of Invective." *The Journal of Hellenic Studies* 121: 154–58.

Strubbe, J. H. M. 1991. "Cursed Be He That Moves My Bones." In *Magika Hiera: Ancient Greek Magic and Religion,* edited by C. A. Faraone and D. Obbink, 33–59. Oxford: Oxford University Press.

Taillardat, J. 1962. *Les images d'Aristophane.* Paris: Les Belles Lettres.

———, ed. 1967. *Suétone: Des termes injurieux: Des jeux grecs.* Paris: Les Belles Lettres.

Tambiah, S. J. 1969. "Animals Are Good to Think and Good to Prohibit." *Ethnology* 8: 424–59.

Tasinato, M. 1982. *Elena o della velenosa bellezza.* Padua: Cleup.

Thompson, D. W. (1895) 1936². *A Glossary of Greek Birds.* Oxford: Clarendon.

———. 1947. *A Glossary of Greek Fishes.* London: Oxford University Press.

Todd, S. C. 1993. *The Shape of Athenian Law.* Oxford: Clarendon.

Toynbee, J. M. C. (1973) 1996². *Animals in Roman Life and Art.* Baltimore and London: Johns Hopkins University Press.

Tosi, R. 1991. *Dizionario delle sentenze latine e greche.* Milan: Rizzoli.

Trinquier, J. 2004. "Les loups sont entrés dans la ville: De la peur du loup à la hantise de la cité ensauvagée." In *Les espaces du sauvage dans le monde antique: Colloque Besançon, 4-5 mai 2000,* edited by M.-C. Charpentier, 85–118. Besançon: Presses universitaires de Franche-Comté.

Turpin, J.-C. 1980. "L'expression ΑΙΔΩΣ ΚΑΙ ΝΕΜΕΣΙΣ et les 'actes de langage.'" *Revue des Études grecques* 93: 352–67.

Tutrone, F. 2012. *Filosofi e animali in Roma antica.* Pisa: ETS.

Unterbeck, B., M. Rissanen, T. Nevalainen, and M. Saari, eds. 1999. *Gender in Grammar and Cognition.* Berlin and New York: Mouton de Gruyter.

Vérilhac, A.-M., and C. Vial. 1998. "Le mariage grec, du VIe siècle av. J.-C. à l'époque d'Auguste," supplement, *Bulletin de Correspondance Hellènique* 32. Athens and Paris: École Française d'Athènes.

Vermeule, E. 1979. *Aspects of Death in Early Greek Art and Poetry.* Berkeley: University of California Press.

Vernant, J.-P. (1980) 1988. "Marriage." In *Myth and Society in Ancient Greece,* 55–78. Translated by Janet Lloyd. New York: Zone Books. Originally published as "Le mariage en Grèce archaïque." *La parola del passato* 148 (1973): 51–79. Republished in *Mythe et société en Grèce ancienne,* 57-81. Paris: Maspero, 1974.

———. 1983. "Hestia-Hermes: The Religious Expression of Space and Movement in Ancient Greece." In *Myth and Thought among the Greeks,* 127–75. Translated by Janet Lloyd and Jeff Fort. London and Boston: Routledge and Kegan Paul. Originally published as "Hestia-Hermès." *L'Homme* 3 (1962): 12–50.

———. 1988. "Between the Beasts and the Gods." In *Myth and Society in Ancient Greece,* 143–82. Translated by Janet Lloyd. New York: Zone Books. Originally published as the introduction to *Les Jardins d'Adonis,* by M. Detienne. Paris: Gallimard, 1972.

———. 1989. "At Man's Table." In *The Cuisine of Sacrifice among the Greeks,* edited by M. Detienne and Vernant, 21–86. Translated by Paula Wissing. Chicago: University of Chicago Press. Originally published as "À la table des hommes." In *La cuisine du sacrifice en pays grec,* edited by Detienne and Vernant, 37–132. Paris: Gallimard, 1979.

———. 1991. "A 'Beautiful Death' and the Disfigured Corpse in Homeric Epic." Translated by Andrew Szegedy-Maszak. In *Mortals and Immortals: Collected Essays,* edited by F. Zeitlin, 50–74. Princeton: Princeton University Press. Originally published as "La belle mort et le cadavre outragé." In *La mort, les morts dans les sociétés anciennes,* edited by G. Gnoli and Vernant, 45–76. Cambridge and Paris: Cambridge University Press, 1982.

Vetturini, C. 1996. "Simbolismo animale in Giappone." In *Bestie o dei? L'animale nel simbolismo religioso,* edited by A. Bongioanni and E. Comba, 155–79. Turin: ANANKE.

Vigne, J.-D. 2004. *Le débuts de l'élevage.* Paris: Le Pommier.

Vilatte, S. 1986. "La femme, l'esclave, le cheval et le chien: Les emblèmes du 'kalòs kagathòs' Ischomaque." *Dialogues d'Histoire Ancienne* 12: 271–94.

Violi, P. 2001. *Meaning and Experience.* Translated by Jeremy Carden. Bloomington: Indiana University Press. Originally published as *Significato ed esperienza.* Milan: Bompiani, 1997.

Visintin, M. 1992. *La vergine e l'eroe: Temesa e la leggenda di Euthymos di Locri.* Bari: Edipuglia.

Visser, M. 1980. "The Erinyes: Their Character and Function in Classical Greek Literature and Thought." PhD thesis, University of Toronto.

———. 1986. "Medea: Daughter, Sister, Wife and Mother: Natural Family versus Conjugal Family in Greek and Roman Myths about Women." In *Greek Tragedy and Its Legacy: Essays Presented to D. J. Conacher,* edited by M. Cropp, E. Fantham, and S. E. Scully, 149–65. Alberta: University of Calgary Press.

Visser, T. 2001. "Grabrelief vom Ilissos." *Der Altsprachliche Unterricht* 44, nos. 4–5: 90–91.

Von Rudloff, R. 1999. *Hekate in Ancient Greek Religion.* Victoria, B.C.: Horned Owl.

Vox, O. 1983. "Solone nero." *Quaderni di storia* 9: 305–21.

———. 1984. *Solone: Autoritratto.* Padua: Antenore.

Wade-Brown, A. 1974. "Il significato sociale dei nomi di cane tra gli Nzema." *La critica sociologica* 29: 163–68.

Walter, P., ed. 1999. *Mythologies du porc.* Grenoble: Jérôme Millon.

Weber, D. 1999. "On the Function of Gender." In *Gender in Grammar and Cognition,* edited by B. Unterbeck, M. Rissanen, T. Nevalainen, and M. Saari, 495–509. Berlin and New York: Mouton de Gruyter.

West, M. L. 1978. *Hesiod: Works and Days.* Oxford: Clarendon.

———. 1990. *Studies in Aeschylus.* Stuttgart: Teubner.

———. 1997. *The East Face of Helicon: West Asiatic Elements in Greek Poetry and Myth.* Oxford: Clarendon.

White, D. G. 1991. *Myths of the Dog-Man.* Chicago and London: University of Chicago Press.

Whittaker, C. R., ed. 1988. "Pastoral Economies in Classical Antiquity," *Proceedings of the Cambridge Philological Society,* supplement 14. Cambridge: Cambridge Philological Society.

Wijeyewardene, G. 1968. "Address, Abuse and Animal Categories in Northern Thailand." *Man* 3: 76–93.

Williams, F. 1999. "Daphne's Hounds: Gender and Feminism in Parthenius 15." *Eikasmos* 10: 137–42.

Williams, G. 1959. "Dogs and Leather." *Classical Review,* n.s., 9: 97–100.

Willis, R. 1974. *Man and Beast.* New York: Basic Books.

———. 1990. *Signifying Animals: Human Meaning in the Natural World.* London: Routledge.

Wissman, J. 2012. "Angry Dogs and Stones: A Proverbial Simile in the Homeric Scholia." *Rheinisches Museum* 155: 291–309.

Wolfe, C. 2010. *What Is Posthumanism?* Minneapolis: University of Minnesota Press.

Woodbury, L. 1978. "The Gratitude of the Locrian Maiden: Pindar, *Pyth.* 2. 18–20." *Transactions and Proceedings of the American Philological Association* 108: 285–99.

Worman, N. 2001. "This Voice Which Is Not One: Helen's Verbal Guises in Homeric Epic." In *Making Silence Speak: Women's Voices in Greek Literature and Society,* edited by A. Lardinois and L. McClure, 19–37. Princeton and Oxford: Princeton University Press.

Worthington, I. 1990. "Aristophanic Caricature and the Sam Wide Group Cups." *Eranos* 88: 1–8.

Woysch-Méautis, D. 1982. *La représentation des animaux et des êtres fabuleux sur les monuments funéraires grecs de l'époque archaïque à la fin du IVᵉ siècle avant J. C.* Lausanne: Bibliothèque historique vaudoise.

Wüst, E. 1956. "Erinys." In *Realencyclopädie der classischen Altertumwissenschaft,* edited by A. F. Pauly and G. Wissowa, suppl. 8, 82–166. Stuttgart: Druckenmüller.

Zambon, S. 2007. "Una voce sei tu null'altro: L'usignolo nella tradizione culturale del mondo antico." Doctoral thesis, Università di Siena.

Zatta, C. 1997. *Incontri con Proteo.* Venice: Istituto veneto di scienze, lettere ed arti.

Zeitlin, F. I. 1978. "The Dynamics of Misogyny: Myth and Mythmaking in the *Oresteia.*" *Arethusa* 11: 149–81. Reprinted in *Playing the Other: Gender and Society in Classical Greek Literature,* 341–74. Chicago: University of Chicago Press, 1996.

———. 1995. "The Economics of Hesiod's Pandora." In *Pandora: Women in Classical Greece,* edited by E. Reeder, 49–56. Princeton: Princeton University Press.

Zlotogorska, M. 1997. *Darstellungen von Hunden auf griechischen Grabreliefs.* Hamburg: Dr. Kovač.

Zucker, A. 2005. *Les classes zoologiques en Grèce ancienne, d'Homère à Élien.* Aix-en-Provence: Publications de l'Université de Provence.

———. 2006. "Sur l'extension de certains noms d'animaux en grec: Les zoonymes pluriels." *Métis,* n.s., 4: 97–122.

cultural taxonomy of, 162; divisive elements in, 176; food pact in, 45–46, 50–51, 67, 170; gender in, 183; hierarchical, 183; historical dynamics of, 179; Homeric, 192nn2–3,6,10; human responsibility in, 184; imitation in, 176; metonymic, 15, 156; reciprocity in, 176; reification of, 175; in rural society, 27, 38–39, 195n39; saming/othering in, 175; shared environment of, 169–70, 174; sites of resistance in, 183; social expectations in, 162; subjugation in, 175, 177; with undesired species, 183–84

human-animal studies, viii, ix; anthrozoology and, 174–78

human-canine relationships: affordances in, 170; autonomy in, 44; coevolution of, 247n21, 250n50; collaborative, 80, 170; ethical-normative aspects of, 44–45, 46–47; food pact in, 40–41, 64; insults in, 11–12; names in, 14–16, 191n31; recognition in, 67, 73; structuralist analysis of, 248n32; unmediated, 44

human-canine relationships, Greek, 4; in Aelian, 233n11; aidōs in, 122; ambiguity in, 75, 91–93, 98–99; asymmetry in, 48–49, 173, 178, 204n127; authority in, 66, 128; autonomy in, 122, 170; bonding in, 37–40; business model of, 41, 45; companionship in, 102; competence in, 170; contractual model of, 41–42, 44–46, 50; control in, 38; cultural representations of, 54, 66; dependence in, 38; emotional investment in, 178; ethical norms of, 49–50, 80–82, 122, 123, 157, 178; familial model of, 41, 45, 123, 205n133; female metaphors in, 107; food in, 23–27, 38, 165; food pact in, 40–43, 45–47, 170; funerary symbols of, 73–74; Greek conceptualization of, 162; human behavioral rules in, 80–82; identity in, 73, 74, 178, 212n74, 233n8, 235n27; individuality of dogs in, 110; inversion of, 61, 63, 64; loyalty in, 47, 50, 93, 116, 123–25, 204n125; matrimonial model of, 123; nurturing in, 38, 64, 66; origin myths of, 43; paradoxes in, 156; perspective on males through, 172; philia in, 48–51, 138; recognition in, 91, 123, 166, 236n34; ritual cannibalism in, 61; self-perception in, 64; social partnership in, 169–71, 177; spaces of freedom in, 183; structural constants of, 16; subordination in, 78–79, 81, 84–85, 106, 127–28, 131, 166, 173, 178, 215n15, 216nn23,25; symbolic elaborations of, 177; transgression in, 27, 92; in vase painting, 212n84

human-canine relationships, Homeric, 18–23, 161; contradictions in, 55–56; synergy in, 19–20. See also Argus (Odyssey)

humanism, Western: limitations of, 249n43

humanity: continual formation of, 250n52; debt to other species, 250n51, 252n73; ecological crisis of, 174; interaction with environment, 176, 247n14; Zeus's punishment of, 2, 188n5

hunger, canine, 206n17, 210n54; death from, 67–68; in Homer, 118; in Homeric Hymn to Demeter, 119; role in wolfish behavior, 30, 42; types of, 194n35. See also feeding habits, canine

hunting dogs, Greek, 36; in Aesop, 196n51; aggressive, 30, 37, 93; apsychoi/eupsychoi, 220n67; Atē as, 240n78; calming of, 200n80; Cassandra as, 141; charopoi eyes of, 229n164; as cognitive prosthetics, 170; death of, 217n34; enjoyment felt by, 29; freedom of movement, 39; grammatically gendered feminine, 145, 241n93; in Homer, 18–19, 20; intelligence of, 198n69; madness of, 97; Orion's, 113, 114; rewards for, 29, 196n50; signals of, 131, 231n180; training of, 40, 247n22; treatises on, 247n22; value of, 202n113

hybridization, 180

hyenas, corpse-eating, 207n10

Hyginus (mythographer), on faithful women, 233nn9–10

hypagein (to subdue), 224n106

hypharpazein (to snatch from below), 68–69

hypothōpeuein, 239n68

hys (sow): grammatical gender of, 148, 149–50, 243n113; as sexual metaphor, 150, 243n112. See also pigs

Icarius, daughter's devotion to, 124

identity, human: animals' role in, 180; annihilation of, 58, 63, 64, 66; dogs' role in, 73, 74, 178, 212n74, 233n8, 235n27; postmodern, 175; women's, 140

ideology: of gender, 172; in response to social tensions, 248n25

Iliad: adultery in, 101–5; aeikia in, 211n61; canine necrophagy in, 55–57, 64–66, 162, 206n1, 208n29; conflict of gods in, 82–84, 89; dog insults in, 75–79, 82–84, 86–87, 89, 101–2, 143–44, 150, 216n23; dogs in, 18, 19–20, 22; Dog Star in, 112; Erinyes in, 222n87; funeral rites in, 72–73, 212n80; guard dogs in, 19–20, 65–66; hunting dogs in, 19; kingship in, 120; lion imagery in, 84; lyssa in, 31, 99, 113, 197n63, 207n19, 223n94; paraenetic insults in, 223n94; ritual cannibalism in, 58–60, 69; woman as insult in, 240n86